The Struggle for Labour's Soul

'New Labour' is often accused of being obsessed with style rather than substance and with image rather than ideology. *The Struggle for Labour's Soul* examines how the Party's political thought has developed from 1945 to the present day. It explores the divisions in the Labour Party between the Old Left, the New Left, Centrists, the Old Right and 'New Labour'. These ideological positions are examined in the context of the key political issues of the 21st century including constitutional reform, markets, equality, internationalism and globalisation. The book concludes with commentaries by renowned experts on the various competing traditions within the Party. Featuring contributions by leading academics, journalists and politicians, this is the first major analysis of Labour's political thought for a generation. It will be essential reading for students of British politics and Labour Party members, as well as for the general reader.

Raymond (Lord) Plant is a Labour peer and Professor of Jurisprudence at Kings College London. **Matt Beech** is a visiting Research Fellow in politics at the University of Southampton. **Kevin Hickson** lectures at Manchester and Liverpool Universities.

The Struggle for Labour's Soul

Understanding Labour's political thought since 1945

Edited by Raymond Plant, Matt Beech and Kevin Hickson

Routledge
Taylor & Francis Group

LONDON AND NEW YORK

First published 2004
by Routledge
11 New Fetter Lane, London EC4P 4EE

Simultaneously published in the USA and Canada
by Routledge
29 West 35th Street, New York, NY 10001

Routledge is an imprint of the Taylor & Francis Group

© 2004 selection and editorial matter: Raymond Plant, Matt Beech
and Kevin Hickson; individual chapters: the contributors

Typeset in Baskerville by Taylor & Francis Books Ltd
Printed and bound in Great Britain by TJ International Ltd,
Padstow, Cornwall

British Library Cataloguing in Publication Data
A catalogue record for this book is available from the British Library

Library of Congress Cataloging-in-Publication Data
A catalog record for this book has been requested

ISBN 0–415–31283–3 (hbk)

ISBN 0–415–31284–1 (pbk)

Contents

List of Contributors   vii
Acknowledgements   x
Introduction   1
KEVIN HICKSON, MATT BEECH AND RAYMOND PLANT

PART I
Positions   **5**

1 **The Old Left**   7
   ANTHONY ARBLASTER

2 **The New Left**   24
   MARK WICKHAM-JONES

3 **The Centre**   47
   NOEL THOMPSON

4 **The Old Right**   68
   KEVIN JEFFERYS

5 **New Labour**   86
   MATT BEECH

PART II
Themes   **103**

6 **Ends, Means and Political Identity**   105
   RAYMOND PLANT

7 **Equality**   120
   KEVIN HICKSON

8 **Globalisation**   137
   ANTHONY G. MCGREW

9   Ownership, Planning and Markets   163
STUART HOLLAND

10   Labourism: Myths and Realities   187
ERIC SHAW

11   Constitutional Reform   206
DILYS M. HILL

12   Internationalism   229
BRIAN BRIVATI

PART III
Commentaries   **245**

13   The Old Left   247
TAM DALYELL

14   The New Left   251
FRANCES MORRELL

15   The Centre   257
JOE HAINES

16   The Old Right   261
AUSTIN MITCHELL

17   New Labour   268
POLLY TOYNBEE AND DAVID WALKER

Afterword   274
ROY HATTERSLEY

Bibliography   278
Index   288

Contributors

Anthony Arblaster was Reader in Politics at the University of Sheffield and previously worked for *Tribune* and lectured at the University of Manchester. He has written widely on political theory and the politics of culture and is opera correspondent for the *Independent*.

Matt Beech was a Thorneycroft scholar and completed his PhD on the political philosophy of New Labour at the University of Southampton in 2003. He is a visiting research fellow in politics at the University of Southampton.

Brian Brivati has recently been appointed Professor of Contemporary British History at Kingston University. He is the biographer of *Hugh Gaitskell* (1996). His recent work has focused on the Labour Party's attitude to overseas policy.

Tam Dalyell has been an MP since 1962 and he is now the Father of the House. He was Parliamentary Private Secretary to Dick Crossman 1964–5. He is a regular contributor to parliamentary debates, especially on foreign policy and devolution. He is author of *Dick Crossman: A Portrait* (1989).

Joe Haines was Press Secretary to Harold Wilson 1969–76. He was for many years a senior journalist with the *Daily Mirror* newspaper. He is the author of *The Politics of Power* (1977) and *Glimmer of Twilight: Murder, Passion and Intrigue in the Court of Harold Wilson* (2003).

Roy (Lord) Hattersley was Labour MP for Birmingham Sparkbrook 1964–97 and was Deputy Leader of the Labour Party (1983–92) and Secretary of State for Prices and Consumer Protection (1976–9). He is a frequent contributor to the *Guardian* and is author of over 15 books including his statement of social democratic values *Choose Freedom: The Future of Democratic Socialism* (1987) and his memoirs *Who Goes Home?* (1995).

Kevin Hickson was a Thorneycroft scholar and obtained his PhD on the 1976 IMF Crisis from the University of Southampton in 2002. He lectures at Manchester and Liverpool Universities. He is joint editor of *Governing Before New Labour*, on the 1974–9 Labour Governments (2004, with Anthony Seldon).

Dilys M. Hill is Emeritus Professor of Politics at the University of Southampton. She has published widely on British and US politics and is recognised as a major authority on urban politics and regeneration issues.

Stuart Holland is Professor of Economics at the University of Coimbra, Portugal, and was MP for Vauxhall 1979–89. His books include *The Socialist Challenge* (1975) and *The European Imperative: Economic and Social Cohesion in the 1990s* (1993), which was the basis of Jacques Delors's 1993 White Paper on Growth, Competitiveness and Employment.

Kevin Jefferys is Reader in History at Plymouth University. He wrote *Anthony Crosland: A New Biography* (1999) and is editor of two collections of Labour Party biography – *Leading Labour: From Keir Hardie to Tony Blair* (1999) and *Labour Forces: From Ernest Bevin to Gordon Brown* (2002).

Anthony G. McGrew is Professor of International Relations and Chair of the Politics Department at the University of Southampton. He is a leading authority on globalisation. His major text is *Global Transformations*, with David Held (1999).

Austin Mitchell has been Labour MP for Great Grimsby since 1977. He previously worked as a journalist and broadcaster with the BBC and Yorkshire Television and was also a lecturer in political science in New Zealand. He has written several books including *The Case for Labour* (1983) and *Four Years in the Death of the Labour Party* (1983).

Frances Morrell is joint chief executive of Arts Inform. She was policy adviser to Tony Benn (1974–9) and Leader of the Inner London Education Authority (1983–7). She was the founding Director of the Institute for Citizenship Studies in 1991, and was Secretary to the Speaker's Commission on Citizenship. Her books include *The Community Sphere* (2002) and *Children of the Future* (1989).

Raymond (Lord) Plant is a Labour peer and Professor of Jurisprudence at King's College London, and was Master of St Catherine's College, University of Oxford. He was Chairman of the Labour Party Commission on Electoral Reform (the 'Plant Report') and of the Fabian Commission on Taxation and Citizenship. He was awarded the PSA Lifetime Achievement award in 2003.

Eric Shaw is Senior Lecturer in Politics at Stirling University. He has written several major studies of the Labour Party including *Discipline and Discord in the Labour Party* (1988); *The Labour Party Since 1979: Crisis and Transformation* (1994) and *The Labour Party Since 1945* (1996).

Noel Thompson is Professor of Modern History and Head of the History Department, University of Wales, Swansea. He has published widely on Labour Party history and politics including *Political Economy and the Labour Party: The Economics of Democratic Socialism 1884–1985* (1996) and *Left in the Wilderness: The Political Economy of British Democratic Socialism Since 1979* (2002).

Polly Toynbee writes for the *Guardian* and was previously Social Affairs Editor of the BBC. She is co-author of *Did Things Get Better? An Audit of Labour's Successes and Failures* (2001, with David Walker) and has recently written an account of her experiences living on the minimum wage, *Hard Work: Life in Low-Pay Britain* (2003).

David Walker writes for the *Guardian* and is co-author of *Did Things Get Better? An Audit of Labour's Successes and Failures* (2001, with Polly Toynbee). He has authored several chapters and pamphlets.

Mark Wickham-Jones is Senior Lecturer in Politics at the University of Bristol. He wrote the major study of the Alternative Economic Strategy, *Economic Strategy and the Labour Party: Politics and Policy-making 1970–83* (1996) and has published widely on New Labour.

Acknowledgements

The original suggestion for writing a book on the political thought of the Labour Party since 1945 bringing together discussions of the Old Left, New Left, Centre, Old Right and New Right (New Labour) was made by Matt Beech. The idea to develop it into a longer edited volume bringing together leading writers on the Labour Party, with the introduction of cross-cutting thematic issues and commentaries from those involved in the formation of policies and thinking at the highest level, was then made by Kevin Hickson. The input of Raymond Plant has been crucial – intellectually in terms of reading and commenting on each chapter and improving the quality of thought of the other two editors, and also by ensuring through his reputation that the book secured the support of a leading publisher and distinguished contributors.

We would like to thank first and foremost the contributors. The task of the editor is impossible to fulfil without the commitment of the contributors to the project. We have been very blessed with the enthusiastic support of the contributors. This has made our task much easier.

We would also like to thank the publisher; particularly Craig Fowlie and his staff for all of their support and advice along the way.

Matt Beech and Kevin Hickson would like to add two further personal notes of appreciation. The first is to Raymond Plant, our chief source of intellectual inspiration. We have both been blessed with having his support, both as editor in this project and as a PhD supervisor. The second is to Claire Beech, who has not only had to endure seemingly endless conversations, often lasting well into the night, and learnt more than she cares to know about the political thought of the Labour Party, but has also given generously of her time in editing the book in its final stages.

Last but certainly by no means least we would like to acknowledge our families and friends, with love.

Introduction

Kevin Hickson, Matt Beech and Raymond Plant

The Labour Party is a party of values, but often not of ideas. That is to say that those in the Labour Party have a set of unarticulated values which shape their approach to politics. But these values often remain little more than intuitive. They have, to borrow our terminology from Henry Drucker, an ethos but not a doctrine.[1] Often these values shape not only the approach of individuals within the Labour Party, but also the Party as a whole. At crucial times in the history of the Party, this ethos, defined by Lesjek Kolakowski as 'an obstinate will to erode by inches the conditions which produce avoidable suffering',[2] combined with a desire to achieve power, has been enough to see the Party through.

Any book on the political thought of the Labour Party must recognise the relevance of the less doctrinaire aspects of social democratic (or democratic socialist) ideology. Yet this book is also about the Party's doctrines. Although serious debate and reflection on democratic socialist ideology are often limited to a narrow band of the Party's intellectuals, their thinking has reached a wider audience.[3] It is from these reflections and debates that the Party and the various groups within it have variously defined their purpose and their policies. Prior to 1945 the strands of opinion in the Labour Party were much more fluid and imprecise than post-1945. The turning point was partly the War, but mainly the 1945–51 Government. Whatever the achievements and failures of that government were, it has continued to hold pride of place in the folklore of the Party. Debate after 1951 has often been a struggle between left and right of the Party, with one eye to the future, defining a credible way forward in the face of new problems, new issues, and the other eye looking backwards to that government.[4] This was certainly true of the debates between the Revisionists and the Bevanites in the 1950s, but it is also true of the New Left in the 1970s and early 1980s. Even New Labour, which has often sought to distance itself from Labour's past, has cited the achievements of 1945–51 and talked of the failure of Labour in the 1960s and 1970s to live up to those achievements.[5]

Ideas are therefore important to the Labour Party. This is not surprising. Social democracy rests on values. These values are subject to articulation and defence through the democratic process. In this respect, social democracy is similar to the Hayekian New Right, which was also at root a set of values to be articulated and defended, the great ideological rival of British social democracy since at least the mid-1970s. It is this emphasis on values which distinguishes social democracy both from the structuralist Marxism of the traditional East European kind and from British conservatism, or at least the earlier Oakeshottian variety of conservative political thought with its emphasis on tradition and practice. If we want to change the world, as social democrats do, then it is necessary to argue from first principles.[6] What is therefore surprising, then, is not the emphasis on values within the Labour Party, but rather that it has been little studied.[7]

The first aim of the book is to improve our understanding of the political thought of the Labour Party since 1945. We identify five basic positions. The first is the 'Old Left'. Although associated with the dominant personality of Nye Bevan, the intellectual direction was given by Dick Crossman and his group of younger followers including Michael Foot and Barbara Castle. The 'Old Left' interpreted 1945–51 as a limited success, but noted that the initial radicalism of the early years gave way to inertia, and Crossman and others argued for the need to 'Keep Left',[8] going on to oppose the Revisionists in the 1950s and emphasising the need for further nationalisation and a 'third way' between Communism and Atlanticism abroad. However, the concrete achievements of the Old Left were difficult to identify.

According to those who maintained a left-wing position, the demise of the 'Old Left' was due less to internal weaknesses of the argument they presented than to the weakness of the Old Left leaders themselves. Nye Bevan's public support for Gaitskell's multilateralist nuclear policy, calling unilateralism an 'emotional spasm', and Crossman's loyalty to Harold Wilson in government between 1964 and 1970 were both seen as signs of weakness, if not betrayal. Enter the 'New Left'. Inspired in part by the authors of the New Left Review in the 1960s and events in continental Europe, the New Left advocated industrial reform, protectionism and further public ownership in the form of the Alternative Economic Strategy and the politics of participation at home and withdrawal from the EEC. In order to achieve these aims, the New Left, broadly under the leadership of Tony Benn from the mid-1970s, attempted – and in some crucial ways achieved – reforms to the Party's constitution.

Throughout the history of the Party since 1945, a critical mass of MPs held the balance of power in the Parliamentary Labour Party. This is the elusive yet crucial 'Centre' of the Party. The need to win elections ensures that the Party presents itself as united – the need to achieve a balance in the Party. This involves both a critical section of MPs and the leadership of the Party, best symbolised by the cautious pragmatism of Harold Wilson and to a lesser extent Jim Callaghan. The existence of the Labour Party centre is crucial yet is often overlooked. It informs us of both the balance of power within the Party and the uses of the Party's ethos; hence its inclusion in this book.

The 'Old Right' of the Party, unlike the Left in old or new guises, has been a consistent presence in the Labour Party since 1945. Originating in the contributions of Hugh Dalton, Douglas Jay and Evan Durbin in the immediate pre-war era and shaping the conduct of policy 1945–51, it reached its peak in the work of Hugh Gaitskell as leader between 1955 and 1963 and the writings of the Old Right's chief intellectual figure, Tony Crosland. Emphasising the importance of values, stating that socialism is 'about equality' and employing the economic doctrines of Keynes, the Old Right carved out a distinctive approach which, at least to some extent, conditioned the policies of Labour in power in the 1960s and 1970s. Although the Croslandite perspective came under attack not only from a resurgent Labour left, but also from a younger generation of revisionists, many of who joined the Social Democratic Party (SDP), it still had advocates in the 1980s, notably the Party's Deputy Leader, Roy Hattersley.

The timing of the transition from 'Old Right' to 'New Right' – the creation of New Labour – is hard to pinpoint. The Labour Party underwent several phases of revisionism, particularly after the 1987 General Election defeat in the form of the Policy Review and again after yet another defeat in 1992 with the Social Justice Commission, but it can be argued that the Labour Party under John Smith still had some Old Right emphases, thus pointing to the importance of Tony Blair's leadership since 1994. Similarly, the nature of the difference between the Old Right and New Labour is controversial. It largely comes down to political economy – the 'supply-side' approach of New Labour replacing Keynesian economics, with the result that New Labour allows for a greater role for the market than many on the 'Old Right' would accept; but it may also be possible to identify a difference over the amount of justified inequality.

The second aim of the book is to provoke some debate. The editors do of course have their own views, but have sought to provide a balanced account, giving equal space to each of the ideological perspectives. Debate in recent times has been almost non-existent, something which this book seeks to rectify. The current strength of each position is difficult to ascertain, although each has its advocates; and we have managed to assemble some in the final section of this book. It is therefore hoped that, in addition to providing analytical clarity to Labour's political thought in the post–war era, this book will also provoke a wider debate within and beyond the Labour Party.

Structure of the book

The book is divided into three parts. Part I outlines the key features of each of the five positions this book identifies: the leading personalities, key texts, ideas, organisation and policies, together with an assessment of their successes and failures. The arguments contained within the chapters on the Old Left by Anthony Arblaster, the New Left by Mark Wickham-Jones, the Centre by Noel Thompson and the Old Right by Kevin Jefferys can all to some extent be made with the sense of reflection which historical space permits. The conclusions of the New Labour chapter by Matt Beech must in contrast be provisional.

Part II contains a number of discussions on various themes which cut across the positions outlined in the first section. Raymond Plant discusses the complex relationship between values and policies (ends and means) inherent in social democratic political thought. Kevin Hickson examines some of the theoretical and social policy issues surrounding the idea of equality, so central to democratic socialist thought. Tony McGrew examines the recent transformation of the international economy and the response of the Labour Party to these changes in its approach to domestic economic management. The role of economic policy is discussed further by Stuart Holland in his examination of ownership, planning and markets. The vital link between the Labour Party and the trade unions is discussed by Eric Shaw, broadening out into a wider discussion of class-based politics. Dilys Hill examines the constitutional reforms of New Labour. Finally, Brian Brivati examines the contrasting approaches to foreign policy within the Party since 1945. The selection of themes covers both philosophical issues and the full range of public policy areas, always linking these debates to the divergent ideological positions within the Party.

Part III consists of five personal commentaries written by authors who are broadly sympathetic to each of the positions: the Old Left by Tam Dalyell, the New Left by Frances Morrell, the Centre by Joe Haines, the Old Right by Austin Mitchell and New Labour by Polly Toynbee and David Walker. The commentaries consist of both the personal recollections of those involved and a statement of what ought to be done now in new conditions and with new issues. Readers may or may not agree with one or more of these positions, but will hopefully find them provocative.

Notes

1   Drucker, H.M., *Doctrine and Ethos in the Labour Party* (Allen and Unwin, London, 1979).
2   Quoted in Healey, D., *The Time of My Life* (Penguin, London, 1990, 2nd edition) p.472.
3   The largely neglected issue of the Labour Party's intellectuals and their relation to the broader Party has been given a boost by the work of Radhika Desai. See Desai, R., *Intellectuals and Socialism. 'Social Democrats' and the Labour Party* (Lawrence and Wishart, London, 1994).
4   See the contribution by Austin Mitchell in this volume, who makes a similar point.
5   See in particular Blair, T., '1945 Anniversary Lecture' delivered to the Fabian Society (5/07/1995).
6   See Plant, R., 'Democratic Socialism and Equality' in Lipsey, D. and Leonard, D., (eds.) *The Socialist Agenda: Crosland's Legacy* (Cape, London, 1981) pp.135–55.
7   See Foote, G., *The Labour Party's Political Thought: A History* (Macmillan, London, 1996, 3rd edition).
8   The name given to the group established by Crossman and others to campaign within the Labour Party for the sorts of policies they wanted, especially in foreign policy.

Part I
Positions

1   The Old Left

Anthony Arblaster

The year 1945 was, and remains, the most significant in the history of the British Labour Party. It was not only that the general election of that year was the first to produce a clear parliamentary majority for Labour, based on a popular vote of nearly twelve million – two million more than were cast for the Conservatives. It also remains the case that none of the three later periods of Labour government, each lasting about five or six years, including the post-1997 Blair Governments, have a record of substantial, reforming achievement comparable to that of the Attlee Governments of 1945–51. This was, as Ralph Miliband called it, 'the climax of Labourism'[1] not to be surpassed.

The word 'socialist' was not then the embarrassment it was later to become, for many of Labour's leading politicians. Labour had gone into the election with a manifesto which proclaimed defiantly 'The Labour Party is a Socialist Party and proud of it. Its ultimate purpose at home is the establishment of the Socialist Commonwealth of Great Britain ... ' But the energy and resolution with which Labour proceeded to enact its programme were in some respects surprising. For even after the war in Europe was over in May 1945, Attlee, Bevin, and Dalton were all inclined to accept Churchill's suggestion that the wartime coalition should continue in being until Japan was defeated. But the Party's National Executive Committee refused to accept this, and preferred to face an early general election instead.

As for the Party's programme, the public ownership proposals were there against the inclinations of at least some of the Party's leaders. They had been included as a result of a motion passed, despite pleas from the platform, at the Party's Conference in December 1944. The mover of the motion was Ian Mikardo, who recalled that Herbert Morrison, the Party's leading electoral strategist, told him after the debate: 'you do realize, don't you, that you've lost us the general election.'[2]

There had been plenty of signs in by-election results in the later years of the war, in the popular response to the Beveridge report on employment and national insurance, and in much else, that the electorate was moving left, and such opinion polling as there then was confirmed this:

According to opinion polls, a majority approved of the nationalization of land, state control and ownership of the mines and railways, state control of the post-war purchase and distribution of food, and general state direction of the transition from war to peace.[3]

So the defeat of Churchill and the Conservatives at the election need not have come as quite so much of a surprise. But it is all the more to the credit of Labour's leaders that, despite their own pessimism, they moved so quickly and firmly to implement most of the programme on which they had been elected, showing a respect for Party conference decisions which later Party leaders seldom have.

The result was that in relation to domestic issues the new government enjoyed a protracted honeymoon with its supporters, both in the House of Commons and in the Party as a whole, while its wider popularity was also well sustained. After the economic and political crisis of 1947, things were rather different. The Government seemed to lose much of its confidence and momentum. Much of the basic programme had been implemented or, as with the creation of the National Health Service, was in the process of being realised, and ministers seemed uncertain as to where to go, what to do next. Discontent in the ranks began to grow, and it focused on the key issue of the nationalisation of the steel industry. It was a key issue because earlier nationalisations had covered two kinds of enterprise: basic utilities, such as gas and electricity, and industries which, though central to the economy, were neither particularly profitable nor well-run, such as coal and the railways. These state take-overs represented about 20 per cent of the economy as a whole. But what was to happen to the other 80 per cent? The question of the purpose and future of public ownership was to be central to the debate and conflict between left and right in the Labour Party for the next decade and more.

Steel was thus a test case because it was neither a failing industry nor a basic utility. To take steel into public ownership would be a major incursion into the heartland of the successful, productive economy. It was far more of a challenge to capitalism and private property than the nationalisation of coal or electricity. So it was seen as an indicator of the future direction of the government and the Party. This was recognised by the group of left-wing MPs who produced *Keep Left* in May 1947:

> The determination of the Government to go forward with this plan will be the proof of its resolve not to be content with half-measures in the renovation of British Industry. It will, incidentally, involve a challenge to the citadel of capitalist power in this country.

The authors of *Keep Left* were R.H.S. Crossman, Michael Foot and Ian Mikardo. It was written over the Easter weekend and it was, according to Mikardo, a completely harmonious process: 'It all went very smoothly and happily.'[4] But surely that 'incidentally' is either a little joke or else misplaced?

It was not only the 15 signatories of *Keep Left* who were concerned about steel. At a meeting of the Parliamentary Labour Party in August 1947 a petition in favour of steel nationalisation was presented which had been signed by nearly 150 backbenchers.[5] This followed a period of intense debate within the cabinet in which Morrison, always lukewarm and cautious about public ownership, argued against further state take-overs. The following year, he promised the Party conference that Labour's future programme would contain further proposals for public ownership, but meanwhile there must be time for ministers 'to consolidate, to develop, to make efficient the industries that have been socialized in the present parliament.' 'Consolidation' became the watchword of the Party leadership, certainly as far as public ownership was concerned.[6]

This certainly did not satisfy the left, either in parliament or in the constituencies. The *Keep Left* pamphlet, which had enjoyed considerable success among the Party rank-and-file, had asked:

'Is there too much Socialism or too little?' and had suggested in reply that, 'present difficulties are not the result of socialist planning: they are the result of not enough boldness and urgency and too much tenderness for vested interests. You can't make socialist omelettes without breaking capitalist eggs.

Much the same point was made by the first delegate to respond to Morrison's speech at the 1948 conference, as Ralph Miliband pointed out:

I want to see the present tempo maintained. ... I do not feel that anybody can say that we are going too fast. Many of us think we are going to slow. ... ownership gives control. The only way in which we can get control is by getting ownership. So I want it to be made quite clear in our programme that we stand for control through common ownership.[7]

This fundamental assertion that 'ownership gives control' was, as we shall see, exactly what was disputed by the revisionist right in the debate over public ownership that rumbled on sporadically throughout the 1950s and early 1960s.

The steel industry was eventually nationalised in 1950. It was the one nationalised industry which the Conservatives returned to private ownership when they came back into power in 1951. It remained a symbol of the struggle over public ownership, and Harold Wilson, when he became Prime Minister in 1964, duly took steel back into the public sector. But by then re-nationalisation was no more than a gesture to his old friends and supporters on the left. It was not followed by substantial or systematic extension of the public sector in the years of the Labour government that followed.

When it came to drawing up the programme for the next period of Labour government, to be presented to the electorate at the 1950 general election, it was clear that there was confusion, or division, in Labour's ranks, about what public ownership was for. This was demonstrated by the randomness of the 'shopping list' of industries proposed for public ownership. Apart from iron and steel, the list included cement, sugar, the wholesale meat trade, and insurance – the last not then so powerful and significant as it has since become. The narrowness of Labour's victory in 1950 led to the abandonment of even these modest proposals, apart from iron and steel.

It is obvious, at least in retrospect, that there was a fundamental division between left and right within the Party over public ownership. For the left, the steady extension of public ownership, certainly over all of what Aneurin Bevan was to call 'the commanding heights' of the economy, was a necessity if elected governments were to be able to enact the popular will and meet the needs and demands of the people as a whole. Socialists were socialists precisely because they had no faith in capitalism, or what Labour leaders now prefer to call 'the market', to meet those needs and demands. Public ownership was supposed to lead also to the development of industrial democracy, or workers' control, within nationalised industries; and there was growing anxiety on the left in the late 1940s about the fact that this was not really happening.

But public ownership was seen as integral to democracy in a more basic way: an elected government without the power over the economy which public ownership would provide would be hamstrung in its efforts to direct the economy in the public interest, hemmed in by the power of private property in its monopolistic and oligopolistic forms: Bevan made this point in *In Place of Fear*, the reflections on democratic socialism he published in 1952:

> If confidence in political democracy is to be sustained, political freedom must arm itself with economic power. Private property in the main sources of production and distribution endangers political liberty, for it leaves Parliament with responsibility and property with power.[8]

Thus public ownership was seen by the Labour left at this time as integral to the socialist project. It was this assumption that was to be challenged by the 'revisionists' of the right in the 1950s.

So there were growing misgivings on the left about the Party's plans for the future, and about its commitment to challenging capitalist power and capitalist priorities, as the Labour government lost momentum after the first burst of legislative and reforming zeal. But on balance pleasure and satisfaction at the domestic achievement of Labour in power outweighed the anxieties aroused by talk of 'consolidation' which was code for slowing down and doing less.

As far as Britain's international position and foreign policy were concerned, left-wing responses were always rather different: doubts about and opposition to the essentially traditional and conservative foreign policy of Ernest Bevin were there from the beginning. Labour's foreign policy was consistent with the basic bias of most British, and indeed, Western foreign policy since 1917: it was dominated by anti-communism. Hostility to communism was the mainspring of the Western policies of appeasing the various Fascist states in the 1920s and 1930s. It was of course the preoccupation, indeed obsession, of the post-1945 Cold War. The four years in which the Western powers joined the Soviet Union in war to defeat Nazism and German expansion across Europe can be seen in retrospect as a brief, uncharacteristic break in the long Cold War against communism, which began with the Russian Revolution and only ended with the collapse of European communism in 1989–91.

Bevin and Attlee had no hesitation about signing up for the Cold War. Indeed, a US Secretary of State James Byrnes later recorded, Bevin rather shocked the Americans by the fierceness of his hostility to the Russians in post-war negotiations.[9] When Churchill, in his notorious speech at Fulton, Missouri on 11 March 1946 announced that the Soviets had lowered an 'iron curtain', across Europe, Attlee, in response to a question from MP Tom Driberg, pointedly refused to disown its sentiments.[10]

In the immediate aftermath of the war against Nazism the Labour left had its own distinctive perspective on Britain's position in the world. It wanted the Labour government to avoid taking sides in the Cold War. It had a vision of a democratic socialist third way between the authoritarianism of Soviet communism and the relatively unbridled capitalism of the United States. By the autumn of 1946 there was much anxiety that this possibility was disappearing, and that the government was aligning itself with the United States in the global polarization between capitalism and communism. That October 21 MPs sent a private letter to Attlee proclaiming the virtues of a 'genuine middle way' between America and the Soviet Union, and warning against the Labour Government 'being infected by the anti-Red virus which is cultivated in the United States'.[11] The letter was signed by, among others, Michael Foot, Crossman, and Jennie Lee – Bevan's wife. There was no substantial response from Attlee, so an amendment to the King's Speech was put down, calling on Britain to 'provide a democratic and Socialist alternative to an otherwise inevitable conflict between American capitalism and Soviet Communism.' Bevin was furious, and accused the amendment's 57 signatories of 'treachery'.[12]

The *Keep Left* pamphlet, which appeared six moths later, in May 1947, continued to develop this theme. It denounced the idea of 'collective security against Communism' as 'a counsel of despair': 'Its advocates assume an unbridgeable gulf between Western and Eastern Powers and argue that the only way to stop Communism spreading is to organize the world against Russia'. Against this polarization, the pamphlet looked towards Europe. 'We are Europeans Now' was the heading of one substantial section:

> … strategically, we British have become Europeans whose prosperity and security depend on that of the rest of Europe, Working together, we are still strong enough to hold the balance of world-power, to halt the division into a Western and Eastern bloc, and so to make the United Nations a reality.

Europe as a third force between the Cold war rivals, a Europe which would 'renounce the manufacture and use of atomic bombs' – it is a remarkable vision, which contrasts sharply with the strong anti-European tone of the Labour left in the 1970s and thereafter.

It would be agreeable to think that the Labour left was united in its refusal to be drafted into the anti-communist crusade, and persisted in its advocacy of a third way, independent of the two rival super-powers. Alas, this was not the case. *Tribune*, at this time under the editorship of Michael Foot and Evelyn Anderson, adopted a fiercely anti-communist line. When a reader wrote to complain of the imbalance between the paper's constant criticism of Soviet Russia and its relative silence about the evils of American foreign policy and American capitalism, *Tribune* replied that 'the major threat to democratic socialism and the major danger of war in Europe arises from Soviet policy and not from American policy.' It also claimed that the Marshall Aid Plan offered 'Western Europe' (not Europe as a whole, be it noted) the chance to 'be reconstructed as a Third Force in the world.'[13] Mervyn Jones records in his biography of Foot that, as early as 1946, Foot was 'convinced that Stalin was aiming to achieve political domination of other nations – Persia or Poland, perhaps even France or Italy – wherever it was a feasible goal and by any available means of pressure.'[14]

Two dramatic events in 1948, the communist take-over of Czechoslovakia and the Soviet blockade of West Berlin, reinforced this belief, and *Tribune* consequently refused those 37 left-wing Labour MPs who sent a telegram of support to Pietro Nenni, the Italian Socialist leader who was fighting the 1948 election in alliance with the Italian Communist Party. A Socialist victory would lead to 'the extinction of democracy by the same methods recently employed in Czechoslovakia.'[15] Foot and *Tribune* preferred, in effect, victory for the Christian Democrats, as did the CIA and the United States, which was prepared to intervene militarily if necessary to prevent the communists becoming the government if they won the election. *Tribune* apparently took the view that even the largest communist party in Western Europe, which regularly won 30 per cent of the votes in general elections, was no more than a tool of Kremlin expansionism.

After this it came as no surprise that *Tribune* welcomed the creation of NATO in 1949 – a 'pact for peace' – and supported the immediate American military response to North Korea's attack on South Korea in 1950. But *Tribune*'s support for NATO did not go unchallenged. Ian Mikardo resigned in protest from the paper's board, although he continued to write for the paper. In reply to Mikardo's protest, Foot asserted that 'The major purpose of Soviet policy has been the complete subjection of as many countries as possible to the Soviet will.'[16]

By the time that *Keeping Left* was published in January 1950, there had been a substantial retreat from the positions taken up in the *Keep Left* pamphlet of nearly two years before. The 12 signatories to *Keeping Left*, who did not include Foot, claimed that events had rendered the policies set out in the earlier pamphlet 'out-dated'. 'Instead of mediating between the blocs, we have become a member of the Atlantic Pact.' Our economic dependence on Washington was one reason why, 'however much we disliked it, we had in the end to take sides in the Cold War.' The pamphlet referred to 'Russian control' of Western communist parties, and the signatories were 'resolutely opposed' to 'the participation of any Stalinist Party in a Western coalition.' It looked as if a substantial section of the Parliamentary Labour Party had signed up for Cold War anti-communism.

Tribune even supported the Transport and General Workers' Union's ban on communists holding office within the union, scoffing at the suggestion that the ban was 'undemocratic.'[17]

There were many dangers in this course, which the Cold War left did not always avoid. One was that, as Ellen Schrecker has recently pointed out:

> for all its diversity, anti-communism was indisputably a movement of the political Right. Although liberals and even socialists joined the network, they did not set its tone. Instead, they enlisted in an ongoing crusade whose parameters had long been set by conservatives.[18]

As a consequence, the persecution, not only of avowed communists, but of large numbers of independent leftists and socialists, most of all in the United States, but also in Britain and elsewhere, either went unnoticed or was even endorsed by the British anti-communist left. I.F. Stone, the independent radical American journalist, was chronicling this persecution from its beginnings after the end of the War, and his work was certainly known to the British left, since his books were published by the *New Statesman*'s publishing company, Turnstile Press.[19] Yet we find little echo of his campaign in the left-wing press in Britain.

On the contrary, there was a very marked tendency to idealise the Truman administrations, to exaggerate the strength of the American left and labour movement in relation to the Democratic Party. *Tribune* described Truman's re-election in 1948 as a 'great victory for American labour' and for 'the common people all over the world'. Stone's response was far cooler.[20] Crossman in 1950 hailed both the Marshall Plan and the American response in Korea as 'enormously encouraging experiments in collective democratic action' and declared that 'the strongest potential ally' of British socialism was 'the American labour movement and the Fair Dealers in Washington'.[21]

One particular unpleasant episode involved no less a figure than George Orwell. In the post-war years, Orwell was a zealous anti-communist and, like many such, was free with accusations of being 'crypto' communists or communist sympathisers. In a report from London for *Partisan Review*, he referred to the left-wing MP Konni Zilliacus as an 'underground' communist. Zilliacus wrote to *Tribune*, for which Orwell then regularly wrote, to protest:

> I am not a member of the CP, never have been a member of the CP, and would consider it a disgraceful thing to do, to be secretly a member of any party or organisation, membership of which was not compatible with membership of the Labour Party.

Far from retracting his innuendo, Orwell effectively repeated it in his reply to Zilliacus, albeit in a way which kept him clear of the libel laws.[22] It is an exchange which reveals Orwell at his bullying worst. Ironically, a few years later in 1950, Zilliacus was being denounced by the British Communist Party for his open support for Yugoslavia in its dispute with Moscow.[23]

Much of the pro-American and anti-communist enthusiasm on the left faded away in the early 1950s. On the international plain the catalyst for this was the protracted and dangerous war in Korea, and the massive re-armament programme which the Attlee Government agreed to in response to American pressure in 1951. This led to the resignation of Aneurin Bevan, Harold Wilson and John Freeman from the Labour Government in April 1951, and the beginning of the bitter internal war between the Gaitskellite right and the Bevanite left which consumed so much of the Party's energy and time between 1951 and 1957.

Bevan was, as Minister of Health from 1945 to 1951, the architect of the National Health Service. He was justifiably proud of this great achievement, and he was ready to defend its principles against allcomers. So when the newly appointed Chancellor of the Exchequer, Hugh Gaitskell, decided to impose charges on teeth and spectacles in order to help pay for the projected vast programme of re-armament, Bevan let it be known to Attlee that this was for him a resigning issue. Gaitskell knew this well enough, but persisted with his plan. Indeed it may have been one reason why he persisted, for when Hugh Dalton said that John Strachey might resign over the charges along with Bevan and Wilson, Gaitskell replied that 'we will be well rid of the three of them.'[24] The charges would raise 23 million pounds in a year – a trivial sum in relation to the planned arms budget of £4,700 million over three years – but 'by insisting on pressing health service charges Gaitskell knowingly and unnecessarily provoked the crisis.'[25] Bevan and his supporters were right about the re-armament programme, too. It proved, as they said, to be a burden too heavy for the British economy, and the Conservatives, once they returned to power in 1951, lost no time in cutting back. Churchill grudgingly conceded that on this occasion Bevan had been right, but only 'by accident'.[26]

Of course Bevan had personal as well as political reasons for resigning. He was indisputably one of the Government's most prominent and talented members, but he had been passed over for promotion three times by Attlee, for the post of colonial secretary, as Chancellor in succession to Stafford Cripps, and for the foreign secretaryship when the dying Bevin was forced to resign in March 1951. What alienated some people in his resignation speech the following month was his bitter attack on Gaitskell, but what was of more substance was his reiteration of the third way perspective: ' … we have allowed ourselves to be dragged too far behind the wheels of American diplomacy' – words which have not lost their relevance more than 50 years later. He claimed that Britain since the War had 'been engaged … on the most remarkable piece of social reconstruction the world had ever seen', which had given the country 'the moral leadership of the world'. This was hyperbolical stuff, which indicated that the left shared in the illusions of the age as to Britain's global importance. But it also indicated Bevan's continuing belief that democratic socialism offered something distinctive which ought not to be sacrificed to the priorities of the Cold War. Gaitskell on the other hand took the quite different view that the most important task of the moment was to 'keep the Labour Party behind the Anglo–American alliance.'[27]

Bevanism came into existence with Bevan's resignation from the Government, and the conflict between left and right dominated and damaged the Labour Party for the next five years. It was both an ideological conflict and a struggle over the Party leadership. The latter was finally resolved at the end of 1955, when Attlee finally retired, and Gaitskell succeeded him, winning the leadership election with an outright majority of Labour MPs' votes over his two rivals, Bevan and Herbert Morrison, who came a humiliating third. In the course of the following year Bevan came to terms with Gaitskell as leader, and began to play a major part once more in the Party's leadership, but in the end at a devastating cost to his standing as the champion of the left within the Party.

Personal rivalries and antipathies undoubtedly exacerbated the ideological clash. Bevan at least initially despised Gaitskell[28] and Gaitskell in turn disliked Bevan's style of politics. Crossman reported that in 1955 Gaitskell was even comparing Bevan to Hitler: 'They are demagogues of exactly the same sort … there are minor differences but what's striking is the resemblance.'[29] What is even more striking is the extraordinary intolerance and inflexibility of the Party's dominant right. The recognition that left and right had always existed within the Party and simply had to co-exist seemed anathema to many of them, not least Gaitskell himself.

At the Party conference at Morecambe in 1952 the Bevanites enjoyed an extraordinary success in winning six out of seven seats on the NEC reserved for representatives of the constituency Labour parties. Dalton, Morrison and Gaitskell were among the unsuccessful candidates. That, and the passing of a number of radical motions, caused great alarm on the right. Two days after the conference Gaitskell hit back with a speech that was McCarthyist in both substance and tone. He denounced *Tribune* in strident terms: 'it is time to end the attempt at mob rule by a group of frustrated journalists' – although it is not clear in what way such influential figures as Foot and Crossman could be described as 'frustrated', nor in what way a small-circulation weekly could achieve 'mob rule'. Even more sinister was his charge that many speeches and resolutions at the conference were 'communist-inspired', and the claim that 'about one-sixth of the constituency Party delegates appear to be communist or communist-inspired'. Gaitskell was careful not to make the claim himself – 'I was told by some observers' – but of course by repeating it he gave it currency and plausibility. This was entirely characteristic of the smear rhetoric which typified the anticommunist witch-hunt of that period, but it is still shocking to find it used by a future leader of the British Labour Party.

The battle between left and right ground on for the next three years culminating in the attempt in 1955 by Gaitskell and others on the right to have Bevan expelled from the Labour Party after he challenged the Party line on the issue of the British H-bomb. It is amazing, looking back, that the outright expulsion of so prominent and popular a member of the Party should even have been attempted – and that only weeks before a general election. But the attempt failed. Attlee did not support it, and some of Gaitskell's closest 'revisionist' supporters such as Anthony Crosland and Roy Jenkins also advised against it – obliquely.[30] After this, and after Gaitskell had won the leadership, the tide of intolerance against the left began to recede, although Gaitskell always retained the Cold War mentality which searched incessantly for 'Reds under the bed'. His reference, in his defiant speech against the Party conference decision to support British nuclear disarmament in 1960, to 'pacifists, neutralists, and fellow-travellers' was typical of the man and the mentality.

Bevan was a hugely charismatic figure, a natural figurehead for the left. But he was strongly individualistic in both temperament and behaviour. He was not a committee person and he was not an organiser. Mikardo later wrote that 'The trouble with Nye was that he wasn't a team player.'[31] He was a spellbinding speaker who could draw great crowds to political meetings. But it was for others to organise those meetings and, indeed, to give 'Bevanism' its structure and continuity as a movement. And, as Mark Jenkins has shown, there was a lot going on beyond the rows and tensions at Westminster, which have tended to attract the most attention from political historians.[32]

Although Labour lost the general election of October 1951, it accumulated its highest ever vote of nearly 14 million, 200,000 more than the Conservatives, who nevertheless won more seats in the Commons. So six years of Labour government had, if anything, enhanced Labour's electoral popularity. What is more, individual membership of the Party peaked at over one million in the years 1952 and 1953, just when the Bevanites achieved their first success in getting elected as constituency representatives on the NEC. This suggests that there was no tension between building a mass party and support for the left, while the 1951 election vote suggests that, initially at least, the emergence of Bevanism did no harm to the Party's wider popularity. There is thus a case for saying that Bevan, the 'Leftwing firebrand', might have proved to be more electorally attractive than Gaitskell, contrary to the orthodoxy, which claims that only parties which hold to the 'moderate' centre ground can win elections.

Tribune's pamphlet *One Way Only*, which appeared in July 1951, with a foreword by the ex-ministers, Bevan, Wilson and Freeman, was a great success. It quickly sold 100,000 copies. Also very successful were the *Tribune* Brains Trusts, at which a panel of left-wing MPs would respond to audience questions. Support for these also indicated the popularity of the Bevanite position with rank-and-file Labour supporters and members. The right, usually with the support of Attlee, denounced the Bevanites as 'a party within the party', and did everything they could to make it difficult for the left to organise.

But, apart from providing support for Bevan himself, and for the left in parliament, what exactly did Bevanism stand for? The obvious place to look for an answer might seem to be Bevan's own book, *In Place of Fear*, which appeared in the spring of 1952, attracted much attention and was widely read. And the book does indeed tell us a great deal about Bevan himself, the experiences and education that made him a socialist, and the democratic socialist philosophy which provided the basis of his politics. But it is a rambling, disjointed text which at times shows signs of having been hurriedly dictated (which some of it was),[33] and, most seriously, it failed to provide the Labour left with the clear sense of direction and arguments they needed in their battle with the revisionist right. It was, as John Campbell says, a missed opportunity 'to stake out the agenda for the next Labour government'[34] at a time when much in the Party was moving in favour of the left. Intellectually, it offers no substantial competition for Crosland's *The Future of Socialism*, which appeared four years later and was immediately recognised as 'the bible' of the new revisionism.

It is not necessary to agree with Crosland's analysis or his conclusions to recognise the seriousness and quality of what he had produced. He argued that the changes within capitalism, and the shift in the balance of economic power from capital to government and the trade unions – some of this the work of the Labour Governments – made public ownership unnecessary as a means of control over the economy. Indeed, in his earlier contribution to the *New Fabian Essays* of 1952, he had gone further than this, and had argued that Britain, like Sweden, had 'by 1951 ... in all the essentials, ceased to be a capitalist country.'[35] Socialists should therefore focus on other, less economic and institutional goals, above all the attainment of real social equality. Equality was, in principle, as dear to the left as to the right. But in fact it received very little attention from the left in this period. For example, the Labour Party had committed itself to the principle of comprehensive secondary education at its conference in 1942, but the post-war government showed no interest in implementing it, and the left did not agitate for them to do so. It was left to two education ministers from the right of the Party, Crosland himself and Shirley Williams, to lead the Labour campaign for comprehensive schools in the 1960s and 1970s.

The truth was that too much Bevanite energy was consumed by relatively unimportant issues, such as (West) German re-armament, and in reacting to plans and proposals coming from the revisionist right. The left did not have a clear and coherent agenda of its own. It would continue to defend the principle of public ownership, and its extension; but there was no answer comparable in substance to Crosland's argument that public ownership had lost its relevance and its centrality to the socialist project. Bevan had not provided it: Crossman might have done, but he did not develop his ideas with the same pertinacity and sustained attention as Crosland.

In the essays he wrote in the 1950s, collected as *Planning for Freedom* (1965), Crossman claimed that 'the communist countries demonstrate with ever increasing force the efficiency of nationalization'[36] and that through 'the planned socialist economy' they would 'outpace and overtake the wealthy and comfortable Western economies.'[37] With hindsight we can see that Crossman, writing in the wake of the Sputnik launch in 1957, which certainly startled the West, was over-impressed by the apparent efficiency of the communist economies. But his was in any case not the best or the most appealing argument to put forward in support of public ownership. In addition to this he conceded a good deal to the revisionist case, accepting with them that the trade unions were now 'an essential institution of the modern mixed economy. Trade unionists are no longer denied their proper status and their leaders are always welcome at Downing Street, whatever Government is in power.'[38] He accepted, too, that

Keynesianism had enabled capitalism to avoid mass unemployment and produce a 'workable' type of society.[39] Since capitalism was susceptible to reform, the case for socialism had to be made in other terms, in terms of 'values'. 'Keynesianism may have undermined the old-fashioned economic case for socialism, but it has left the political and moral case for it completely unaffected.'[40] But this kind of formulation, like Bevan's *In Place of Fear*, left it very unclear what the programme of the next Labour government should be.

The question of what direction in internal policy Labour should take after 1951 was not really answered by the Bevanite left. The running was made by the revisionists. When the Party published *Industry and Society* in 1957, and it was approved by the Party conference, it was clear that the right had won the day on the issue of public ownership. The document committed the next Labour government to the nationalisation of steel and long-distance road haulage, but there were no further specific plans. It added that 'we reserve the right to extend public ownership in any industry or part of industry which, after thorough enquiry, is found to be seriously failing the nation.' This was a classic fudge: it was open to the left to put an optimistic interpretation on this if it wished to delude itself. But what it implied was that the general socialist case for public ownership had been jettisoned. Each act of nationalisation would require a specific and pragmatic justification. The principle of public or common ownership and control would not be enough. Privately, Bevan considered it 'a lousy document but one can't spend all one's time fighting.'[41] He commended it to the Trades Union Congress, and his one-time ally Harold Wilson presented it with enthusiasm to the Party conference.

After the 1959 electoral defeat, Hugh Gaitskell wanted to go a step further and revise the Party constitution in a way which would marginalise or at least qualify the commitment in Clause IV of the constitution to common ownership. It was a step too far. He was warned against it by Crosland and others among his right-wing allies and supporters, but with characteristic obstinacy insisted on presenting the proposal to Labour's special post-election conference.[42] It generated vast controversy within the Party and the trade unions, and had to be abandoned. It was left to Tony Blair, 35 years later, to push this symbolic change through a demoralised party, desperate for electoral success, and willing to pay almost any price for it.

The 1957 Party conference, at which *Industry and Society* was endorsed, was, however, most widely and painfully remembered for an even more devastating blow to the Labour left – one dealt by its own undisputed leader, Bevan himself. For this was the occasion when Bevan had to speak on behalf of the Party's National Executive against a motion urging that Britain, then only the world's third nuclear power, should take the lead by ceasing to manufacture or test such weapons. It was a traumatic moment for the Bevanites, and a turning point in the history of the British left.

The shock of Bevan's rejection of immediate unilateralism was all the greater because no politician had done more than he in the previous years to make 'the Bomb' a major issue in British politics. So much so, indeed, that Labour was already officially committed to halting nuclear testing, and Bevan undoubtedly intended, if he became Labour's foreign secretary, to take the lead in trying to negotiate a halt to the production of these appalling weapons.

The only surprise is that it took the left so long to recognise nuclear disarmament as a major issue. Admittedly the first decisions to manufacture nuclear weapons had been taken secretly by Attlee, Bevin and a tiny inner circle of confidants in October 1946. Bevin said he wanted a bomb 'with a bloody Union Jack on it', which sums up, crudely enough, the basic motivation for the decision. The Cabinet was neither consulted nor informed, although both Dalton and Cripps argued that the project could not be afforded.[43] In May 1948 the Defence Minister, A.V. Alexander, referred casually in parliament to the fact that atomic weapons were among those being developed; but no one seems to have caught on to the significance of this admission. Only in 1952, with the first weapons test off Australia, was the existence of a British nuclear programme made public, although it is possible that Bevan and other left-wing ministers knew about it before then. But it still took time for a public and political response to emerge.[44]

When it did, Bevan was one of its most passionate spokespeople, even if his position was not entirely clear or consistent. Sometimes he adopted a unilateralist position, at others not.[45] But in general terms he was at one with the unilateralists. He, like them, believed that Britain was in a unique position to take the initiative in promoting nuclear disarmament, whether by renouncing nuclear weapons unconditionally, or, less dramatically, by offering to do so if the big two powers, the US and the USSR, would respond appropriately. It was the latter position which he took up at the Brighton conference. But this involved rejecting a demand for immediate unilateral action, and Bevan, as a speaker who preferred spontaneity to a carefully prepared script, rejected unilateralism in terms which could only cause deep and lasting offence. Unilateral renunciation would be, he said, 'an emotional spasm'. Equally offensive but also absurd was the claim that a British Foreign Secretary, committed to unilateralism, would be sent 'naked in to the conference chamber'. This phrase in particular inspired several mocking cartoons.

As we have seen, Bevan's position was in fact more nuanced, closer to the unilateralist position, than this ill-judged speech and its impact suggested. But the damage was done. It was clear that the campaign against British nuclear weapons had lost a leader, and probably could not look to the stunned Labour left to fill the gap. Within weeks of Bevan's speech meetings were being held which led to the creation of CND, the Campaign for Nuclear Disarmament, which then became the first, and the most durable, of the many independent radical protest campaigns which have played so important a part in British politics in the past four decades and more.

Other factors contributed to the emergence of CND. The gratuitous Anglo–French attack on Egypt in the autumn of 1956 had had a radicalising effect, like the comparably gratuitous Anglo–American attack on Iraq in 2003. And in the same year Nikita Khruschev's sensational denunciation of Stalin who had died less than three years earlier, coupled with the Russian suppression of the Hungarian uprising at the same time as the Suez crisis, led to a mass exodus from the British Communist Party of intellectuals and activists. Unlike many earlier ex-communists, most of these defectors did not become reflex Cold War anti-communists, but remained on the left, and were active in left-wing politics.

From this time the pattern of left-wing politics in Britain was quite different from what it had been in the previous 40 years. It was no longer dominated by the Communist Party and the Labour left, both of which had suffered such damaging blows. Revolutionary, or 'Trotskyist', groupings flourished as they had not done before. An independent non-party New Left emerged, and CND undoubtedly attracted the kind of idealistic, even visionary commitment which would, in earlier decades, have been channelled into the Labour or Communist parties. 'Idealistic people went sour on the Labour Party, and a genuine public tide of moral feeling was broken on the unyielding rocks of the Labour leadership.'[46]

Bevan's defection was thus a turning-point in the politics of the British left. The left inside the Labour Party did not, of course, disappear or dissolve after the Brighton conference. *Tribune* identified itself wholeheartedly with CND, and the fight against Gaitskellite revisionism continued, most strongly after the 1959 election, when the revisionists were floating such notions as the overt renunciation of public ownership, or a change of name for the Party. But the accession of Harold Wilson to the leadership of the Party, after Hugh Gaitskell's sudden death in January 1963, cut much of the ground from beneath the feet of the left. Wilson was the nearest thing there was to a left-wing candidate in that leadership election, and his success was seen, not least by Wilson himself, as a kind of posthumous victory for Bevan (who had died in 1960) and Bevanism. Foot, Crossman and others saw it as a kind of 'opening to the left', and it took some time for them to shed this illusion – if they ever entirely did.

As so often in its history, the Labour left in this period was swimming against the tide within the Parliamentary Party. The leadership of the Party was, as it normally is, in the hands of the right; it was cautious, even timid in some ways, and conservative in much of its foreign policy. Sometimes this careful moderation seems to be electorally appropriate. But in the period after the Second World War it certainly was not. Morrison was wrong in thinking that a commitment to large-scale public ownership would prove an electoral liability in 1945. The electoral strength of Labour in 1950 and 1951, and the steady rise of individual Party membership up to 1952 together with the growth in trade union membership, which continued beyond 1952, all suggest that, notwithstanding the Conservative recovery, the tide of public opinion was still with Labour, if only Labour had known what to do with it. Alas, Labour's leadership had little idea of where to go once the major reforms planned and promised in 1945 had been implemented. Talk of 'consolidation' and endorsement of the so-called 'mixed economy' were coded announcements that further radical changes were not envisaged.

There was a vacuum where a future programme should have been, and while a centre-left intellectual like Crossman could see the problem[47] he did not have much of substance with which to fill the gap. So it was left to the revisionists of the right, and above all the formidably thorough Anthony Crosland, to offer a coherent perspective and strategy based on it. This gave the right a dynamic sense of direction which was as much political as intellectual. The left was strong enough to block Gaitskell's plan to sideline Clause IV in 1959, just as it was strong enough to win the conference vote on nuclear disarmament in 1960. But neither victory made a lasting difference to the future direction of the Party. The disarmament decision was reversed the following year, and Britain has to this day retained its nuclear weapons capability, although it depends on the United States for their means of delivery. Public ownership was quietly marginalised and under successive leaders Labour has steadily adapted to the far more modest and conservative role of providing efficient management support for a capitalist economy, while following in recent years the Thatcherite Conservative pattern of privatising and commercialising services and enterprises, some of which were in public hands long before Labour came to power in 1945.

On public ownership, the Labour left fought a long, if sometimes erratic, rearguard action against the revival of market philosophy and practice in the 1950s; but without making a really strong or well-developed case in favour. As to Britain's international position, the record is again erratic, with Foot and Crossman in particular showing themselves all too susceptible at times to the anti-communist obsessions of the early Cold War.

But broadly speaking we can discern one continuous thread of concern and hope: that a democratic socialist Britain should carve out an alternative third way between the capitalist United States and the authoritarian communism of the Soviet Union; that it should attempt to mediate or bridge the gulf between them; and that it should be strongly oriented towards what came to be known as the Third World, the world of the poor but developing societies which, like post-war Britain, adopted neither the capitalist nor the communist pattern of economic development. Bevan's personally close relations with Marshall Tito of Yugoslavia and Pandit Nehru of India were indicative of this orientation. It was a perspective which, like that of many people in CND, tended to overestimate Britain's global importance and influence. But nevertheless it offered a genuine viable alternative to the subservience to America which remained and still is the cornerstone of foreign policy for British governments of both parties. After Bevan had turned his back on unilateralism in 1957, it was left to CND and the New Left to keep this dream alive for a few more years. And it is worth noting that, in the first post-war years at least, this alternative perspective implied a far more positive view of Britain's relations with Europe than was current on the left in the 1960s and 1970s in relation to British membership of the EEC.

It could also be argued that the Labour left in this period was too focused on a single charismatic leader, Bevan, too dependent on his initiatives and his rhetoric. Yet the Labour left, both at Westminster and in the constituencies, had a life independent of Bevan's foibles and impulses; and when he failed on 'the Bomb' to provide the leadership they needed, an organisation of popular protest sprang up which more than filled the gap he left behind. The Labour left after this was often outflanked, and left looking rather old-fashioned and conventional – as when *Tribune* denounced the use of direct action against the Bomb as espoused by Bertrand Russell and the Committee of the One Hundred in 1961. After 1956, and after CND erupted onto the political scene with the first Easter march, from London to Aldermaston in 1958, the pattern of left-wing politics in Britain changed radically. It became more diverse, more pluralist, less party-dominated, and less politically conventional, and, nearly half a century later, looks likely to remain so.

Notes

1 Miliband, R., *Parliamentary Socialism*, (Allen & Unwin, London, 1961), ch. 9.
2 Mikardo, I., *Back-Bencher*, (Weidenfeld & Nicholson, London, 1988), p. 77.
3 Addison, P. *The Road to 1945*, (Pimlico, London, 1994), p. 264.
4 Mikardo, I., *Back-Bencher*, p. 110.
5 Rubinstein, D., *Socialism and the Labour Party 1945–50*, (ILP Publications, London, 1979), p. 5.
6 Miliband, R., *Parliamentary Socialism*, p. 298.
7 *Ibid.* p. 299.
8 Bevan, A., *In Place of Fear*, (Quartet, London, 1978), p. 49.
9 Nairn, T., *The Nature of the Labour Party* in *Towards Socialism*, (Fontana, London, 1965), p. 194.
10 See Morgan, K.O., *Labour in Power 1945–1951*, (Oxford University Press, Oxford, 1985), pp. 245–6.
11 Jones, M., *Michael Foot*, (Gollancz, London, 1994), p. 150.
12 *Ibid.*
13 Hill, D. (ed.), *Tribune 40*, (Quartet, London, 1977), p. 69.
14 Jones, M., *Michael Foot*, p. 149.
15 *Ibid.* p. 160.
16 See Hill, D., *Tribune 40*, p. 71.
17 See Jenkins, M., *Bevanism: Labour's High Tide*, (Spokesman, London, 1979), p. 75.
18 Schrecker, E., *The Age of McCarthyism*, (St Martin's, Bedford, 2002), p. 12.
19 See Stone, I.F., *The Truman Era*, (Turnstile Press, London, 1953).
20 See Jenkins, M., *Bevanism: Labour's High Tide*, pp. 66–7 and Stone, I.F., *The Truman Era*, pp. 60, 71–2.
21 See Crossman, R.H.S., *Planning for Freedom*, (Hamish Hamilton, London, 1965), pp. 165–7.
22 See Orwell, S., Angus, I. (eds), *The Collected Essays, Journalism and Letters of George Orwell*, (Secker & Warburg, London, 1968), pp. 191–4.
23 See Jenkins, M., *Bevanism: Labour's High Tide*, pp. 54–6.
24 See Brivati, B., *Hugh Gaitskell*, (Richard Cohen Books, London, 1996), p. 119.
25 See, Campbell, J., *Nye Bevan: A Biography*, (Hodder & Stoughton, London, 1987), p. 250.
26 See, Foot, M., *Aneurin Bevan 1945–1960*, (Paladin Books, London, 1975), pp. 352–3.
27 See Brivati, B., *Hugh Gaitskell*, p. 279; and for Bevan's speech see Campbell, J., *Nye Bevan: A Biography*, p. 242.
28 See Campbell, J., *Nye Bevan: A Biography*, p. 219.
29 *Ibid.* pp. 299–300; and see Lee, J., *My Life with Nye*, (Penguin, London, 1981), p. 241.
30 See Williams, P. (ed.), *The Diary of Hugh Gaitskell 1945–1956*, (Jonathan Cape, London, 1983), pp. 394–5.
31 Mikardo, I., *Back-Bencher*, p. 151.
32 See Jenkins, M., *Bevanism: Labour's High Tide*, chapters 5–6.

33 See Foot, M., *Aneurin Bevan 1945–1960*, p. 365.
34 Campbell, J., *Nye Bevan: A Biography*, p. 271.
35 Crosland, C.A.R., *The Transition from Capitalism* in Crossman, R.H.S. (ed.), *New Fabian Essays*, (Turnstile Press, London, 1952), p. 42.
36 Crossman, R.H.S. *New Fabian Essays*, p. 120.
37 *Ibid.* p. 95.
38 *Ibid.* p. 68.
39 *Ibid.* p. 60.
40 *Ibid.* p. 63.
41 See Campbell, J., *Nye Bevan: A Biography*, p. 329.
42 See Brivati, B., *Hugh Gaitskell*, pp. 332 and 339.
43 See Morgan, K., *Labour in Power 1945–1951*, p. 282.
44 *Ibid.* p. 284.
45 See Campbell, J., *Nye Bevan: A Biography*, pp. 331–2.
46 Hoggart, S., Leigh, D., *Michael Foot: A Portrait*, (Hodder & Stoughton, London, 1981), p. 121.
47 See Crossman, R.H.S., *New Fabian Essays*, pp. 126–7.

2   The New Left

Mark Wickham-Jones

Introduction

In the last week of February 1984, a young back-bench Labour MP spent the day campaigning at a parliamentary by-election in Chesterfield before returning to London that evening.[1] To be sure, the MP had family reasons for being there: his father-in-law was a friend of Labour's candidate. It was, however, something of a surprise that he should have made the journey north: politically at odds with the candidate, it was a visit he could have easily avoided. In all probability, despite doubts about the contestant's views, the MP felt an obligation to contribute. In so participating, the MP, Tony Blair, offered what was probably the only, albeit limited, practical support he gave to the career of the veteran left-winger Tony Benn, who was duly re-elected to the Commons on 1 March that year. Later, Blair's judgement about the period was savage: 'while I was growing up in the Labour Party and he [Ken Livingstone] and Arthur Scargill and Tony Benn were in control of the Labour Party they almost knocked it over the edge of the cliff into extinction.'[2]

Fourteen years before the Chesterfield by-election, on 18 June 1970, Harold Wilson's Labour Government lost office. As with any general election defeat, the outcome left the Party in a dispirited state. On this occasion, however, Labour was especially demoralised. The extent of the Party's dejection reflected, in part, that the defeat had been unexpected. More significantly, it signalled a pervasive sense of deep dissatisfaction with the Wilson administration's record since 1964, an impression heightened by the rhetoric surrounding Labour's accession to power in that year. Within weeks, debate was underway within the Party as to what were the key lessons of the Government's experiences and what should be the consequences of the defeat for Labour's policies and outlook. During the next four years or so, a 'New Left' gradually emerged based around a cohesive group of the Party's leading figures. They insisted that Labour take a more radical, focused and socialist approach to policy issues. Their demand marked a break with the Party's well established, essentially Revisionist trajectory.

I use the term New Left advisedly: the phrase can be applied to other group-ings within the Party's history (most obviously too much of the opposition that Revisionism encountered during the late 1950s). The significance of the term in this chapter is to emphasise the extent to which Labour's left after the 1970 defeat articulated a different set of ideas and took on a different organisational form to those so often associated with the left in the past. Other labels might be used to characterise the new grouping: for example, either Tribunism or Bennism.[3] The former does not capture the diversity of the left in this period, associating it with a single Parliamentary faction and newspaper (noteworthy though they were). The latter over-identifies the left with one individual, Tony Benn (albeit one of the most important personalities of the period). Just how cohesive was the New Left is an open question, of course: as an assemblage, it was made up of many different groups and individuals with a considerable diversity of support, emphasis and outlook. I argue here, however, that there was a core of goals and policy issues around which the New Left was based.

Between the early 1970s and the early 1980s, the New Left dominated Labour Party politics. It became entrenched within many of the constituency parties and established in many of the trade unions that were affiliated to Labour. Many of the Party's officials were openly identified with it, as were many of the intellectuals and commentators who were sympathetic to Labour whilst working, for the most part, outside of it. Just as Thatcherite values and ideas came to be associated with a wider societal discourse during the late 1970s and 1980s, so the New Left was linked to such a kind of dialogue, though a less pervasive one, for around a decade. Its ideas permeated socialist discourses inside and outside Labour in a range of areas, including of course economic matters. The New Left had less success in winning over the Parliamentary Labour Party but nevertheless it was able to cement a firm base amongst MPs. By contrast, it was able to dominate the Party's policy-making processes and, for a time, it shaped Labour's organisational structure in a dramatic and new fashion. In the early 1980s, for a variety of reasons, it fractured into several distinct groupings, the most important of which are commonly labelled the 'hard' and 'soft' left. Thereafter it had far less influence in directly shaping Labour's outlook. I do not address the decline of the New Left in this chapter; I do indicate, however, that its legacy was of considerable relevance for the contemporary Labour Party fashioned under Tony Blair's leadership.

For most, the New Left's legacy is not perceived to be a positive one. Many academics and journalists have described it as a group of manipulative and intolerant individuals who intended to drive out all dissenters from the Party. In this depiction, the New Left's fundamental concern was with issues of power and organisation: their aim was to design and impose a set of structures upon the Party within which their control would be secure. Policy issues and political ideas were secondary, epiphenomenal matters: they existed to be used in an instrumental fashion to attain that over-riding goal. Weapons with which to take control of the Party, policy promises could be thrown out at whim without any consequence as part of the ongoing battle between left and right that consumed Labour for much of the 1970s and 1980s. The focus of this conventional account is on the civil war within the party between 1979 and 1983: the constitutional demands of the New Left to reform Labour's structure are portrayed as a vicious and irrational attempt to recast the organisational character of British social democracy. Writing in the *Guardian* newspaper in October 1979, the commentator Peter Jenkins concluded acerbically: 'the dispute about democracy within the Labour movement is really, of course, a dispute about power.'[4] A related criticism was that the New Left's theoretical issues were divorced from practical matters. A decade or so later, David Marquand asserted that 'neo-socialism is surprisingly uninteresting' in terms of political strategy; the left's approach, he claimed, was 'silent'.[5] These are the judgements of those associated with Labour's right. There is a sense, however, in which they have become part of an accepted discourse, even within Labour, one that was well captured by the novelist Sue Townsend in *The Growing Pains of Adrian Mole*. Her character Ivan Braithwaite's letter of resignation from the Labour Party concluded: 'and finally and sadly your own comments about Tony Benn I find absolutely repellent. Calling a member of your own Party a "goggle eyed goon" is just not on.'[6]

The orthodoxy concludes that the New Left failed: its members were unsuccessful in their attempt to take over Labour. More than that, they did considerable damage to the Party's electoral prospects. The New Left is blamed for the internal struggle, for the conflict, and so for the electoral decline experienced by Labour in this period. Paul Hirst's blunt judgement is emblematic in this regard: 'the rise of Bennite leftism led to civil war within the Party.'[7] Ian Aitken was contemptuous: 'in my eyes, Benn's crew not only came close to destroying the Labour Party in the early eighties, they also created the conditions for Mrs Thatcher's triumphant onslaught on the Keynesian consensus.'[8]

Unsurprisingly, many within New Labour's leadership characterise the New Left in such a fashion. Scheming left-wingers are blamed for the Party's wilderness years between 1979 and 1997. Benn and others, Blair asserts, made Labour 'unelectable'. He claimed that 'at that time the Labour Party was a byword for extremism. We were hopelessly divided and deeply unpopular. MPs and council leaders routinely attacked the leadership. The atmosphere in meetings was poisonous.'[9] Philip Gould, a close lieutenant of Blair, echoes such assertions: 'from 1970 onwards, the left began their slow, inexorable assault. Labour's long death march had been begun. The centre of gravity inside the Party was shifting decisively to the left.'[10]

In this chapter, I take issue with these claims. First, I argue that the New Left was not motivated primarily by a desire to take control of Labour by any means, whether they be manipulative or not, democratic or not. I claim that the New Left is much better defined by the ideas and values to which its members were attracted. It was the failure of many within the Party's existing leadership to discuss and accede to those ideas within Labour's policy processes that led to the New Left's concern with organisational issues. From this perspective, far from being a secondary matter, ideas and policy commitments are the defining feature of the New Left. For much of the chapter, I examine the ideas that underpinned the objectives and policies adopted by the New Left.

Second, I conclude that leading actors within the New Left alone should not be blamed for Labour's electoral decline during the 1970s and 1980s. Moreover, and more importantly in the context of New Labour, I argue that the New Left played an important part in shaping the Party that is New Labour. To be sure, many of its leading figures disavow Blair's project. But I argue that there are links between the New Left and New Labour. I explore these connections in my conclusion.

The development of the New Left

The New Left emerged in response to a number of developments within and outside of the Labour Party. Of course, activists and others have often turned leftwards in the aftermath of electoral defeat. What is striking about Labour's trajectory after 1970 is the extent of the Party's radicalisation and the degree to which a new, much more coherent left-wing programme was adopted. The policy performance of the 1964–70 Wilson administration was pivotal to the materialisation of the New Left. Manifest disappointments ranged widely from domestic matters, especially economic policy, to foreign affairs. The economic growth promised with so much dramatic fanfare in 1964 had never materialised: far from it: Labour's National Plan had collapsed in ignominious failure, giving way to successive deflations that culminated in the devaluation of 1967 (accompanied by further deflation). A proposed planned growth of wages collapsed into a wages freeze and further severe restraint. Labour had undertaken to end the apparently destabilising cycles of 'stop–go': in a sense the administration had done so, but only by resorting to 'stop–stop'.[11] The conclusion drawn by left-wingers was that the extent of failure was such that new policy instruments were needed if socialist objectives were to be met. In particular, they concluded that Keynesian demand management could no longer be the basis for a successful socialist economic strategy. Economic failures, critics indicated, necessitated a reconsideration of the Party's existing social democratic trajectory. Incidentally, Crosland and the Revisionists were also critical of the Wilson administration's record. But they blamed policy errors (the failure to devalue) and the resolution of ministers rather than the policy tools that were at the Government's disposal.

Progress in social policy, long anticipated, was also discouraging. A range of pressure groups such as Shelter and the Child Poverty Action Group identified social problems that the Government had failed to tackle adequately. Such organisations provided detailed criticisms of the Wilson Government and their members fed directly into some of the groupings that came to characterise the New Left. The rise of these single-issue pressure groups during the 1960s was an indication of dissatisfaction. Many tackled issues that might have been considered to be the preserve of Labour, an indication that the Party was not fulfilling its natural roles.[12] (Of course, the late 1960s saw an upsurge of protest movements in universities, in unions and in civil society generally: much of such activities fed, in time, into the New Labour Left as well as other left-wing groupings.)

Policy failures were not confined to domestic matters. To the extent that the Wilson administration was perceived to have failed in standing up to United States involvement in Vietnam, foreign policy was equally disappointing to Party activists. Alan Warde catalogues the assortment of disappointments: 'Tribunite [left-wing MPs] disenchantment was also expressed in back-bench revolts which reached enormous proportions, over public expenditure, immigration, health charges, Vietnam, Nigeria, reform of the Common Market and social provision.'[13]

Labour had been elected on an ambitious and rhetorical programme. To offer such a manifesto, one that pledged so much and appeared to deliver so little, added to the disillusionment. In retrospect, the 1964 programme had papered over cracks within the Party and united some of the varied elements of British social democracy that had been long engaged in policy disagreements and other bitter disputes during the 1950s. In so doing unresolved problems were put to one side. After 1970, such quarrels erupted once again, as bitter and as far-reaching as ever. Policy failures strained relationships within the Party. Activists felt ignored by the Party leadership and Labour's membership fell precipitously between 1964 and 1970 from 830,000 to 680,000. On joining the Party in 1969, Ken Livingstone wrote later, 'I was swimming against a tide of disillusionment.'[14] By 1970, relations between the Wilson Government and many of the senior figures within Labour's affiliated unions were exceptionally poor. The tension reflected Wilson's attempt to recast the legal framework surrounding industrial relations, proposals contained in the White Paper, *In Place of Strife*. Many trade unionists felt they had been made scapegoats by the Wilson administration for Britain's relative economic failure. After 1970 they were to be much more supportive of the Party's left than they had been in the past. Policy fiascos were accompanied by contextual developments: structural change within the trade unions meant that certain left-inclined unions had become stronger within the Party (for example, the Transport and General Workers Union and the Engineers now controlled 31 per cent of the vote at the Party conference), whilst new unions emerged that were less accommodating of Labour's predominantly right-wing leadership (such as NUPE and ASTMS). In any case, retirements saw the appointment of a new cohort of more assertive trade union leaders such as Jack Jones and Hugh Scanlon. Taken together, such factors meant that the trade unions were much less deferential and less loyal to the norms and traditions of Labour's past: an aggressive union movement was prepared to support left-wing demands. Arguably, a more militant trade unionism had emerged, one evidenced by a growth in strikes during the 1960s (2.2 million days lost in 1964; 11.0 million in 1970).

The Party context was also much more favourable than in the past. Labour's list of proscribed organisations was abandoned in 1973. In a tolerant atmosphere, it was easy for the New Left to campaign, organise and put together new ideas.

The character of the New Left

Labour's New Left is not defined by a single text, in the same way that, arguably, Labour's Revisionist right was during the 1950s. The Revisionists owed much to Tony Crosland's *The Future of Socialism* (though other texts by Evan Durbin,

Douglas Jay, the Socialist Union and the Fabians were important). Two comparative points can be made about the Revisionist canon. The first concerns the status enjoyed by Crosland's volume: it is hard to over-estimate its import. The second is that many of the Revisionist texts, including Crosland's, range widely and freely as comprehensive accounts of what it is to be a social democrat. For the New Left, there is no defining text of such unchallenged weight and, for the most part, such volumes as exist are focused and discrete. This point should not be taken to indicate that the writings of the New Left are unimportant; rather as a sign that they are not as all-embracing as those produced by a previous generation of Labour intellectuals. A plethora of material defines the New Left. In terms of economic policy, Stuart Holland's *The Socialist Challenge* remains the seminal account.[15] Regarding civil society and democratic reform, Tony Benn's collected essays are important.[16] The specific case for import controls is made in the reports of the Cambridge Economic Policy Group. The material produced by the Institute of Workers' Control (IWC), published by Spokesman, focuses upon a variety of matters including industrial democracy (a particular interest of the periodical, *Workers' Control Bulletin*, re-launched as *Workers' Control*) and the peace movement (a concern of the journal *Spokesman*). Many of the New Left's arguments and claims and much of its vision and outlook is to be found in a plethora of sources including newspaper articles, conference debates, pamphlets and interviews as well as in books and chapters.

Stuart Holland's book is the most significant economic text, one that came to define the Alternative Economic Strategy (AES) advocated by the New Left. A variety of other publications dealt with the AES: most of the groupings that contributed to the New Left produced a version, as books or pamphlets, of the Left's economic approach and further support was to be found in the annual TUC Economic Review. That *The Socialist Challenge* dominates the New Left's economic discussion, however, is easily understood. The volume was the most complete account of the left's economic thinking and one of the first to be published (in the summer of 1975). Holland was the principal architect of the New Left's thinking as practised in the Labour Party's policy-making committees during the early 1970s and one reviewer described him as 'Tony Benn's guru'.[17] Writing in *The New Statesman*, Alan Ryan noted, 'for what it [*The Socialist Challenge*] offers is a full dress statement of the economic thinking of the Labour Party's left wing'.[18] *The Economist* described it as 'the new socialist orthodoxy.'[19] Robert Skidelsky was more forthright: 'it is arguably the most important book from the British left since Anthony Crosland's *The Future of Socialism* whose central thesis it explicitly sets out to disprove.'[20] Reading *The Socialist Challenge*, one is struck by the extent to which Holland's volume, littered with references to Crosland, is a direct response to the Revisionist model. Michael Brody described it as:

A clear attempt to draw up a massive, closely-argued and wide ranging analysis of the way forward for economic and industrial policy in Britain, which is intended to have the same overwhelming effect within Labour Party circles as did Anthony Crosland's moderate manifesto *The Future of Socialism* twenty-five years ago.[21]

Holland's arguments not only shaped Labour Party documents for the decade between 1973 and 1983: his themes influenced much of the subsequent debate (though different versions of the AES existed).[22] Reviewing Tony Benn's *Arguments for Socialism* in 1979, Ferdinand Mount noted the author's debt to Holland for his data.[23]

Alongside texts such as Holland's, individuals were important in shaping the New Left. Especially significant was Tony Benn, who had been Minister for Technology in the Wilson Cabinet. Disillusioned with that Government's performance, he moved sharply left in its aftermath. A skilled and persuasive orator, he galvanised the left and became a focal point for the discussions around which the New Left emerged. Benn was, of course, especially important in mobilising and offering encouragement: for one participant, during the 1970s, he was 'the most formative influence in the Labour Party'.[24] Michael Meacher remembered him as 'an inspiration, who had a grand vision, who had a sense of purpose and who was a brilliant communicator.'[25] Benn chaired the Party's Home Policy Sub-Committee which reported to its National Executive Committee and was responsible for the content of Labour Party policy documents. (As an aside, it should be noted that in general left-wingers were assiduous in attending the internal policy-making committees of the Party). Other Parliamentarians who were sympathetic to the ideas of the New Left included Judith Hart, Joan Lester, Ian Mikardo and Brian Sedgemore.

Stuart Holland's role has been noted earlier. Ryan described him as 'one of the intellectual custodians of the tough interpretation of Labour's industrial policy'.[26] Michael Meacher, a member of Labour's left and an MP, remembered later, 'he [Holland] had a great impact on Party consciousness.'[27] An academic at Sussex University, Holland was by no means alone, of course. Michael Barratt Brown advocated similar ideas though he had less direct impact upon the Labour Party. Members of the Cambridge Economic Policy Group, one of whom (Francis Cripps) worked for Tony Benn for a period, shaped the case for import controls whilst arguments for increased worker participation were made by Ken Coates and others associated with the Institute for Workers' Control (IWC) and the Spokesman publishing house, based in Nottingham. Support for nationalisation came from the Public Enterprise Group of which the seemingly tireless Holland was chair in the early 1970s. Party officials who were sympathetic to the left included Terry Pitt, Geoff Bish (successive policy directors) and Margaret Jackson (later, as Margaret Beckett, a Labour MP).

Support for the New Left came from some of Labour's affiliated trade unions and other groupings within the Party.[28] Benn wrote of one IWC meeting in 1973: 'it was a mixed bunch, a sort of market place of the extreme left.'[29] The Campaign for Labour Party Democracy was a significant body, assiduous in promoting the cause of conference sovereignty. It was followed in 1978 by the Labour Co-ordinating Committee, which subsequently became identified with the soft left before being made over into a Blairite force during the mid-1990s (an indication of the transformation of the left over the last 25 years). Other groups included the Rank and File Mobilising Committee and Independent Labour Publications (a small successor to the Independent Labour Party but which contained a few elderly, loyal members who had been expelled from the party during the 1930s, an indication of a pre-Bevanite, indeed pre-war left). Some of those involved on Labour's left in the 1970s had been involved in other earlier lefts: Michael Barratt Brown and John Hughes, for example, had been involved in the New Left that criticised Revisionism in the late 1950s and 1960s. Others had been involved in the May Day Manifesto group which organised in response to the deflations of the Wilson administration.

The New Left that developed in Labour politics after 1970 was markedly different from its radical predecessors. The Party has, of course, always had a dissenting wing of those impatient with and disenchanted by the leadership. But earlier lefts had been characterised by very different features. They usually enjoyed less support, they were often based on personalities, and they were frequently reactive and rather emotional in outlook. Above all, the left that challenged the Party's leadership during the 1940s and 1950s lacked a theoretically coherent set of ideas for the domestic agenda. The Bevanites were very focused on international concerns. More nationally oriented, the New Left of the 1970s was less concerned with an ethical socialism and more interested in practical measures.[30] It also enjoyed closer links to the trade unions than in the past. A last point of contrast is that the Bevanites were firmly wedded to the Parliamentary process (for critics such as Ralph Miliband the defining feature of their impotence). Whilst Parliament was the focus for their strategy, the New Left was ambiguous on this subject and accepted that extra-parliamentary action might be necessary (strikes, protests, local-level activities might all play a part alongside Parliamentary methods).

Labour's New Left should not be defined purely in terms of the ideas and values that it espoused. I realise in making this point I might be interpreted as conceding some ground to those who depict the New Left largely as part of an organisational struggle. I am not: my analysis indicates that ideas and values were central to the New Left. But the New Left was a complex phenomenon and its support for Labour's ethos, that is for the norms and rules that define the Party's character, should be noted alongside doctrinal matters.[31] The New Left accepted much of the labourist tradition that identifies the Party: for example it supported striking workers and those engaged in industrial actions as a matter of principle. In his collection, *Arguments for Socialism*, Benn noted how the experiences of the labour movement had shaped the Party's character.[32] But the policy debates and theoretical disputes of the 1970s and 1980s, particularly during the first half of that period, demonstrate that the doctrinal character of the New Left should not be neglected. This commitment to ideas, organised in a coherent package, marked a new development for the Labour left and is an important defining feature of the politics of the left during the 1970s.

The objectives of the New Left

What objectives did the New Left seek? Broadly, the New Left sought a society defined by a number of key features. These included: considerable equality (and a sweeping redistribution of wealth and income); a greater efficiency in the production of goods and services; a set of democratic processes and procedures throughout all aspects of decision-making by which all could participate and through which those in authority could be held to account; and an internationalism in foreign affairs which promoted disarmament. Benn claimed, 'the Labour Party exists to bring about a shift in the balance of power and wealth ... We also aim to make economic power more fully accountable to the community, to workers and the consumer. We aim to eliminate poverty, to achieve a far greater economic equality and meet urgent social needs.'[33]

Equality

The New Left's notion of equality was a tougher one than that of the Revisionists: it was more directly linked to equality of outcome and to a determination to eradicate significant inequalities of income and wealth through redistributive measures. Holland noted, 'if income equalisation were introduced as an explicit strategy ... it would have to include income from wealth, where the greatest inter-personal and inter-family disparities lie.'[34] Revisionists had toyed with the idea of wealth taxes: for the most part, they concluded them to be of limited import as means of securing equality. Benn asserted 'a belief in basic human equality and freedom.'[35] Despite this reference to freedom, most members of the New Left placed less emphasis on this aspect of socialist theory than did either Revisionist thinkers or Neil Kinnock and Roy Hattersley in the Party statement of the socialist creed that they drafted a decade or so later. For the most part, liberty was taken to be an implicit feature of an egalitarian society in which an equitable distribution of resources empowered individuals to realise their full potential in a positive fashion (a freedom to develop their capabilities). Critics regarded the New Left's commitment to equality coupled with its desire to replace material incentives with more selfless motivations as impractical.

Efficiency

The New Left doubted whether the existing pattern of market processes and private ownership could secure efficient economic outcomes. It claimed that an alternative, much more interventionist and socialist set of arrangements could be designed to attain a better rate of growth. In one sense a reflection of the United Kingdom's persistent economic difficulties and its generally disappointing performance for much of the post-war period, efficiency was a more important goal for many members of the New Left than was equality.[36] The attainment of growth was pivotal and, broadly, there was none of the complacency about economic issues that marked some of Crosland's work. The emphasis on growth was a contrast with Bevanism as well: Alan Budd noted that 'the problem with capitalism became not that it is immoral but that it is inefficient'.[37] As Benn asserted, these contradictions [economic difficulties] are fundamental to the economic system under which we operate; and that system [the market one] is deadlocked and log-jammed by contradictory interests that cannot be resolved without basic economic and political reforms.[38]

He continued, 'indeed we believe that the nation can earn its living effectively and profitably only if there is a new balance of wealth and power in favour of working people.'[39] It is important to remember that Benn and others wrote at a time of sustained economic difficulties for the British and other similar economies. The notion that a more interventionist model of economic policy might be more efficient than that of a market-based approach was a commonly held, though not uncontested one.

Democracy, accountability and participation
Members of the New Left were far more interested in issues of participation than the Party had been hitherto. Crosland had been lukewarm about industrial democracy: it was 'remote from the vicissitudes of life on the factory floor'.[40] He claimed: 'we surely do not want a world in which everyone is fussing around in an interfering and responsible manner, and no one peacefully cultivating his garden.'[41] By contrast, thinkers of the New Left such as Benn and Holland concluded that workers should be able to participate fully in decisions that shaped the environments in which they worked. The term 'participation' needs to be deployed with care: in general many members of the New Left were uncertain about what form workers' participation might take. Some within the Institute for Workers' Control objected to the term (as well as to workers' management) as being insufficiently radical and implying that employees might be co-opted into existing arrangements. They favoured 'workers' control'. This claim is captured by comments by Neil Kinnock, then in a more radical phase than that associated with his later leadership of Labour. He argued, 'no strategy for industrial democracy could work if based on "consultation" or "participation" because both of these implied that workers had no right or power to take decisions about how industry was run.'[42] Predictably, members of the New Left were lukewarm about the Bullock committee's modest proposals for industrial democracy during the 1974–9 Labour Government.

The key point about participation and accountability, however, is that the New Left's goals were not confined to economic and social outcomes as defined by efficiency and equality but referred also to the processes and arrangements by which such aims were secured. Moreover, participation was a general, ill-defined ambition, one not confined to the workplace. Those with power should be held to account in order that society was more democratic. Accordingly, decisions should be made openly and transparently. So, for example, in order for society to be democratic, the powers of the British Prime Minister should be constitutionally defined and limited by a variety of mechanisms of accountability, including a greater lucidity in their exercise. Of course, this feature of the New Left's political thought had considerable bearing upon the organisational structure of the

Labour Party during the early 1980s. Benn argued, 'the real problem is that Labour MPs have fallen under the control of the parliamentary leadership through patronage, official secrecy and demands for total loyalty to the leader personally.'[43] Such patronage needed to be curbed if Labour was to be a democratic and, effectively, a socialist party.

Internationalism

The New Left's internationalism was organised around pacificism and disarmament. It represented a marked contrast to the pro-deterrence stance taken during much of the Cold War by the Party. This internationalism was equivocal and several commentators have portrayed the New Left as a nationally oriented one.[44] At times the New Left appeared to be dominated by national concerns and to be exceptionally insular in its outlook. Joan Lestor berated the left's failure to pay 'serious attention to internationalism'.[45] Tony Benn's hostility towards the European Economic Community was motivated, in large part, by an anxiety that British membership of it involved too great a loss of national political and economic sovereignty, a fear that was shared by many other left-wingers. Indeed, on occasion Benn's model of socialism was presented in a rather blinkered fashion:

> this [socialism] is very much a home-grown British product ... We have been wise enough not to seek to impose a common socialist dogma on anyone. Indeed our socialism grew out of our experience and was not handed down from above or received from outside.[46]

Holland wrote: 'the advocacy of workers' control by Tony Benn in the seventies has owed more to his experience of the limits of technocracy and the example of Upper Clyde Shipbuilders than to any foreign model.'[47] Interestingly, aspects of Holland's own work (essentially non-socialist elements) were influenced by European economic arrangements, especially those in Italy. The ambiguities of the New Left's internationalism provides an important point of contrast with the earlier Bevanite left for whom a realignment in prioritisation of foreign policy in a socialist direction was a defining feature.

These features were inter-related in significant ways and as goals they merged together. The New Left held that a society based around the principle of accountability and participation would be a more efficient one. Workers who were engaged in what their firms did would work more productively. Likewise an egalitarian society would be an efficient one: there was no trade-off between fairness and efficiency.

The New Left's goals were, arguably, unremarkable. How far they differed from those articulated by Labour before the early 1970s is an open question. The objectives of equality, efficiency, democracy and internationalism had long defined the socialist project. Just how much Stuart Holland's basic definition of socialism is at odds with that of Tony Crosland is by no means obvious. Holland argued: 'socialism is the creation of a society in which it is easier to secure self-fulfilment through serving society than through the exclusive pursuit of self alone.' Such a society demanded 'maximum democracy' and the 'maximum disposal of economic resources for the welfare of all the people'.[48] Transparently, there was much in such bland statements with which Labour's Revisionists might agree and at times members of the New Left claimed congruence between their goals and those of Revisionism: what had changed, Holland argued, was the means by which such goals might be achieved. The Crosland model of social democracy presumed a competitive economy, an erroneous assumption given the growth of monopolistic firms:

> the main reason for the crisis [of the British economy] has been not so much the misapplication of Keynesian techniques of demand management as their erosion by a new mode of production which has divorced macro policy from micro structure.[49]

Holland continued later in his book: 'it is on this key question of state power and government control that the Crosland analysis has been proved wrong, and with it the "revisionist" thesis.'[50]

There are some significant differences, however, between the detailed goals of the New Left and those of the revisionists. One significant point to be emphasised is that the New Left's model implied a transformation of capitalism: the kind of goals to which its adherents aspired could only be attained with far-reaching reforms to the structure of the economy and of society. The implication was that, once such reforms had been implemented, society would no longer be a capitalist one dominated by a free market economy, unfettered individualistic decision-making and private ownership. In part this difference reflected a contrasting perception of the British economy and the nature of capitalism. Crosland (and other Revisionists) continued to assert that governments were not threatened by the power of firms, especially of multinationals. Holland, however, made frequent reference to the 'increasing threat which multinationals can prove to national economic sovereignty.'[51]

Taken together such goals led most members of the New Left to doubt that their goals could be secured within a capitalist society. A wholesale transformation was needed to attain their goals. In short, socialism and capitalism were incompatible: Judith Hart wrote: 'the needs of the nation cannot be met by using capitalist methods in a capitalist economy'.[52] Such an approach could secure neither an equal society nor economic growth. This conclusion challenged the assertion of Labour's Revisionists that social democratic goals could be achieved in a capitalist framework, albeit one that was regulated. Joan Lestor argued: 'if our ambition is no greater than to modify some of the harsher consequences of the capitalist system we should cease to call ourselves socialists.'[53] A similar point was made by Benn towards the end of his collected essays:

> it [the labour movement] must now decide whether the aspirations of British socialism are to be narrowly redefined as the desire to hold those

gains we can expect as a by-product of a successful capitalism that can afford them in the rare boom years. The alternative is to set our sights higher, to decide to transform capitalism by democracy into socialism.[54]

In comparable vein, Holland concluded that any incomes policy (something that had become a staple of the Revisionist policy armoury by the early 1970s) could only work if linked to tough controls on prices and profits. For society, the implication was comprehensive: 'pursued in the wider context of socialist transformation, such equalisation policy would aim to abolish class society.'[55] The goals of the New Left and the revisionists were fundamentally different.[56] (Interestingly, Holland claimed that his were in alignment with 'traditional Labour policy'.[57])

Perhaps it should be observed here that different visions and different policy programmes existed within the New Left. These ranged from modest interventions directed at improved growth to much more far-reaching strategies. Indeed, some proponents of such measures indicated that such an approach would be unlikely to succeed but would pave the way for yet more radical policies. In a sense most members of the New Left combined these positions: Benn told Eric Hobsbawm, 'I don't say that this is a comprehensive transformation strategy, but at least it's got the twin goals of running it and changing it.'[58]

The policies of the New Left

To achieve these goals, the New Left came up with a different set of policy measures to those advocated by Labour in the past. The economic failures of 1964–70 coupled with the reassertion of more definitively socialist goals demanded new policies, and the programme articulated by the Labour left became known during the 1970s as the Alternative Economic Strategy. Alongside Keynesian reflation, Stuart Holland concluded that Labour needed to use nationalisation and planning to secure its aims. His reasoning was straightforward: the kind of competitive market that Crosland and other Labour theorists had assumed the British economy to be no longer existed. The most significant development was the monopolisation of the economy: a hundred or so firms dominated manufacturing production, producing half of the overall output, as well as other sectors of the economy.[59] Monopolisation was coupled with an internationalisation of the economy, characterised by the growth of multinational firms. In this regard, Labour's New Left anticipated later discussions of globalisation. The last defining feature of the economy was that a class-based elite dominated these monopolistic multinationals. It was a fallacy to assume that managers acting in society's general interest ran private firms. Managers and owners worked together, motivated by private profit regardless of any more general consequences for society. It was not just the trend to monopolisation therefore that necessitated new policies: power remained concentrated within the hands of a business class. Class antagonism was, according to Holland, a defining feature of the UK's social structure.

The impact of these changes was to erode an economic policy based upon demand management. The necessary prerequisites for Keynesianism no longer existed. Monopolistic multinationals did not respond to injections of demand into the economy by a government with increased production (and employment); they simply raised prices. Their investment decisions were immune to the orthodox Keynesian policy battery of fiscal, monetary and regional measures. Accordingly, new instruments were needed. These instruments included nationalisation, planning and workers' control.

The basis of nationalisation should be 'competitive public enterprise' which involved the takeover of one private firm per sector of the economy: the company would then be run in a competitive fashion to challenge the private monopolies. Rather than raise prices to extract abnormal profits, public firms would cut prices and compel private companies to match their decisions. Barratt Brown and Holland claimed 'productivity in the public sector has in fact often grown faster than in private manufacturing.'[60] Recently nationalised companies would be managed from a new state holding company, the National Enterprise Board. It would ensure 'an active penetration of private capital though public ownership and a transformation of the nature of power in industry.'[61] Whilst growth was the central objective of nationalisation, public ownership would improve equality and accountability. Judith Hart noted that previous nationalisations had had little impact upon equality, 'because it has not embraced the profitable, but, indeed has underwritten the unprofitable, it [public ownership] has had very little effect on the distribution of economic power and wealth'.[62] Nationalisation would enhance democracy, a *Tribune* editorial proclaimed: 'those who control them [private firms] are totally unresponsive to the needs of the nation'.[63]

For planning individual agreements, a form of contract between companies and the state would in essence seek to attain the same goal, that of a more competitive, faster growing economy. Firms would be obliged to divulge information on pricing policies and map out their plans for the future.

Like the Revisionists, the New Left claimed that it did not advocate nationalisation for its own sake. Benn wrote, 'we are not interested in ownership just for the sake of ownership. We are concerned with the power that ownership carries with it to shape our future.'[64] The New Left's attitude to the matter was essentially an empirical one. Hart proclaimed that 'every proposal [for public ownership] must be justified on its merits and shown to be relevant to national needs.'[65] Nationalisation was, however, pivotal. Hart described it as 'a first essential if we are to move towards a socialist society'.[66] Without such interventionist policies, Holland claimed that 'in international policy, the state will increasingly see its sovereignty undermined by multinational capital rather than reinforced by international agencies.'[67] *Tribune* was blunt: 'without a doubt, it [Labour Party policy] hinges on the need for a massive extension of public ownership.'[68] Twenty-five companies was the 'minimum necessary to put the next Labour government in a position to master economic events'.[69]

In June 1973, the Party published *Labour's Programme 1973* outlining the New Left's policy promises and for the next decade or so formal documents were dominated by these commitments. In the summer of 1973, perhaps unsurprisingly, much of the focus within Labour and in the press was on the plans for the nationalisation of 25 of the leading profitable companies in the economy, mostly in manufacturing sectors. Speaking at a conference just after the February 1974 general election, Holland defended them:

> Labour's public ownership proposals were not irrelevant luxuries ... a powerful National Enterprise Board had to be central to Labour's strategy and must not be allowed to become merely the glorified Industrial Reorganisation Corporation that some Labour leaders wanted ... The public ownership of twenty-five companies in these conditions would be a real lever for radical change.[70]

When *The Socialist Challenge* was published two years later, David Marquand commented: 'for what Mr Holland has done is to pour new wine into the old bottles of Clause IV: to provide for the first time for twenty-five years an at least faintly plausible theoretical justification for the prejudices of the Labour left.'[71] Holland argued:

> it [monopolisation of the economy] supports the traditional socialist argument that without public ownership and control of the dominant means of production, distribution and exchange, the State will never manage the strategic features of the economy in the public interest.[72]

Investors' Chronicle noted: 'Holland is also realistic in pulling no punches over what would be the implications of the sort of massive state intervention in industry which the left sees as essential.'[73]

Given the increased monopolisation of the British economy, Stuart Holland described Crosland's opposition to the new policies as surprising: 'with a bit of foresight, Mr Crosland might have claimed credit for the leaven in Labour's new public enterprise proposals.'[74] Ryan expressed 'surprise at the ferocity of the [Party] opposition the proposals [of Holland] aroused'.[75] Later, Holland remembered, 'when it was put to him that he might well be considered the godfather of the idea [Competitive Public Enterprise] ... Crosland rejected the idea, saying, "I never considered anything on this scale or of this kind." '[76] Indeed, in proposing that public firms should make profits some older left-wingers were hostile to the thrust of Holland's outlook. Eric Heffer wrote later that they 'smelt too much of Tony Crosland's concept of only developing publicly owned companies in profitable sectors'.[77] Alan Budd concluded: 'if the intention is to convert the Revisionists the time is far too hostile ... It is thus unlikely to shift moderate opinion in the Labour Party while it could well be regarded as too generous to capitalism by the left.'[78]

The New Left's economic strategy was not confined to public ownership and planning. A battery of policies would be required to secure socialist goals. These included price controls, measures for industrial democracy and, for a time at any rate, import controls. Industrial democracy would, of course, be important in the promotion of accountability. A 1981 internal Party document stated that as 'a matter of principle … key decisions which affect the future of society should not be taken in private by unelected bodies.'[79] Quite what industrial democracy would entail remained uncertain and there was a further question mark concerning whether such a measure could be reconciled with a *dirigiste* planning system. Holland noted that there were 'many possible variants on the means whereby workers themselves should give shape to the endorsement of greater industrial democracy'.[80] Protectionist measures did not figure in the original AES but by the mid-1970s had become a staple, though controversial, element of it. Concern surrounded them most obviously because potentially they would damage the living standards and prospects of workers elsewhere by reducing trade (and so reflected badly on the New Left's internationalist credentials). Holland qualified their inclusion in the AES: 'I am not wholly persuaded about the import controls case, which is always isolated by the press, but it may be necessary.'[81] The New Left was hostile to the European Economic Community and most members advocated withdrawal (Holland, again, was ambiguous on the matter). One reviewer commented:

> he [Holland] echoes Tony Benn's carpings about the Community, though it is not clear when one has finished the book whether he is objecting to the Community because it has developed supranational powers and so threatens national sovereignty, or because it has not developed these powers and is therefore ineffective to tackle the problem.[82]

Alongside an interventionist economic strategy, defence was a policy issue of considerable import for the New Left: its members were tireless advocates of unilateral nuclear disarmament. The left's commitment to internationalism, however, was often rather submerged. Benn was hostile to the notion that Labour might learn from elsewhere in its economic strategy, criticising one internal document in 1981: 'it was a real bureaucrats' paper – let's copy France and Japan. There was nothing about social justice and socialism'.[83]

The structure of the Labour Party became a particular focus for the New Left's policy programme. The New Left was committed to an extension of accountability and participative processes throughout the economy and civil society. Such processes should, of course, be introduced within the organisation of the Party. That the Party's largely right-wing leadership was able to ignore much of the New Left's policies, especially during the 1974–9 government, added to the importance of transforming Labour's internal configuration. Given the failure of the Labour leadership to endorse the left's programme either in opposition (between 1970 and 1974) or in government (between 1974 and 1979) it is unsurprising that betrayal was a recurrent theme. Many members of the New Left repeatedly levied such a charge against senior figures within the Party.

After 1979, given the disappointments of office, it was unsurprising that so much effort should be focused on constitutional reform. Benn was forthright: 'unless this power balance is redressed by the introduction of new democracy within the Party and the movement, we shall never resolve the pressures which have built up, the nature of which it is so easy to misinterpret.'[84] Members of the New Left emphasised the importance of popular support within the Party in the articulation and implementation of their measures: Holland wrote: 'if the Labour leadership in Parliament is to be forced to implement the radical heart of the programme, it will have to be pressured by organised Labour – both at a national level and on the shop floor'.[85]

It is important to note that the New Left's commitment to constitutional reform stemmed from its programmatic demands. A coherent policy programme was articulated during Labour's period in opposition between 1970 and 1974. Before the 1979 general election defeat, policy matters, with a few exceptions, dominated the New Left. A glance at the pages of *Tribune* in this era indicates the range of policy debates and the relative unimportance of constitutional matters within the Party. Only in the aftermath of defeat and the rejection of the New Left's measures, what was official Labour Party policy, did constitutional reform become the central issue. The exceptions are noteworthy. *Tribune*, long associated with policy demands, published a pamphlet on organisational change in 1972. More significantly, having been floated a year earlier, the Campaign for Labour Party Democracy was launched in the aftermath of Harold Wilson's refusal to accept the proposal that a Labour government nationalise 25 of the top 100 companies.[86] The causal link from policy to power here is manifest: policy development and theoretical debate within the Party preceded the struggle for constitutional reforms.

It is clear that, despite some surface similarities, members of the New Left held different goals and espoused contrasting policies to Labour's Revisionists. Their analyses were based on different theories: the New Left acknowledged an explicit debt to Marx and theories of monopoly capitalism whilst the Revisionists continued to espouse Keynesianism. They took different views of the empirical nature of the economy and of what was a realistic reformist strategy. There were significant differences between the New Left and the Bevanites as well. Poorly developed in policy terms, Bevanism articulated a complex and sweeping set of interventionist measures, including a wages policy, in a rather loose fashion. One further point on this issue should be noted. Whilst Crosland and others concluded that the Party's policy platform must be limited to meet the perceived moderate preferences of the electorate, the New Left concluded their strategy to be electorally viable regardless of its content. Benn claimed: 'campaigning for democracy within the Party will continue in the future because these reforms are intrinsically linked with Labour's integrity and credibility as a party trying to win popular support.'[87] Elsewhere he claimed: 'if – but only if – the electorate vote for a Labour government, the Party expects its elected MPs to implement this policy.'[88]

Conclusions

Having dominated Labour politics for much of the 1970s and early 1980s, the New Left's influence dissipated dramatically thereafter. The most significant reasons for this development concerned its fragmentation into different group-ings, the resurgence of the Party's right, and the realignment of many of Labour's affiliated unions. The splits had been presaged as far back as the early 1970s. For example, Michael Foot, strongly committed to socialist goals as Labour leader in the 1980s, was more cautious than others about what kind of commitment the Party should give to public ownership in 1973. In the 1980s, he was critical over the emphasis placed upon constitutional reform. Benn's campaign to win the deputy leadership of the Party in 1981 was especially important, dividing the New Left in a dramatic and what was to be an irreconcil-able fashion.

What responsibility the New Left played in Labour's electoral decline between 1970 and 1983 is uncertain. Of course, they must take some blame for the Party's difficulties. But it is by no means obvious that a party was unelectable on the kind of policies that they articulated in this period. Labour won the February 1974 General Election on a radical manifesto, albeit in difficult circumstances. Electoral decline probably owed much more to the ideological conflicts and the fratricidal disunity that characterised Labour politics than to the values and beliefs of the New Left *per se*. Many of the indicators of decline (falling Party membership, a diminishing electoral base, severe economic prob-lems and policy uncertainty) were well advanced before the New Left emerged. Although left-wingers failed to reverse Labour's difficulties, they cannot causally be blamed, as Ian Aitken has done demonstrating a tenuous grasp of history, for the surfacing of those problems. The judgement of Heath, Jowell and Curtice is germane in this regard: 'if anything, the British electorate dislike a divided party even more than they dislike an ideologically extreme party.'[89]

The arguments of the New Left seem far removed from the policies articu-lated by New Labour during the last decade. Stuart Holland's economic programme has been subjected to a barrage of criticisms and no longer appears faintly realistic. Even at the time numerous objections were made. Skidelsky pointed out that the relationship between corporate power and economic decline was under-theorised: 'any such link is inherently implausible given the fact that the growth of corporate power is general while Britain's failure is unique.'[90] Revisionists were in general scathing. Peter Stephenson, the editor of the Revisionist journal *Socialist Commentary*, reviewed Holland: 'the Party is being asked to march up a blind alley'.[91] For David Marquand, the success of Stuart Holland reflected the poverty of intellectual discussion within Labour:

> In the country of the blind, the one-eyed is king. In a labour movement starved of theory, Stuart Holland is rapidly becoming an ideological guru. His *Socialist Challenge* is glib and cocksure in approach, grating in style and sloppy in argument; if it could be considered solely on its intellectual merits,

no one would have to take it seriously. But it cannot be considered solely on its merits.[92]

Marquand concluded: 'it is, of course, a fantasy – and a sick, destructive fantasy at that.' There is something in Marquand's claim: the quality of debate within Labour was limited during the early 1970s and the adoption of Labour's Programme 1973 owed much to the institutional character of the Party's policy-making procedures. Members of the New Left later accepted that their policies lacked support within the labour movement. Holland commented: 'you could with hindsight say that the way in which the policies were initially debated and fought for within the Party was inadequate.'[93]

Further criticisms concerned the interpretation of the data about monopolisation: Mount noted 'serious shortcomings and contradictions'.[94] Moreover, a strategy designed to reduce monopoly profits was ill-designed to deal with the economic difficulties with which many firms were confronted from the mid-1970s onwards. The proposals for competitive public enterprise and planning agreements seem with hindsight to be optimistic to say the least. The New Left's thought is riven with a tremendous faith in the state, a faith that appears misplaced now but was not atypical of economic thought at the time. The role of industrial democracy in the strategy was not fully thought out: arguably a commitment to workers' control is at odds with one to national planning as well as with uniform standards. The objectives of the strategy were ill-defined and open to interpretation: was it about a socialist transformation or about the renovation of capitalism? Reflecting the way that European arrangements had influenced Holland's thought, Warde's conclusion was that it was 'hardly revolutionary'.[95] At times its socialist character appeared to rely on its more peripheral aspects (industrial democracy). Aspects of the strategy were controversial: there was considerable opposition to import controls from within the New Left whilst debate persisted about what form workers' control might take.[96] Underlying such concerns was the question as to what kind of opposition the strategy might generate from capitalists and others hostile to such measures.

In the 1970s and 1980s these criticisms were not quite so obvious. Much of the disparagement appeared partisan. In a period of economic crisis and international tension, many commentators accepted that the post-war consensus needed to be re-forged, if not yet replaced. Years later, Peter Jenkins commented perceptively: 'if I had to have chosen one of them in that year [1975], Thatcher or Benn, rival exponents of decline and the twins of their age, I think I would have given the future to Tony Benn.'[97] It was by no means certain what the form of any re-arrangement of the policies and institutions that governed the United Kingdom would take. At the time it was the right within British politics that appeared to be defensive. Debating Labour's plans, Judith Hart commented laconically: 'we hear no demands – even from the Monday Club – for restoring the mines and the railways to private ownership.'[98] Alan Ryan concluded his review of Holland:

in the absence of a crystal ball, one cannot guess whether *The Socialist Challenge* will prove to be the Bible of a successful and reinvigorated Labour Party or merely the latest monument to the Party's inability to break the will of the Treasury.[99]

What is the New Left's legacy? Has it had any impact upon New Labour? On the face of it the two positions seem far removed from each other, in terms either of policy or of organisational outlook. A few qualifications might be made to this judgement. There are important links of personnel between the New Left and the administrations headed by Tony Blair from 1997 onwards. Five members of Blair's first Cabinet voted for Benn in the 1981 deputy leadership contest, an event of emblematic importance in the fragmentation of the Labour left. They were Robin Cook, Frank Dobson, John Prescott, Gavin Strang and Jack Straw. Margaret Beckett was out of the Commons at the time, Clare Short was yet to be elected, whilst Michael Meacher, closely associated with Benn, never quite made the Blair Cabinet. Other members of the Blair Government, some identified with New Labour, were actively involved on the Party's left during the 1970s and 1980s. These include such figures as Stephen Byers, David Blunkett and Alan Milburn. Of course, for some, their experiences on the left, especially in local government, shaped their outlook about what was a realistic approach to policy and strategic matters. In policy matters there seem to be few links. The New Left raised questions concerning gender and race issues that persist today (though on neither issue is the record as good as it might have been). Gordon Brown's pre-budget report and his focus on the supply side of the economy can be linked indirectly to the New Left's rather tortured attempts to find a solution to inflationary pressures and to their rejection of the Keynesian economic model respectively.

New Labour adherents are scathing about the constitutional demands and the internal reforms promoted by the New Left during the 1970s and early 1980s. The kind of 'activist democracy' articulated by the left is ridiculed. But it is by no means certain how attractive Labour was before the 1970s in terms of its organisational structures and participatory processes, what Eric Shaw terms 'social democratic centralism'.[100] To give one example, when Joe Ashton arrived at the House of Commons, having won a seat outside his native Sheffield, his home MP in whose constituency he had been an active Party member for years did not recognise him.[101] Aspects of Ashton's portrait of 'Old' Labour are unappealing: elements of the Party displayed an entrenched sexism and were xenophobic. Racial issues were often ignored. Votes at meetings could be easily manipulated, while unions were able to intervene during candidate selections (to be sure such practices continued under the New Left). In such circumstances, coupled with policy failure and the leadership's capacity to ignore debates, it is easy to understand why so many left-wingers wanted to introduce reforms to the Party's constitution in order to alter its character and open up some of its procedures.

The turmoil of the 1970s and early 1980s challenged the entrenched beliefs and practices of Old Labour as never before. In this sense, the Bennites of the 1980s and the modernisers of the 1990s are united in their rejection of so much of what characterised Labour politics and policies in the post-war period. In challenging moribund structures, the New Left raised important questions about what should be Labour's internal structure. In debating socialist goals and policies, they challenged an ingrained model of social democracy that was struggling in the context of economic crisis and political change. The New Left did not, to be sure, provide durable answers for these matters. They did open up Labour to debate, change and reform. From this perspective there is a positive dimension to the New Left's legacy. In his history of the Labour Co-ordinating Committee (LCC), Paul Thompson wrote: 'but in its own way this agenda [of the LCC] was a modernising one. Serious work by good people went into the AES. Tony Benn then had interesting and serious things to say about opening up the political process.'[102] It is, perhaps, no accident that so many members of the Blair administration came from the left of the Party (of one form or another; of one grouping or another). Having come far from the housing estates of Chesterfield, Tony Blair has more in common with Tony Benn and owes a bigger debt to him than either might wish to acknowledge.

Notes

1 This chapter develops arguments contained in Wickham-Jones, M., *Economic Strategy and the Labour Party* (Macmillan, Basingstoke, 1996). It has also been shaped by two excellent, contrasting volumes: Panitch, L. and Leys, C., *The End of Parliamentary Socialism* (Verso, London, 1997) and Seyd, P., *The Rise and Fall of the Labour Left* (Macmillan, Basingstoke, 1987). Thanks to Kevin Hickson.
2 Quoted by the *Guardian*, 19 November 1999.
3 On the former see Warde, A., *Consensus and Beyond* (Manchester University Press, Manchester, 1982); on the latter see Foote, G., *The Labour Party's Political Thought* (Macmillan, Basingstoke, 1997).
4 Reprinted in Jenkins, P., *Anatomy of Decline* (Cassell, London, 1995), p. 109.
5 Marquand, D., *The Unprincipled Society* (Jonathan Cape, London, 1988), pp. 69 and 72.
6 Townsend, S., *The Growing Pains of Adrian Mole* (Puffin Books, Harmondsworth, 2002), p. 105.
7 Hirst, P., 'Miracle or Mirage? The Thatcher Years', in Tiratsoo, N. (ed.), *From Blitz to Blair* (Phoenix, London, 1998), pp. 195–6.
8 Aitken, I., 'Gospel Truth', *The London Review of Books*, 19 February 1998, pp. 17–18.
9 Quoted at www.bbc.co.uk, 19 November 1999.
10 Gould, P., *The Unfinished Revolution*, (Abacus, London, 1998), p. 35.
11 Artis, M., 'Fiscal Policy for Stabilisation', in Beckerman, W. (ed.), *The Labour Government's Economic Record 1964–70* (Duckworth, London, 1972), pp. 262–99, p. 265.
12 Whitehead, P., *The Writing on the Wall* (Michael Joseph, London, 1985), p. 25.
13 Warde, A., *Consensus and Beyond*, p. 169.
14 Livingstone, K., *If Voting Changed Anything They'd Abolish It* (Hutchinson, London, 1987), p. 11.
15 Holland, S., *The Socialist Challenge* (Quartet, London, 1975).
16 Benn, T., *Arguments for Socialism* (Jonathan Cape, London, 1979); and Benn, T., *Arguments for Democracy* (Jonathan Cape, London, 1980).
17 Stephenson, P., 'Tony Benn's guru', *Socialist Commentary* (October 1975), pp. 18–19.
18 Ryan, A., 'The companies we keep', *New Statesman*, 25 July 1975, pp. 113–14, p. 113.
19 2 August 1975, p. 104.
20 Skidelsky, R., 'A Call to Arms', *The Spectator*, 9 August 1975, pp. 187–8, p. 187.

21 *Investors' Chronicle*, 25 July 1975.
22 For reasons of space I do not discuss these different versions.
23 Mount, F., 'Arguments for Me', *The Spectator*, 29 September 1979, pp. 21–2, p. 22.
24 Whitehead, P., 'Tony Benn', in Rosen, G. (ed.), *Dictionary of Labour Biography* (Politicos, London, 2002), p. 38.
25 BBC, 'The Wilderness Years', 1996.
26 Ryan, A., 'The Companies We Keep', p. 113.
27 Prior, M., 'Problems in Labour Politics', Interviews, *Politics and Power 2* (1980), pp. 3–36, p. 6.
28 Wickham-Jones, M., *Economic Strategy and the Labour Party*, p. 132.
29 Benn, T., *Against the Tide* (Hutchinson, London, 1989), p. 15.
30 Warde, A., *Consensus and Beyond*, p. 183.
31 My debt to Drucker, H.M., *Doctrine and Ethos in the Labour Party* (George Allen and Unwin, London, 1979) will be apparent here.
32 Benn, T., *Arguments for Socialism*, p. 44.
33 *Ibid.* pp. 48–9.
34 Holland, S., *The Socialist Challenge*, pp. 171–2.
35 Benn, T., *Arguments for Socialism*, p. 44.
36 See Hodgson, G., *The Democratic Economy* (Penguin, Harmondsworth, 1983).
37 Budd, A., *The Politics of Economic Planning* (Fontana, London, 1978), p. 125.
38 Benn, T., *Arguments for Socialism*, p. 142.
39 *Ibid.* p. 147.
40 Crosland, C.A.R., *The Conservative Enemy* (Jonathan Cape, London, 1962), p. 225.
41 Crosland, C.A.R., *The Future of Socialism* (Jonathan Cape, London, 1956), p. 255.
42 London, 20 July 1974, *The Spokesman*, no. 29 (Winter 1974/75), p. 102.
43 Benn, T., *Arguments for Democracy*, p. 188.
44 Foote emphasises the national side to the New Left, especially to Benn and Holland.
45 *Tribune*, 25 May 1973, p. 5.
46 Benn, T., *Arguments for Socialism*, p. 146.
47 Holland, S., 'Whither Labour Now?', *Workers' Control Bulletin*, 1978, no. 5, pp. 2–4, p. 3. The approach was 'specifically, if not, idiosyncratically British'.
48 Holland, S., *The Socialist Challenge*, p. 37.
49 *Ibid.* p. 14.
50 *Ibid.* p. 26.
51 *Ibid.* p. 75.
52 *Tribune*, 8 June 1973, p. 5.
53 *Tribune*, 25 May 1973, p. 5.
54 Benn, T., *Arguments for Democracy*, pp. 217–18.
55 Holland, S., *The Socialist Challenge*, p. 173.
56 'We are not talking about minor changes', Benn, T., *Arguments for Socialism*, p. 162.
57 Holland, S., *The Socialist Challenge*, p. 174.
58 Benn, T., 'Interview with Eric Hobsbawm', *Marxism Today* (October 1980), pp. 5–13, p. 12.
59 Holland, S., *The Socialist Challenge*, pp. 48–52.
60 Barratt Brown, M. and Holland, S., *Public Ownership and Democracy* (IWC, Nottingham, 1973), p. 5.
61 Prior, M., 'Problems in Labour Politics', Interviews, p. 20.
62 *Tribune*, 4 May 1973, p. 5.
63 *Tribune*, 8 June 1973, p. 5.
64 Benn, T., *Arguments for Socialism*, p. 53.
65 *Tribune*, 8 June 1973.
66 *Tribune*, 25 May 1973, p. 5.
67 Holland, S., *The Socialist Challenge*, p. 140.
68 *Tribune*, 18 May 1973, p. 1.

69 Holland, S., 'Press statement', in Barratt Brown and Holland, *Public Ownership and Democracy*, p. 3.
70 Report on Birmingham conference, *The Spokesman*, no. 29, (Winter 1974–5), p. 98.
71 Marquand, D., 'Clause Four Rides Again', *Times Literary Supplement*, 26 September 1975, p. 1095.
72 Holland, S., *The Socialist Challenge*, p. 15.
73 *Investors' Chronicle*, 25 July 1975.
74 Holland, S., *The Socialist Challenge*, p. 24.
75 Ryan, A., 'The companies we keep', p. 113.
76 Prior, M., 'Problems in Labour Politics', Interviews, p. 19.
77 Heffer, E., *Labour's Future*, (Verso, London, 1986), p. 14.
78 Budd, A., *The Politics of Economic Planning*, p. 125.
79 'National planning', RD: 1046/September 1981, p. 6.
80 Holland, S., 'Press statement', in Barratt Brown and Holland, *Public Ownership and Democracy*, p. 3.
81 Holland, S., 'An Alternative Economic Strategy', *The Spokesman*, 34, Winter 1977–8, pp. 133–6, p. 136.
82 Stephenson, P., 'Tony Benn's Guru', p. 18.
83 Benn, T., *End of an Era* (Hutchinson, London, 1992), p. 150.
84 Benn, T., *Arguments for Democracy*, p. 38.
85 Holland, S., *Workers' Control Bulletin*, December 1973, p. 2.
86 Mullin, C., *How to Select or Reselect your MP* (CLPD/IWC, Nottingham, 1981), p. 19.
87 Benn, T., *Arguments for Democracy*, p. 194.
88 Benn, T., *Arguments for Democracy*, p. 38.
89 Heath, A., Jowell, R. and Curtice, C., *The Rise of New Labour* (OUP, Oxford, 2001), p. 84.
90 Skidelsky, R., 'A Call to Arms', p. 187.
91 Stephenson, P., 'Tony Benn's Guru', p. 18.
92 Marquand, D., 'Clause Four Rides Again', p. 1095.
93 Prior, M., 'Problems in Labour Politics', Interviews, p. 20.
94 Mount, F., '*Arguments for Me*', p. 22.
95 Warde, A., *Consensus and Beyond*, p. 190.
96 Foote, G., *The Labour Party's Political Thought*, p. 322.
97 Jenkins, P., *Mrs Thatcher's Revolution* (Jonathan Cape, London, 1987), p. 58.
98 Hart, J., 'Labour's plans for public ownership', *Tribune* 4 May 1973, p. 5.
99 Ryan, A., 'The Companies We Keep', p. 113.
100 Shaw, E., *Discipline and Discord* (Manchester University Press, Manchester, 1988).
101 Ashton, J., *Red Rose Blues* (Macmillan, Basingstoke, 2000), p. 88.
102 LCC, *The Forward March of Modernisation* (LCC, London, no date), p. 3.

3   The Centre

Noel Thompson

Chapters on the Old Right, New Labour, Old Left and New Left can discuss the work of broadly homogeneous groups of thinkers who have contributed to and shaped distinctive traditions of political and economic thinking, that have informed policy debates and policy-making within the Labour Party. The categorisation of some thinkers may be disputed and the intellectual trajectory of others may result in their movement across the political spectrum (and so between chapters) but there is a set of core beliefs, critical perspectives and policy prescriptions that most commentators would associate with each of these denominations and which give them a measure of ideological coherence.

There is, though, no such solid ground for the commentator who wishes to discuss the political economy of the Centre. Indeed when my contribution to this project was first mooted it was suggested that only with the late Strachey do we have a post-war thinker who might, conceivably, be categorised as centrist. This was an interesting view, though one which suggested that if my chapter was remarkable for anything, if would be its brevity.[1]

And yet 'the Centre' is a categorisation that has been, is and no doubt will continue to be used by those who write about the Labour Party. When it comes to identifying its ideological *differentiae specificae* it may prove snarkly elusive and it certainly has a protean character which precludes the analytical and prescriptive coherence one associates with the old and new, lefts and rights. But, for all that, few would deny the existence of something that might be legitimately termed a centrist political economy; one that has informed public perceptions of the character of the Labour Party and has proved crucial in the determination and articulation of economic and social policies.

Moreover, it can be argued that terms such as 'left' and 'right' only have value when we know, or can hazard a view, as to what constitutes the centre and where it lies. In this regard they have meaning only in relation to an historically defined reference point. Roy Hattersley is on the right of the Party in the 1970s and early 1980s, in the centre of the Party by the mid-to-late 1980s and decidedly on the maverick left of the Party for most of the last decade. But that says as much about the trajectory of the centre as it does about the ideological path that Hattersley has trodden. The Liberal Democrats are clearly to the right of the Labour Party in the 1980s but may be seen as to its left at the present juncture. But this is clearly a consequence of a profound ideological shift in the Labour Party (centre) rather than any radical change in where the Liberal Democrats stand.

For these and other reasons it is, therefore, vitally important to make some attempt to furnish an historical analysis of the political economy of Labour's centre, however difficult it may be to establish its defining characteristics and to identify those theorists who have given it theoretical substance. It is also important to hazard some explanation as to its post-war ideological trajectory given the defining role it plays as regards the political spectrum as a whole.

Let me begin then with a crude definition. In ideological terms the centre represents that matrix of values, aspirations, analysis and prescriptions to which, at any point in time, a critical mass of the Party gravitates. Of course as with all definitions, crude or otherwise, this raises as many problems as it solves. In particular it raises the question of what we mean by critical mass, how we identify it and how we establish its ideational matrix.

As to the former, by 'critical mass' I mean a body of support that can hold within its gravitational field the constellations of both left and right and thence give the Party a greater or lesser measure of stability and unity. Of course there is then the difficulty of who constitutes this centre and how we establish its distinguishing ideological characteristics. Should the focus be on post-war Conference decisions on key economic and social issues? Can these be taken as representative of a critical mass within the Party?[2] In some instances it might be possible to argue this but Conference decisions have frequently represented the victory of either left or right; and further, an attempt to establish the lineaments of a centrist political economy in this way raises old issues as to just how representative those who wield the trade union block vote in Conference are of their memberships, let alone of the Party as a whole. Clearly, in the 1950s and early 1960s, trade unions influenced Conference decisions in a manner that favoured the right and then, in the 1970s and early 1980s, the left.

So perhaps we should cast the net more widely to encompass the values, the rhetoric, the ideas, the critical analysis and the views on policy of the median or modal Labour Party member. Of course this raises formidable evidential and related epistemological difficulties, not least as regards the relative absence of the requisite surveys of opinion for the earlier part of the post-war period. Also, even if consistently available, such evidence would be difficult to distil into an internally consistent political economy and thence a coherent narrative of this aspect of the centre's ideological trajectory.

It might then be better to focus on the Parliamentary Party and identify a 'critical (centrist) mass' within *its* ranks. Here again, though, there is the problem of establishing what constitutes and who represents such a centre. Of course the problem might be simplified by taking the leaders of the Party as guardians and embodiments of the Party's middle ground and the unifying role it plays. It is, after all, the role of leaders to draw together the elements of the broad Labour church and reconcile its warring elements through the positions that they take up and the policies that they advance. Of course the ideological basis of these may reflect the leader's own predilections but, at the same time, s/he must be seen to articulate and represent a set of policies to which a critical (centrist) mass of the Parliamentary Party can subscribe. Approached in this way, a history of the political economy of the centre will become a history of the political economies of successive Party leaders; an interesting exercise in comparative intellectual history but a problematic one when it comes to netting the shark. For a while, in theory, the leader should iterate and represent a set of core positions around which the Party may rally. There have clearly been occasions when leaders have occupied positions to the right or left of the Parliamentary Party.

At such junctures the leader has often sought to shift the Party's centre of ideological gravity. Their aim has been not merely to represent but to redefine the centre in their own political image. Gaitskell in the late 1950s and early 1960s, over nuclear weapons and Clause IV, sought to steer the Party rightwards towards a new centre ground that would attract elements of middle-class support lost to the Conservatives in the context of burgeoning post-war affluence. Wilson may be seen as trying to steer the Labour Party towards a more strategic, leftish vision of the conduct of macroeconomic policy than that represented by Keynesian demand management. Tony Blair can be regarded as playing a crucial role in shifting the Party to a centre position well to the right of the one which it occupied even in the early 1990s. In these cases the leader does not so much occupy the centre as seek to re-define it. To the extent that they succeed, they once again become representative of a critical mass of the Party. To the extent that they prove unsuccessful, they cease to embody the centre's values and aspirations and, in such circumstances, as with Michael Foot in the early 1980s, they lose the capacity to give the Party unity and leadership. In the case of Wilson, failure to deliver the National Plan (1965) required a partial strategic reversion to the expedients of Keynesian macroeconomic management; re-occupation of the centre ground from which he had sought to nudge the Party.[3]

So if there are significant problems with using the political economy of Labour leaders as a reflection of middle opinion, where can we find a more representative articulation of the ideology of the centre? If the quest involves the search for a political economy to which a critical mass of the Party can subscribe, that connects at its margins with the Party's left and right and that gives it the greater or lesser measure of unity that it enjoys, then there would seem some utility in considering the Party's manifesto. The political economy embedded in the manifesto emerges, in some measure, from the crucible of the struggle of disparate viewpoints and power blocs within the Party and, in this regard, it must be seen as a product of their relative strength or capacity for political manoeuvring.[4] That said, the manifesto must furnish an analysis of problems and proffer a related set of economic and social policies to which a critical mass of the Party can largely subscribe. It must, in effect, generate the centripetal forces necessary to give the Party the unity necessary to fight and, ideally, win an election.

Of course, it can again be argued that there are occasions when such literature reflects an attempt to shift the Party's ideological centre of gravity; occasions when it reflects the ascendancy of a particular element, left or right, within the Party. *A New Hope for Britain*, 1983, would certainly fall into this category. In so far as the left's Alternative Economic Strategy (AES) could be distilled, it was distilled into that document. It represented a definite attempt to redefine the ideological core of Party political economy and its publication epitomised the dominance of the left within the Party in the late 1970s and early 1980s.[5]

In a sense, though, *A New Hope for Britain*, and key policy documents published in the early 1980s, were evidence of the centre's atrophy and fragmentation. Indeed in that period, it will be argued, what the Party signally lacked was a centre, or at least a centre with a political economy that could attract a critical mass of support within the Party. The Keynesian social democracy that had provided the ideological bedrock of the centre for three decades had, by that point, been so eroded by the critiques of both left and right and by the economic experience of the 1970s, that an ideological vacuum had been created which the AES-left could and did fill. At this historical juncture the centre experienced a paradigm crisis; one that was not fully resolved until the 1990s. What occurred after 1983 was, in this reading, a profound paradigmatic shift that reconfigured the whole ideological basis of the centre; one which, by the mid-1990s, once again allowed it to offer a political economy which could secure that support within the Party necessary for the centre to play a unifying role. This fundamental reconstitution of the centre ground was also one that, of course, redefined the meaning of left and right, both within the Party and more generally within British politics.

To fulfil its role, as it has been defined here, a centrist political economy must do a number of things. It must articulate an economic analysis and an economic programme in tune with the Party's core aspirations and values. It must, in some measure, establish its social democratic pedigree by drawing on recognisable traditions of thinking within the Party. Even New Labour, with its desire to eschew the legacy of the past, has none the less felt it necessary to establish its affinity, however spuriously, with Tawneyite ethical socialism. It must also be seen to address what are regarded as the pertinent issues of the day; issues that, in some considerable measure, will be determined by the nature and success (or otherwise) of contemporary capitalism. In this regard it can also be argued that it must generate a policy programme that can accommodate cross-class aspirations and objectives. As Prezworski and Sprague have suggested 'given the minority status of workers' in all Western industrial societies, 'leaders of class-based parties must choose between a party homogeneous in its class appeal but sentenced to perpetual electoral defeats or a party that struggles for electoral success at the cost of diluting its class orientation.' In effect, 'in search of electoral support, socialists must present themselves to different groups as an instrument for the realisation of their *immediate* economic interests, immediate in the sense that these interests can be realised when the party is victorious in forthcoming elections.'[6] In effect, social democratic objectives must be altered, diluted or configured in ways congenial to those who have a material interest in the continued, smooth functioning of a capitalist system. Almost inevitably this means that a centrist political economy of a social democratic party such as Labour must convince a broad social constituency that it can engage constructively with contemporary capitalism, respond to its discontents and secure its continued smooth functioning.

This does not rule out the possibility of social democratic progress. Social democracy and, specifically, a centrist articulation of it, will not necessarily be rendered impotent by the need to secure electoral support. But it is also the case that that need requires the dilution of social democratic objectives to differing extents and these are dependent upon the nature and ethos of contemporary domestic and international capitalism. Thus, post-war, Bretton-Woods capitalism and late-twentieth-century Nordic and Rhineland capitalism all had the ideological space necessary to permit the articulation of manifestly social democratic programmes. But capitalism has assumed other forms; forms where accommodation must severely circumscribe anything that could legitimately be categorised as social democratic progress. This, it will be argued, is what has occurred in the case of its late-twentieth-century Anglo–American variant, with profound consequences for the political economy of the contemporary centre. It is with these shaping forces and pressures in mind that the post-war manifestos of the Labour Party, as representative of centre opinion, will now be considered.

One of the salient characteristics of the immediate post-war literature of the Labour Party and, in particular, its manifesto – *Let us Face the Future* – was the clear sense of the failure of inter-war capitalism, and the essentially Fabian explication of the nature of that failure, that it conveyed. These failings were seen as consequent, in large measure, upon the existence of monopolistic concentrations of economic power.

> The great economic blizzards [which] swept the country in those years. The great inter-war slumps were not acts of God or of blind forces. They were the sure and certain result of the concentration of too much economic power in the hands of too few men ... bureaucratically-run, private monopolies which may be likened to totalitarian oligarchies within our democratic state.

It was these entities, with their economic power wielded by the self-interested few, that had created the chaos of the inter-war period. The language and litany of critique was as familiarly Fabian as the solution.[7] The Labour Party 'st[ood] for order against chaos';[8] for the public ownership and public control that alone would prevent the re-emergence of the economic anarchy which had followed the abandonment of controls and planning after the Great War. The language of planning, of the conscious ordering and control of economic life, runs throughout the manifesto – 'Labour would plan from the ground up'. Private enterprise would have a role to play in a mixed economy but very much in the context of 'a national plan'.[9]

In the 1930s, Labour Party literature began to reflect the influence of economic thinking that saw in deficient aggregate demand a major precipitant of general economic depression and considered that the state could utilise fiscal and monetary policy in a manner that ensured the maintenance of full employment. The provenance of these ideas was not uniquely Keynesian but, certainly, both Keynes's *Treatise on Money* and his *General Theory* left their imprint on Party thinking.[10] At a general, theoretically imprecise level, *Let us Face the Future* took such ideas on board. The questions of whether and to what extent the Labour Government assimilated and acted on the Keynesian revolution in economic thinking, and if so when, have been much debated, with answers determined in no small measure by how that revolution is defined.[11] As one recent commentator has seen it, Labour 'politically … seemed to have embraced the Keynesian creed in the key wartime policy statement *Full employment and financial policy*'.[12] But as he also points out, this was a 'product of Labour's economists' and was different in tone from the 1945 manifesto. If, however, we adopt a loose definition of Keynesianism as a willingness to manage aggregate demand with an eye to macroeconomic objectives such as full employment and a dampening of inflationary pressures, then Keynesianism can be said to have increasingly informed both the policy documents and policy conduct of post-war Labour governments.

What is also apparent, though, in the 1945 manifesto, is a belief that macroeconomic management by itself would not cure the ills that afflicted contemporary capitalism.

> All parties [paid] lip service to the idea of jobs for all. All parties [were] ready to promise to achieve that end by keeping up the national purchasing power and controlling changes in the national expenditure through Government action.

But 'where agreement cease[d] [was] in the degree of control of private industry that is necessary to achieve this desired end'.[13] *Let us Face the Future* made clear, therefore, that what distinguished the political economy of the Labour Party was not its adherence to the pursuit of full employment by fiscal means but the public ownership, public control and conscious planning of economic activity. 'If the slumps in uncontrolled private industry are too severe to be balanced by public action, *as they will certainly prove to be*', the Labour Party would, as its 'opponents' would not 'draw the conclusion that the sphere of public action must be extended'.[14] And for the Labour Party of the immediate post-war period, as for that of the inter-war period, this meant a substantial extension of the public sector. It required 'public ownership of fuel and power industries. Public ownership of gas and electricity undertakings. Public ownership of inland transport. Public ownership of iron and steel', with moves towards land nationalisation.[15]

What also comes across clearly from *Let us Face the Future* is the post-war Labour emphasis on the supply side. Confronted by a dollar gap of alarming proportions, it was clearly needful if living standards were to be maintained, and if a substantial increase in social welfare expenditure was to be made possible, then the productivity and thence the competitiveness of British industry should be significantly enhanced. This necessitated planning, it required:

the shaping of suitable economic and price controls to secure that first things shall come first in the transition from war to peace. There must be priorities in the use of raw materials, food prices must be held, homes for the people must come before mansions, necessities for all before luxuries for the few. *It is either sound economic controls or smash.*[16]

Such views represented the bedrock of party political economy. They constituted a core of analysis and prescription to which a critical mass of the Party adhered. This centrist political economy was self-consciously and avowedly a socialist political economy. Its language was that of planning, organisation, order, control, public ownership, the public good, and it was articulated by 'a Socialist Party' that was 'proud' to call itself such. A party whose 'ultimate purpose at home [was] the establishment of a Socialist Commonwealth'.[17] This political economy was a function of the profound influence of a radical Fabianism within the post-1931 Labour Party but it also represented a political economy that was consistent with the general experience of the manifest failings of early-twentieth-century capitalism. It was also a product of the peculiar circumstances and distinctive pressures and constraints under which British capitalism laboured in the immediate post-war period. Like all such centrist political economies articulated by the Labour Party, it emerged from an iterative engagement with contemporary capitalism that fundamentally influenced, if it did not finally determine, its distinguishing characteristics. And it was the case that, as the nature of post-war British capitalism changed – in part as a consequence of the policies implemented by the Labour governments of 1945–51, in part as a result of the new international economic order that came out of Bretton Woods and, in large measure, as a consequence of the high, sustained, full-employment level of economic growth that post-war (even British) capitalism enjoyed – so this ongoing process of iterative engagement was to effect a revision of the political economy of the centre.

The achievements of the first post-war Labour Government have been discussed at length and its merits or demerits need not detain us here.[18] It is, however, necessary to make mention of the kind of British capitalism that Labour policies had helped to construct by the early 1950s. This was characterised by a mixed economy with a significant public sector; an economy in which a substantial part of the national income was devoted to public expenditure of a kind that had a material bearing on social welfare. It was an economy where rationing and price controls still existed but where such intervention in its workings had been substantially reduced as relative abundance replaced scarcity, as the dollar gap was closed and as economic growth laid the basis for a rise in living standards. It was too, by the early 1950s, a more stable, confident and successful, if 'managed', British capitalism and one that by the end of the decade had established a track record for delivering the economic goods and delivering them in ever-increasing quantities to an increasingly affluent population. In short, the capitalism with which the Labour Party engaged in the 1950s was different in important respects from that which it had confronted in the inter-war and immediate post-war period.

There is a sense of this as early as *Let us Win Through Together*, and the Labour manifestos for the 1950 and 1951 general elections. For, in essence, what these documents did was to defend the kind of mixed and managed capitalism to which Labour had played midwife. Thus the focus was not so much on extending public ownership as making existing 'public enterprise ... a model of efficiency and of social responsibility'.[19] As regards 'social legislation', 'what [was] needed now [was] not so much new legislation as the wise development, through efficient and economical administration, of the services provided by ... Acts' already passed.[20] In addition, macroeconomic management had a higher profile and the language of demand management was more in evidence than in 1945. Certainly there could still 'be no advance without planning' or without price control, 'control over capital investment' and 'control over financial forces'. But such terms as 'control' and 'planning' acquired a less Fabian resonance and their prescriptive reach was extended to embrace everything from regional economic policy to import and foreign exchange control. In this regard, planning and public ownership were often conceived of in terms of the adjuncts necessary to deal with the external constraints upon the effective pursuit of full employment.

> Subject to the will of Parliament, we shall take whatever measures may be required to control financial forces, so as to maintain full employment and promote the welfare of the nation; while publicly owned industry will be ready to expand its investment when employment policy demands it.[21]

Further, while the *patois* of Fabianism was still apparent, so was the language of individual freedom, initiative and enterprise. Labour was concerned to create the conditions necessary for 'the full and free development of every individual person', 'releas[ing] ... all the finer impulses of man'.[22] It would give 'encouragement to enterprise', setting 'private enterprise ... free from the stranglehold of restrictive monopolies', giving 'everybody in industry' 'a fair chance'.[23] Moreover, in contrast to Fabian perceptions of capitalism as characterised by an increasing concentration of economic power in monopolies and oligopolistic arrangements, the only antidote for which was the extension of social ownership, Labour Party literature in the 1950s saw effective anti-monopoly legislation as the primary means of maintaining vigorous competition in the private sector.

Keynesian social democracy involved a belief in the capacity to achieve certain macroeconomic objectives – full employment, relative price stability and balance of payments equilibrium – through the management of aggregate demand; an acceptance of a mixed economy whose commanding heights were in public ownership but where the balance between public and private, post-1951, would change only at the margins; the pursuit, on grounds both of equity and the maintenance of a high level of aggregate demand, of a fairer distribution of income and wealth and a commitment to substantial, and increasing (in line with the Gross Domestic Product (GDP)), public expenditure on social welfare and social infrastructure.

These distinguishing features of Keynesian social democracy, which were present in the manifestos of 1950 and 1951, loomed even larger in those of 1955 and 1959. These documents made mention of the need for redistributive policies, though emphasis was placed less on the increase of direct taxation than the removal of those existing tax privileges enjoyed by the British bourgeoisie.[24] The manifestos of 1955 and 1959 emphasised the pursuit of full employment, while recognising the challenge of delivering it in a context of stable prices:[25] a challenge that could only be met by a Labour government that was 'prepared to use all measures, including the Budget, in order to expand production and simultaneously to ensure that welfare is developed and prosperity fairly shared' and was 'able to win full [wage restraint] co-operation from the unions by such measures as a fair-shares Budget policy and the extension of the Welfare State'.[26] Thus in both manifestos the Budget was seen, in classically Keynesian social democratic fashion, as a means of delivering both socially egalitarian and employment objectives. That said, the Fabian, anti-market resonances in Labour's 1955 manifesto should not be ignored with mention made of 'cutting out waste in the present antiquated system of food distribution and ... reimposing price-controls on essential goods where necessary.'[27]

This literature expressed the need for high levels of public expenditure on social welfare and the nation's social and industrial infrastructure – education, housing, health, pensions and transport.[28] There was also support for the public sector in the context of a mixed economy; though a mixed economy where it was envisaged that the balance between public and private would not be significantly altered.[29] As the 1959 manifesto made clear, the Party had 'no other plans for further nationalisation', except where 'an industry is shown, after enquiry, to be failing the nation'.[30] In this period, therefore, Keynesian social democracy came to furnish the principles and practice of a distinctively centrist political economy to which a critical mass of the Party subscribed.

The advent of Wilson as Labour Party leader was to see an attempted revision of the political economy of the Centre. An increasing recognition of the problem of relative economic decline, and a related perception of Britain as the sick man of Europe, played an important part in this.[31] In effect, the growing recognition of the relative failure of British capitalism precipitated a retrieval of a rhetoric of planning: one interwoven with the patois of science and technology. This shift is apparent in policy documents such as *Signposts for the Sixties* and certainly so in the 1964 manifesto *Let's go with Labour for the New Britain*, which declared the need for 'a New Britain – mobilising the resources of *technology under a national plan*';[32] 'only a major change of attitude to the *scientific revolution*, including an acceptance of the need for *purposive planning*, will enable us to mobilise the new resources technology is creating and harness them to human needs.'[33] A Plan would therefore be formulated with the co-operation of 'both sides of industry operating in partnership with the Government'.[34] It was such a strategy that would allow Britain to break out of 'the defeatist Stop/Go cycle' that had reduced her trend rate of growth well below that of most of her major industrial rivals.[35]

There is here, clearly, a resonance with the kind of Fabianism to be found in the social democracy of the 1930s and the immediate post-war period. Indeed the manifesto made specific and approving reference to the 'purposive planning of the post-war Labour Governments'.[36] Fabian too was the role which the document gave to an emerging technocracy, highlighting the contribution to economic well-being that might be made by science and those 'technicians and technologists, designers and production engineers with the expertise to utilise its potential.[37] In the 1964 manifesto there was also a sharper stress on the role to be played by the public sector. Though when it came to the crunch there were no specific proposals for its extension apart from the re-nationalisation of steel.[38]

The failure of the National Plan is well documented and has been discussed at length. Most commentators would agree that that failure was, in significant measure, a consequence of the absence of instruments and powers by means of which the Plan could be implemented.[39] Of course pre-war Fabian socialism had also been unclear as to how planning was to be effected. It did, though, advocate municipalisation and nationalisation to create the institutional basis and provide the means through which planning might be co-ordinated and made effective. In the 1964 manifesto, however, we have the Fabian rhetoric of 'socialist planning'[40] without the Fabian means of delivery; or, perhaps more accurately, we have Keynesian social democracy with a Fabian veneer.[41] In this context it is interesting to note that the language of planning was easily and frequently transposed to the sphere of demand management with, for example, the notion of a 'planned growth of incomes' seen as central to preventing the build-up of inflationary pressures in the pursuit of full employment.[42] Equally telling here was the multiplicity of policy contexts in which the rhetoric of planning was deployed but where the substance of policies remained unchanged from those advanced in the 1950s. Thus there was to be a 'plan for the regions', a 'plan for transport', 'a plan for stable prices', a 'plan for tax reform'.[43] These amounted to a regional policy, an integrated public transport system, anti-monopoly legislation, the taxation of capital gains and the closure of tax loopholes. All were policies that had been advanced throughout the 1950s.

As to the Welfare State, there was a continued strong commitment. And, although reference is made to a 'New Welfare State' along with a 'New Britain', this was expressed in terms, and was to be delivered by means, that remained largely unchanged in Labour literature throughout the 1950s and early 1960s. Labour would furnish the worker with:

> the opportunity to work and to be fairly rewarded for it … to make provision against the day when age, sickness, industry or redundancy impairs his capacity to earn … to know that during the misfortunes of ill health, the facilities of a modern and well equipped service will be available … to have a home for his family, and to be able to buy or rent it at reasonable terms.[44]

It was the case, therefore, that despite the forays into the rhetoric of science and purposive planning to be found in the manifestos of 1964 and 1966 and despite the appeal to the values and skills of the contemporary technocracy, the substance of centrist political economy remained substantially the same into the 1960s as it had been in the 1950s. And, in this regard, it played a similar kind of unifying role in both periods, providing Fabian fundamentalists and Keynesian social democrats with a single hymn book from which to sing. In effect the centrist political economy of the 1960s was Fabian in spin and social democratic Keynesianism in substance.

By 1970 and the general election of that year the National Plan was dead in the water. The manifesto, *Now Britain's Strong: let's make it great to live in*, expressed the need for planning and, specifically, mention was made of creating a National Manpower Service that would engage in 'forward planning of our manpower needs' but, for the most part, the notion of planning was expressed in vague and undeveloped terms. It also co-existed (and was sometimes fused) in the manifesto with the language of 'economic management'.[45] Moreover, 'the central aim' of an incoming Labour government was to be classically Keynesian: 'a steady and sustained increase in output with secure and rising employment', that avoided 'the violent stop-go cycles that have done so much to damage our economy in past years'.[46]

Two themes in this literature are, however, worthy of note. As unions became more militant in the late 1960s and as their activity was considered by many to be jeopardising both the maintenance of full employment by Keynesian means and the rising Welfare-State-related expenditure that full employment helped to sustain, Labour's relations with them became a matter for concern. Union support for the broad outlines of Keynesian social democracy had helped to constitute that critical mass that formed the centre ground of the Party in the 1950s and 1960s. *Per contra* union militancy called that support into question. Within the Labour Party, therefore, some came to see a refinement of the Keynesian social democratic model as imperative; a revision that would secure from unions the requisite restraint to enable a Labour government to continue to deliver its objectives. *In Place of Strife* represented one approach to the problem, seeking as it did legislative constraints on the use of strike action. In addition, the manifestos of 1966 and 1970 pointed in the direction of a corporatist solution to the difficulty of relating wage claims to price increases in a manner that would break what was seen by many as a wage-push inflationary spiral. Further, reference was made to industrial democracy as a means to 'greater industrial harmony'; 'involv[ing] the worker through his union more closely in the decisions which affect[ed] his working life', thereby 'eliminat[ing] the grievances that are the cause of many strikes'.[47] So, in the late 1960s, we can see an attempt to reconfigure the Keynesian social democratic model in ways which accommodated the pressures, in particular the inflationary pressures, which were becoming an increasingly prominent feature of Western industrial capitalism.

With difficulties in giving practical expression to the principles of Keynesian social democracy increasing, the political economy of the centre was beginning to alter. Its theoretical substance and policy objectives remained essentially what they had been but the former became less securely based[48] and the latter more difficult of attainment. In consequence, disagreements grew, in particular over the adjuncts (particularly in relation to the control of prices and incomes) necessary to deliver its policy prescriptions. Faultlines were apparent in the centrist position to which the greater part of the Party had adhered for over two decades. Also, at an international level, the managed capitalism of the 'golden age' was beginning to disintegrate; something apparent in the demise in the early 1970s of the fixed-exchange-rate regime that had underpinned economic progress since Bretton Woods.

It was from the left, however, that a comprehensive response to rapidly changing economic circumstances and a disintegrating Keynesian social democratic paradigm was to come.[49] This took the form of an Alternative Economic Strategy to restore to a Labour government the power necessary to conduct an economic policy that had at its core the pursuit of democratic socialist objectives; power that had been significantly eroded by the rapid, contemporary growth of Transnational Corporations (TNCs).[50] This was to be achieved by a substantial expansion of public ownership, the use of planning agreements between private corporations and government to ensure they acted in a manner consistent with the government's planning aims[51] and the extension of industrial democracy.[52] In addition, Party literature highlighted the need for 'a drastic redistribution of wealth and income'.[53]

The strategy was given its first, and in some respects its most lucid, expression in Party literature in *Labour's Programme for Britain* 1973, and key elements filtered into the two manifestos for 1974 – *Let us Work Together – Labour's Way out of the Crisis* and *Britain will Win with Labour*. As regards the extension of public enterprise, this was to include 'shipbuilding, ship-repairing and marine engineering, ports, the manufacture of airframes and aeroengines' and would also involve:

> taking over profitable sections or individual firms in those industries where a public holding is essential to enable the Government to control prices, stimulate investment, encourage exports, create employment, protect workers and consumers from the irresponsible multi-national companies and to plan the economy in the national interest.[54]

This would be done, initially, in relation to the 'pharmaceuticals, road haulage, construction, [and] machine tools' industries, with a National Enterprise Board acting in the role of a holding company along the lines of the I.R.I. in Italy.

The economic crises of the mid-to late1970s and, in particular, the crisis of British capitalism, meant that Labour had to engage with a different beast from that of the 'golden age'. Keynesian social democracy *tout seul* was no longer sufficient and this created imperatives and opportunities for the left to redefine the party's ideological centre of gravity. In this context the changing nature and relative failure of capitalism allowed an avowedly socialist political economy to be articulated;[55] one that would 'bring about a fundamental and irreversible shift in the balance of power in favour of working people and their families'.[56]

There are good reasons for seeing all this as representing the disintegration of the centrist political economy to which Labour had previously adhered and that had exercised such a profound influence on the its economic and social policies. Yet until the early 1980s many Keynesian social democrats continued to believe that the Party's manifestos and other policy documents of the mid-to late 1970s could be viewed as advancing policies that were primarily designed to furnish the powers necessary to rejuvenate, not bury, their economic philosophy. In effect, these documents could be, and were, read according to political taste by both the Keynesian social democratic centre and the AES left. For example, the Social Contract[57] could be understood, by Keynesian social democrats, as a means of rendering effective a demand management solution to the problem of unemployment, through a prices and incomes policy; a means of 'restor[ing] and sustain[ing] [non-inflationary] full employment'.[58] Moreover, it could be seen by them as an opportunity of confronting trade unions with their responsibilities to 'the community as a whole', by making them address the price and other impact of their wage claims.[59] On the other hand it could be portrayed as an instrument for ensuring a 'planned expansion of incomes' that would effect a redistribution of income in favour of working people and their families. It could be regarded by Keynesian social democrats as a key component of macroeconomic management, while the AES left could see it as an instrument for the purposive planning of a socialist economy; planning that would involve the working class through the role played by trade unions in establishing and attaining a range of macroeconomic targets and objectives. After all, the October 1974 manifesto had made clear that 'the Social Contract … [was] not concerned solely or even primarily with wages … [but] the whole range of national policies'.[60] As with the term 'planning' in the 1950s, therefore, the Social Contract could be interpreted according to ideological taste. If for the left the 'aims set out in [the] manifesto' (of February 1974) were 'socialist aims', that manifesto and the manifesto of October could still be seen, by others, as keeping alive the essential principles and practice of the centrist political economy dominant in the 1950s and 1960s.

As late as 1979, the manifesto still embodied key elements of the old centrist political economy, though by that time it had come to reflect an uneasy compromise between the AES left, Keynesian social democracy and, in some measure, a 'punk monetarism' that had secured a temporary foothold in the higher echelons of the Party. Thus, as with the 1974 manifestos, *The Labour Way is the Better Way* evinced the language of a corporatist Keynesianism, with 'the Government's Industrial Strategy' being 'about how to create more wealth and more jobs through a constructive national partnership with unions and management'.[61] This was to be achieved by means of institutions and practices that approximated to those of the *Konzertierte Aktion* of the German Federal Republic.[62] Such a partnership would, it was believed, secure the traditional social democratic objective of full employment while preventing the exacerbation of those inflationary pressures that had been all too apparent in the late 1970s. Yet the manifesto also gave *equal* priority to the defeat of inflation and the return to full employment. 'The Labour government [would] pursue policies which [would] give a high priority to a return to full employment' but this must 'go hand and hand with keeping down inflation'.[63] It should be noted too that any Phillips curve notion of a trade-off between jobs and inflation was replaced by a causal sequence that ran from inflation to unemployment. 'One must keep a curb on inflation and price' because 'inflation causes loss of jobs'. Similarly 'nothing under-mine[d] a nation as inflation … it is a threat to jobs'.[64]

At the same time the manifesto contained much of an AES-left provenance, with reference to the need to 'expand the work and finance of the National Enterprise Board, using public ownership to sustain and create new jobs'; to 'planning agreements with the necessary back up statutory powers'; to the encouragement of co-operatives through a Co-operative Development Agency; to the need for protectionist measures and capital controls to ensure the success of an expansionary strategy, with, in addition, veiled threats as regards the role of the financial sector and the commitment of a Labour government 'to a major extension of industrial democracy'.[65]

However, in the late 1970s and early 1980s, with the left in the ascendant within the Party, with some of those who had previously subscribed to the princi-ples of Keynesian social democracy succumbing to 'punk monetarism' and with others defecting from the Party to establish the SDP, those Keynesian social democrats still in its ranks clearly came to despair of rendering the AES in their own image. And certainly many were in sympathy with Gerald Kaufman's cate-gorisation of the 1983 manifesto – *A New Hope for Britain* – as the longest suicide note in history. By that date the Party lacked a centrist political economy that could attract that critical mass of support that Keynesian social democracy had engendered. It was a Party without a centre ground. Indeed it could be argued that such a centre ground had shown marked signs of fragmentation and atrophy as early as the mid-1970s; manifestos reflecting a volatile mix of economic ideolo-gies while lacking sufficient and sustained coherence to furnish an adequate basis for a centrist political economy. In this period there was no longer a centre that could hold left and right within its gravitational field.

The heavy electoral defeat of 1983 and the advent of Neil Kinnock as Labour Party leader led to an attempt to reconstruct that ground. Though what one sees also in the 1987 and 1992 manifestos is an effort to engage with the realities of an increasingly globalised capitalism very different from that which Keynesian social democracy had confronted; a capitalism characterised by the rapid growth of foreign direct investment, a dramatic increase in the volume of short-term capital movements; a related abandonment of foreign exchange controls by all the major Western industrial nations; a marked expansion in the ratio of trade to GDP in particular as a consequence of intra-regional trade liberalisation and a capitalism characterised too by the increase in the size and relative economic importance of TNCs which, by the 1990s, accounted for approximately 75 per cent of interna-tional trade. This was a capitalism with enhanced opportunities for investors and corporations to exit when policy-makers failed to accommodate their wishes and one which demanded from policy-makers a more rigorous adherence to the goal of international competitiveness if short- and longer-term capital flows were not, swiftly and inexorably, to undermine the value of a nation's currency.[66]

So while the 1987 manifesto proposed to tackle the problem of mass unemployment by means of a conventional Keynesian strategy of increasing public investment on the social and industrial infrastructure of the nation, it was also characterised by a particular emphasis on creating the supply-side preconditions for honing the competitive edge of enterprises located in Britain.[67] In this regard much was made, in this and subsequent manifestos, of the quality of labour inputs. 'People' were identified as the nation's 'most precious resource' and in recognition of this Labour offered a National Training Programme.[68] The 'right skills' would make the country 'more efficient, more competitive and more socially just'.[69] One should not perhaps read the construction of this sentence as involving prioritisation but it is interesting to note in passing that efficiency and competitiveness do come before social justice. The stress though was on the synergistic relationship between upgrading human capital and enhancing social justice; again a theme that was to loom large in subsequent New Labour manifestos and economic policy documents.

There was too in this and later manifestos an attempt to retrieve for social democratic purposes the rhetoric of freedom that, in the 1980s, the New Right had come to monopolise and utilise to considerable political effect.[70] Thus an effective supply-side strategy would create '*Freedom* and fairness for all Britain's people'.[71] And 'Labour's objective' should certainly be 'to broaden and deepen the *liberty* of all individuals in our community: to *free* people from poverty, exploitation and fear; to *free* them to realise their full potential; to see that everyone has the *liberty* to enjoy real chances, to make real choices'.[72]

Some of the fundamental themes of a new centrist political economy began, therefore, to emerge in the late 1980s and early 1990s. Fairness is linked with efficiency; the former finding its justification by reference to its positive impact on the latter and freedom itself is prioritised as an objective. Thus the 1992 manifesto again put 'at the core of [its] convictions [a] belief in individual liberty', and offered policies that represented 'a practical commitment to freedom' and 'equality of opportunity'. In addition, the country was to be made 'more *competitive* ... and *just*'.[73]

In the 1992 manifesto too, with Britain 'facing the intensifying pressures of European and global competition', the themes of a supply-side social democracy became even more apparent,[74] the objective of enhancing national and corporate performance assuming a particular prominence. 'Britain [was] in a race for economic survival and success. Faced with intense competition companies can succeed only by constantly improving their performance', and the manifesto therefore placed a particular emphasis on creating the conditions and supplying the quality and quantity of factor inputs necessary to attain this.[75] Labour would furnish 'a government which business can do business with ... It is the government's responsibility to create the conditions for enterprise to thrive.'[76] To this end a Labour government would provide 'a stable economic environment' with 'consistently low inflation', 'stable exchange rates and steady and competitive interest rates' and the 'education and training' that would ensure an adequate supply of skilled labour.[77] Labour should be in the business of creating a knowledge-drive and a supply-side social democracy, and the key to this was 'a well-educated and motivated workforce'.[78]

Yet even in 1992 a residual Keynesian social democracy characterised the new centrist political economy that the manifesto sought to construct.[79] The Party proposed a National Recovery Programme that was to have an immediate impact on the level of employment and aimed to seek support for a co-ordinated, European expansion of aggregate demand to effect 'a swift reduction in unemployment'.[80] Increased public expenditure was also to play an important part in upgrading the nation's social infrastructure with the 'phased release of receipts from the sale of council houses' used 'to build new homes and improve old ones'.[81] There was to be a substantial increase in investment in public transport and the NHS as well as education.[82] Further, the use of fiscal policy for redistributive purposes was mentioned. Thus, while the 25 per cent and 40 per cent tax rates would remain unchanged, 'a new, top rate of tax of 50 per cent' would be introduced.[83] Moreover government would act to 'halt the deterioration which has taken place in the pay and conditions of public sector workers'.[84] Keynesian social democracy was in its death throes. It had now long ceased to be able to furnish a centrist political economy. But even in 1992 its influence and its memory lingered on.

With the advent of New Labour, and with the policy reviews of the mid-1990s, this residual influence was to all but disappear. By the 1997 manifesto, certainly, the centre ground had been reconstituted in a form from which all the essential elements of Keynesian social democracy had been excised; one that was consistent with an almost unqualified acceptance of an increasingly globalised and untrammelled international capitalism that was generating a marked intensification of competitive pressures. What New Labour now overtly offered was '*a new centre* and *centre-left* politics' that would 'put behind us the bitter political struggles of left and right that have torn our country apart for decades'.[85]

More specifically, New Labour sought to formulate a political economy that was predicated on an acceptance of the Anglo–American model of corporate capitalism; a model that prioritised capital mobility, labour flexibility and shareholder interests. This was a political economy that was focused on delivering an economic environment congenial to the interests of transnational corporate capitalism; an environment where infrastructural investment lowered corporate costs and where an adequate supply of flexible, highly-trained, high-productivity labour was readily available; one that would allow Britain to bid successfully for, and retain, foreign direct investment and therefore one where neither individual nor corporate taxation would act as a disincentive. In this latter regard New Labour was adamant in 1997 and remained so thereafter – 'There will be no increase in the basic or top rates of income tax.'[86] It was also to pride itself in its 2001 manifesto in having cut corporation taxes 'to their lowest levels ever'.[87] In that document too the overriding economic objective was clearly stated: Britain should be made 'the best place to do business in Europe'. It must become 'a dynamic economy founded on skills and knowledge' and 'that mean[t] investment by private and public sector in infrastructure and skills, and the right competitive framework to support enterprise small and large'.[88]

As regards 'economic management', New Labour 'accept[ed] the global economy as a reality'.[89] This meant, in effect, that other than ensuring stability,[90] there was little that could be done by way of the conduct of macroeconomic policy. The pursuit of *full* employment was to be replaced by the maintenance of '*high and stable* levels of employment':[91] an objective that was to be attained by the successful delivery of supply-side goals rather than through the macro use of fiscal policy. In this regard too New Labour proposed to eschew the future use of monetary policy by giving a degree of autonomy to the Bank of England that would 'free [it] from short-term political manipulation'.[92] In 2001 mention was made of 'full employment' but in the context of discussing measures to promote a more efficient functioning of the labour market, particularly at the lower end, through the use of welfare measures to 'encourage' participation.[93]

In the 1997 manifesto New Labour also expressed a commitment to 'enhancing the dynamism of the market, not undermining it';[94] in effect embracing the intensification of competitive pressures and all that these demanded, particularly of the workforce, in terms of greater flexibility of hours, work practices and decentralised and performance-related pay bargaining.[95] It looked to 'partnership not conflict between employers and employees', but a partnership predicated upon an acceptance of the global economy as a reality and the constantly improving corporate and national performance that that demanded. This partnership was also to be constituted on the basis of 'the main changes of the 1980s in industrial relations'; with these being linked in the next sentence to the need for 'healthy profits as an essential motor of a dynamic market economy'.[96] Labour therefore accepted that flexibility precluded any restoration of the trade union rights that the labour force had enjoyed for the greater part of the post-war period under the dispensation of Keynesian social democracy.

As to social welfare objectives, 'a modern welfare state' was directly linked to equipping 'Britain … to prosper in a global economy of technological change'.[97] 'An imaginative welfare to work policy' would go some way to achieve that modernisation and would certainly mitigate the fiscal burden that resulted from a reluctance to seize the employment opportunities that a more flexible labour market furnished.[98] Moreover, as regards public expenditure in general, 'New Labour [would] be wise spenders not big spenders' and indeed they offered to 'stick to planned [by the Conservatives] spending allocations for the first two years in office'.[99] Compassion and care might still be important but they were to be set in a context 'in which ambition and compassion [were] seen as partners not opposites'.[100] Enhanced social welfare, like greater fairness, was to be a means to the end of greater economic efficiency and enhanced performance. And, in any case, 'fairness and efficiency [went] together'.[101]

New Labour's attempt to engage with and accommodate the kind of international capitalism that was emerging in the late twentieth century has therefore led to the formulation of a new centrist political economy, radically different from that of the 1950s and 1960s. This is a political economy that privileges competitiveness, entrepreneurship,[102] flexibility and free market forces, and embraces the salient characteristics of Anglo–American corporate capitalism. It is one that has shifted Labour's centre to ground which even the Liberal Democrats are hesitant to occupy; but ground which the Party seems unlikely to depart in the foreseeable future.

Notes

1 Others might have been added to the list – the early Roy Jenkins and the later Tony Crosland with, in the late 1980s, Roy Hattersley and, possibly, Austin Mitchell. Certainly Strachey's critical review of *The Future of Socialism* delineates a position that separates him from the social democratic right while differentiating him from the fundamentalist Left; see 'The new revisionist', *New Statesman*, 6 October 1956.
2 For a detailed study of how such decisions emerge see Minkin, L., *The Labour Party Conference: a Study in the Politics of Intra-party Democracy* (Manchester University Press, Manchester, 1978).
3 As Tomlinson points out the demise of the plan did not mean a complete abandonment of the 'modernisation' agenda; J. Tomlinson, 'Labour and the Economy', in Tanner, D., Thane, P. and Tiratsoo, N. (eds), *Labour's First Century*, (CUP, Cambridge, 2000), pp. 62–3.
4 On the formation of some of the post-war Labour Party manifestos see Minkin, L., *The Labour Party Conference* pp. 293–5; pp. 311–14.
5 The best study of the Alternative Economic Strategy and its fate is Wickham-Jones, M., *Economic Strategy and the Labour Party: Politics and policy-making, 1970–83*, (Macmillan, London, 1996).
6 Przeworski, A., and Sprague, J., *Paper Stones: A History of Electoral Socialism*, (University of Chicago Press, Chicago, 1986), p. 3; p. 52.
7 On the distinguishing characteristics of Fabian political economy see McBriar, A., *Fabian Socialism and English Politics, 1884–1918*, (CUP, Cambridge, 1962) and Thompson, N., *Political Economy and the Labour Party*, (UCL Press, London, 1996), pp. 15–24.
8 Labour Party, *Let us Face the Future*, in Craig, F.W.S. (ed.), *British General Election Manifestos, 1918–1966*, (Political Reference Publications, Chichester, 1970), p. 97.
9 *Ibid.*, pp. 98–9.
10 On this see Durbin, E., *New Jerusalem: The Labour Party and the Economics of Democratic Socialism*, (Routledge & Kegan Paul, London, 1985), pp. 133–59, and Thompson, N., *Political Economy and the Labour Party*, pp. 129–33.
11 For differing views on the 1947 budget in this regard see Cairncross, A., *Years of Recovery: British economic policy, 1945–51* (Methuen, London, 1985), pp. 419–29; Booth, A., 'The Keynesian revolution in economic policy-making', *Economic History Review*, 36, 1983, p. 123 and Rollings, N., 'British budgetary policy, 1945–55: A "Keynesian revolution"?' *Economic History Review*, 41, 1988, pp. 283–98.
12 Tomlinson, J., *Democratic Socialism and Economic Policy, the Attlee years, 1945–51*, (CUP, Cambridge, 1997), p. 214.
13 Labour Party, *Let us Face the Future*, p. 99.
14 *Ibid.*
15 *Ibid.*, p. 101, p. 103.
16 *Ibid.*, p. 102, my emphasis.
17 *Ibid.*, p. 101
18 See in particular Tomlinson, J., *Democratic Socialism and Economic Policy* and Cairncross, A., *Years of Recovery.*
19 Labour Party, *Let us Win Through Together*, 1950, in Craig, F.W.S., (ed.), *British General Election Manifestos 1918–1966*, p. 128.
20 *Ibid.*, p. 132.

21 *Ibid.*, p. 128.
22 *Ibid.*, p. 127.
23 *Ibid.*, p. 129.
24 Labour Party, Britain belongs to you: The Labour Party's policy for consideration by the British people, 1959, in Craig, F.W.S. (ed.), *British General Elections Manifestos, 1918–1966*, p. 197.
25 *Ibid.*
26 *Ibid.* See also Labour Party, *Forward with Labour: Labour's Policy for the Consideration of the Nation*, 1955, in Craig, F.W.S. (ed.), *British General Election Manifestos, 1918–1966*, p. 180.
27 *Ibid.*, p. 178.
28 Labour Party, *Britain Belongs to You*, p. 198, p. 201, and Labour Party, *Forward with Labour*, p. 179.
29 Labour Party, *Forward with Labour*, p. 180 and Labour Party, *Britain Belongs to You*, p. 201; except as regards the re-nationalisation of steel, road haulage and strategic sections of the chemical and machine tools industries: Labour Party, *Forward with Labour* 1955, p. 180; the latter two receiving no mention in 1959.
30 Labour Party, *Britain Belongs to You*, p. 201.
31 Though so too did the influence of economists such as Thomas Balogh and Nicholas Kaldor.
32 Labour Party, *Let's go with Labour for the New Britain*, 1964, in Craig, F.W.S. (ed.), *British General Election Manifestos, 1918–1966*, p. 230, my emphasis.
33 *Ibid.*, my emphasis.
34 *Ibid.*, p. 229.
35 *Ibid.*, p. 230.
36 *Ibid.*
37 *Ibid.*, p. 234; see also Labour Party, *Time for decision*, 1966, in Craig, F.W.S. (ed.), *British Election Manifestos, 1918–1966*, p. 272. Fabian too was the manifestos stress on the need for new expertise in government itself.
38 See Labour Party, *Let's go with Labour for the New Britain*, p. 233.
39 Labour Party, *Time for Decision*, listed instruments of policy necessary for 'national economic planning' as control over building and the movement of capital abroad! p. 268. For a critical account of this episode see Ponting, C., *Breach of Promise: Labour in power, 1964–70* (Hamish Hamilton, London, 1987).
40 Labour Party, *Let's go with Labour for the New Britain*, p. 233.
41 In substance, therefore, Shaw is right to categorise the period 1964–70 as 'Keynesian social democracy in power': Shaw, E., *The Labour Party since 1945*, (Blackwell, Oxford, 1996), pp. 68–107.
42 And, indeed, one planning institution that was successfully established after Labour came to power in 1964 was the Prices and Incomes Board.
43 Labour Party, *Let's go with Labour for the New Britain*, p. 234.
44 Labour Party, *Time for Decision*, p. 276.
45 Labour Party, *Now Britain's strong. Let's make it great to live in*, 1970, in Craig, F.W.S., *British General Election Manifestos, 1959–87*, (Dartmouth Press, Aldershot, 1990), pp. 132–4.
46 Labour Party, *Let's go with Labour for a New Britain*, p. 234.
47 Labour Party, *Now Britain's Strong, Let's Make it Great to Live in*, p. 149.
48 For example, the challenge to the Phillips-curve trade-off between unemployment and inflation.
49 For a discussion of the intellectual origins of this see Wickham-Jones, M., *Economic Strategy and the Labour Party* and Hatfield, M., *The House the Left Built*, (Gollancz, London, 1978).

50 On this the classic texts were Holland, S., *The Socialist Challenge*, (Quartet, London, 1975) and Brown, M.B., *From Labourism to Socialism: A Political Economy for Labour in the 1970s*, (Spokesman Books, Nottingham, 1972).

51 On these see, for example, Labour Party, *Britain Will Win With Labour*, 1974, in Craig, F.W.S. (ed.), *British General Election Manifestos, 1918–1966*, p. 245.

52 As regards the public sector Labour 'intend[ed] to socialise existing nationalised industries. In consultation with the unions we shall take steps to make the management of existing nationalised industries more responsible to the workers in the industry', Labour Party, *Let Us Work Together – Labour's Way out of the Crisis*, 1974, in Craig, F.W.S. (ed.), *British General Election Manifestos, 1918–1966*, p. 192. As regards the private sector:

> Our aim is to make industry democratic – to develop joint control and action by management and workers across the whole range of industry [and] commerce … This objective involves strong trade union organisation and widening the scope of collective bargaining.
>
> (Labour Party, *Britain Will Win With Labour*, p. 246.)

53 Labour Party, *Let Us Work Together*, p. 187; see also Labour Party, *Britain Will Win With Labour*, p. 247.

54 Labour Party, *Let Us Work Together*, p. 191; see also Labour Party, *Britain Will Win With Labour*, p. 245.

55 'The aims set out in this manifesto are Socialist aims, and we are proud of the word', Labour Party, *Let Us Work Together*, p. 193.

56 Labour Party, *Let Us Work Together*, p. 193; Labour Party, *Britain Will Win With Labour*, p. 255.

57 See in particular Labour Party, *Britain Will Win With Labour*.

58 *Ibid.*, p. 242.

59 *Ibid.*, p. 243.

60 *Ibid.*, p. 242.

61 Labour Party, *The Labour Way is the Better Way*, in Craig, F.W.S. (ed.), *British General Election Manifestos, 1918–1966*, p. 284

62 Thus,

> each year there [would] be three-way talks between Ministers, management and unions to consider the best way forward for our country's economy. Germany's Social Democratic Government has proved that this is a good way to reach agreement on how to expand output, incomes and living standards.
>
> (*Ibid.*, p. 285)

63 *Ibid.*, p. 287.

64 *Ibid.*, p. 284, p. 286.

65 *Ibid.*, p. 288, p. 289, pp. 295–6.

66 On this see Thompson, N., *Left in the Wilderness. The Political Economy of British Democratic Socialism since 1979*, (Acumen, Chesham, 2002), pp. 214–23.

67 Labour Party, *Britain Will Win*, 1987, in Craig, F.W.S. (ed.), *British General Election Manifestos, 1918–1966*, p. 459.

68 *Ibid.* p. 458.

69 *Ibid.*

70 For an interesting discussion of New Labour's use of language see Fairclough, N., *New Labour, New Language*, (Routledge, London, 2000).

71 *Ibid.*, p. 463

72 *Ibid.*

73 Labour Party, *It's Time to get Britain Working Again*, Labour Party, London, 1992, p. 7, p. 8, my emphasis.

74 *Ibid.* p. 7.

75 *Ibid.* p. 11.

76 *Ibid.*

77 *Ibid.*, p. 7, p. 11, p. 7.

78 'The key to a successful modern economy is a well-educated and motivated work-force ... Britain's future must be high skill, high wage and high tech', *Ibid.*, p. 13. On this see Thompson, N., *Left in the Wilderness, the Political Economy of British Democratic Socialism since 1979*, pp. 214–32.

79 On the lingering influence of a Keynesian full-employment strategy in the Labour Party literature of the early 1990s, see Anderson, P., and Mann, N., *Safety First: The Making of New Labour*, (Granta, London, 1997), pp. 88–90.

80 Labour Party, *Its Time to get Britain Working Again*, p. 11.

81 *Ibid.*, p. 10.

82 *Ibid.*, pp. 10–11.

83 *Ibid.*, p. 11.

84 *Ibid.*

85 Labour Party, *New Labour: Because Britain Deserves Better*, London, Labour Party, 1997, p. 3, p. 2.

86 *Ibid.*, p. 4.

87 Labour Party, *Ambitions for Britain: Labour's Manifesto 2001*, Labour Party, London, 2001, p. 11.

88 *Ibid.*, p. 8.

89 Labour Party, *New Labour: Because Britain Deserves Better*, p. 3.

90 The need for a 'stable economy' or 'economic stability' is expressed no fewer than seven times in nine pages in the 2001 manifesto.

91 Labour Party, *New Labour: Because Britain Deserves Better*, p. 11.

92 *Ibid.*, p. 13.

93 *Ambitions for Britain: Labour's Manifesto*, 2001, p. 26.

94 Labour Party, *New Labour: Because Britain Deserves Better*, p. 3.

95 'Britain believes in a flexible labour market that serves employers and employees alike', *Ibid.*, p. 15.

96 *Ibid.*, p. 15.

97 *Ibid.*, p. 3.

98 *Ibid.*, p. 15; on this see also *Ambitions for Britain*, p. 26.

99 Labour Party, *New Labour: Because Britain Deserves Better*, pp. 12–13.

100 *Ibid.*, p. 3.

101 Labour Party, *Ambitions for Britain*, p. 11.

102 In 2001 New Labour insisted on the need 'to promote the development of entrepreneurship in the school curriculum', *Ibid.*, p. 8.

4   The Old Right

Kevin Jefferys

Introduction

In 1974 Tony Crosland was asked what he meant by socialism:

> I have always thought that Socialism was fundamentally about greater
> equality, and by greater equality I don't mean simply more equality of
> opportunities so that the strong can get to the top more easily ... I meant a
> wider social equality which would also cover the distribution of property,
> which would also cover the educational system and would also cover rela-
> tionships in industry. ... I think to me that is what Socialism means, that we
> should have a more equal and more egalitarian, which I would consider a
> more just society.[1]

With hindsight, Crosland's words have a hollow ring. He came last of the six
contenders in the race to replace Harold Wilson as Labour leader in 1976 and
less than a year later he died suddenly, aged only 58. Callaghan's Government,
battered and bruised by the IMF crisis and the 'Winter of Discontent', was
crushingly defeated by Margaret Thatcher at the 1979 general election,
heralding a long period in opposition for Labour and the end of the road for
Croslandite socialism. Any notion of seeking to create a more equal society
through the redistribution of income and high public spending on social services
was thoroughly discredited; the era of Thatcherism beckoned.

The 'Old Right' provides a convenient label for those who, like Crosland,
belonged to the revisionist or social democratic wing of the Labour movement.
The main aims in what follows are to identify the key contributors to the
thinking of Labour's Old Right since the 1930s and to outline their core ideas
and values, thereby establishing the context for a more detailed analysis of
concepts such as equality in later chapters. In addition, an attempt is made to
assess the success or otherwise of the Old Right in influencing Labour policy. As
this influence has varied over time, a chronological framework has been adopted
in line with the main phases of the Party's leadership. Two particular themes
permeate the chapter as a whole. The first is to point up the fluidity of social
democratic ideology. To identify with a particular wing of the Party, whether

right or left, did not mean adherence to a static and unchanging set of views and policies. Just as the balance of power *between* sections of opinion inside the Party was always changing, so was the balance *within* ideological groupings. As we shall see, there were crucial disagreements on the Old Right over nationalisation, over Europe and over the very nature of the revisionism of which Crosland was the chief exponent. The second theme of the chapter is to suggest that while social democratic ideas had a powerful influence at various times – and an emotional appeal for many Labour activists that still persists – such ideas never entirely captured Party thinking. Even in the apparent 'golden age' of social democracy in the 1950s and 1960s there was a case for saying that revisionism, certainly as defined by Crosland, 'had not been tried'.[2]

Revisionist antecedents during the Attlee years, 1935–55

Social democracy had a long pedigree dating back to the nineteenth century when the German 'revisionist' Eduard Bernstein attempted to rethink Marxist socialism. British politicians and intellectuals sought to follow Bernstein's lead in the 1930s. The downfall of Ramsay MacDonald's government in 1931 exposed the paucity of serious thinking about domestic policy that characterised the early Labour Party. Against the backcloth of the 'hungry thirties', it seemed for a while that the Party might move towards advocacy of direct confrontation with the capitalist system. Pressure from the grass roots was channelled through the left-wing Socialist League and Labour conferences resounded to calls for whole-sale central planning. The challenge of the quasi-Marxist left was gradually contained, though it had a powerful appeal. After the post-1929 economic collapse, writers such as Harold Laski and John Strachey made forceful claims that capitalism was in terminal decline. At Oxford in the late 1930s, three of the figures later prominent on the Old Right – Roy Jenkins, Tony Crosland and Denis Healey – were all flirting with Marxism, which appeared to be the most persuasive alternative to Fascism. For idealistic young undergraduates, Communism – despite Stalin's purges in the Soviet Union – offered the hope of a brave new world. 'We lived in a world of pamphlets, meetings, marches, demonstrations – and very exhilarating it was', Crosland later recalled. He and his friends would frequently march off to the Labour Club in Oxford, where there was great sympathy for the communist cause, 'pausing only to spit through the Trinity gate as we went past'.[3]

For the most part, however, the political and industrial wings of the Labour movement were dominated by figures of more moderate persuasion. The emergence of an Attlee–Bevin axis at the top of the Party was followed by a reshaping of policy. In place of the old-style rhetoric of MacDonald, a talented group of Labour economists evolved a new programme which promised to combine Keynesian demand management with physical control economic planning. The key figure in this process was the ebullient ex-Etonian Hugh Dalton, who led the way with the publication of his 1935 book *Practical Socialism for*

Britain. Dalton was determined to develop what Labour had lacked in the past: a coherent and workable economic strategy. Many of his ideas found their way into Labour's *Immediate Programme of 1937*, a pragmatic yet radical policy document that foreshadowed much of the Party's policy in office after 1945. Although dedicated to the 'immediate', Dalton also had a profound longer-term influence. His energetic support for younger intellectuals led many to regard him as the 'grandfather' of the revisionists, though most of those who benefited from his patronage showed little gratitude. Crosland, who turned against communism as the war against Hitler intensified ('I am engaged on a great revision of Marxism & will certainly emerge as the modern Bernstein', he wrote to a friend in 1941), received enormous encouragement from the doting Dalton. Yet Crosland almost damned his mentor with faint praise, later describing *Practical Socialism for Britain* as just one of 'a number of non-analytical works of a practical reformist nature' which 'contained no long-run analysis of the future of capitalism'.[4]

Two other Dalton protégés were important in developing his ideas before 1945. Douglas Jay, a member of the 'XYZ Club' of Labour supporters in Fleet Street and the City, published *The Socialist Case* in 1937, a book he described as seeking to counter 'the flood of quasi-Marxist volumes pouring forth in the 1930s from Gollancz's Left Book Club and proclaiming the imminent collapse of capitalism'.[5] Jay put forward three main arguments: that the case for social justice rested on redistribution of wealth, contrary to the Marxist concern with ownership; that redistribution could be achieved peacefully and democratically; and that unemployment and cyclical depression were monetary phenomena which could be overcome by intelligent management of 'total effective demand'. Although overshadowed by war, an even more wide-ranging critique was made by another Oxford-trained economist – Evan Durbin – in his work *The Politics of Democratic Socialism*, drafted in 1938–9 and published in 1940. Durbin's aim was nothing less than to restate Labour's view of capitalism, class and strategy and so to 'break the spell' of Marxism in intellectual circles. The growth of suburbia and rise of the lower middle classes, Durbin noted, made a mockery of Marxist notions of ever-increasing revolutionary consciousness. The economic recovery of the mid-1930s also indicated that capitalism was not facing inevitable collapse as Marxists claimed: 'the walls of Jericho will not fall at a shout nor crumble from within'.[6]

Durbin's book was greeted with contempt by the likes of *Tribune* and the *New Statesman*; he admitted that in the eyes of Laski he was regarded as a 'pseudo-Conservative'. This hostile response overlooked parts of Durbin's work that were in line with thinking on the Labour left. While he was against dogmatic hostility to capitalism, and so accepted the need for private enterprise, he agreed that for Labour to be more than just 'an old reforming party', it would need to rely heavily on physical planning and public ownership. Prior to his sudden death in a tragic drowning incident in 1948 (when he saved his daughter and her friend off the Cornish coast), Durbin wrote of Labour's nationalisation programme as a 'triumph of democracy' and the Party's 'main success' in office after the war.[7]

It would therefore be misleading to label Durbin simply as a forerunner of 1950s-style revisionism. While he foreshadowed later thinking on the changing nature of capitalism, his attachment to public ownership placed him firmly in the Party mainstream of the 1940s. In spite of Durbin's reputation as the author of the 'bible of revisionism', he did not agree with Jay's 1937 view – later a cornerstone of the revisionist faith – that nationalisation of efficient private companies might produce unhealthy monopolies, and would not in itself promote social equality or economic security.[8]

In effect the non-Marxist majority in Labour ranks during the 1930s and 1940s were united around a 'corporate socialist' ideology – one that accorded a central place to public ownership.[9] For most of Attlee's tenure of the leadership arguably the key figure on the right was Herbert Morrison, architect in the 1930s of a nationalisation programme based on his experience of creating the London Passenger Transport Board. It was Morrison who championed the view that planned public enterprise would be more efficient than the bloated and ill-managed private monopolies that had failed the British economy in the 1930s. Hence it was Morrison who took much of the credit for the measures implemented after 1945, which ranged from a massive electrification programme to public ownership of the mines. He did, though, become increasingly concerned that many of the nationalised industries were reluctant to modernise outdated working practices. Morrison's advocacy of 'consolidation' in the late 1940s was not a call for Labour to rest on its laurels; rather he wanted to find ways of ensuring that state industries played a full part in developing the economy.

After Labour limped back to power in 1950 Morrison conceded: 'It is … quite clear that the majority of the electorate are not disposed to accept nationalisation for the sake of nationalisation.' He added, in words that pointed towards the revised view of public ownership that was to characterise the Labour right after 1951, that 'it was more important to pay attention to making effective and efficient the existing socialisation rather than to proceed with a further nationalisation programme at the present time.'[10]

In the meantime, much of the reshaping of Britain in the immediate post-war years was welcomed by all shades of Party opinion. But implementation of Labour's domestic programme – combining extensive welfare reforms such as the NHS with planning of a mixed economy in which the public sector figured large – left an obvious problem: what should come next? Debate about this question intensified after Attlee lost power in 1951. His final years as leader were marked by factional in-fighting of a sort largely absent since 1935. What followed was a protracted civil war between the so-called 'fundamentalist' supporters of Aneurin Bevan, who remained attached to further nationalisation as a cornerstone of policy, and right-wing backers of Morrison and the increasingly powerful ex-Chancellor, Hugh Gaitskell. Although Bevan spoke of a 'basic conflict over party purpose', ideological divisions were limited at this point. Most disputes were over foreign policy, and both sides struggled to produce freshly-formulated programmes to apply to domestic politics. What this left, at the heart of the bitterness in the early 1950s, were differences of political style and emphasis, compounded by a rapid hardening of individual loyalties. The whole dispute became, in the words of Douglas Jay, 'a notable case of what Thucydides, in his account of the civil war in Corfu calls "statis": faction for faction's sake in which the protagonists know which side they are on, but usually cannot remember why it all started.'[11]

The uneasy nature of the relationship between left and right was illustrated in the *New Fabian Essays*, published in 1952. This collection contained contributions from younger MPs on the Labour right such as Jenkins, Healey and Crosland. The latter's contribution, 'The Transition from Capitalism', picked up Durbin's assessment by arguing that Attlee's government had produced a new type of post-capitalist society. In one of the most well-received of the essays, marking him out as a serious theoretician, Crosland added that despite such changes Britain in the 1950s had not yet begun to approach the ideal of a 'classless or egalitarian society', as was evident both from social data and the 'deplorable' persistence of class antagonisms. The way ahead was to switch attention from economic to social reform, notably in the sphere of education.[12] Yet the collection was not conceived as some form of Gaitskellite tract. The book contained essays by left-wingers such as Ian Mikardo and John Strachey, as well as by the editor Richard Crossman, a forceful advocate of Bevanism on the Labour backbenches. The project was planned and initiated well before the Bevanite controversies erupted, though the unity the volume presupposed had largely disappeared by the time of publication in the summer of 1952. The *New Fabian Essays* not only looked back fondly to shared assumptions about the achievements of the Attlee governments; they also pointed forward to an era in which left-right divisions were brought sharply into focus.

The triumph of revisionism? Gaitskell as leader, 1955–63

Hugh Gaitskell's election as Labour leader in December 1955 was a critical moment in the evolution of the Old Right. Following Labour's defeat at the general election in May 1955, it was obvious that Attlee – after 20 years at the helm – would soon retire. Yet instead of going immediately he clung on for several months, his critics convinced that this showed his determination to spite his long-term rival, Herbert Morrison. In the interim Hugh Dalton launched 'Operation Dynamo', a public attempt to dislodge ageing members of the shadow cabinet, nine of whom were over 65. By encouraging others to follow his own lead in making way for youth, Dalton helped to encourage the view that Morrison, in his late sixties, was too old for the leadership.[13] In the ballot among Labour MPs that followed Attlee's decision to quit, 49-year-old Gaitskell comfortably emerged as the standard-bearer of the centre-right, defeating Bevan and leaving Morrison humiliated in third place. Morrison's bitterness at his treatment was such that he refused to continue as deputy leader. His exclusion from the senior ranks underlined the eclipse of nationalisation as a tenet of the Labour right. With Morrison out of the way, the ideological running was now made by Gaitskell's personal and political intimates, the 'revisionists' or 'Hampstead Set', as they were known, as a result of frequent visits to the leader's home in Frognal Gardens.

Gaitskell's cause was greatly strengthened by the publication in 1956 of what for many remains the finest work of its kind since the war, Crosland's *The Future of Socialism*. Defeated at the election in 1955, Crosland was free to put the finishing touches to the book he had been working on for several years. The early chapters went over ground already covered in his essay in *New Fabian Essays*. In analysing changes since the war, Crosland again argued that pre-war capitalism had been changed beyond recognition. In moving on to look at how socialism needed to be redefined in the light of such changes, Crosland introduced a key aspect of the new revisionism: a distinction between ends and means. Too often, he felt, particular groups – notably Marxists, but also others like the Fabians – had appropriated the term 'socialism' to describe the means by which they would bring about reform. But as the proposed means had never commanded universal assent, it was best that any definition should stick to the ends in view. On this definition, socialism for Crosland was primarily about equality and welfare. It remained a relevant creed because in spite of post-war improvements, social distress and squalor were still widespread in 1950s Britain, class antagonisms remained strong, and the distribution of rewards and privileges was still highly inequitable. This constituted the 'ethical basis for being a socialist'.[14]

What then was to be done? The core of *The Future of Socialism* contained Crosland's ideas for future policy. As well as continuing to improve the welfare services introduced after 1945, he hoped to see a 'social revolution' achieved through egalitarian reforms, notably to the education system and to the distribution of property. While wishing to go beyond equality of opportunity, he was not in favour of equality of outcomes. He did not wish to see 'the Queen riding a bicycle'. Society would look very different if his proposed changes were carried through, and it would be for a 'younger generation' to look at the arguments afresh. As far as economic policy was concerned, Crosland noted the importance of growth for the realisation of socialist objectives, though more attention was given at the time to his trenchant view that, while further measures of public ownership were needed, old-style state monopolies were 'wholly irrelevant to socialism as defined in this book'. They were not essential, he believed, to establishing social equality, increasing social welfare or eliminating class distinctions. The conclusion to the book contained some of its most striking passages, underlining Crosland's libertarianism and his conviction that social rather than economic issues should be accorded top priority in future. He urged not only cultural changes that might make Britain 'a more colourful and civilised country to live in', but also – in what amounted to a blueprint for the type of legislation introduced a decade later – the updating of restrictive laws on divorce, homosexuality, censorship and rights for women.[15]

Bevanites were outraged by Crosland's assertion that nationalisation should henceforth play only a minor role in socialist advance. Nevertheless for many activists the brilliance of Crosland's writing and analysis made his book a vital reference point for a generation to come. Gaitskell was immensely proud of his friend's work, which was lauded in reviews as an exciting synthesis of reformism and radicalism, going beyond Morrisonian 'consolidation' and making socialism look relevant to the circumstances of the day. Bevan's reluctant acceptance that the leadership issue had been settled for the time being, and his willingness to serve in Gaitskell's shadow cabinet, meant there was only a negligible intellectual challenge to revisionism inside the Party. Indeed in the late 1950s the tide appeared to be moving in one direction. Even former Marxists such as John Strachey appeared to have undergone a change of heart. In his 1956 work *Contemporary Capitalism*, Strachey conceded that Marx had underestimated the ability of progressive forces to harness the powers of the state and agreed that a planned market economy was feasible in a way that did not seem attainable before the war. Although important differences remained – with Strachey continuing to emphasise economic planning and nationalisation where Crosland spoke of equality and social justice – *Contemporary Capitalism* suggested the revisionist tide might sweep all before it.[16]

Further support for Gaitskell came in the pages of *Socialist Commentary*, the Labour right journal edited by his friend Rita Hinden, a firm exponent of a mixed economy as a 'third way' between Soviet communism and American capitalism. *Socialist Commentary* originated in the early 1950s as a monthly publication aimed at countering *Tribune*. It shared Morrison's view that Labour needed to remain a national rather than a class party, though it went ahead of Morrison in claiming that demands for public ownership were a hindrance to such a development. By 1955 the journal had become the unofficial mouthpiece of the Gaitskellites, promoting all the causes the new leader was associated with – the Atlantic alliance, strong anti-communism, a mixed economy and social equality. The self-effacing Rita Hinden, though in the shadow of more powerful personalities around her, became a key figure in the development of revisionism. As well as co-editing *Twentieth Century Socialism* – in which the themes of liberty, fellowship and equality were given prominence – she commissioned a series of policy supplements for the journal on topics such as incomes policy, social services and education, so providing further ammunition for the reshaping of Party policy in the late 1950s.[17]

The revisionist tide ebbed – at least temporarily – when Labour suffered a third successive election defeat in 1959. Gaitskell's view that defeat stemmed from a failure to modernise Labour's image – especially its association with wholesale nationalisation – was bitterly resented in some quarters. He encountered stiff opposition when he proposed to amend 'Clause IV' of the Party's constitution, with its reference to the 'common ownership of the means of production, distribution and exchange'. It was not only the left who felt it was outrageous for Gaitskell, having dictated policy over recent years, to claim that defeat necessitated moving further still to the right. Mainstream opinion, including that of trade unionists hitherto loyal to the leader, also regarded Clause IV as non-negotiable. This historic symbol convinced members that, come what may, their socialist faith remained intact. Unaware that union leaders would desert him, Gaitskell embarked on a fight he was unable to win, unleashing a period of renewed blood-letting which appeared to confirm the worst fears about Labour's future. After backing down in 1960, Gaitskell's leadership itself was challenged by the ex-Bevanite Harold Wilson, and he was forced to acknowledge that revisionism had not captured the Party in the way he hoped. Crosland told his friend that morale on the Labour right was 'appallingly low', with no positive reforms in sight and the prospect of further electoral defeat ahead unless things changed.[18]

After seeing off Wilson's challenge, Gaitskell began an impressive fightback in 1961. He reversed an earlier conference defeat over unilateralism, and he benefited from the economic difficulties facing Macmillan's Tory government. Labour's revival at the ballot box – in by-elections and local elections – was such that Gaitskell was widely regarded as being well placed to become the next Prime Minister. His efforts were greatly assisted by the emergence of the pressure group the Campaign for Democratic Socialism (CDS), which sought to promote revisionist ideas among constituency activists. The revisionist tide appeared to be swelling once more. In November 1962 Crosland brought together much of his thinking since 1956 in *The Conservative Enemy*, aimed at providing a 'programme of radical, social-democratic reform for the middle 1960s'. In what he described as 'much the angriest of his books', he attacked not just the Macmillan government, but also the extra-parliamentary New Left for clinging to 'an out-dated semi-Marxist analysis of society'. Where *The Future of Socialism* concentrated on state education, Crosland's egalitarianism now showed itself in his attack on private education, which he called 'the greatest single cause of stratification and class-consciousness in Britain'.[19] Despite lacking the freshness of his previous book (most of essays in the collection had been published beforehand), *The Conservative Enemy* won high plaudits. This was partly because Crosland's reputation as the high priest of revisionism was firmly established by 1962, though it also stemmed from the concern even of his detractors not to rock the boat ahead of what looked like an inevitable Gaitskell premiership.

But there was no Gaitskell premiership. Weeks later the Party leader died suddenly from a rare disorder of the immune system. It was a huge blow to the revisionist project. Crosland in particular had relied heavily on his friendship with 'Gaiters', as he called him, and was left politically high and dry when, as expected, Labour MPs plumped for Harold Wilson – Gaitskell's arch-enemy – as the new leader. Within weeks, Crosland went from 'the inner sanctum to outer darkness'.[20] The 'royal court' around the new leader consisted mostly of former Bevanites such as Richard Crossman and Barbara Castle. It was too early to tell if, as Crosland feared, all the painstaking efforts to promote revisionism would go to waste. In effect Gaitskell's death left Labour in a state of flux, demonstrating that the long civil war of the 1950s had never been satisfactorily resolved. Despite Gaitskellite domination of Party institutions since 1955, revisionism had never completely captured Labour opinion. Fundamentalist socialism may have been down, but it was not out. As the Clause IV controversy illustrated, there remained deep-seated attachment to traditional symbols and rhetoric. It thus remained unclear which of the Party's main traditions would prevail, especially as the early indications were that Wilson would use the novel idea of 'scientific socialism' to bind the main factions together while avoiding the hard question: was Labour in the 1960s a party of socialism or social democracy?[21]

The disintegration of social democracy under Wilson and Callaghan, 1963–80

In spite of his background as a Bevanite who had resigned over health service charges in 1951, Wilson essentially belonged to the moderate centre of the Party. He believed, like Attlee, that Labour was best led by maintaining unity; in other words, that he should not follow Gaitskell's more abrasive style. In policy terms, this meant playing down both the revisionist emphasis on social equality and the left-wing commitment to extending public ownership. Instead he argued that the Party should champion a managerial revolution, identifying Labour as the Party of modernisation, in contrast to the tired 'grouse-moor' image of the Tories under Macmillan and Douglas-Home. In the short term this proved brilliantly successful. The annual conference of October 1963, compared with the last time the Party met in Scarborough in 1952, was a 'positive love-feast', uniting around Wilson's call to harness the 'white heat' of the technological revolution.[22] With his confident television manner, Wilson came across as an engaging and fresh face, carrying Labour to a narrow victory at the general election in 1964. By linking socialism with science, Wilson appeared to have succeeded in modernising the Party in a matter of months, where Gaitskell had struggled for years. 'With one bound Jack was free – or so … it was possible to believe.'[23]

In retrospect, it became clear Labour's victory in 1964 was won at the cost of greatly raising expectations, within the Party and the electorate at large. The folly of this strategy became evident when, after a second and larger election success in 1966, the government was faced with a series of debilitating economic crises. Devaluation, tax increases and cuts to cherished social programmes all took an enormous toll on Wilson's popularity. For many who placed their hopes in Labour's vision of a 'New Britain', the late 1960s were a time of bitter disillusionment – a period that brought a lower growth rate than during the 'wasted years' of the Conservatives. The left found little evidence of any serious attachment to economic planning, and the government's much-vaunted 'National Plan' was quietly sidelined. There were some successes associated with revisionist ministers such as Crosland – notably with moves towards comprehensive secondary schooling – and Jenkins, who backed moves to liberalise the law on issues ranging from abortion and equal pay for women to homosexuality. Jenkins's record at the Home Office was offset, however, by his performance as an orthodox Chancellor who presided over cutbacks in social expenditure, the reimposition of charges for health prescriptions and increases in unemployment.[24]

Labour's loss of power in 1970 was followed by renewed in-fighting between the inheritors of the old fundamentalist and revisionist traditions. But the arguments of the 1970s were conducted in a markedly different framework from those of the 1950s. Wilson's premiership left a legacy of uncertainty, with both main traditions feeling they had been let down. Crossman, as an ex-Bevanite one of those who most welcomed the leadership change in 1963, concluded that Wilson had no 'profound thoughts' about the direction of the Party, having aspired to nothing more than to 'stay in office'.[25] Revisionists were convinced Wilson had paid only lip service to their cause. For Crosland, Wilson had no real interest in socialist or political theory, no governing set of principles, and no serious concern for equality.[26] Labour, it seemed, had fudged the answer to the 'hard question': it was neither the Party of socialism nor social democracy. This identity crisis was compounded by a recognition that Labour was on the defensive to a greater extent than at any time since the war. In spite of successive defeats at the polls in the 1950s, the faithful – looking back with pride at the record of the Attlee years – could trust that, one day, the forward march of progressivism would inevitably be resumed. This spirit of optimism was harder to detect when Wilson left office. Instead, as left-wing views gained ground among the rank-and-file, the social democratic wing of the Party, far from reasserting itself as it did in the 1950s, began to disintegrate. Underpinning this process was the economic malaise of the 1970s, with inflation rampant, growth minimal and trade unions apparently 'out of control'. Other policy issues, however, also proved critical, as did the decay in the relationship between key individuals on the Old Right.

Europe played a key role in the fragmentation of the Old Right. The first two years of opposition after 1970 were overshadowed by protracted disputes over Labour's attitude towards membership of the European Community. A minority of pro-Market MPs, grouped around Roy Jenkins, decided to back Heath's Tory government in pushing for British entry, despite suspicions about the value of membership in the eyes of many MPs and activists. In an effort to reconcile divisions, Wilson proposed that a Labour government would renegotiate the terms of entry and hold a referendum on British membership – a formula which prompted the resignation of Jenkins from the shadow front bench. As well as undermining Jenkins's hopes of one day becoming Party leader, the whole episode seriously damaged the social democratic cause, especially as the staunchly pro-European views of Jenkins and his acolytes were not shared by Crosland, who abstained in the crucial Commons vote.[27] Jenkinsites were incensed by this 'betrayal' of the high-priest of revisionism, especially when a newspaper leaked Crosland's view that an 'elitist' faction of right-wing intellectuals were in danger of becoming separated from the main body of the Labour movement. 'Their idea of a Labour Party is not mine', Crosland confided in his wife. 'Roy has actually come to dislike socialism.'[28] After 1972 the Jenkinsites, numerically the strongest element among social democrats inside the PLP, were becoming increasingly detached from the mainstream.

By the time Labour won a narrow election victory in the spring of 1974 Crosland had become almost a one-man champion of egalitarian socialism. Wilson's return to Downing Street coincided with the publication of Crosland's last book *Socialism Now*. The introductory essay, drafted in 1973, addressed the issue of whether traditional revisionism required a complete overhaul in the wake of the oil crisis that had sent shockwaves through the world economy. While he stuck to his earlier definition of socialism, Crosland acknowledged that, with Britain facing unprecedented challenges, it was legitimate to question if greater equality was still attainable. On this issue he insisted that revisionism remained more persuasive than the revived 'semi-Marxist thought' of the Labour left. While increased public ownership might help in some areas, the failures of the past decade had little to do with nationalisation; there was no indication that massive transfers of ownership would help to achieve equality. What was needed was not a move to Clause IV socialism but a 'sharper delineation of fundamental objectives', with careful costing and planning of reforms to make them part of a coherent package, not isolated achievements as when Labour was last in power. He then listed his own priorities: the reduction of poverty, the provision of decent homes, nationalisation of development land, the redistribution of capital wealth, elimination of selection in secondary schools and the extension of industrial democracy. Such a programme would require higher taxes among the better-off, including workers such as dockers and printers who instinctively favoured pay differentials in place of equality.[29]

Crosland was lucky in the timing of his book, which gave it much prominence and publicity, though he encountered sterner criticism than he had in the past. He was attacked for being hazy not only about how to achieve higher growth, but also about how to secure the reduction of poverty that he said was the top priority. Some of the sharpest critiques came from those who were seeking more far-reaching redefinitions of revisionism. John Gyford and Stephen Haseler in a Fabian pamphlet, *Social Democracy: Beyond Revisionism*, argued for a more populist strategy, aimed at reducing inequality by a more localised, grass-roots approach. A similar theme was taken up by Dick Taverne – who had resigned in protest against left-wing activity and secured election as a Democratic Labour MP in the Lincoln by-election of 1973 – in his book *The Future of Labour* (1974), which called for Labour to break with the unions and cultivate community politics. Younger Jenkinsites such as Giles Radice, frustrated that the rift over Europe meant Crosland gave them little encouragement in their own efforts to think out new strategies, concluded that *Socialism Now* did not provide a *Future of Socialism* mark II: 'but that does not mean that it does not need to be done'. This clearly touched a nerve, for Crosland bluntly said at one point that he was 'too bloody busy' to rethink his whole philosophy. On another occasion he remarked: 'Keynes didn't write another General Theory'.[30]

The experience of government after 1974 saw the effective demise of egalitarian socialism. The leadership contest that followed Wilson's resignation in 1976 underlined the point that there was no natural heir-apparent on the social democratic right. Jenkins, Healey and Crosland were all soundly beaten by Jim Callaghan, the pragmatic 'safety first' candidate. When Jenkins decided to leave British politics to take up the presidency of the European Commission, the future leadership of the Labour right appeared to rest between Crosland, promoted to become Foreign Secretary, and Chancellor Denis Healey, neither of whom attracted the levels of back-bench support claimed by Jenkins in his prime. Crosland and Healey found themselves at loggerheads during the IMF crisis, when the Foreign Secretary attempted to resist the draconian cutbacks required as the price of international support for the ailing British economy. The crisis did not, as some have claimed, mark a watershed in which Labour turned towards monetarism. Healey never had to draw on more than half the available loan, and economic recovery in 1977 enabled him to celebrate 'Sod Off Day' – when Britain became free of IMF control – much earlier than anticipated. In most respects economic policy after 1976 'differed little from what it had been before the arrival of the IMF'.[31] But as well as damaging Labour's credibility, the IMF had shattering effects on the Old Right. When Crosland died suddenly in February 1977, the revisionist notion of achieving equality via economic growth and redistributive taxation looked to be dead in the water.

In the last phase of the Callaghan Government, the number of articulate exponents of the social democratic cause dwindled further. After Crosland's death, his friends argued that since 1964 his brand of socialism had never become the overarching ideology that would have been likely under a Gaitskell administration, especially as Crosland had been denied the Chancellorship – the one post which would have put him in a position to propose alternatives to periodic bouts of deflation. Others were more critical of Crosland's legacy. The most detailed effort to refurbish revisionism from a sympathetic perspective was made by John Mackintosh, a leading light in the loyalist Manifesto Group of Labour MPs, who claimed that the growth of corporatism in the 1970s was the underlying cause of Britain's economic weakness. Parliamentary government and the independence of MPs needed to be reasserted, Mackintosh claimed, while devolution to the regions was essential if faith in democracy was to be revived. In 1978 he attacked what he saw as the 'basic error' of Croslandism in talking 'endlessly about the distribution of wealth, its taxation and use for this and that but very little about the creation of wealth'. The task of creating a productive mixed economy remained, though Mackintosh himself was unable to come up with any new economic theory of growth. He was still working on a full restatement of revisionist socialism when he too died in July 1978. According to Greg Rosen, although Mackintosh had not formulated all the answers before his death, he had at least 'asked the questions'.[32]

The final nail in the coffin for the social democratic right was the failure of Labour's strategy for working with the trade unions, culminating in the misery of the 'Winter of Discontent' in 1979. In place of Attlee's corporate socialism, Gaitskell's revisionism and Wilson's scientific socialism, Callaghan offered only an old-fashioned Labourism that had manifestly gone out of fashion. When this was made brutally apparent at the 1979 election, a resumption of bitter infighting for the ideological heart of the Party became unavoidable. 'To pretend in this situation that socialists and social democrats are all part of the same great Movement', wrote the disenchanted former MP David Marquand, 'is to live a lie'. It was a lie that many were no longer prepared to live. Confronted with what they saw as 'Bennery' at Westminster and 'entryism' in the localities, the Labour right were unable and unwilling to launch a counter-attack. After Callaghan's replacement as leader by Michael Foot, the breakaway Social Democratic Party was formed by the nucleus of those who cut their teeth as revisionists in the 1950s – Jenkins, Bill Rodgers and Shirley Williams, joined by David Owen. Within months the new Party could claim over 20 MPs, mostly defectors from Labour ranks, committed to 'breaking the mould' of British politics by replacing Labour as the main opposition. The few remaining adherents of Croslandite socialism were left to ask, more in hope than expectation, whether 'the humane and flexible vision of the democratic socialists' might one day 'rise again from the ashes'?[33]

The Old Right since 1980: risen from the ashes?

In spite of its early success, the ultimate failure of the SDP owed something to its lack of a coherent ideology. Its claim to be a radical party of renewal disguised the essential caution of its views: old revisionist notions of welfare and equality were replaced by new concerns with decentralisation, freedom and ecology, tacitly acknowledging that low economic growth was a fact of life.[34] Another reason why the SDP was unable to break the mould was that most of the Labour right did not join the new Party. Defections tended to be heaviest in cities where the left was strong, notably London and Liverpool; in some areas – for example Scotland – the SDP never got off the ground. Among those who stayed were key figures such as Healey, Roy Hattersley and Gerald Kaufman. With Foot as leader, the Old Right was too enfeebled to block the left-influenced manifesto of 1983 – 'the longest suicide note in history' as Kaufman called it – which was followed by crushing electoral defeat, with Labour recording its lowest share of the popular vote since 1918. Yet the right could take some comfort from Foot's replacement after the election by Neil Kinnock, when Roy Hattersley secured the post of deputy leader. In spite of his Tribunite past, Kinnock saw the need to move Labour back towards the centre ground of politics in order to regain power. By the time of the 1987 election the Party offered more moderate policies: the earlier pledge to withdraw from the EC had been dropped and promises to reduce high levels of unemployment had been scaled down. This was not enough to seriously dent the ascendancy of the Thatcher government, but it was sufficient to see off the challenge of the Liberal–SDP Alliance, so confirming Labour's survival as the main alternative government.

The compromises contained in the 1987 manifesto left uncertain what ideological basis Labour policy now rested upon. Some clues came in a series of major pronouncements over the following two years. 'Surprisingly rapidly after its apparent demise,' argues Andrew Thorpe, 'revisionism was back on the agenda'.[35] Kinnock's reaction to defeat was to press on with the process of what he called 'modernisation'. He sanctioned the Party's first comprehensive policy review since the 1950s, establishing seven review groups to rethink Labour's approach to domestic and international affairs. In 1988 an interim *Statement of*

Democratic Socialist Aims and Values was produced, pointing towards an acceptance of the irreversibility of many Thatcherite reforms and recognising that the market economy should be regarded as innocent until found guilty, rather than vice versa. The operation of the market, it was claimed, 'where properly regulated, is a generally satisfactory means of determining provision and consumption.'[36]

The *Statement* had been drafted by the deputy leader, Hattersley, who a year earlier had published a fuller exposition of his ideas in *Choose Freedom*. The subtitle of the book, *The Future for Democratic Socialism*, recognised the huge debt Hattersley owed to Crosland. While Hattersley broadly endorsed the role of markets, he took a traditional social democratic approach to their practical limitations. 'In education and health,' he argued, 'scarce resources must be distributed according to need, not purchasing power'. By giving prominence to freedom as a concept at the heart of socialist thinking, Hattersley was attempting to challenge the association of the term with the Thatcherite right. He argued that liberty and equality were closely linked and that Labour, instead of being regarded as a patronising force that sought to interfere with people's lives, needed to make the case for extending choice and opportunity as far as possible. Democratic socialism, in Hattersley's view, was about 'an extension of freedom brought about by a more equal distribution of resources', so leading to the 'emancipation of previously powerless citizens'.[37]

The Policy Review culminated in 1989 in the publication of *Meet the Challenge, Make the Change*, a document which underlined two key themes in the evolution of Labour thinking. The first, already signalled in the interim statement, was a commitment to a regulatory role for government: 'to help the market system work properly where it can, will and should – and to replace it where it can't, won't or shouldn't.' The second key theme was the sidelining of public ownership as a major instrument of policy; an explicit recognition that Thatcher's privatisation programme of the 1980s could not be easily undone. In many ways, the review was a testament to how far Kinnock had reversed the left-wing tide of the early 1980s. He brushed off accusations of betrayal and welcomed the support he received from MPs such as Giles Radice, who welcomed in his 1989 book *Labour's Path to Power* the recognition that 'the competitive model, provided it is adequately regulated, works well in the allocation of goods and services.'[38] Much of the discussion of the policy review, however, failed to capture the public imagination, and press critics noted the absence of a 'big idea' to replace corporate socialism or Wilsonian technocracy. 'The most effective way of attacking Labour', wrote Colin Hughes and Patrick Wintour, 'continued to be the insult that socialism was an out-dated creed. The review modernised the Labour Party – or started to – but failed to make socialism modern.'[39]

Such accusations dogged Kinnock until after his resignation following defeat at the 1992 general election. They resurfaced also during the leadership of John Smith, who cautiously maintained his predecessor's commitment to the modernisation of Party policies and organisation. Although associated with the Labour right in his earlier career, Smith earned respect from all sections of the Party for a more inclusive approach than his predecessor. Where Kinnock had often confronted his critics, Smith disarmed them. As Labour pulled ahead of the discredited Major government after Black Wednesday in September 1992, mutterings about Smith's leadership came less from 'traditionalists' but from 'modernisers', those on the new right who believed the Party still needed to reform itself drastically if it were ever to regain a wider appeal. It would not be enough, the argument ran, simply to rely on Tory unpopularity and 'one more heave' to bring Labour back to power. One such critic, the shadow Home Secretary Tony Blair, frequently told friends: 'John is just so cautious – it's a disaster.'[40] Smith had, however, positioned Labour skilfully with a real prospect of returning to power when he died in May 1994; an unexpected development without which the era of Blair and New Labour would never have been ushered in.[41]

In reflecting on the development of policy after 1983, many commentators and political observers spoke of a revival of revisionist social democracy. According to David Marquand, the 1980s had seen an ideological transformation. As in the 1950s, public ownership had been downplayed and the emphasis had been placed on selective intervention in the economy to ensure fairer or more efficient outcomes. Within a few years of the 1983 debacle, Labour had turned itself around to commit itself to further European integration, to continued membership of NATO and to a market-oriented mixed economy. Kinnock, in the words of Marquand, 'was now a better – or at any rate, a more successful – revisionist than Gaitskell had ever been'.[42] Yet the differences between the 1950s and 1980s were arguably more striking than the similarities. As Kinnock himself was to concede, there was no 'central philosophical theme' to the policy review he sanctioned. In contrast to Crosland's work, there was no attempt to ground findings in systematic analysis of recent social and economic change. Throughout his tenure of leadership Kinnock was unable to shake off his fear that too bold or rapid change could 'have fractured the developing consensus and retarded the whole operation'.[43]

One of the strongest critiques of the 1980s policy review has been made by Eric Shaw, who presents it not as a belated conversion to European-style social democracy but as 'the dilution or renunciation' of Keynesian ideas. In the first place, the emphasis on 'supply-side' measures – on the need for selective intervention on the supply-side of the economy – implied a retreat from demand management and a recognition of the constraints on public expenditure. Unlike in the 1960s, Labour had abandoned the view that macroeconomic intervention could be vigorously pursued to promote growth and full employment. In addition, with electoral calculations in mind, the Party no longer adhered to the strategy of pursuing egalitarian and welfare goals based upon high levels of public spending and sharply redistributive taxation. What Labour doctrine amounted to, Shaw claims, was 'post-revisionist social democracy', a stunted orthodoxy that had achieved little more than renegotiating the historic compromise between capitalism and the state – on 'terms much more favourable to capitalism' than in earlier years.[44]

While others reach a less harsh judgement, noting that Labour's ideological adaptations after 1983 made it more electorally appealing than it had been for a generation, the emergence of New Labour after 1994 appeared to confirm that the left had entered a 'post-revisionist' phase. 'The political fact of the age', John Gray wrote in 1996, 'is the passing of social democracy.' The use of tax and welfare systems for egalitarian redistribution was no longer possible in Britain, he noted, owing to institutional changes since 1979, voter resistance and the globalisation of economic activity. Any attempt to develop a successor to Thatcherism as a viable governing philosophy could not go back to 'assumptions and modes of thought that belong to an historical context that has vanished beyond recovery'.[45] As Brian Brivati has noted, Gordon Brown – the Chancellor who determined much of New Labour policy in office after 1997 – frequently used language that struck a chord with Party activists, expressing his ambition to tackle poverty, unemployment and international debt. Yet very few of his initiatives could be described as socialist. Brivati says that 'the approach of the government and the new British political consensus, is based on a combination of European social democracy and North American New Democratic ideology'. Such an approach was justified, in Brown's eyes, because it promised what previous Labour governments could not deliver: sustained electoral success.[46]

But if revisionist social democracy has not – as its adherents hoped – 'risen from the ashes', its legacy remains. Indeed it still has a strong sentimental appeal for many Labour activists and supporters. In July 2002 Chancellor Brown poured huge new sums of money into public investment, prompting commentators to talk of the great 'social democratic moment' after five frustrating years of waiting. 'Now there is less old Labour and New Labour', wrote Polly Toynbee in the *Guardian*, 'just social democratic Labour taxing and spending for better public services.' Toynbee admitted, however, that this interpretation involved a degree of wishful thinking. What was missing, she conceded, was any political passion to accompany the new spending announcements. Unless voters became emotionally committed to making public services work, there remained the danger that they would simply demand ever more and make the ballot box the customer complaints desk. As Prime Minister, Tony Blair continued to give little sense of an underlying commitment to social justice; his language remained 'magesterially-managerial but ... ideology-free'.[47] In this Toynbee was echoing those who believe that at the start of the twenty-first century socialism and social democracy have both been replaced by nothing more than 'enlightened managerialism'.[48] Social democracy is dead; long live social democracy.

Notes

1 Transcript of interview with Llew Gardiner, Thames Television Programme, 'People and Politics', cited in Jefferys, J., *Anthony Crosland* (Richard Cohen, London, 1999), pp. 227–8.
2 Lipsey, D. and Leonard, D. (eds), *The Socialist Agenda: Crosland's Legacy* (Jonathan Cape, London, 1981), p. 26. For the idea of a post-war 'golden age', see for example Callaghan, J., *The Retreat of Social Democracy* (Manchester University Press, Manchester, 2000).

3　Cited in Jefferys, J., *Anthony Crosland*, p. 7.

4　Howe, S., 'Hugh Dalton', in Jefferys, K. (ed.), *Labour Forces. From Ernest Bevin to Gordon Brown* (IB Tauris, London, 2002), pp. 43–59.

5　Jay, D., *Change and Fortune. A Political Record* (Hutchinson, London, 1980), p. 63.

6　Durbin, E., *The Politics of Democratic Socialism* (Routledge & Sons, London, 1940), pp. 142–4.

7　Brooke, S., *Labour's War: The Labour Party during the Second World War* (OUP, Oxford, 1992), p. 300.

8　Foote, G., 'Evan Durbin', in Rosen, G., (ed.), *Dictionary of Labour Biography* (Politicos, London, 2002), pp. 178–80.

9　Foote, G., *The Labour Party's Political Thought: A History* (Macmillan, Basingstoke, 1997), pp. 149–86.

10　Rosen, G., 'Herbert Morrison', in Jefferys, K. (ed.), *Labour Forces*, pp. 25–38.

11　Jay, D., *Change and Fortune, A Political Record*, p. 221.

12　Crosland, C.A.R., 'The Transition from Capitalism', in Crossman, R.H.S. (ed.), *New Fabian Essays* (Turnstile, London, 1952), pp. 33–68.

13　Pimlott, B., *Hugh Dalton* (Jonathan Cape, London, 1985), pp. 622–3.

14　Crosland, C.A.R., *The Future of Socialism* (Jonathan Cape, London, 1956), p. 116.

15　*Ibid.*, pp. 216–17 and 520–4.

16　Strachey, J., *Contemporary Capitalism* (Victor Gollancz, London, 1956); P., Larkin, 'John Strachey', in Rosen, G. (ed.), *Dictionary of Labour Biography*, pp. 550–3.

17　Morgan, K.O., 'Rita Hinden', in *Labour People. Leaders and Lieutenants* (Oxford University Press, Oxford, 1987), pp. 239–45.

18　Jefferys, K., *Crosland*, pp. 74–5. On the Clause IV controversy see Jones, T., *Remaking the Labour Party. From Gaitskell to Blair* (Routledge, London, 1996), pp. 41–64.

19　Crosland, C.A.R., *The Conservative Enemy. A Programme of Radical Reform for the 1960s* (Jonathan Cape, London, 1962), pp. 174–82.

20　Jefferys, J., *Anthony Crosland*, p. 89.

21　Jones, T., 'Labour Revisionism and Public Ownership 1951–63', *Contemporary Record*, 5, 3 (1991), pp. 443–6.

22　Howard, A. and West, R., *The Making of a Prime Minister* (Jonathan Cape, London, 1965), p. 38.

23　Clarke, P., *A Question of Leadership. Gladstone to Thatcher* (Hamish Hamilton, London, 1991), p. 255.

24　Ponting, C., *Breach of Promise. Labour in Power, 1964–70* (Hamish Hamilton, London, 1987); Coopey, R., Fielding, S. and Tiratsoo, N. (eds), *The Wilson Governments, 1964–70* (Pinter, London, 1993).

25　Howard, A. (ed.), *The Crossman Diaries. Selections from the Diaries of a Cabinet Minister 1964–70* (Hamish Hamilton, London, 1979), pp. 253–4: diary entry for 11 December 1966.

26　Jefferys, J., *Anthony Crosland*, p. 133.

27　Desai, R., *Intellectuals and Socialism. 'Social Democrats' and the British Labour Party* (Lawrence and Wishart, London, 1994), pp. 141–52.

28　Crosland, S., *Tony Crosland* (Jonathan Cape, London, 1982), pp. 227–8.

29　Crosland, C.A.R., *Socialism Now and Other Essays* (Jonathan Cape, London, 1974), pp. 17–48.

30　Radice, G., 'Revisionism Re-visited', *Socialist Commentary*, May 1974, pp. 25–7; Jefferys, J., *Anthony Crosland*, p. 176.

31　Burk, K. and Cairncross, A., *'Goodbye Great Britain'. The 1976 IMF Crisis* (Yale University Press, London and New Haven), 1992, p. 228.

32　Rosen, G., 'John P. Mackintosh', in Rosen (ed), *Dictionary of Labour Biography*, pp. 373–6.

33　Marquand, D., 'Inquest on a Movement', *Encounter*, July 1979, p. 134; Lipsey, D. and Leonard, D. (eds), *The Socialist Agenda*, pp. 42–3. In his final years Crosland himself preferred the label 'democratic socialist', describing a 'social democrat' as someone who was about to join the Tory Party.

34 Foote, G., *The Labour Party's Political Thought*, pp. 259–60.

35 Thorpe, A., *A History of the British Labour Party* (Macmillan, Basingstoke, 2001), p. 201.

36 Labour Party, Statement of Democratic Socialist Aims and Values (London, 1988), p. 10.

37 Hattersley, R., *Choose Freedom: The Politics of Democratic Socialism* (Penguin, London, 1987), p. 148; Lewis Baston, 'Roy Hattersley', in Jefferys, K. (ed.), *Labour Forces*, pp. 221–34.

38 Radice, G., *Labour's Path to Power: The New Revisionism* (Macmillan, London, 1989), p. 14.

39 Hughes, C. and Wintour, P., *Labour Rebuilt. The New Model Party* (Fourth Estate, London, 1990), p. 205.

40 Cited in Naughtie, J., *The Rivals: The Intimate Story of a Political Marriage* (The Fourth Estate, London, 2001), p. 45.

41 Jefferys, K., *Finest and Darkest Hours. The Decisive Events in British Politic from Churchill to Blair* (Atlantic Books, London, 2002), pp. 283–306.

42 Marquand, D., *The Progressive Dilemma: From Lloyd George to Kinnock* (Heinemann, London, 1991), p. 201. See also Smith, M.J., 'A Return to Revisionism? The Labour Party's Policy Review', in Smith, M. J. and Spear, J. (eds), *The Changing Labour Party* (Routledge, London, 1992).

43 Kinnock, N., 'Reforming the Labour Party', *Contemporary Record*, 8, 3 (1994), p. 545; Jones, T., *Remaking the Labour Party*, pp. 127–30.

44 Shaw, E., *The Labour Party since 1945* (Blackwell, Oxford, 1996), pp. 102–6.

45 Gray, J., *After Social Democracy* (Demos, London, 1996), pp. 7–8.

46 Brivati, B., 'Gordon Brown', in Jefferys, K. (ed.), *Labour Forces*, pp. 237–49.

47 The *Guardian*, 17 July 2002.

48 Brivati, B. 'Gordon Brown', in *Labour Forces*, p. 249. For the view that the left has 'entered an ideological wilderness from which there seems little prospect of return', see also Thompson, N., *Left in the Wilderness. The Political Economy of British Democratic Socialism since 1979* (Acumen, Chesham, 2002).

5   New Labour[1]

Matt Beech

The election of Tony Blair as leader of the Labour Party in 1994 has proved to be the beginning of an epoch in Labour Party history. Blair's leadership and his desire to modernise and reform the internal and external politics of the Labour Party have been nothing short of radical. This chapter attempts to provide an account of New Labour's political philosophy. Initially, one must make the point that New Labour is not the political agenda of either the entire national or the Parliamentary Labour Party. New Labour can be understood as being the politics and the political project of a group of powerful modernisers.[2] The chief protagonists are obviously Tony Blair, Gordon Brown, their respective advisers, press secretaries and most members of the Blair Cabinets since 1997. As for the political project associated with the term 'New Labour', a generally accepted interpretation appears to be the project of making the Labour Party nationally electable and capable of forming majority governments for more than a single term, as was not the case throughout the twentieth century when the Labour Party held office as a majority government for only nine years.[3] However, to leave an understanding of New Labour as merely the politics of modernisation by a powerful clique and as the project of electability and sustainable power would be to overlook some significant changes in political philosophy and re-interpretations of the Labour Party's social democracy. This chapter does not argue that New Labour has one cogent and generally accepted philosophy, because the Labour Party is a broad philosophical church that often includes contradictory and conflicting ideas and principles. Furthermore, the brief history of New Labour has demonstrated that certain ideas and philosophical frameworks suddenly germinate but last only for a short period, such as the one-time interest in the 'stakeholding' ideas in society and economy.[4] Nevertheless, this chapter rejects the cynicism of some commentators who view New Labour as being purely pragmatic and committed solely to being the natural party of government, and argues that New Labour is social democratic and is the new right wing of the Labour Party.[5]

The political viewpoints of politicians can change over time due to various factors ranging from circumstance to powerfully-put counter-arguments and modifications of personal conviction. A famous Labour Party example of this is Tony Benn who began his career in the 1950s as a Gaitskellite, then appeared to become a Wilsonian technocrat during the 1960s and ended up as the figure-head for the New Left during the 1970s and 1980s.[6] Many New Labour acolytes were once ardent followers of various ideational factions in the Labour Party. For example, some such as Margaret Beckett, Robin Cook, John Prescott and Jack Straw were supporters of the Bennite New Left. Others, though fewer in number, were on the Labour right and would describe themselves as occupying the social democratic wing of the Party, such as Peter Mandelson and the late Donald Dewar. This brief summary of previous political commitments illustrates that individual political belief can shift to a greater or lesser extent. All of the aforementioned politicians could today be regarded as examples of New Labour and although they may differ on specific policies they would share the main thrust of New Labour's politics. New Labour's politics is a form of social demo-cratic politics shaped by historical events of the previous two decades. These events include the 1979, 1983 and 1987 general election defeats, the political and intellectual hegemony of Thatcherism, the notable policy reforms of the Policy Review and the narrow victory of Major's Conservative Party in 1992. Therefore, New Labour is a product of the recent history of internal, external and philosophical changes in the nature of British social democracy.

When New Labour came to power in 1997, 18 years after last holding office, it entered a world significantly altered by economic, technological and geo-polit-ical change. New Labour holds to a specific economic and sociological thesis of globalisation, which informs its aspirations and policy objectives. In the Western world, mainstream politicians of all persuasions generally accept this thesis, although it is strongly criticised by some notable academics.[7] To refer to it as the 'globalisation thesis' is partly problematic as the term is contested and has become deeply politicised. However, for the sake of this chapter it will suffice. The globalisation thesis argues that the economic, technological and geo-political changes are all part of an observable phenomenon that has evolved in the last quarter of the twentieth century.

With regard to economics, the decline in operation of the doctrine of Keynesianism in the Western world and the dominance of market forces has opened national economies to large flows of tradeable goods and services. In short, many more countries are active in trading partnerships and are economi-cally dependent on each other. Another change in economics is the expansion of world financial markets. These markets trade in actual time due to sophisticated telecommunications systems that allow huge flows of capital to be traded by vast numbers of traders in markets throughout the world. In each day of trading on the world financial markets over one trillion dollars is 'turned-over' in trans-actions of currency. Likewise, companies choose to invest in states whose workforces are well trained and highly skilled. Therefore, investor confidence in a national economy is central to companies staying in that state and central to the availability of jobs in the private sector. The flexible nature of capital means that multinational companies can easily shut down factories and plants, making job instability a significant aspect of the globalised economy. The positive side of such a situation is that firms wanting to harness favourable economic conditions in specific countries can create jobs rapidly. In the chapter entitled *The Global Economy* in his book *New Britain: My Vision of a Young Country*,[8] Blair affirms this belief in the globalisation thesis:

> The driving force of economic change today is globalisation. Technology and capital are mobile. Industry is becoming fiercely competitive across national boundaries. Consumers are exercising ever-greater power to hasten the pace of this revolution. Travel, communications and culture are becoming more international, shrinking the world and expanding taste, choice and knowledge. The key issue facing all governments is how to respond.[9]

Another aspect of the globalisation thesis that has contributed to the economic interdependence of nations in the global market is the communications revolution. By the term 'communications revolution' one is referring to the growth in information technology ranging from the widespread use of personal computers and email to website and satellite technologies. All of these types of technology create a world of immediate communication and immediate flows of information.[10] For example, the 24-hour money markets depend on satellite and computer technology, television is now a global medium which provides information, entertainment and interactive communication due to digital technologies. *Ibid.* p. 31. Therefore, globalisation is not only transforming the business sector of nations but also the entertainment and leisure sector and the nature of public institutions such as the NHS which runs a 24-hour, nurse-led, internet and phone-based helpline known as NHS Direct which answers people's concerns about illness and health issues.

Geo-political change is a further aspect that has occurred due to globalisation. Economic blocs such as the European Union, NAFTA, OPEC and the Asian Tiger economies exert significant power over national economic policies. For Britain in particular, the decision either to join or withhold from the Euro is another crucial globalisation decision to face. Military defence, global crime prevention and political convergence are all issues that the world faces through the lens of co-operation and partnership rather than as solitary island nation-states. Global fragmentation has occurred partly as a reaction to the collapse of the traditional political boundaries of the Cold War and the ensuing democratisation and economic liberalisation in regions such as eastern and south-eastern Europe, and partly as a reaction to the political instability that a globalised world brings. Globalisation has shrunk the world in terms of finance, time and space. This gives rise to opportunities for wealth creation inside and outside the Western world, it reduces the detachment the West used to have from global social problems, it means that different races, religions and cultures mix together in a smaller and more diverse world, and it means that national and international co-operation becomes a necessity not an optional extra. However, globalisation also raises the spectre of cultural and religious clashes and international terrorism, and it highlights the ever-widening wealth gap between the

North and the South. Political and economic instabilities have been exacerbated because of the world's interconnected and interdependent character. It is within this globalised world that New Labour has constructed its revised form of social democracy.

New Labour, as this chapter will argue, is the politics of the new right wing of the Labour Party. In some sense, New Labour's members are the current revisionists in the Labour Party because they have revised their policies in accordance with global economic and societal changes in much the same way as the Gaitskellite revisionists of the mid-1950s did in light of the changes in the nature of capitalism, and in the post-Welfare State society. This position, outlined by Tony Crosland in the mid-1950s, saw capitalism partly reformed due to the rise in power of the industrial left, the anti-capitalist classes and the Labour Party.[11] Crosland also noted the role played by technical change in the management of capitalism from owners to managers who, along with swathes of the middle classes, were repulsed by the degradation and squalor which a large section of the British working class had to endure during the ills of laissez-faire capitalism in the early part of the century.[12] Nevertheless, although these factors were contributory in weakening the faith in traditional laissez-faire capitalism, Crosland thought that such factors had a relatively small impact on changing the character of capitalism. He posited the view in *The Future of Socialism* that it was the Second World War and the need for economic and social reconstruction which reformed the nature of British capitalism more than any other specific factor. The moral change amongst the electorate kept out the Conservative Party and enabled a radical Labour administration to reconstruct welfare capitalism with widespread social provision through Keynesian demand management, the likes of which had never been seen before.[13]

None the less, that is where the phrase 'revisionist' should stop, as it is used synonymously for the 'Old Right' of the Labour Party, in other words the traditional social democratic wing of the Labour Party. Perhaps more explicitly, the term 'revisionist' conjures up the ideas of the thesis and political model put forward by Crosland. New Labour is not revisionist in the sense of being Croslandite. If anything, the modernisation and changes in political philosophy made by New Labour are changes away from traditional Croslandite social democracy. It is because of the abandonment of much of Crosland's thesis, and thus of the mainstay of traditional social democratic politics in the Labour Party, that such resentment on the British left has built up surrounding New Labour. In particular, New Labour's desire to encourage entrepreneurial energy in the business community[14] has contributed to the antipathy towards it. As a modernised social democratic government, New Labour would never have found significant support from either of the main groups on the Labour left, namely the 'Old' or 'Bevanite left' which in reality ceases to exist in the Parliamentary Labour Party, and the 'New' or 'Bennite left' which still exists on the Labour left although it is greatly reduced in number. However, New Labour courted the support of the remaining advocates of the 'Old Right'. The radical change and abandonment of much of Crosland's revisionist agenda prompted some notable individuals of the 'Old Right' such as Roy Hattersley to claim, as he did in a newspaper article, that 'It's no longer my party.'[15] It is the purpose of the remainder of this chapter to provide an account of New Labour's political philosophical principles and to interpret what has been abandoned and what has been adopted by the new right wing of the Labour Party.

The first political principle that defines New Labour is its version of equality. However, this is difficult to ascertain because it is apparent that New Labour is quite vague about the principle of greater equality of outcome. New Labour's vagueness is heightened by conflicting messages about equality coming from both numbers 10 and 11 Downing Street. Traditional social democrats such as Crosland and in more recent times Hattersley have maintained that social democracy is centrally about a belief in greater equality of outcome between individuals and groups in society. Crosland expressed the central tenet of social democracy when he said:

> Socialism, in our view, was basically about equality. By equality, we meant more than a meritocratic society of equal opportunities in which the greatest rewards would go to those with the most fortunate genetic endowment and family background; we adopted the 'strong' definition of equality – what Rawls has subsequently called the 'democratic' as opposed to the 'liberal' conception.[16]

This principle of greater equality of outcome as understood by the 'Old Right' has proved to be the philosophical bone of contention for some who doubt New Labour's social democratic credentials. For now the pertinent question is whether New Labour holds to greater equality of outcome as a principle or whether it considers it a noble ideal but one which is impractical in a globalised economy and electorally unfeasible in Britain's aspirational society. At times New Labour appears to assert that social democrats need to aim slightly lower in their ambitions and commit themselves to a strong version of equality of opportunity, or, as some describe it, equality of opportunity and fairness of outcome, as opposed to the traditional principle of greater equality of outcome.[17]

Akin to this debate surrounding the principle of greater equality of outcome is the issue of whether New Labour favours an absolute, a relative or what is sometimes referred to as a rising absolute level of measuring poverty. In one sense, these two discussions are two sides of the same coin. Once again, New Labour appears to be sending out conflicting signals. Prime Minister Blair famously stated that the absolute level of poverty is what he considered important when questioned by Jeremy Paxman in an interview on the BBC's *Newsnight*, and came close to advocating the neo-liberal trickle-down theory.[18] The Chancellor, Gordon Brown, then confused the debate further by using relative measurements in outlining his strategy for combating child poverty and then subsequently announced figures showing a significant reduction in the absolute level of child poverty.[19]

To some, such observations may appear petty, but they can be seen as evidence of the uncertainty within New Labour concerning its commitment to the principle of greater equality of outcome. It is also an ambiguity that some suggest goes right to the heart of New Labour, inasmuch as both the Prime Minister and the Chancellor share different versions of equality. This is purely conjecture and will perhaps only be definitively resolved well into the future when memoirs are published. However, in a recent interview discussing New Labour's political ideas with a senior civil servant I was told that New Labour, or at least the Treasury, holds to the Croslandite conception of greater equality of outcome but is applying that principle in a modern economic context.[20] The interviewee stated that the Treasury is applying greater equality of outcome through targeted tax credits, educational allowances and specific skills and education training opportunities such as *Surestart*, but also through the *Working Families Tax Credit* which has secured fairer outcomes to families with two children earning around £13,000 or half the national average earnings whereby they are roughly £3,500 better off per year. The interviewee informed me that this was done not merely to make work pay, but to provide fairer outcomes and therefore greater equality of outcome for such low-income families.[21]

In a discussion of equality it is useful to distinguish between the following positions: a commitment to greater equality of outcome; a commitment to giving priority to the worst-off members of society; a commitment to raising people to a particular level, where they have 'enough' to lead a satisfactory life. These three positions respectively can be termed the strict egalitarian conception of equality, the priority conception of equality and the sufficiency conception of equality.[22] This chapter argues that New Labour conceives greater equality to consist of two different components, neither of which is the strict egalitarian conception of equality. The first component is a commitment to giving financial priority to the worst-off members of British society. This, as we have noted above, can be referred to as the priority conception of equality. Examples of the priority conception of equality by New Labour are the Chancellor's *Pensioner Guarantee* and *Working Families Tax Credit* programmes to the poorest pensioners and poorest families with children.[23]

The second component in New Labour's conception of equality is a commitment to raising people to a particular level whereby they have 'enough' to lead a satisfactory life. One can refer to this (as is noted above) as the sufficiency version of equality. Of course, this is problematic, because what is meant by the term 'enough'? What is 'sufficient'? There is no general understanding or consensus in British society about the minimum needs that must be met before one can claim to lead a satisfactory life. Nevertheless, the sufficiency conception of equality is understood as providing a sufficient level of income and services. Historically, this has been the job of the Welfare State through a variety of welfare payments and entitlements. In one sense, this conception of equality is greater equality up to a sufficient level, at which point permits individuals to earn incomes unreservedly. The *National Minimum Wage* is an example of the sufficiency conception of equality inasmuch as it regulates that labour is paid at a sufficient minimum level.[24] Therefore, one could argue that New Labour has abandoned its commitment to the strict egalitarian conception of greater equality of outcome and adopted a strong version of equality of opportunity, sometimes referred to as equality of opportunity and fairness of outcome which is comprised of the priority and sufficiency conceptions of equality.

However, were the traditional social democrats on the 'Old Right' (such as Crosland and Hattersley) actually ever strict egalitarians? Did they not just hold commitments to priority and sufficiency conceptions of equality like those of New Labour? If the answers are 'no', they were never strict egalitarians and 'yes', they hold to priority and sufficiency conceptions of equality like those of New Labour, then traditional social democrats are far more similar to New Labour than they may think.

New Labour's espousal of equality of opportunity and fairness of outcome (which characterises its commitment to priority and sufficiency conceptions of equality) could be understood as being the same as greater equality of outcome espoused by Crosland, for two reasons. First, if equality of opportunity and fairness of outcome are taken together as two component parts of one principle, then it would seem that the emphasis of 'fairness of outcome' transforms the notion of equality of opportunity and transforms New Labour's notion of strong equality of opportunity at every level in a person's life by adding a redistributive character and a guaranteed outcome of a minimum level. If this is how 'fairness of outcome' is intended to be perceived and applied, then one could make a case to say that it is a modern version of the traditional social democratic concept of greater equality of outcome because the Croslandite position also sought to guarantee people a greater degree of equality through redistribution from progressive levels of direct taxations, high levels of investment in public services and welfare payments, whilst at the same time championing opportunity for all in the form of comprehensive education.[25] Obviously, the means of establishing the principle will be different as the economic systems are different, but the principle, if analysed in this way, could be viewed as being the same.

Second, Crosland's brand of socialism was to him essentially about equality and the equality termed by John Rawls as 'democratic equality'. Rawls's position is what he termed 'justice as fairness' and it is comprised of his two principles of justice. The first principle is that each person is to have an equal right to the most extensive basic liberty compatible with a similar liberty for others. The second principle asserts that social and economic inequalities are to be arranged so that they are both reasonably expected to be to everyone's advantage and attached to positions and offices open to all.[26] In addition, Rawls argues that when the two principles conflict the first principle or the 'liberty principle' must take priority over the second or 'difference principle'.[27] Therefore, from Rawls's inference that there will be social and economic inequalities in society and in certain circumstances they will be just, in other words when they have complied with the difference principle, it is clear that Rawls is not advocating strict egalitarianism. What the difference principle does allude to is that Rawls is an advocate of a priority conception of equality, as he desires that all forms of inequalities be arranged 'to the greatest expected benefit of the least advantaged'.[28] Therefore, Crosland cited Rawls's approach to equality as best representing his own approach and, because Rawls is a prioritarian and not a strict egalitarian, one can see areas of overlap and similarity with New Labour's conception of equality.

New Labour's ambiguity over its version of equality is unfortunate but its emphasis on education, skills and opportunity at every stage of life is a pragmatic and electorally expedient response to the changing attitudes and demographics of British society. For example, the very high levels of income taxation during the Wilson–Callaghan Governments of 1974–9, namely a lower tax rate of 25 per cent, a basic tax rate of 33 per cent, a higher tax rate of 83 per cent and a higher tax rate for unearned income of 98 per cent, would simply not be electorally feasible today. This is not to say that the British public opposes all forms of increased taxation. As in the 2002 Budget, the increase in taxation (notably through National Insurance Contributions) to invest vast sums of money in public services such as the National Health Service proved popular with the majority of the public (at the time of writing and based on available polling data).[29] Nor does this scepticism towards what can be termed traditional social democratic levels of direct taxation dismiss entirely the prospect of a higher tax band for the very highest earners in society. The Fabian Society's *Commission on Taxation and Citizenship*[30] recommended that a 50 per cent tax band be created above a threshold of £100,000 per annum in taxable income that would affect approximately 200,000 citizens. The Inland Revenue calculated that such a tax band would yield £2.9 billion in the year 2000–1 and it would be expected to rise by approximately £200 million per year over the next few years as more people enter the £100,000 income bracket.[31]

The second main philosophical principle that defines New Labour and is indicative of its modernised social democracy is its belief in the need for more cohesive communities. For example, in his Fabian Pamphlet, *The Third Way: Politics for the New Century*,[32] Blair outlined his belief in the principle of community. He argues that:

> Strong communities depend on shared values and a recognition of the rights and duties of citizenship – not just the duty to pay taxes and obey the law, but the obligation to bring up children as competent, responsible citizens, and to support those – such as teachers – who are employed by the state in the task. In the past we have tended to take such duties for granted. But where they are neglected, we should not hesitate to encourage and even enforce them, as we are seeking to do with initiatives such as our 'home-school contracts' between schools and parents.[33]

New Labour has rediscovered the traditional social democratic principle of community or what Christian socialists termed 'fellowship' and what some Ethical socialists described as 'fraternity'. The typology of the term is less important than the historical salience of embracing 'community' as a philosophical principle, because in doing so, New Labour has yet again set clear water between itself and the 'Old Right' of the Labour Party. Jose Harris comments that New Labour's ideas surrounding the political and philosophical value of community are akin to those of the Labour Party before the Second World War and that those similar conceptions of fraternity and fellowship were lost during mid-twentieth century social democracy. She argues that:

> The Edwardian concern with 'duty and citizenship', largely sidelined by the technocratic culture of the mid-century, resonates strongly through many New Labour documents, as do Edwardian ideas about reciprocal relationships between welfare and work, punishment and fraud. Although ideas about what constitutes virtue have changed beyond recognition, early Labourites would certainly have endorsed the New Labour view that policies should be 'ethical' and citizens 'virtuous'.[34]

The principle of community can exist at different levels. For example, much of New Labour's belief in the principle of community has been a commitment to community at the level of the state. It involves a communitarian conception of citizenship that emphasises responsibilities to the community as well as individual rights within that community. Another level of community is regional community. New Labour has shown interest in issues and problems within specific regions and the establishment of the *Regional Development Agencies* is evidence of this interest. Furthermore, the discussion about regional assemblies, especially by the Deputy Prime Minister John Prescott, highlights the fact that regions in Britain are cultural, social and economic communities that may benefit from greater devolved power and a regional focus to solving problems and managing public services. A further level of community is that of the local community. New Labour promotes its conception of community at the local level through its financially decentralist programme; the *New Deal for Communities*.[35]

There are several factors which illustrate why New Labour has re-emphasised a principle that has in effect been lying dormant in the textbooks of social democracy for the last 60 years. First, as Stephen Driver and Luke Martell argue in their book, *New Labour: Politics after Thatcherism*,[36] New Labour is a post-Thatcherite party. It has witnessed the neo-liberal philosophy of the Thatcher and Major Governments with their reticent attitude towards community, social co-operation and collective action. The neo-liberal philosophy gave political and moral primacy to the individual and was deliberately silent about the social responsibility of individuals. Driver and Martell suggest that communitarian political ideas provide New Labour with an alternative social philosophy to neo-liberalism.[37]

Second, a factor to consider in understanding New Labour's penchant for community is that mid-twentieth-century social democratic thought was dominated by an ethos of political, economic and social individualism. The main political and economic concern was the position of the individual worker and the inequalities he suffered and what the remedies were for reducing this wage inequality. The individual ethos in the social realm was rightly concerned with extending individual rights to women in the workplace, protecting the rights of the disabled and citizens of ethnic origins, de-stigmatising the homosexual lifestyle, as well as removing the illegality of homosexual practice from English law. All of these acts, which are often categorised as part of the drift into the 'permissive society', are associated with the British left, the Labour Party and with a preference towards a liberal, not a communitarian social philosophy. For the Croslandite revisionists of the late 1950s to the 1970s the philosophical value of fraternity or community was hardly mentioned within the gamut of social democratic ideas.[38] The value of greater equality took centre-stage and consumed the philosophical discussion surrounding principles.

Third, the communitarian instinct of the Labour Movement and of the majority of Labour MPs had diminished.[39] Liberalism, not communitarianism, had become the dominant set of social ideas and therefore personal and communal responsibilities and duties were relegated, if not completely discarded, in favour of individual rights.[40] New Labour wanted to reclaim social and moral policy prescriptions consistent with a communitarian left approach to social theory. Such policies would perhaps include tough sentencing for young offenders but with education and rehabilitation, teenage curfews in violent neighbourhoods but with government-funded support for youth projects; and in addition, welfare-to-work schemes which give the individual the right of state benefits for a fixed period of time and expect the individual to take responsibility for his or her own future through one of several options, ranging from further training or education, to voluntary work, an environmental project or an organised job placement.

This easily fits in the rubric of communitarianism on the left. In short, people as individuals have rights because they are citizens and their citizenship guarantees them certain political, economic, social and legal rights. However, in some specific cases, citizens have to fulfil responsibilities in exchange for these guaranteed rights.[41] Therefore, New Labour still guarantees certain entitlements as rights, as well as emphasising a contingent responsibility to reciprocate a duty to the state in certain spheres. A communitarian left account may suggest that people as citizens have responsibilities to the state in keeping the law, responsibilities to their families and to their communities in taking a role in improving the quality of life where they live. For example, this could be achieved through active vigilance against crime and anti-social behaviour, and through mutual help and voluntarism to those in their communities who need support. According to Blair and other leading communitarians in New Labour, the Labour Party had been for too long the Party of liberal rights for all, without expecting and expressing the commitment individuals have as citizens, and the responsibilities they owe in exchange for certain benefits and rights they are entitled to.[42]

Many Labour MPs would perhaps still describe themselves as liberals not communitarians, but the debate is not as simplistic as liberal social democracy versus communitarian social democracy because most people believe in liberal rights and in communitarian responsibilities.[43] It is, in fact, not a conflicting dichotomous relationship but it can be a useful way to distinguish the social philosophy of individuals, political groups and political factions. Perhaps it is more accurate to say that many Labour MPs would regard themselves as more liberal than communitarian or even as 'liberal communitarians' or as 'communitarian liberals' rather than exclusively labelling themselves as liberals or as communitarians.[44] One could suggest this is a false debate in setting up an irreconcilable social cleavage because no liberal would disregard the importance of community and no communitarian would disregard the importance of the individual. There may well be a grain of truth in such an evaluation; however, the discussion is about emphasis and it does represent a clear difference in social theory and this same divide on social and moral issues can be noted in the Labour Party. However, the centre of gravity in the social thought of New Labour has returned to the communitarian standpoint. One could say that New Labour's re-emphasis on the political philosophical value of community within social democracy is echoing R.H. Tawney's form of Christian socialism that sees other political principles not as ends in themselves but as means of achieving a more ethical and fraternal society.[45] New Labour has not imported a new principle into its modernised social democracy, but re-discovered a traditional social democratic principle that has not been given much attention since the Edwardian era.

The third main philosophical principle that characterises New Labour is its commitment to a positive conception of liberty or freedom. The principle of positive liberty is continued by New Labour in the same mould as that of its traditional social democrat predecessors.[46] New Labour, like the Croslandite social democrats of the 1960s and 1970s, would adhere to the value of liberty expressed as a positive right to a set of political, social and economic entitlements. The debate about the principle of freedom is not quite so straightforward as to be able to label the left's side of the debate as 'freedom to' and the right's side of the debate as 'freedom from'.[47] This is because Marxist thinkers, who occupy the extreme political left, can couch their arguments of 'true' freedom for the proletariat in negative libertarian terms. For example, they may argue that 'true' freedom is freedom from the bourgeois state and freedom from the exploitative economic relationship that the capitalist system imposes on the proletariat. In addition, it invites the MacCallum type of rejoinder, that X is free from Y to do Z.[48] In other words, freedom is a triadic relationship and political groupings disagree over what they understand to be the ranges of the X, Y, and Z variables. However, in mainstream political theory, those on the left are usually positive libertarians and those on the right are usually negative libertarians; but this is not always the case.[49]

An important factor in the different conceptions of freedom between thinkers on the left and the right is the issue of obstacles that impede freedom and count as constraints on freedom.[50] For thinkers on the right such as Sir Keith Joseph and Fredrich von Hayek obstacles that are deliberately and intentionally imposed can restrict individual freedom. Hayek believes that freedom exists providing there is no interference by an outside human force.[51] Bosanquet suggests that this can be understood through two propositions. First, an individual is free if he can make important decisions. Second, only human interference affects the freedom of an individual. All other types of social pressure and economic status are omitted from this analysis.[52] Conversely, thinkers on the left assert that any obstacles that are the result of human action or social and economic forces can constitute a restriction on individual freedom. For example, poverty would count as a restriction on freedom whether or not the individual in poverty was responsible for his state of affairs, and whether or not it had been imposed intentionally on him. Raymond Plant suggests that:

> The limitations on individual freedom are not just those imposed deliberately by the intentional actions of others and which the liberal tradition rightly wishes to resist and restrict, but also those limitations which are imposed by natural differences of birth and genetic inheritance, together with those which are the result of human action whether deliberate or not, in the field of family background, economic resources, welfare and education.[53]

A further example of the positive conception of liberty is that a social democrat believes that all people should have the freedom to obtain a free state education. Liberty is enabling and from this positive conception, social democracy can build a framework of opportunities through which individuals can fulfil their potential. Conversely, many of those on the right conceive of liberty as freedom from state intervention in one's life. This could perhaps be expressed through the policy of favouring low direct taxes to administer only basic social provisions such as pavements and street lighting rather than progressive graduated taxes which could provide free high-quality education and skills training for whoever would like the opportunity of improving their life chances and market employability. Therefore, New Labour has a positive conception of liberty that it has not adopted nor abandoned, but instead is consistent with the conception of liberty held by its traditional social democratic predecessors.

An understanding of the philosophical principle of freedom or liberty is important for social democracy for several reasons. First, because throughout its history social democracy has been unsure and ambiguous in terms of its relationship with the value of freedom, particularly as the right has attempted to claim it for itself. For too long the right made social democrats feel that freedom was the uncomfortable relation in the family of social democratic principles – equality, liberty and community. Second, the intellectual capital of Thatcherism was largely provided by Friedrich von Hayek. The philosophy of neo-liberalism can perhaps be best expressed in Hayek's books *The Constitution of Liberty* and *Law, Legislation and Liberty Vol. II: The Mirage of Social Justice*.[54] Throughout the neo-liberal era of political hegemony, the left and the Labour Party failed to provide a social democratic alternative to the myth of neo-liberal freedom. For example, greater equality was much regarded as the absolute end of social democracy's mission. Third, on its own greater social and economic equality is a

level of improvement, a degree of provision which one has attained, a quant-
ifiable measurement of material goods and wealth in comparison to one's class
or the previous generation, or comparable with the lot of a neighbouring
country. Does more equality equate to more fulfilling lives for citizens? Possibly,
but two points need to be considered. The first point is that reducing the gap
between the better-off and the poor does not necessarily provide poorer people
with greater economic freedom. The gap between classes may be reduced but
simply taking more from the rich and investing it in public services will not
directly benefit the poor: as we have been aware for many years, the middle
classes benefit disproportionately from public services.[55] Therefore, the poor are
not necessarily empowered by the better-off losing a bit more of their pay
packets. Redistributive programmes must target specific groups, especially
society's very poorest, and more faith needs to be placed in helping people to
help themselves. The second point is that the principle of greater equality
enables citizens to lead a more fulfilling life only in that it gives them greater
economic and social freedom, which in turn provides them with greater opportunities and experiences. Therefore, greater equality can be a means for securing
greater freedom but is not greater freedom in itself.

Similarly, significant numbers of social democrats would espouse the desire
for a socially just society as their ultimate goal for social democracy.[56] This again
is difficult to discern because social justice is closely intertwined with notions of
greater equality and the correction of market injustice. Therefore, one could
either revert to the arguments alluded to above for the one-dimensional benefit
of greater equality as an end for social democracy, or one could assert that social
justice is principally concerned with the structural ills of the market economy
and, because markets can never be made perfect, there will always be a degree of
market injustice and on its own social justice is not an end in itself. Social justice,
important as it is, does not appear to guarantee individuals a more fulfilling life;
like the principle of greater equality it requires one to view it as part of a collection of principles which aim at empowering individuals to be freer and fostering
a sense of community at local, regional and state level.[57] Therefore, considered
separately, the principles of greater equality of outcome and social justice can
never be the endgame for the philosophy of social democracy.

New Labour seems to differ slightly from traditional social democrats in its
ideas of ends and goals of social democracy. New Labour asserts the combination of liberty and community in expressing its hope for a citizen to be free to
lead a fulfilling and autonomous life. In addition, such a statement presupposes
that the citizen feels empowered as an individual within his or her neighbour-
hood and community. Thus, individual freedom to fulfil one's potential is half of
the goal for many New Labour social democrats. The other half of the philosophical picture is that an integrated cohesive nation will consist of individuals
and families who regard themselves as full citizens within their own communities
because they have rights and entitlements in that community and owe duties and
obligations to that community. Through this ethical and social framework, the
individual feels significance and purpose as part of the community at local,
regional and state level.

Whilst, yet again, such a view may appear vague and wordy to some, it holds a sensible understanding of the essential difference between the natures of certain philosophical principles. Certain principles are 'assisting principles': they assist collectively with other principles in contributing to 'definitive principles'. Often, 'assisting principles' relate to the betterment of the human condition, such as greater equality of outcome. This principle collectively assists contributing to individual liberty and community. The other types of principles are 'definitive principles' inasmuch as they stand on their own as desired goals. Such principles for modernised social democracy would include individual liberty and community. New Labour, this chapter contends, is committed to such 'definitive principles' and this is evident in its emphasis on the rights and responsibilities of individual citizens and ensuring community participation in decision-making, especially on social and economic programmes for neighbourhoods, such as the *New Deal For Communities*.

This chapter has attempted to provide an account of New Labour's principles of political philosophy, and to highlight what it has kept and what it has abandoned from the traditions of social democratic thought. New Labour does advocate philosophical principles and, among them, the definitive principles appear to be individual liberty and community. New Labour still believes in a version of equality to enable government to provide individuals with the freedom they deserve to lead a fulfilling life. However, it is here that New Labour is ambiguous, possibly divided, and perhaps departs from the traditional social democratic position. Whereas Crosland and Hattersley claimed to hold to a belief in greater equality of outcome, New Labour is unsure whether it sees itself in that same tradition. However, in this chapter doubt has been cast upon whether traditional social democrats such as Crosland and Hattersley were actually ever strict egalitarians. One could say that New Labour holds a commitment to the priority and sufficiency conceptions of greater equality. Its brand of equality provides state education and skills programmes for all at every conceivable stage of life. Furthermore, it focuses on making citizens employable in an increasingly competitive global market. It has and does redistribute wealth, and tax rises may well continue to fund further public service investment. New Labour, unlike any Parliamentary Labour Party or Labour Government for more than half a century, views the principle of community extremely highly. From its social philosophy of communitarianism, which pervades all of its social policy prescriptions, to the rights and responsibilities maxim which is fast becoming a mantra for the modernised left, New Labour's emphasis on local, regional and state-level community participation and collective social and personal responsibility for others has been re-emphasised. Regarding the principle of liberty, New Labour is well within the mould of traditional social democrats in its view of liberty as positive freedom for all, which the active hand of the state can and should guarantee. Furthermore, individual liberty has taken a central role along with community as marking out the definitive social democratic principles of this new right wing of the Labour Party.

Notes

1 I am very grateful to Kevin Hickson, Michael Jacobs, Andrew Mason and Raymond Plant for comments on an earlier draft of this chapter and to my wife Claire for proof-reading the volume. Any errors are of course my own.

2 For detailed accounts of the New Labour project see Gould, P., *The Unfinished Revolution: How The Modernisers Saved The Labour Party*, (Abacus, London, 1998) and MacIntyre, D., *Mandelson and the Making of New Labour*, (Harper Collins, London, 1999).

3 See, Gould, P., *The Unfinished Revolution: How The Modernisers Saved The Labour Party*, p. 231.

4 New Labour appeared to embrace 'stakeholding' as a framework for its modernised social democracy between 1995 and 1996 but then reneged on it and a discussion surrounding Third Way ideas blossomed soon after that. For more on the stakeholding thesis see Hutton, W., *The State We're In*, (Jonathan Cape, London, 1995).

5 See Austin Mitchell's commentary in this volume (chapter 16. p. 261).

6 Foote, G., *The Labour Party's Political Thought*, (Macmillan, Basingstoke, 1997) p. 315.

7 See Hirst, P. and Thompson, G., *Globalization in Question*, (Polity Press, Cambridge, 1999).

8 Blair, T., *New Britain: My Vision Of A Young Country*, (Fourth Estate, London, 1996).

9 *Ibid.*, p. 118.

10 Giddens, A., *The Third Way: The Renewal Of Social Democracy*, (Polity Press, Cambridge, 1998) p. 31.

11 Crosland, C.A.R., *The Future of Socialism*, (Jonathan Cape, London, 1956) p. 56.

12 *Ibid.*, p. 57.

13 *Ibid.*, p. 59.

14 Mandelson, P. and Liddle, R., *The Blair Revolution: Can New Labour Deliver?*, (Faber and Faber, London, 1996) pp. 3–4.

15 Hattersley, R., 'It's no longer my party', *Observer*, Sunday 24 June 2001.

16 Crosland, C.A.R., *Socialism Now and Other Essays*, (Jonathan Cape, London, 1974) p. 15.

17 The absence of traditional social democratic rhetoric that implies a desire for greater equality of outcome such as redistribution could help to support the change in New Labour's attitude towards equality.

18 Jeremy Paxman interviewed the Prime Minister on BBC's Newsnight, on 5 June 2001.

19 On 18 March 1999, Blair gave the Beveridge Lecture at Toynbee Hall, London, to mark the 750th anniversary of University College, Oxford. In the speech he set out the Government's desire to abolish child poverty by 2020, halve it by 2010, reduce it by a quarter in 2004 and reduce it by 1.2 million in 2001. However, on 11 April 2002, the Chancellor announced that the Government had reduced child poverty by 0.5 million (in relative terms), which was a reduction from 4.4 million in 1996–7 to 3.9 million in 2000–1. Therefore, the target was missed by 0.7 million in relative terms but it was exceeded in absolute terms in a reduction of 1.5 million.

20 Interview with senior civil servant, London, December 2002.

21 *Ibid.*

22 See Parfit, D., 'Equality and Priority', in Mason, A. (ed.), *Ideals of Equality*, (Blackwell, Oxford, 1998).

23 Other examples of New Labour's commitment to the priority conception of equality include its £580 million investment in *Surestart* for young children, nursery places for every four-year-old; £450 million in the Children's Fund for children's charities to spend; £5 billion investment in *The New Deal* for 18–25-year-olds, *New Deal* for the over-25s; *New Deal Plus* for the over-50s, *New Deal* for single mothers and for disabled people; also, *Action Teams* for jobs in the 2000 poorest areas; high levels of spending on

secondary schools; and the *Connexions* programme for 11–25-year-olds who fail to gain educational attainment and skills training. For a thorough examination of New Labour's social legislation see Toynbee, P. and Walker, D., *Did Things Really Get Better?*, (Penguin, London, 2001) pp. 10–44.

24 Legislation and social programmes that endorse the priority conception of equality may well also endorse the sufficiency conception of equality and vice versa. The *National Minimum Wage*, the *Pensioner Guarantee*, and the *Working Families Tax Credit* are all appropriate examples of this.

25 The problem political theorists have is one of definition. Does 'fairness of outcome' automatically mean greater equalisation of outcome? If it does, then there is an argument to say that initiatives such as the *Working Families Tax Credit* are measures aimed at producing greater equality of outcome. If, on the other hand, 'fairness of outcome' means a 'fair outcome', then we are back where we started because 'fair' is a relative term and its value is not universal but particular.

26 Rawls, J., *A Theory of Justice*, (OUP, Oxford, 1999), p. 53.

27 *Ibid.*

28 *Ibid.*, p. 72.

29 According to the April 2002 *Guardian*/ICM poll, 72 per cent of respondents said they approved of the Chancellor's decision to raise national insurance contributions to fund more spending for the NHS. See Travis, A., 'Popularity of Budget halts Tory revival', *Guardian*, 23 April 2002.

30 The Commission on Taxation and Citizenship, *Paying For Progress: A New Politics of Tax for Public Spending*, (Fabian Society, London, 2000).

31 *Ibid.*, p. 235.

32 Blair, T., *The Third Way: New Politics for the New Century*, (Fabian Society, London, 1998).

33 *Ibid.*, p. 12.

34 Harris, J., 'Labour's Political and Social Thought', in Tanner, D., Thane, P. and Tiratsoo, N. (eds), *Labour's First Century*, (CUP, Cambridge, 2000), p. 39.

35 The *New Deal for Communities* promotes local communities, first, within the decision-making process of the programme, enabling them to speak as individuals, community organisations, churches, businesses and voluntary groups within their community instead of through a delegate or solely through a local government officer; and second, because it provides local communities with a fixed grant to spend as they see fit.

36 Driver, S. and Martell, L., *New Labour: Politics After Thatcherism*, (Polity Press, Cambridge, 1998).

37 *Ibid.*, p. 29.

38 See Haseler, S., *The Gaitskellites: Revisionism in the British Labour Party 1951–1964*, (Macmillan, London, 1969).

39 The social philosophy of the Labour Party in the mid-twentieth century had been exclusively linked to the theories of Liberalism and according to the right had in part led to the 'permissive society' standpoint of the 1960s whereby the Wilson Labour Government, under the guidance of the Home Secretary Roy Jenkins, posited a raft of liberal reforms of social legislation which modernised British law in line with cultural, sexual and economic changes happening in the Western world.

40 For a good discussion of the Liberal/Communitarian debate see Mulhall, S. and Swift, A., *Liberals and Communitarians*, (Blackwell, Oxford, 1996).

41 An example of this is the *New Deal* for the unemployed, which focuses on unemployed 18–25-year-olds in neither work nor education. In exchange for their benefit allowance individuals have to meet with civil service advisers who spend four months assessing them and aiding them in their search for employment. If that fails, then the *New Deal* states that the individuals have one of four options; an educational course, a job with an employer, work on an environmental project or work with a voluntary

organisation. For more on the *New Deal* see Toynbee, P. and Walker, D., *Did Things Get Better?* pp. 14–15.

42 Driver, S. and Martell, L., *New Labour: Politics After Thatcherism*, p. 15.

43 For a good discussion on the complexities of the debate surrounding liberals and communitarians and, in particular, the areas of agreement see Selznick, P., 'Foundations of Communitarian Liberalism', in Etzioni, A., *The Essential Communitarian Reader*, (Rowman & Littlefield Publishers, Oxford, 1998).

44 However, there is no up-to-date survey of the social attitudes of MPs and in particular no specific study of Labour MPs, therefore this issue is speculation and not an established fact.

45 See Tawney, R.H., *Equality*, (George Allen & Unwin, London, 1931).

46 Although, perhaps there is a debate to be had here concerning the possible difference in the connection between the principles of liberty and community between New Labour and the traditional social democrats. One could argue that New Labour emphasises a social reciprocity in exchange for certain state entitlements and the traditional social democrats appear to have prioritised the citizen's right to entitlements regardless of any notion of social or communal reciprocity. I am grateful to Kevin Hickson for this thought.

47 For a thorough discussion of positive and negative liberty and rights, in the context of the Labour Party, see Plant, R., *Citizenship, Rights and Socialism*, (Fabian Society, London, 1988).

48 See MacCallum, G.C., 'Negative and Positive Freedom', in Flathman, R.E. (ed.), *Concepts in Social & Political Philosophy*, (Macmillan, London, 1973).

49 Certain types of Liberal hold a positive conception of liberty as a principle commitment; in Britain, they would traditionally be known as Social Liberals. Liberal Conservatives may also hold a commitment to a positive conception of liberty; in Britain they would be termed One-nation Conservatives.

50 I am grateful to Andrew Mason for discussions on this subject.

51 See Hayek, F., *The Constitution of Liberty*, (Routledge and Kegan Paul, London, 1960), ch.1.

52 Bosanquet, N., *After the New Right*, (Heinemann, London, 1983) p. 92.

53 Plant, R., *Equality, Markets and the State*, (Fabian Society, London, 1984) p. 6.

54 Hayek, F., *The Constitution of Liberty*; and *Law, Legislation and Liberty Vol.II: The Mirage of Social Justice*, (Routledge and Kegan Paul, London, 1979).

55 See Le Grand, J., *The Strategy of Equality*, (Allen & Unwin, London, 1982).

56 Particularly social democrats and others on the left who would follow Rawls's version of justice. See Rawls, J., *A Theory of Justice*.

57 Although stating that justice is the first and the most important virtue of institutions, Rawls also asserted that one conception of justice is preferable to another when its broader consequences are more desirable. See Rawls, J., *A Theory of Justice*, p. 6. I assert that social democracy must hold social justice and greater equality to be necessary 'assisting' principles but on their own they are not preferable as 'definitive principles' to individual liberty and community.

Part II

Themes

6 Ends, Means and Political Identity

Raymond Plant

The Third Way stands for a modernized social democracy, passionate about its commitment to social justice and the goals of the centre left, but flexible, innovative and forward looking in the means to achieve them ... The Third Way is not an attempt to split the difference between Right and Left. It is about traditional values in a changed world ... What of policy? Our approach is 'permanent revisionism', a continual search for better means to meet our goals, based on a closer view of the changes taking place in advanced industrialized societies.

T. Blair, *The Third Way: New Politics for the New Century*

The distinction between ends and means, between values and policies, has been absolutely critical for New Labour. The claim has been, as exemplified in the quotation from Tony Blair as the epigraph to this chapter, that New Labour is still committed to the historic values of the Labour Party while being radical and revisionist in the means it has used and proposes to use in the pursuit of those values. It is argued that the values or the aims or the ends remain constant and that this preserves the political and ideological continuity of the Party in both its Old and New Labour forms; the means, however, are radically different as one would expect since circumstances change and the ways in which values have to be pursued reflect this change. So far, this claim might appear to be unexceptionable and to have a great deal of political force: securing the political continuity of the Party while sanctioning a range of policies to realise the Party's traditional values which are not normally seen as typical of Labour's historical approach to policy-making.

However, the distinction between ends and means raises many deep issues about what might be called the political theory of the Labour Party and its political identity and indeed the whole question of how the historical identity of the Party, construed in terms of its beliefs, is to be understood. If we are to be intellectually honest we have to go some way behind the beguiling politics of the ends/means distinction and look at issues which are both historical and philosophical which lie behind the political debate about ends and means.

Historical background

The very first point to make in this exploration of the distinction is that it is not at all *new*. While it has been of central importance to New Labour, it is a distinction which has a history – indeed a controversial history – inside the Labour

Party and indeed outside it in the wider European socialist movement. The distinction between ends and means has been absolutely central to European revisionist social democracy, which from its very beginning has been linked to a set of basic values such as social or distributive justice and the achievement of greater social and economic equality to parallel the formal political and legal equality which was coming to be conceded in the Western democracies in the course of the late-nineteenth and early-twentieth centuries justice. It was this idea – the extension of the idea of civil and political equality into the social and economic realm – that accounts for the *social* in social democracy. The aim of a social democratic party was not that of a revolutionary challenge to the basis of economic power but rather the achievement of political power, so that power thus secured and the will to exercise it could gain for the working class a more equitable distribution of resources and opportunities. Social democracy was seen essentially as a matter of gaining political power and then using it in the interests of social justice. Socialism, in its social democratic form, was thus to be defined in terms of ends, goals and values; it was not to be seen in the context of a general theory of history and human development such as that developed by Marx. It was also to be empirical about the choice of means to achieve the ends of greater social justice and was not committed to the idea that any particular means like the common ownership of the means of production or nationalisation was absolutely essential. A wide range of means might enable a more equal and just society to be developed and these were empirical and contextual judgements to be made. Ends were permanent; means were contextual. This was a central theme of German social democracy in the nineteenth century and particularly in its Gotha Programme, which Marx criticised so vehemently.

In Marx's view social democracy is an illusion because it mistakes the relationship between politics and economics. Marx's view – embodied in his overall materialist theory of history and society – was that power is essentially economic. The economic basis of society consisting of the means of production (labour, tools and raw materials etc.) and the relations of production (the work relationships which allow the means of production to be exploited to their greatest extent) have the most decisive effect of the possession of both economic and political power in society. Economic interests are the most basic and will dominate the exercise of political power in society. From this it follows in Marx's view that the pursuit of social justice in the absence of an agenda to overthrow capitalist forms of ownership and capitalist social relations is impossible because these basic power relations cannot be overcome by purely political means. The maldistribution of resources in society and the social injustice of that maldistribution are   a reflection of the dominant power relations in terms of the ownership of the means of production. Social injustice is a reflection of something much deeper which cannot be addressed without dealing with that deeper problem which is the private ownership of the means of production and the dominance of capitalist economic interests. This is how Marx puts the point in *The Critique of the Gotha Programme*:

Any distribution whatever of the means of consumption is only a consequence of the distribution of the conditions of production themselves. The latter distribution, however, is a feature of the mode of production itself ... If the elements of production are so distributed then the present distribution of the means of consumption results automatically. Right can never be higher than the economic structure of society and its cultural development conditioned thereby.[1]

Hence for Marx the attempt to define the socialist project essentially in terms of values such as social justice or equality is an illusion: it deals only with the symptoms of what is wrong with capitalist society (the maldistribution of the means of consumption) without addressing the causes of this maldistribution, namely the structure of ownership of the means of production. If you have the private ownership of the means of production then you will get a distribution of the means of consumption which favours the rich. Social justice can only be attained when there is a replacement of private ownership in favour of common ownership of the means of production and, given the strength of capitalist social, economic and political power, this transition can only come about by revolutionary rather than evolutionary and political means.

So social democracy is an illusion for Marx in that the social democrat either does not see or denies the intertwining of the issues of social justice and ownership. For a Marxist, the New Labour idea of social justice and a market economy with predominantly privately owned goods is just the most recent version of this mistake. Ends and means cannot be separated in the way that is central to the revisionist social democratic project. If the end is social justice then certain means, namely the common ownership of the means of production, are necessary conditions of achieving the end. It is not that we have a constant value like social justice and a choice between different means in different contexts. Because of the general nature of the relationship between politics and economics for Marx there has to be this interlinking of social justice and common ownership.

One way of putting this point rather more specifically and in a way that has been central to the history of social democracy is the idea that there is a clear distinction to be drawn between production and distribution, that the way things get produced and the ownership of the means of production can be regarded as independent of the distributional issue. For Marx, on the contrary, production and distribution are inextricably intertwined and there is no way of splitting means and ends. This issue over the pattern of distribution of resources, power and opportunities and the pattern of ownership of the means of production has been central to disputes between social democrats and Marxist socialists for the past one hundred years. Different answers have been given to questions about the relationship between political and economic power, about the common ownership of the means of production and the pursuit of social justice and the kind of politics that would have to be pursued to achieve the ends in question, or from a Marxist perspective to facilitate the overthrow of capitalist relations of production. Social democrats have often favoured a citizenship and inclusive approach to political action whereas socialist parties which have seen the private ownership of the means of production as central have tended to opt far more for a class-based approach to politics while recognising the limitations of politics embedded in the Marxist analysis of the relationship between political and economic power. Because the social democrat has eschewed the Marxist analysis of the relationship between political and economic power and the necessity of revolutionary transformation of society there has been an imperative need to build a political party that could gain power through parliamentary means and use a political majority to secure a more equitable distribution of resources. This has meant that social democratic parties, largely as the result of their rejection of the intertwining of means and ends, have taken a more citizenship, rather than a class-based approach to politics and thus have sought a basis of political support outside the working class and in so doing have had to situate a view of distributive justice in a project that has wider appeal. This is a point to which we shall return later.

These debates emerged first of all in response to the issues raised by the German social democratic thinker Eduard Bernstein. Bernstein had spent a part of the period when the social democratic party had been banned in Germany by Bismarck in England and had become familiar with the early Fabians and with non-Marxist approaches to socialism. This led him to reflect on the basis of Marx's dismissal of the social democratic project and in this context Bernstein's focus was on the materialist theory of history. This is not the place to go into detail about Bernstein's critique of Marx. Suffice it to say that he rejected the materialist theory of history because it did not in fact explain actual historical developments, and when it had sought to predict such developments such as the growing immiseration of the working class under capitalism and the polarisation of classes it had been proved wrong. For Bernstein socialism and social democracy had to be about the realisation of rather ill-defined ends and values, including economic justice, while being empirical and contextual about means. As he says in his book *The Preconditions of Socialism*:

> At any given time we could draw up a set of general political principles of Social Democracy which could claim universal validity, but we could not draw up a plan of action that would be valid for all countries.[2]

Here is the reassertion of the separation of means and ends with the consequential demotion of the Marxist claim that one set of means, namely common ownership, was a necessary condition of attaining the end in question. This approach produced a furious reaction from Lenin, Kautsky and Luxemburg – a set of debates which are of great importance for understanding the history of socialism but which are not of direct relevance to the salience of the means/ends distinction for modern politics. It is however worth pointing to one tension in Bernstein's account, and that is in relation to the role of democracy and the goals of social democracy. Is it the case that democracy is an essential means to the goals of social democracy for Bernstein? Indeed, given that the term democracy is incorporated into the name of the political position it might be argued that democracy and greater democratisation are either an essential means to social democratic ends or part of the end of social democracy itself. However, whether an end in itself or an indispensable means, the idea of democracy sits rather in tension with the idea that social democracy can be defined in terms of a set of very specific values, say to do with social justice, because what is the guarantee that democratisation will lead society in the direction of some social democratically preferred system of distribution? If democracy is central to the value system of social democracy, does this not mean that other values or ends cannot be too definite otherwise they will not themselves be subject to democratic assessment and judgement? There is quite a lot of evidence that Bernstein saw this and this is probably why his own account of the ends of social democracy is rather woolly and indefinite. As we shall see, this issue of the relationship between democracy and other social democratic goals has not gone away for the modern Labour Party.

It is arguable that at its inception the Labour Party's position on means and ends found itself somewhere between Marxism and Bernsteinian revisionism. The totemic Clause IV of the Labour Party Constitution linked in an indissoluble way the pursuit of social justice with the common ownership of the means of production.

> To secure for the producers by hand and brain the full fruits of their industry, and the most equitable distribution thereof that may be possible, upon the basis of the common ownership of the means of production ... [3]

This link between the ownership of the means of production and the pattern of distribution could hardly be stated more clearly and the insistence that the pursuit of justice in distribution required the common ownership of the means of production shows the influence of the Marxist position. However, the clause, and indeed the political practice of the Labour Party, was non-Marxist in its assumption that this move to common ownership could be achieved by political and parliamentary means and not by a revolutionary challenge to the position of the owners of capital. So it could be said that Clause IV of the Constitution did make the case for the link between production and distribution in the context of the pursuit of social justice. A good deal of subsequent revisionism in the Labour Party has turned on this point.

The most extensive revisionist theory, which involved dwelling a good deal upon the means/ends distinction, was C.A.R. Crosland's *The Future of Socialism* published in 1956.[4] Indeed in correspondence with his friend Philip Williams, Crosland had professed a youthful wish to be regarded as the second Bernstein and there is certainly a very compelling case to be made that Crosland's book certainly equalled if it did not surpass Bernstein's work. Although the book is penetrating and original, his views were shared by many in the Labour leadership at the time, including its leader Hugh Gaitskell. The revisionist case developed by Crosland was undoubtedly an important factor influencing

Gaitskell's ultimately unsuccessful attempt to get the Party to drop Clause IV of its Constitution following the election defeat in 1959. It would, however, also be fair to say that Douglas Jay's *Forward* article had an important effect too.[5] In that article Jay emphasised the distinction between means – of which common ownership or nationalisation was only one and which had to be assessed in context – and ends, such as equality and social justice which are constant. In the revisionist view Clause IV linked ends and means in too indissoluble a manner. Ends have to be stated clearly and are enduring; means were to be judged contextually and empirically and indeed discarded when political and economic circumstances changed.

Crosland's revisionism turned on two things: first, the claim that the basic aim or end of socialism is greater social equality; second, a denial of the Marxist claim that socialist aims such as equality and social justice could not be pursued in a capitalist economy. Crosland claimed that in fact capitalism had changed out of all recognition since Marx's time and that in the context of modern capitalism (if that is what it should still be called in his view), and that social democratic objectives could be pursued without further extension of common ownership; although it has to be said that he showed no inclination to argue that the post-1945 structure of public ownership of basic utilities should be changed.

For Crosland post-war capitalism had fundamentally changed its nature and this meant that social democratic ends had to be pursued in new ways. He argued that capitalism had changed as the result of a whole range of developments which in parallel with Bernstein he regarded as having invalidated Marx's predictions about the future development of capitalism. So what were these factors? They included the following:

Capitalism had changed first of all because the ownership of the means of production which Marx attributed to a class of capitalist owners was now much more dispersed and this dispersal was a continuing process. Hence, a Labour government pursuing an agenda of social justice would not confront a number of individual owners of the means of production who formed an homogeneous class with homogeneous interests opposed to such an agenda.

In any case the sector of private ownership had been diminished as the result of the 1945 Labour Government's programme of nationalisation of coal, steel, railways, electricity, telephony etc. It seemed to a revisionist of Crosland's persuasion that the public ownership of these infrastructural industries was here to stay and that this had diminished private ownership. They also argued however, that further nationalisation was unnecessary in the pursuit of social justice.

Because of the dispersal of ownership it was argued that ownership and control were not synonymous. The practical control of business and industry was in the hands of managers. The main task was to ensure that managers ran business in the light of desirable social objectives.

Crosland also argued that the greater democratisation of British life had put severe constraints on the power of the private owners of capital. Democratic institutions and practices were now a clear countervailing power against that of the power of private owners.

In parallel to this there had been a growth of unionism which had diminished the power of private owners and managers and compelled them to take into account far more the interests of the workforce.

In addition there was the post-1945 development of the welfare state which meant that in terms of a set of basic goods such as health, education and welfare, citizens were no longer subject to the vagaries of the market or charity but also the collective responsibility for meeting need.

The revisionists also argued that while the sense of class was still strong in Britain and reflected the life chances of citizens there had neither been the growing polarisation of classes nor the immiseration of the working class as predicted in Marx's theory.

Finally, there was the prospect, the detail of which will be explored in more detail below, that new instruments, identified by Lord Keynes in his *General Theory*,[6] were available to enable capitalism to be managed in the interest of greater social justice.

All of this meant that modern capitalism was fundamentally different from late-nineteenth century capitalism and that Marxist assumptions about the means necessary to achieve socialist/social democratic values had to be rethought for the modern world.

However, I want for a moment to dwell upon a feature of social democracy which we saw in the context of Bernstein. That is to say the link between the social and democracy in social democracy. A heavy emphasis on the democratic side of social democracy might imply that the other goals of social democracy (in Crosland's view greater social equality) would have to be subject to demo-cratic endorsement. This does not seem to be how Crosland himself saw it and it is interesting to look at two linked aspects of his approach. As we have seen he was an egalitarian – greater social equality was his goal, his basic value. One reading of *The Future of Socialism* and his other writings however would lead one to the belief that he did not think that it was a necessary condition for the achievement of that goal to create a popular democratic consensus in favour of greater equality because greater equality could be attained indirectly rather than by the need to create a society of committed egalitarians. It could be achieved indirectly by economic growth, the fiscal dividends of which would allow the better-off to at least maintain their absolute position while improving the relative position of the worst-off. So the egalitarian strategy did not have to rest on a strong popular endorsement or strong democratic credentials because it could be achieved in a situation of growth by means of this indirect strategy which did not require a distributive consensus of any great width or depth. Essential to this growth-based strategy was the availability of Keynesian economic techniques which we shall discuss next, but it did mean that once these techniques became unavailable for the indirect approach to greater equality there was no distributive consensus to sustain an egalitarian policy in a much colder economic climate.

One key feature of Crosland's argument is that aims like greater social equality can be achieved by political management of the economy by using Keynesian techniques of demand management which were unknown to previous generations of social democrats and which made it redundant to argue for the common ownership of the means of production and economic planning in any physical sense as a means of securing social justice. Social justice could be attained by demand management rather than by nationalisation and physical controls of the economy. This approach therefore entailed a clear distinction between ends, greater social justice and equality, and means demand management together with the existence of the post-1945 nationalised industries. This was the solvent to the social democratic dilemma as set out so clearly by Marx in *The Critique of the Gotha Programme*, namely how was it possible to pursue a project of social justice in the context of an economy dominated by private ownership? The answer was Keynesian economic techniques.

Of course the impact of Keynes was absolutely critical to the post-Second World War revisionist rejection of Marx, as Adam Przeworski in his classic book *Capitalism and Social Democracy* has argued:

> Social democrats everywhere soon discovered in Keynes' ideas, particularly after the appearance of the *General Theory* something they urgently needed: a distinct policy for administering capitalist economies. The Keynesian revolution – and this is what it was – provided social democrats with a goal and thus a justification for their governmental role, and simultaneously transformed the ideological significance of distributive politics that favoured the working class.[7]

In a sense it could be said that Keynesian economic management was as indispensable a means to the intellectual coherence of the social democratic project of securing social justice as common ownership was to Marxists. Indeed, it was precisely Keynes's theories that rendered common ownership irrelevant for social justice. As Keynes himself argued:

> It is not the ownership of the instruments of production which it is important for the state to assume. If the state is able to determine the aggregate amount of resources devoted to augmenting the instruments and the basic rate of reward to those who own them it will have accomplished all that is necessary.[8]

By the 1970s, however, it was clear that this view was mired in difficulties. A full analysis of these difficulties is way beyond the scope of this chapter and any full analysis would have to cover the collapse of the Bretton Woods agreements in 1971, following President Nixon's decision to allow the dollar to float; the growing globalisation of the world economy and the openness of world markets; the growth of multinational companies which were not amenable to being influenced to the degree assumed by the revisionists in terms of national economic and political agendas; the oil price shock; the growth of union militancy etc. If Keynesianism was a key means to achieving social democratic ends in the context of a market economy then the problems with Keynesianism seemed to betoken the collapse of post-Second World War revisionist social democracy. The need for the IMF loan in 1976 and Callaghan's speech to the Labour Party conference of that year which implicitly rejected some central aspects of Keynes's theory were seen by many to indicate the passing of this particular phase of social democratic revisionism. In the same way as both Bernstein and Crosland had argued that capitalism had changed fundamentally since Marx's day, so it seems that globalisation and the complex strands of economic, political and social development caught by that term have transformed capitalism again, but in ways that made both the goal of social democracy, particularly social justice and greater equality, more difficult and the means, namely Keynesian economic management, seemingly of diminishing applicability. The alternatives seemed to be stark. Either the programme of economic liberalism as was to be found in the writings of thinkers like Hayek and Friedman and followed to a large extent by the Thatcher Government, or a reversion to a more marxsiant approach as exemplified in the Left's Alternative Economic Strategy. At the same time, an attempt at Keynesian social democracy in one country, as initially attempted by President Mitterand after he came into office in 1981, failed and that in turn added to the widespread belief that the social democratic moment was over. This sort of judgement seemed to imply something about the nature of the link between means and ends, namely that the achievement of social democratic ends depended, so it seemed, on the availability of one set of means, that is to say Keynesianism. So on this view, far from being permanent or enduring, the salience of social democratic ends could be extinguished by the unavailability of means to achieve them.

The fact is, however, that New Labour has come to power in a context in which it has acknowledged the fundamentally changed nature of capitalism, which, it might be argued, has invalidated Croslandite social democracy, but at the same time New Labour has wanted to endorse the claim that the ends of social democracy are enduring and indeed that it is the enduring nature of these ends that makes the Labour Party the same Party. So, how has this been done? Is there a new set of means available for achieving social democratic ends to replace the dominance of Keynesian means in the 1960s, or have social democratic ends been modified in order to align them with the only available political and economic means? So our next question is: given that modern market economies have in New Labour's view been fundamentally changed, have the ends or goals been changed to accommodate them to these new realities despite the ostensible claim that New Labour shares its goals with the historic goals of the Party?

The identity of ends

The ends of social democracy are essentially seen as drawing on the progressive values in European politics following the Enlightenment and the French Revolution: personal liberty, equality, community/fraternity/solidarity. It is arguable that it is this commitment to these values which secures the identity of the social democratic tradition. The philosophical problem here is that this can be seen as a very thin form of identity and continuity, since while the words invoked may be the same, these words are the names of complex and contested underlying ideas and we have to go beyond the words to the conceptual complexities and ambiguities which they embody to see whether there is a thicker form of identity other than that secured just by the shared commitment to the words. This point was well made by John Rawls in *A Theory of Justice* when he drew a useful distinction between a concept and conceptions of that concept.[9] So, for example, at a thin definitional level 'democracy' means 'rule by the people' but only a richer conception or interpretation of the concept can tell you what you want to know: who are the people? how do they exercise their rule? is democracy direct or representative? and so on. At the level of *concepts* identity will be thin and trivial, we have to move to *conceptions* which are richer and deeper but also contested. To put the point simply and starkly: is the same thing meant by the words denoting their goals and purposes as between Old and New Labour? This is not a new way of posing the problem as Bernstein, for example, posed it in the context of a similar analysis on page 140 of *The Preconditions of Socialism*.[10]

Let me give some examples of the complexities here to show how it bears upon the question of political identity and continuity.

Freedom

As is well known, freedom can mean freedom from (negative freedom) and (or) freedom to (positive freedom). If by freedom is meant negative freedom, that is to say freedom from coercion and unjustified interference by others, then the political task is to ensure that the individual is kept free from coercion whether by another individual, the government or some corporate/public body. It is not, as positive freedom is, about ability and the possession of resources. If by freedom is meant positive freedom, then freedom is not secured only by being made free from coercion. Freedom is about the possession of resources and opportunities as well. It involves the ability to act on the choices that we make and to have a significant range of alternatives from which we can choose. So the term freedom can mean rather different things and depending on how it is used can imply rather different views about the nature and scope of government. So political identity cannot be secured just because the word freedom is used at two different stages of a party's development. Rather we have to know what sort of thick concept of freedom is presupposed in that use of the term. If political identity is to be secured by commonality of values this can be established not by identifying the same term in the political discourse of a party but rather by establishing by analysis that the same conception of the term is being used over time.

Equality

The same point is true about equality. Equality can be understood in a range of ways and in a range of dimensions. It can mean equality of opportunity which may be negative and procedural, as in non-discrimination, or it may be positive, as in securing to individuals resources and opportunities. It may be understood as equality of outcome, that is to say a distribution of resources which will produce more equal outcomes than those thrown up by the free market. There will be complex and contested links between equality and merit/desert and in relation to need. Do we want equality over the whole range of social life and, if not, to which spheres is it relevant? There is also the stern question, equality of what? That is to say what is it that we want to equalise? Again the question of political and ideological continuity cannot be resolved just by appealing to the value of equality *simpliciter*; we have rather to look at the underlying conceptions in all of their complexity.

Community / Fraternity / Solidarity

The term community is just as complex as freedom and equality and can cover ideas of fraternity and solidarity, or what Tawney called 'fellowship'.[11] The word community is particularly linked to New Labour's social policy and I will concentrate on that formulation for the moment. It is very clear that even taking the word community in a rather insulated and restricted sense there are ambiguities. Is community about a normative frame of reference, a source of values, a school for virtue if you like; or is it just a factual way of referring to a specific geographical area which may imply nothing about values? How do both of these relate to what may be thought of as communities of interest, that is to say groupings brought into being without necessarily sharing geographical propinquity but rather sharing a sense of identity through a set of common interests that may just be of a passing nature? How do all of these relate to the way in which community may refer to a particular (ideal?) type of human relationship which is what Tawney had in mind when he talked about fellowship? Again, we have to get below the surface of words to see whether there is commonality in conception.

Of course this is rather general and shortly I will turn attention more closely to the idea of equality, but before then I want to stay with these rather general points for the moment because there are two cognate issues which need to be addressed.

The first has to do with what might be called the *ordering* of values. Is political and ideological continuity in a party to be achieved only by invoking the same values, for example freedom, equality and community? It surely matters whether or not at different times one value is given priority over others and, indeed, the more general question about how the relations between values are to be seen.

Clearly there are tensions between freedom (on some conceptions of it) and equality (on some conceptions of it) and between freedom and the claims of community. If, as Isaiah Berlin argued, it is part of the nature of human life that we lack a general theory which will reconcile values into one harmonious whole we are forced to make choices – and in his view frequently tragic choices – between values. So part of the continuity or otherwise of a political party, if it is to be seen in terms of the goals and values of that party, will depend crucially on whether there is also continuity about how those values have been ordered and prioritised over time. So we not only have to get to some analysis of the conceptions of values employed by a party but also to how these values are ordered during the life of a political party or movement.

Actually the issue is rather important in the history of the Labour Party: let me give two examples of this. In the 1980s Roy Hattersley, the then Deputy Leader of the Party, published a significant book, *Choose Freedom*, in which he argued strongly for seeing equality as a means of achieving greater liberty, and in making this case he also invoked Crosland's work.[12] Leave aside for the purposes of this chapter whether or not the case was convincing. Rather, the point of interest is that within the class of ends, e.g. equality and liberty, these ends can be ordered in such a way that one becomes a means to another. In this case equality becomes a means to liberty. So the question about means and ends in this context is not just that ends are permanent and means are contextual and policy-based but rather that one end is more fundamental than another and that the less fundamental end is a means to the more fundamental one. This is precisely the point at stake in my second example.

The second example goes back to Bernstein but also contains significant political difficulty for New Labour, and that is the role of *democracy* in social democracy. Bernstein certainly gives a very strong impression that democracy is the most fundamental end of social democracy and that as democratisation increases the use of democracy will lead to further kinds of goals which cannot be set out fully prior to their democratic endorsement. So what is the relationship between democracy and the other goals of social democracy if these are understood as freedom, equality and community? If democracy is one of the fundamental ends then surely it has to be *the* fundamental end since other ends would arise out of democratic processes and deliberation. But there is no reason why some preconceived, idea, say of equality would be given democratic endorsement. So in the contemporary context for example, in so far as devolution in Scotland has been a gain in terms of the goal of democratisation it has thrown up a form of national inequality in relation to care for the elderly in that in Scotland personal care will be paid for by the state, in England it will not. Here inequality of outcome is being sanctioned in the name of democracy. Does this mean that in practice democratic values are allowed to trump egalitarian ones? This may be so and would certainly be implied in Bernstein's approach. However it certainly fits rather badly into some of the policy history of the Labour Party and into Crosland's strategy of achieving equality by indirect means which precisely did not require strong endorsement by an electorate of committed egalitarians in his view. It may also be true of the rather indirect approach that Gordon Brown has taken to issues of redistribution.

In closing this essay I want to focus on the issue of equality and the claim that it is this value which over time has given the Labour Party its distinctiveness. Other parties may claim to represent some of the demands of personal freedom and/or the authority of social and community life but on the view that I want to examine it is equality which is crucial to Labour identity. I don't want to focus on the long history of the concept in the Labour Party, although it would be fair to point out that the views of egalitarians within the Party in its history are far more complex and nuanced than can be caught in the very simple-minded contrast between equality of opportunity and equality of outcome. Both Tawney and Crosland were leading egalitarians in the Party but they did believe that functional inequalities were necessary for economic efficiency and were morally justifiable. I want rather to focus on just one issue within the tangle of issues raised by a commitment to equality, namely the relationship between that idea and an increasing gap between rich and poor. Is it the case that the change in the nature of capitalism produced by globalisation and all of its related phenomena has been such that it now no longer is possible to pursue the goal of at least limiting the gap between the rich and the poor (what might very crudely be seen as a form of equality of outcome) and is it the case that the only form of equality that can now be pursued is equality of opportunity? If this is so and explicitly stated in these terms then it would seem that this is a more radical form of revisionism than just a revision of means while ends remain permanent, because if it is argued that at least a concern to reduce that gap is characteristic of the Labour Party historically, then to say that such a concern can no longer be pursued would be a revision of ends as well as means. That is to say, a move to restrict Labour's egalitarian aspirations to equality of opportunity rather than a wider concern with the gap between rich and poor would in fact on this view embody displacing at least one central element of the conception of equality and would be a revision of ends not of means. So how do we seek to answer this question? If we go back to the work of Crosland, the Labour Party's most prominent post-war egalitarian, we can see that a central concern is the gap between rich and poor. In his Fabian pamphlet *Social Democracy in Europe*[13] Crosland argued this case in a very straightforward way by saying that the aim of social democracy was one of greater social equality and that this was to be achieved by economic growth, the fiscal dividends of which could be used to improve the relative position of the worst-off while maintaining the absolute position of the better-off. If the relative position of the worst off is improving in relative terms and the absolute position of the better-off is being maintained the inequality between rich and poor will diminish, assuming that the means employed will be effective. So this argument will go beyond equality of opportunity which in *The Future of Socialism* Crosland argued was 'not enough'[14] in favour of a concern with the overall distribution of income and wealth and a way of narrowing the inequalities found in that distribution. Tackling equality of opportunity alone in Crosland's view was no guarantee that inequalities would diminish, although he was fully in favour of the greatest amount of equality of opportunity and it is worth noting in passing that he believed that comprehensive education was one of the central ways of achieving that.

It is very important in the context of the emergence of New Labour to take notice of the fact that the Crosland position on egalitarian distribution was fundamentally different from that offered by economic liberals and 'New Right' politicians. In their view the relative position of the poor *vis-à-vis* the rich does not matter. Indeed to be concerned to diminish this differential is both economically inefficient (because it will limit the impact of incentives) and morally unjustifiable (because it neglects the claims of desert). Rather, what matters to the poor is not their position relative to the rich but whether they are better off this year than they were last year in their own terms – that is to say their main focus is on their absolute rather than their relative position. This is then combined with the idea that the best way to improve the absolute position of the poor is via the trickle-down effect of the free market and not political interference with market outcomes to improve or rectify what are held (wrongly from this point of view) to be unjustified inequalities. So economic liberal strategy will increase inequality while improving via the trickle-down effect the absolute position of the worst-off. So it can be seen that in this respect economic liberalism is a direct critique not of social democratic means (although it is that as well) but of social democratic ends, at least in so far as they are argued for by a thinker like Crosland. This is important because, if New Labour's view about equality turns out to be very close to that of the economic liberal, then it would be that much more difficult to argue that the aims of the Party have stayed the same and that it has been revisionist about means only. So what is the answer to this question?

The only response that I can make, however unsatisfactory it is, is that the answer is in fact obscure. I don't think that there is any clear or well thought out evidence that New Labour has given up on the idea that inequality in distributional terms is a matter of moral and political concern, whereas for the economic liberal/New Right thinker/politician this would be a matter of indifference or more likely something to be welcomed. It has to be said at the same time however that while Labour has taken very radical steps to improve equality of opportunity ranging from Sure Start to the New Deal, from a concern with skills to reform of the educational system and a great deal more, and indeed has been the most directly redistributive Labour Government ever, these have not had an impact on the gap between rich and poor. If it is argued that it is only as it were from the bottom up – by improving equality of opportunity that the position of the worst-off can be improved, then while this may well have a much more dramatic effect on their absolute position than the economic liberals' reliance on the trickle-down mechanism it has to be accepted, I believe, that this is highly unlikely to make a difference to distributional equality. If the argument against going further, by for example taxing top incomes, is ruled out on grounds of the knock-on effects on incentives and competitiveness in a global economy then it seems to me that we have to accept that the policy restrictions imposed by globalisation etc. have so constrained what is politically feasible that the conception of equality embodied in Labour's history has been reinterpreted in the light of this. I don't want to dwell on the rights or wrongs of this but rather to point out that if this is the case, it is just mistaken to argue that ends are permanent, definitive and identity creating, whereas means are contextual and subordinate to ends, because the argument now would be that it is actually the non-availability of means (in the context of globalisation) that has led to a significant redefinition of the end in question.

Notes

1 Marx, K., *Critique of the Gotha Programme*, in *Marx and Engels, Collected Works, Volume 24* (Lawrence and Wishart, London, 1989), pp.87–8.
2 Bernstein, E., *The Preconditions of Socialism* (edited and translated by Tudor, H., CUP, Cambridge, 1993), p. 159.
3 Quoted in Pelling, H., *A Short History of the Labour Party* (Macmillan, Basingstoke, 1993, 10th edition), p. 44.
4 Crosland, C.A.R., *The Future of Socialism* (Cape, London, 1956).
5 Jay, D., *Forward*, 16 October 1959.
6 Keynes, J.M., *The General Theory of Employment, Interest and Money* (Prometheus, New York, 1997, 1st edition, 1936).
7 Przeworski, A., *Capitalism and Social Democracy* (CUP, Cambridge, 1985), p. 36.
8 Keynes, J.M., *The General Theory of Employment, Interest and Money*, p. 378.
9 Rawls, J., *A Theory of Justice* (OUP, Oxford, 1999, 1st edition, 1971), esp. p. 5.
10 Bernstein, E., *The Preconditions of Socialism*, p. 140.
11 See Tawney, R.H., *Equality* (George Allen & Unwin, London, 1931) and Tawney, R.H., *The Acquisitive Society* (Bell and Sons, London, 1921).
12 Hattersley, R., *Choose Freedom: The Politics of Democratic Socialism* (Penguin, London, 1987).
13 Crosland, C.A.R., *Social Democracy in Europe* (Fabian Society, London, 1975).
14 Crosland, C.A.R., *The Future of Socialism*, chapter 8.

7 Equality[1]

Kevin Hickson

The commitment to equality is the feature of democratic socialism (or social democracy) which distinguishes it from alternative doctrines. This is in contrast to the other values which form the social democratic tripos: community and liberty. Community is a concept capable of many different interpretations so that communitarianism and communitarians can appear across the political spectrum. A positive conception of liberty is shown by both social democrats and the social liberals, with their origins in the late nineteenth century. Equality remains a distinctive socialist commitment. This comment in itself may be questioned since non-socialists may pledge their support for equality. Equality before the law is a value shared by all democrats. Equality of opportunity is similarly a widely held belief. That this is so can be demonstrated by reference to Thatcherism, which even in its most bellicose form still maintained a theoretical commitment to equality of opportunity, defined as freedom from external constraint. However, against this it may be argued that no other doctrine places as much emphasis on equality as democratic socialism. Equality, or more specifically a commitment to a reduction in substantive inequalities, is a core value of democratic socialism. Policies to promote greater equality are central to the social democratic project.[2]

This chapter is therefore concerned with the differing attitudes towards equality expressed by the various strands of Labour Party thought. This book has identified five strands of Labour Party thought: Old Right, New Right, Old Left, New Left and Centre. Of these the Centre lacks a clear ideological perspective and so need not be discussed further here. In the course of my research it has become apparent to me that the main division within the Labour Party towards the issue of equality is between modern social democracy and the Party's traditional perspectives. It is therefore possible to reconstruct, at least partially, an 'Old' Labour/, 'New' Labour divide.

Before going on to look at these attitudes in more detail, it is necessary to make the focus of the chapter clearer. I am not going to discuss equality in terms of race, gender, sexual orientation and so forth, since to do so would require more space and expertise than I possess.[3] Moreover, approaches to these issues are broadly similar across the Labour Party. The Party, generally speaking, has a legislative record of which it can be proud in these areas, as well as some less favourable incidents.[4] Instead, I intend to look at the various philosophical perspectives on equality and how these have manifested themselves into policy approaches to the reduction of income and wealth inequalities. I begin by looking at the revisionist tradition since it is this that has dominated post-war Labour Party thinking.

Old Right

The traditional right-wing revisionist strand of the Labour Party has a long history going back into the pre-war period. It was R.H. Tawney who placed equality at the centre of social democratic political philosophy in his book *Equality*.[5] Tawney argued that the gross inequality in income and wealth that existed in the 1920s and 1930s was morally reprehensible. Extreme poverty had a dehumanising affect by limiting the position of the poorest to a life of mere subsistence. Extreme wealth similarly had a dehumanising affect by pampering the rich. For Tawney equality was linked to liberty. The existence of inequalities limited personal freedom. It was possible to redistribute income and wealth in order to extend individual liberty, by removing the privileges of the rich. This connection of equality to liberty was of significance to later social democratic thinkers. To Tawney, the objective was explicitly greater equality since there was a need to reduce both the extremes of wealth and poverty. But Tawney also made a connection between equality and community, that inequality led to the fragmentation of society and made a mockery of the value of equal worth. It is this connection of equality to community which is of significance when we turn to a discussion of New Labour. Although Tawney was to have an influence on thinkers across the Party, his attachment to equality as the distinguishing value of democratic socialism and his gradual rejection of Guild Socialism were to have a more profound impact on the Labour right, a position which Tawney himself was to occupy in later life.[6] Other pre-war thinkers approached these issues from the perspective of political economists rather than as political theorists. Nevertheless, equality remained a core principle. Douglas Jay, for example, pointed to the high rates of interest paid on large savings so that the rich did not need to work in order to obtain an income.[7] For Hugh Dalton and Evan Durbin too, equality remained the core value.[8] Dalton puts the case succinctly: 'what is necessary is a very great reduction in our present economic inequalities. This implies that, while the average level of well-being must be greatly raised, the rich shall become poorer and the poor richer.'[9]

Dalton had worked closely with a number of younger intellectual politicians in the immediate pre-war years. It is to one of these that I now turn: Tony Crosland. Crosland was, according to one of those who knew him well, the paradigmatic thinker of the post-war generation.[10] Given that Crosland was writing in the post-war period, his perspective was different from the pre-war generation of revisionists.[11] This was so because he was writing after the 1945–51 Labour Government. It must be remembered that the Attlee administration was the first Labour majority government. The record of the Labour Party in power in the pre-war period was rather poor. Two minority administrations had collapsed soon after coming to power amid economic difficulties and the opposition of the right-wing press. The decision of Ramsay MacDonald to form the National Government in 1931 led to a split in the Labour Party. There was therefore much doubt in the Labour Party in the 1930s about what a future Labour government could achieve, and in some quarters an outright fear of right-wing opposition. This even extended into the revisionist right, who thought that only a few positive achievements could be expected by a post-war Labour government. In contrast, the Attlee Government's record was impressive.[12] Crosland was concerned with what social democrats ought to do in the future, given the ongoing debate with the Bevanites in the 1950s. Hence the rationale for *The Future of Socialism*.[13]

Crosland argued that the Attlee Government had ushered in a period of consensus based around a mixed economy, Keynesian demand management and the welfare state. This amounted to nothing less than the transformation of capitalism, with power shifting from the owners of economic wealth to corporate managers, the trades unions and the state. Indeed, Crosland suggested that these transformations had been so significant that capitalism had largely been replaced by a managerialist society.[14] After reviewing socialist thought, Crosland argued that the promotion of welfare and the attainment of greater equality were the appropriate social democratic aspirations.[15] There was a need for greater welfare since poverty still existed in certain geographical areas and at certain times in people's lives. By equality, Crosland meant more than equality of opportunity in which individuals would be given roughly equal starting points from where they could compete for senior positions and higher salaries. For sure, this was preferable to existing inequalities and the continuing importance of privilege. However, for Crosland equality of opportunity was, in his famous phrase, 'not enough'.[16] This was so for several reasons. The first was that the reality of social stratification along class lines would lead to a large division between the elite and the mass in terms of custom, lifestyles and so forth, thus weakening a shared sense of community and threatening the stability of democratic government. Moreover, equality of opportunity is based on ability. Yet, to Crosland differential outcomes based on ability are still unjust, because of unequal starting points such as genetic endowment or family background which are not compensated for in an equality of opportunity society: 'no one deserves either so generous a reward or so severe a penalty for a quality so implanted from outside, for which he himself can only claim a limited responsibility.'[17]

Crosland's strategy for achieving this goal of a more equal society was to use education and social security, financed by the fiscal dividends of economic growth. The former ought to take the form of comprehensive education designed to bring together children from a variety of backgrounds in order to allow for shared social experiences. It was hoped by Crosland that this would reduce social stratification. Social security and taxation would be used to raise the absolute and relative position of the poor. Crosland also favoured the settlement of wages in terms of the rent of ability criterion, by which the amount of income needed to secure for the community particular forms of service would be decided by non-market mechanisms; with the assumption that the resulting inequalities would be less than those produced by the operation of a free-market economy. It was this insertion of the concept of the 'rent of ability' which was to lead to criticisms from the left to which I return below. Crosland argued that, with higher rates at close to 70 per cent in the 1950s, further increases in income tax would act as a disincentive. He therefore argued that little could be done here. In contrast, he did argue in favour of the need to redistribute wealth. This could be done by fiscal means such as a higher rate of wealth tax and a new capital gains tax.

This then was Crosland's thesis, first outlined in *The Future of Socialism* and defended in *The Conservative Enemy*.[18] It can be, and was, attacked from various sources. So, for example, the rise of the Green movement in the late 1960s and 1970s led to a criticism of Crosland's thesis for its dependence on the promotion of economic growth. There were, however, two more serious weaknesses in Crosland's thesis. The first was that Crosland had exaggerated the ability of the British economy to achieve sustained economic growth. Crosland was to acknowledge that he had been overly optimistic in writing in *The Future of Socialism* in 1956 that economic growth would be sufficient to achieve the social objectives he desired. His first acknowledgement of this came only a few years later in *The Conservative Enemy*, but it was in *Socialism Now* that he criticised the record of the 1964–70 Labour Government, which he believed had sacrificed economic growth for maintaining the parity of sterling.[19] The tone of *Socialism Now* was, compared to his earlier works, deeply pessimistic. All that could be achieved during the 1970s was very modest indeed given the low rate of economic growth.

Economic growth was central to Crosland's thesis. It would be easier, he argued, to redistribute income and wealth during periods of economic growth since the higher earners would be more willing to sacrifice a greater proportion of their wealth if they also benefited from economic growth in the first place; that they would be willing to see a decline in their relative position if their absolute position was maintained through economic growth. This leads to the second weakness in Crosland's thesis, arguably greater than the first. Crosland argued that the case for equality was based on subjective moral principle. According to John Vaizey this was due to the fact that Crosland had been influenced by the philosophy of A.J. Ayer.[20] Moral principles, such as equality, lack objective validity. Since they are not subject to proof or disproof, they may or may not be accepted by the reader depending on their own 'moral predilections'.[21] The best that can be done is to state one's own position and then seek to defend this perspective. Crosland then did not attempt to argue for the moral superiority of the egalitarian case. He did however present three justifications for equality.[22] First, the creation of a more equal society reduces social antagonisms. Second, equality is related to social justice – to which I return at the end of the chapter. It should be noted that Crosland related equality to the spread of individual freedom implying a positive conception of freedom. Finally, Crosland related equality to the eradication of social waste, both in terms of reducing social divisions and for creating true opportunities for people to rise to positions of power. This defence of equality, resting as it did on the insistence that moral principles are subjective and relative, lacked both the moral force to persuade wavering voters and to overcome the neo-liberal critique during the 1970s.

The 1970s were a difficult time for social democracy. The persistence of slow economic growth and a volatile international economy in which it became increasingly difficult to implement traditional Keynesian policy, as demonstrated with the 1976 IMF Crisis, undermined social democratic remedies. Moreover, social democracy was critiqued by both a resurgent Labour left, and by the increasingly influential New Right. Nevertheless, Crosland maintained his position. In *Socialism Now*, Crosland argued explicitly for the need to improve the position of the poor in both absolute *and* relative terms.[23] For Crosland, this emphasis on the relative position is significant, and has important implications when considering New Labour. It is first necessary, however, to examine the position put forward by the Labour left.

The Left

I have spent a lot of time so far looking at the case for greater equality put forward by Tony Crosland. This was necessary given his position as the dominant thinker on the revisionist right of the Labour Party in the post-war era. This is both a positive and a negative comment. It is positive in the sense that Crosland was able to produce a book with the intellectual strength of the *Future of Socialism*, and was then able to go on to defend his thesis against all-comers for the following 20 years. His death in 1977 was even more poignant given that this was the time when his thesis was most under attack. Ultimately nobody can be quite sure how he would have responded to the neo-liberal critique.[24] Certainly, there were a number of social democratic responses from those on the Labour right who remained within the Labour Party following the formation of the SDP which were broadly similar to Crosland's thesis. Notable among these were the Socialist Philosophy Group, whose members included Raymond Plant and Bryan Gould, and also the work of Labour's Deputy Leader, Roy Hattersley.[25] The common theme was to reassert the link between equality and liberty made by Tawney and Crosland in order to try to counter the New Right's emphasis on a negative conception of liberty. It is not possible to write from a neutral perspective, and the author should declare his own position. I must confess to a certain admiration for the Crosland thesis. However, in saying that he was the dominant figure on the revisionist right is also an admission that that particular strand of the Labour Party's thought lacked figures of the same calibre. Indeed, looking back it is difficult to see how that position maintained its dominance. But maintain it it did, and the left was always in the position of trying to critique the dominant revisionist element.[26]

In talking about the left it is necessary to distinguish between the 'old' left and the 'new' left. The left was separated by a generation. The Old Left was prominent in the 1950s, searching for a way forward following the 1951 General Election defeat. The New Left came to the fore in the 1970s. However, the two lefts were also separated by their political approach. The New Left was more assertive. This confidence was derived from the possession of a more fully developed theory, and meant that it was willing to go further in its policy proposals than the Old Left had been. The Old Left was, as Tam Dalyell points out in this volume, a rather disparate group of individuals who fell under the term 'Bevanites'. However, it was Richard Crossman who was the leading intellectual in this group.[27] The problem was that Crossman failed to put forward a well-developed case. Although he critiqued the Marxist left, which he felt was not in keeping with the British political tradition and was largely irrelevant given the social reforms of the Attlee Governments, and the revisionist right, which he felt had reduced politics to a set of policy prescriptions and which failed to see the continuing importance of economic ownership; he failed to put forward anything which can be regarded as a positive case of his own. In reading his work one becomes convinced of Geoffrey Foote's assessment that 'Crossman himself was in many ways a political dilettante flitting from idea to idea without ever really considering the full practical consequences or committing himself to fighting them.'[28]

However, in considering Crossman's contribution to the political thought of the Labour Party, two points are relevant here for this discussion of equality. The first is that Crossman, and the Old Left more generally, were committed to equality. The debates of the 1950s between the Gaitskellites and the Bevanites are often abbreviated to a debate between those who believed in equality and those who believed in public ownership. Although this debate rested on the complex relationship between means and ends, about which Raymond Plant has written in this volume and elsewhere[29] and is far more competent to do so than I am, it quickly becomes apparent that the dichotomy between ownership and equality does less than justice to the two positions. The revisionist right clearly believed in equality, but then so too did the Old Left. Similarly, the revisionists did not rule out further public ownership. The debate is better understood as one between those who thought that public ownership was a necessary precursor to greater equality, and those who believed that the levers of monetary and particularly fiscal policy were sufficient to achieve that end, given the extent of central planning introduced between 1945–51. This debate rested on differing perceptions of the nature of economic change. For Crosland recent changes had amounted to nothing less than the transformation of capitalism. The left continued to believe that owners still had significant economic power.

The second point to be made with reference to Crossman is that by equality Crossman meant more than merely raising the absolute position of the poor. As with Crosland, Crossman was concerned with the relative position of the worse-off. This point was made explicit in Crossman's Fabian pamphlet, *Paying for the Social Services*, in which he argued that Income Tax and National Insurance should be central to the financing of the Welfare State in order to incorporate all social classes within state schemes and to narrow the gap between rich and poor.[30] Several leading figures within the Old Left were involved in the implementation of public policies aimed at reducing inequality. For example, Barbara Castle was responsible for introducing the State Earnings Related Pensions Scheme (SERPS) which linked the uprating of pensions to average earnings.

The New Left of the Labour Party launched a full-scale critique of the Croslandite thesis and in so doing continued the onslaught made against Crosland by the extra-Parliamentary commentators of the 1960s in the *New Left Review*.[31] To commentators such as Stephen Lukes, a much greater equality of outcome than Crosland had advocated was both feasible and desirable.[32] According to Lukes, Crosland had supported equality of opportunity only. This was because he had talked a great deal about creating equal starting points through education and welfare reforms, while allowing for inequality of outcome through the 'rent of ability' criterion. For Lukes, this view, what John Rawls had called 'democratic equality', is based on a particular view of human nature. Lukes argued against the need to create incentives through differential wages, although he did allow for non-material forms of incentive. Instead, Lukes called for an approach to equality which emphasised equal worth and the need to tackle social inequalities. Given that Crosland had written a chapter on the limits of equality of opportunity, it would seem a little unfair to say that this was all that he advocated. Indeed, what emerges from the pages of *The Future of Socialism* is in fact rather similar to the position advocated by Lukes, pointing to the fact that the New Left failed to provide a distinctive approach to the issue of equality. Stuart Holland also allowed for a greater role in non-material benefits from work in order to achieve greater equality of outcome. Indeed, Holland felt that psychological factors such as success and prestige were more important to managers than was material outcome. Greater equality of incomes should be related to greater equality of wealth, and its pursuit should be applied across the economy in order to offset trade union demands for wage increases.[33]

The position of the New Left, it should be pointed out, is a little unclear on the issue of equality.[34] Certainly, in terms of rhetoric and policy, it went much further than the Old Left had been prepared to go in its pursuit of greater equality. Although the New Left spoke in terms of equality of result, it is in fact unlikely that they implied a complete equality of outcome. Indeed, the only thinker of the British left to argue for equality of outcome explicitly was George Bernard Shaw: 'the only satisfactory plan is to give everybody an equal share no matter what sort of person she is, or how old she is, or what sort of work she does, or who or what her father was.'[35] The Old Left, New Left and Old Right of the Labour Party were therefore agreed in their belief of greater equality of outcome; although the New Left were prepared to see much greater substantive equality than the two earlier positions. The three factions of the Labour Party argued it out between themselves as to how much equality, or to be more precise inequality, was desirable. Yet it should be pointed out that these debates occurred against the backdrop of a society marked by much less inequality than today.[36]

New Labour

New Labour was elected after 18 years of opposition in 1997 in a society much changed since 1979. The Thatcher Governments had pursued a radically different strategy from that which had gone before: the so-called 'trickle-down' theory.[37] This stated that, by reducing taxes on higher earners, they became incentivised to work harder and to produce more economic wealth. In turn this would allow more of that wealth to trickle down to the poor. The result would be that the absolute position of the poor would improve, but their relative position would decline as the absolute position of the rich increased at a faster rate. The resulting inequality between rich and poor would not matter since the concern of the poor was their absolute position and since inequality was categorically distinct from poverty. The strategy was important since it would be the mechanism through which the poor would accept the free market economy. The strategy, however, was a failure. By the mid-1980s it was clear that in contrast to raising the incomes of the poorest they were actually falling. Even by the end of 18 years of Conservative rule, the position of the lowest income quintile had only slightly improved. In contrast the position of the highest quintile improved substantially. The result was therefore a significant increase in inequality. Measured in terms of the Gini coefficient, inequality in original (pre-tax) income increased from 43 per cent in 1979 to 53 per cent by 1997. Similarly, inequalities in the level of disposable (post-tax and transfer payments) income increased from 28 per cent in 1979 to 33 per cent by 1997.[38]

What then has happened under New Labour? The short answer is that inequality in incomes has remained broadly constant, even taking account of all the measures introduced by the Government since coming to power in 1997.[39] It is clear that New Labour has redistributed substantially over the course of six years. The specific measures introduced since 1997 are many and complex. Space does not permit any detailed examination of these measures.[40] However, two points should be stressed. The first is that the cumulative impact of Gordon Brown's budgets has been strongly progressive. The lowest income decile had gained on average 13 per cent in their net incomes by 2001. The contribution of the budget to the growth of incomes had fallen progressively throughout the income range, with the top 10 per cent benefiting by just 0.1 per cent.[41] According to Alissa Goodman these changes had occurred largely as a result of substantial increases in means-tested benefits targeted at families and pensioners.[42] Those who had benefited less are single people, both in and out of work. The net results of the April 2002 budget, with the 1 per cent increase in national insurance across the income range, are difficult to calculate. However, it is unlikely to alter the current distribution in incomes.

This leads to the second important consideration. This is that much of what New Labour has done has been hidden behind a discourse of social inclusion, which masks the redistributive impact of fiscal policy. Ruth Lister has referred to this as redistribution by stealth.[43] The language employed by New Labour, that it is not a tax and spend party and so forth, fits uncomfortably with what has actually happened. It is probably the case that New Labour employs such language due to the fear of electoral repercussions from a more explicit endorsement of redistribution. However, as Lister goes on to say, this in turn may backfire as an electoral strategy when those who have incurred higher taxes begin to realise, since 'doing good by stealth has the disadvantage of not being seen to be doing good'.[44] To this extent, the 2002 budget may mark a turning-point since Brown's call for a national debate on the funding of the Welfare State makes the issue of redistribution once again explicit, although it may be said that it is not entirely clear what has happened in this debate so far.[45]

The difficulty for New Labour is that although the budget has cumulatively had a redistributive impact it has done little, if indeed anything, to alter the existing income inequalities. It is certainly true that the absolute position of the lowest income quintile has improved more substantially than under the Thatcher Governments, increasing by about 1.5 per cent compared to 0.1 per cent in real terms; although it should be pointed out that this improvement in the position of the lowest income quintile since 1997 is lower than the 1.9 per cent growth achieved under Major.[46] Moreover, the growth in the incomes of the lowest income quintile is below the average growth rate in incomes of 2 per cent, and even the second quintile has experienced a rate below the average.[47] This is despite the introduction of the national minimum wage and the introduction of employment schemes which would impact on lower earners.

There are four reasons why the income growth of the lower earners has not kept pace with others. The first is that average incomes have been rising much faster than previously (2 per cent, compared to 1 per cent between 1990 and 1997). Second, the higher rate on Income Tax – the major means of redistributing income directly – has not been raised since 1997. These two factors together have resulted in the fastest income growth occurring in the top income quintile since 1997 (2.5 per cent).[48] Third, Government action has been focused on attaining higher, if not full, employment. There has not been a substantial increase in welfare payments to the worse-off, with the exception of old age pensions and child benefits mentioned above, and although there has been price indexing of state benefits, there has been no such link to earnings. This has affected the position of those in the lowest income decile, who depend on cash benefits for over 60 per cent of their total income.[49] The final reason is that the timing of the introduction of anti-poverty measures has affected their impact. The decision to maintain Conservative spending plans for the first two years of the Labour Government meant that the level of inequality increased so that measures introduced in the rest of the first term only had the effect of reversing this trend. New Labour has had to do more just to stop inequality increasing. This is not to deny, however, that measures introduced since the end of the last Parliament will not have an impact on reducing further the amount of absolute poverty and indeed the position of the poor relative to the average. There are however two crucial limitations to New Labour's strategy. The first is that the approach to poverty is highly selective with the result that those in poverty but falling outside the targeted groups will be unlikely to see an improvement in their position. Second, Government measures are unlikely to reduce income and wealth inequality without tackling the inequality which exists at the top, which in effect means increases in higher rates of direct taxation.

Moving from policy to the underlying values of New Labour, it becomes apparent that there has indeed been a change in the approach to equality. This has been expressed clearly by Raymond Plant:

> the government wants to restrict its rhetoric of equality to equality of opportunity and to resist developing any other conception of equality to describe its social goals and to restrict the language of greater social and economic equality to social exclusion. Social exclusion is seen very much in terms of opportunity and its denial.[50]

Two concepts are important to New Labour and are mentioned here. The first is equality of opportunity. Blair has listed opportunity as one of his core values, by which he presumably means equality of opportunity since he cites equal worth as another one of his core values.[51] It is the assertion of the principle of equal worth which Blair believes links New Labour to the Party's past, a point to which I return in the next section. New Labour's approach to equality of opportunity is given its clearest expression in Brown's 1997 Crosland Memorial Lecture. Brown argued that 'our commitment to equality is as strong as ever.'[52] However, this belief was expressed in terms of a 'strong' equality of opportunity, which consists of three things. The first is the creation of employment opportunities for all, since this is the most effective way of ensuring that individual aspirations are fulfilled and that the community benefits from economic prosperity. Second, and following on from the first point, the creation of life-long educational opportunities, since the most effective way of creating employment opportunities in a technologically advanced and globalised economy is to educate and train individuals. Finally, access to political power and cultural amenities. This conception of equality of opportunity, it must be stressed, is different from the 'weak' conception of equality of opportunity in which people only have limited life chances. Such a notion of equality of opportunity is related to positive liberty since it is about providing people with the resources and opportunities to pursue their own objectives rather than merely removing external constraints to action – a negative conception of liberty – as promoted by the neo-liberals.

The second important concept here is that of social inclusion. This is also placed at the centre of New Labour's values. The Social Exclusion Unit has been established, and a range of measures introduced at a national and local level to tackle the problem of social exclusion. Social exclusion is defined, as Plant has argued, in terms of the absence of opportunities, such as work. It is seen as a more useful concept than poverty, since poverty implies the absence of a sufficient income. Instead, social exclusion can mean the absence of other things such as decent housing, public transport and so forth. Social exclusion also relates to another value promoted by New Labour, that of community, since it is recognised that the absence of resources and opportunities can often affect communities, such as inner-city housing estates, due to the persistence of high unemployment, drug abuse, higher crime rates, vandalism and so on. Social inclusion has increasingly come to be seen, as Ruth Levitas has pointed out, in terms of paid work.[53] Social exclusion refers to absence from the labour market. The socially included, who can be termed active citizens, are in paid work. One moves from being socially excluded to being socially included by taking paid work; hence the significance New Labour attaches to welfare-to-work schemes. Social exclusion can be recast in terms of paid work for those who can and welfare for those who cannot.

Although New Labour claims to be recasting traditional values in a modern setting, so that values (or ends) remain fixed but policies (or means) have changed, I wish to argue that this framework differs from an egalitarian one. There are two reasons for this. The first relates to those who are not in paid work, not all of whom can be regarded as being 'socially excluded'. For those who cannot work, for example the retired or those with very young children or the severely disabled, New Labour has promised to maintain welfare payments. Even here, however, there has been a shift of emphasis away from a more conventional egalitarian perspective. Levitas points to the problem of equating all work to paid work.[54] She points to the existence of a large number of unpaid workers, such as home carers and charity workers, whose value to the economy is considerable[55] but is not taken into account by New Labour with its concentration on paid work.

The second distinction to be drawn between New Labour's commitment to a strong equality of opportunity and the case for democratic equality, of which we can take Crosland's thesis as the paradigmatic example, is over market outcomes. One may presume that if starting points are deemed to be fair given the existence of a strong equality of opportunity, then market outcomes are also deemed to be fair. New Labour are therefore willing to accept, it seems to me, whatever distributional affects result from the operation of a free market coupled with a strong equality of opportunity, even if this means that income inequality increases. In contrast, market outcomes are still deemed unfair by democratic egalitarians since they depend upon factors beyond the control of individuals. This in turn rests upon a particular understanding of social justice, which I believe to be credible and to which I return in the next section. New Labour therefore accepts a greater role for the operation of the market than the Old Right of the Labour Party.

New Labour appears to reject any concern with market-generated substantive inequalities. Blair came close to endorsing the 'trickle-down' theory, that the generation of high incomes at the top will ultimately benefit the poor as economic activity increases, in his *Newsnight* interview during the 2001 General Election campaign. The 'trickle-down' theory was a key part of economic liberalism. Those close to New Labour have endorsed, at least at the level of rhetoric, New Right theory in two senses. First, New Labour accepts a much greater need for economic incentives than did 'old' Labour. Indeed, Peter Mandelson and Roger Liddle argue that the recognition of the need for incentives is one of the main cleavages between 'old' and New Labour:

New Labour's belief in the dynamic market economy involves recognition that substantial personal incentives and rewards are necessary in order to encourage risk-taking and entrepreneurialism. Profit is not a dirty word – profits are accepted as the motor of private enterprise. Differences in income and personal spending power are the inevitable consequence of the existence of markets.[56]

This point is endorsed by the pioneer of the Third Way, Anthony Giddens, in his acceptance of the key neo-liberal idea of the Laffer Curve: that high tax rates lead to a diminished tax yield as they deter incentives.[57] Second, there is an emphasis in the writing of leading New Labour thinkers on individual responsibility, akin to neo-Conservatism. Again, Giddens sums this up when he advocates 'no rights without responsibilities'.[58] Applied to the unemployed this means no right to welfare payments without the responsibility on the part of the recipient to look for work. Geoff Mulgan, the founder of the think-tank Demos and a key Blair adviser, has also stressed the need to tackle the dependency culture in such language which is reminiscent of the New Right.[59] Thinkers close to New Labour are therefore willing to accept more divergent market outcomes both to increase incentives and to reduce welfare dependency.

The case for equality

I have argued that New Labour's approach to the issue of equality marks a radical departure from the social democratic tradition, and it would appear that New Labour lacks a genuine concern over the level of substantive inequality generated in the market place. I wish to argue, by way of conclusion, that the traditional social democratic belief in social equality is still desirable. It may be argued that New Labour is social democratic in the sense that it maintains a belief in social justice, a positive conception of liberty and the importance of community. Indeed it does, yet New Labour's understanding of equality affects radically its approach to these other principles, so that it can be questioned whether New Labour is in fact social democratic in any meaningful sense. There are four reasons why a more traditional conception of equality, implying as it does a concern with market outcomes, is preferable to a strong equality of opportunity. The first reason for seeking to reduce substantive inequalities can be stated briefly. This is that it undermines the principle of equality of opportunity in itself since the creation of inequalities of outcome produced in one generation removes the equal starting points necessary for the operation of equality of opportunity in the next generation. Although advocates of equality of opportunity tend to argue that inequalities of outcome do not matter, it quickly becomes apparent that they do.

The second reason is that a rejection of the importance of substantive inequalities is inimical to the pursuit of social justice. This is so for two reasons. The first is that market outcomes, even after allowing for a strong equality of opportunity, may not be considered fair. Market outcomes depend on factors beyond the control of individuals. They may not be responsible fully for the outcomes they have attained. Such factors would include luck and so forth, which even the neo-liberal philosopher Hayek has accepted.[60] If we accept that the poor are not necessarily poor as a result of their own actions, as New Labour presumably does by promoting life-long educational opportunities for example, then it can also be accepted that the higher earners are not fully responsible for their high incomes. The second point follows on from this. Even if we accept that market outcomes can be the result of individuals who have sufficient responsibility for these outcomes, then it does not necessarily follow that market outcomes are just. Market outcomes are the result of the promotion of certain human attributes over others, yet it is not clear why one set of attributes should be promoted over others, with the result that society will become marked by inequalities in income and wealth.[61] There is no *a priori* reason why ability to compete in a market economy should be rewarded over other attributes and abilities. Cultural activities and caring for children and the elderly are all valuable to the wider community without sufficient reward within a market economy. There is no reason why those involved in such activities should not see a decline in their relative position under a framework of a strong equality of opportunity, yet such an outcome may be deemed unfair by a majority in society.

Strategies of empowerment have become popular in recent years. The origins of the concept of empowerment are in feminist and radical theories,[62] yet the word has come to have a much wider usage. The New Right spoke of empowering individuals by removing external constraints on their actions. Similarly, New Labour has spoken of empowering people by creating genuine opportunities for them. For example, Blair said of the New Deal programme of reducing long-term and youth unemployment, 'it is empowerment in action and I am proud of it.'[63] Again it should be pointed out that these positions are very different, yet both spoke of empowerment while allowing for significant disparities in income and wealth. I wish to argue that the creation of genuine empowerment is best understood in terms of the need to reduce inequalities. Third Way notions of power, defined as 'power to', or what Giddens calls 'generative power', are limited since they lack an understanding of the relational view of power.[64] Roy Hattersley argues that 'one crucial advantage of moving towards a more equal income level is the opportunity which it provides to allow more citizens to make their own choices.'[65] For Hattersley, then, the ability for individuals to make their own choices, what can be termed the empowering of citizens, is closely related to greater equality of outcome. This is so because of the nature of power. If we take power to mean the power of A over B, then power is clearly relational since it refers to the relationship between A and B, and it is positional since A has power and B does not.[66] Yet if we follow an empowering strategy for all then it becomes apparent that inequality must be reduced. As B is empowered, so A loses his/her relative position. Hence, if we are to see the creation of a society in which people have genuine power over their own lives, then that society must be one marked by a reduction of inequalities, and as Raymond Plant says, 'empowerment has to be concerned with relativities and not just absolutes.'[67]

The final reason why we ought to be concerned with the reduction of substantive inequalities, rather than merely with equality of opportunity, is in fact social inclusion. New Labour, as I said earlier, has made much of the notion of social inclusion. However, as Ruth Lister points out,

> social exclusion is constructed as purely a problem at the bottom of society, ignoring the self-exclusion of those at the top whose massive income and wealth can cut them off from the wider society and from the bonds of common citizenship.[68]

The existence of substantive inequalities damages social cohesion and undermines the principle of equal worth to which Blair says he is committed.[69] In turn this has implications for communitarian politics, with its emphasis on the need to balance rights with responsibilities. Since social exclusion is expressed by New Labour as a problem affecting the bottom of society, it is here where the burden of responsibility mainly falls with no corresponding duties, such as the responsibility to pay higher direct taxation, falling on those at the top. A genuine communitarian politics therefore implies a greater sense of social equality.

Notes

1 I am very grateful to Matt Beech, John Hills, Ben Jackson, Ruth Lister and Raymond Plant for comments on an earlier draft of this chapter. Any errors are of course my own.
2 See Plant, R., 'Democratic Socialism and Equality', in Lipsey, D. and Leonard, D., *The Socialist Agenda: Crosland's Legacy* (Jonathan Cape, London, 1981).
3 For race see Parekh, B., 'Equality in a Multicultural Society', and for gender see Phillips, A., 'What has Socialism got to do with Sexual Equality', both in Franklin, J. (ed.) *Equality* (IPPR, London, 1997).
4 It is interesting to remember that a tough stance on immigration by Labour Governments was common before the advent of New Labour and that the liberal reforms introduced by Roy Jenkins as Home Secretary between 1964–1967 were the exception rather than the norm.
5 Tawney, R.H., *Equality* (George Allen and Unwin, London, 1931).
6 See his 'British Socialism Today' in Hinden, R. (ed.) *The Radical Tradition* (Allen and Unwin, London, 1964).
7 Jay, D., *The Socialist Case* (Faber, London, 1937).
8 Dalton, H., *Practical Socialism for Britain* (Routledge, London, 1935) and Durbin, E.F.M., *The Politics of Democratic Socialism*, (Routledge, London, 1940). For Durbin, it was essential that equality be obtained by democratic means. Equality without democracy was itself an injustice. The significance of *The Politics of Democratic Socialism* was that it demonstrated that equality could be achieved by democratic means, thus providing a useful critique of 1930s British Marxism.
9 *Ibid.*, Dalton, p. 319.
10 Plant, R., 'Social Democracy', in Marquand, D. and Seldon, A., *The Ideas that Shaped Postwar Britain* (Fontana, London, 1996).
11 Henry Drucker argues that there was a fundamental distinction between Tawney and Crosland on the issue of equality, since the former advocated equality of respect, whereas the latter only of opportunity and income. I find Drucker's treatment rather weak. First, I find no such distinction between Tawney and Crosland here, since

Crosland said a lot about equality of respect in terms of class relations and so forth. Second, I prefer to use a distinction between three forms of equality: opportunity, outcome and what can be termed 'democratic' equality, which I go on to explain. I do find Tawney more convincing on the moral case for equality, however. See Drucker, H.M., *Doctrine and Ethos in the Labour Party* (Allen and Unwin, London, 1979), pp. 44–67.

12 For a discussion of the 1945–51 Labour Government see Morgan, K.O., *Labour in Power 1945–51* OUP, Oxford, 1985).

13 Crosland, C.A.R., *The Future of Socialism* (Cape, London, 1956).

14 *Ibid.*, pp. 1–42.

15 *Ibid.*, pp. 43–80.

16 *Ibid.*, pp.150–69.

17 *Ibid.*, p. 168.

18 Crosland, C.A.R., *The Conservative Enemy* (Jonathan Cape, London, 1962).

19 Crosland, C.A.R., 'Socialism Now' in Leonard, D. (ed.) *Socialism Now and Other Essays* (Jonathan Cape, London, 1974).

20 Vaizey, J., 'Remembering Anthony Crosland', *Encounter*, August, 1977.

21 Crosland, C.A.R., *The Future of Socialism*, p. 140.

22 *Ibid.* p. 140.

23 Crosland, C.A.R., 'Socialism Now', p. 46. See also Crosland, C.A.R., *Social Democracy in Europe*, Fabian Tract 438, London, 1975.

24 See Plant, R., 'Democratic Socialism and Equality' in Lipsey, D. and Leonard, D., *The Socialist Agenda: Crosland's Legacy*, for a probable response to the neo-liberals on these issues.

25 Plant, R., *Equality, Markets and the State*, Fabian Tract 494, London, 1984, and Hattersley, R., *Choose Freedom: The Politics of Democratic Socialism* (Penguin, London, 1987).

26 The extent to which revisionist ideas had an impact on Labour when in government has been rightly criticised in this volume by Kevin Jefferys, however.

27 See his main work *Planning for Freedom* (Hamish Hamilton, London, 1965).

28 Foote, G., *The Labour Party's Political Thought: A History* (Macmillan, Basingstoke, 1997), p. 285. Crossman himself came to hold a position dissimilar to revisionism. See *Socialism and Planning*, Fabian Tract 375, London, 1967.

29 See, in particular, 'Blair and Ideology' in Seldon, A. (ed.) *The Blair Effect* (Little Brown, London, 2001).

30 Crossman, R.H.S., *Paying for the Social Services*, Fabian Tract 399, London, 1969.

31 The crucial text here is Holland, S., *The Socialist Challenge* (Quartet, London, 1975).

32 Lukes, S., 'Socialism and Equality' in his *Essays in Social Theory* (Macmillan, London, 1977).

33 Holland, S., *The Socialist Challenge*, pp. 169–74.

34 This is because much of the substantial amount of literature produced by those on the New Left in the 1970s was directed at the issues of economic power and industrial democracy.

35 Shaw, G.B., *The Intelligent Woman's Guide to Socialism and Capitalism* (Constable, London, 1928).

36 The most detailed analysis of the changing pattern of income distribution in the post-war period was the Royal Commission on the Distribution of Income and Wealth chaired by Lord Diamond, which showed that there had indeed been a substantial reduction in inequality, with the biggest reduction occurring between 1938 and 1950, but with a further reduction since 1950 resulting from the operation of public policy (the top 10 per cent had 34.6 per cent of income in 1938, but only 21.4 per cent by the 1970s).

37 For a discussion of the trickle-down theory see Hoover, K. and Plant, R., *Conservative Capitalism in Britain and the United States: A Critical Appraisal* (Routledge, London, 1989), pp. 205–35.

38 See Goodman, A., 'Income Inequality: What has happened under New Labour?' in *New Economy* Vol. 8, No. 2, June 2001, pp. 92–7; p.93.

39 Figures published in March 2003 show that although there was a slight fall in income inequality in the year 2002–03, overall income inequality has increased since Labour came to power in 1997. See, 'Households Below Average Incomes: 2001/02', DWP, London, March 2003.

40 See Glennerster, H., 'Social Policy', in Seldon, A., (ed.) *The Blair Effect* (Little Brown, London, 2001).

41 Goodman, A., 'Income Inequality: What has happened under New Labour?' in *New Economy* p. 96.

42 *Ibid.*, p. 96.

43 Lister, R., 'Doing Good by Stealth: the politics of poverty and inequality under New Labour', *New Economy* Vol. 8, No. 2, June 2001, pp. 65–70.

44 *Ibid.*, p. 66.

45 Blair's first public statement that he believes in redistribution, made in September 2002, can be seen as another contribution.

46 Goodman, A., 'Income Inequality: What has happened under New Labour?' in *New Economy*, p. 95. This was largely due to the redistributive effects of the abolition of the Poll Tax and the introduction of the Council Tax with its associated benefits and rebates for low earners. Income inequality increased after 1995.

47 *Ibid.*, p. 95.

48 *Ibid.*

49 Harris, T., 'The Effects of Taxes and Benefits on Household Income, 1997–1998', *Economic Trends*, No. 545, April 1999, pp. 27–39; p. 32.

50 Plant, R., 'Crosland, Equality and New Labour', in Leonard, D. (ed.), *Crosland and New Labour* (Macmillan, London, 1999).

51 Blair, T., *The Third Way: New Politics for the New Century* (Fabian Society, London, 1998). His other listed values are responsibility and community.

52 Brown, G., 'Equality – Then and Now' in Leonard, D., (ed.) *Crosland and New Labour* (Macmillan, London, 1999), p. 47.

53 Levitas, R., *The Inclusive Society? Social Exclusion and New Labour* (Macmillan, London, 1998).

54 *Ibid.*, p.8.

55 Levitas states a figure within the range of £341 billion to £739 billion. *Ibid.*

56 Mandelson, P. and Liddle, R., *The Blair Revolution* (Faber and Faber, London, 1996).

57 Giddens, A., *The Third Way and Its Critics* (Polity Press, Cambridge, 2000), p. 97.

58 Giddens, A., *The Third Way: The Renewal of Social Democracy* (Polity Press, Cambridge, 1998), p. 65.

59 See Levitas, R., *The Inclusive Society? Social Exclusion and New Labour*, pp. 152–6.

60 Hayek rejects any notion that the market distributes according to any fixed principle. I am grateful to Raymond Plant for discussions on this point.

61 This point was made by Crosland, C.A.R., *The Future of Socialism*, p. 168, in his rejection of equality of opportunity as a sufficient social democratic objective.

62 See Dominelli, L., 'Empowerment: Help or Hindrance in Professional Relationships', in Stepney, P. and Ford, D. (eds), *Social Work Models, Methods and Theories: A Framework for Practice*, (Russell House, Lyme Regis, 2000).

63 Blair, T., 'Beveridge Revisited: A Welfare State for the 21st Century' in Walker, R. (ed.) *Ending Child Poverty: Popular Welfare for the 21st Century* (Polity, Bristol, 1999).

64 Giddens, A., *Modernity and Self-Identity* (Polity Press, Cambridge, 1991), pp. 211–14.

65 Hattersley, R., *Choose Freedom: The Politics of Democratic Socialism*, p. 137.

66 By 'positional' I follow Fred Hirsch who says that certain goods have value derived from their scarcity. The wider dispersal of such goods results in their loss of value. See Hirsch, F., *Social Limits to Growth* (Routledge, London, 1977).

67 Plant, R., 'Why Social Justice?', in Boucher, D. and Kelly, P. (eds), *Social Justice From Hume to Walzer* (Routledge, London,1998), p. 276.

68 Lister, R., 'Doing Good by Stealth', p. 67. See also Lister, R., 'From Equality to Social Inclusion: New Labour and the Welfare State', *Critical Social Policy*, 55, 1998.

69 It's somewhat paradoxical that Giddens accepts this point given his endorsement of the Laffer curve mentioned earlier. See Giddens, A., *The Third Way: The Renewal of Social Democracy*, p. 42.

8 Globalisation

Anthony McGrew

Globalisation is with us. It is not just here to stay. It is here to accelerate.

Rt Hon. Robin Cook, Foreign Secretary.[1]

The driving force behind the ideas associated with the Third Way is globalisation because no country is immune from the massive change that globalisation brings.

Rt Hon. Tony Blair, Prime Minister.[2]

Third way politics should take a positive attitude towards globalisation – but, crucially, only as a phenomenon ranging much more widely than the global marketplace.[3]

Introduction

Globalisation – as both an idea and a historical process – is at the heart of the New Labour project. For its advocates, the 'Third Way' represents a genuine attempt to reconstruct social democracy to fit with the conditions of really existing globalisation. Failure to implement such modernisation, it is argued, makes the outlook for social democracy decidedly grim. To its critics the 'Third Way' represents surrender to the dictates of global capital and a calculated political strategy, resting on the hubris of globalisation, to deny the plausibility of more radical alternatives. What is at issue in this confrontation is a fundamental disagreement about the 'facts' of globalisation and its implications for social democracy and progressive politics. Globalisation, as both process and ideology, is pivotal to explaining the genesis of New Labour, its political programme, its philosophy of progressive governance, and the continuing existential struggle concerning Labour's political identity and future trajectory.

This chapter examines how and why globalisation came to acquire totemic status in the philosophy and project of New Labour. Although strongly associated with the realignment of the Left, following the end of the Cold War and the hegemony of neo-liberalism, the construction of globalisation as a 'modernizing juggernaut' has figured much more explicitly in the rhetoric of New Labour (and the New Democrats) than in that of its European counterparts.[4] This captivation, if not capture, of New Labour by the globalisation discourse requires explaining. Two accounts are offered and explored: the instrumentalist and the neo-revisionist. Whilst the latter is judged more convincing, for reasons which are subsequently discussed, the chapter concludes by examining the stability of the New Labour political settlement confronted by the twin forces of globalisation and European integration. The chapter commences with an exegesis of the principal themes in New Labour's globalisation rhetoric.

Rhetoric

From the 1980s onwards, globalisation – or the process of intensifying world-wide interconnectedness – figured prominently in Labour's internal debates on reform. Responding to the challenge of Thatcherism, monetarism and the significant socio-economic shifts which were underway in Britain, Neil Kinnock initiated a series of policy reviews which sought to redefine Labour's political identity and strategy. In reflecting upon the dissolution of the British post-war political settlement these policy reviews adopted much of the then current orthodoxy, on both the left and right, that global economic integration increasingly made Keynesian-style managed capitalism unworkable.[5] The failure of the Mitterrand experiment in the early 1980s, when France's socialist government abandoned its radical economic strategy partly in response to the reactions of global financial markets, reinforced this presumption. Moreover, this orthodoxy spoke to the deeply rooted suspicion within Labour – especially on the left – of financiers and global capital, captured in Harold Wilson's caustic phrase 'the gnomes of Zurich'; a suspicion deeply ingrained in Labour's political psyche by the 'forced' devaluations of 1949, 1967 and the IMF crisis of 1976. As the 'Big Bang', the communications revolution and the neo-liberal advance combined to create the infrastructure of a more integrated global economy, the conditions for the achievement of 'democratic socialism in one country' appeared to have been radically transformed and the vision itself to be increasingly at odds with the direction of social change. Like its New Democrat counterparts in the US, from whom it borrowed intellectually, Labour sought to adapt to these 'New Times'.

As acknowledged by the 1987 policy review, 'Social Justice and Economic Efficiency', the state's role was increasingly circumscribed not just by the Conservatives' domestic reforms but also by global factors. In effect, as the report stated, the 'freedom of national governments is seriously constrained by international trading agreements, competitive pressures, the huge flows of capital across frontiers, and the decisions of multinational firms'.[6] Hay has admirably documented how this discursive construction of the globalising economy as a distinctive new era increasingly took hold of the policy review process such that by the early 1990s globalisation came to provide a crucial rationale for the modernisation programme of New Labour and the advocacy of Third Way politics.[7] As Schmidt argues, this discourse of globalisation operated simultaneously both strategically, as a coordinative mechanism offering an overarching paradigm which rationalised and gave coherence to the New Labour project, and ideologically by demonstrating and communicating the necessity for, and thus the legitimacy of, the renewal of social democracy.[8] Just as Crosland's revisionism was prompted by the rise of Cold War 'managed capitalism' so the revisionism of New Labour was conceived as a 'progressive' response to the novel circumstances of globalisation and the hegemony of neo-liberal ideas.[9] Whether this revisionism constitutes more of a capitulation to the neo-liberal agenda than a progressive alternative, will be discussed later. At this point it may be valuable to explore in a little more detail the nature and logic of New Labour's globalisation discourse and its connection to the modernisation and renewal of social democracy.

Four distinctive themes can be discerned in New Labour's globalisation discourse as it has evolved from the period of opposition to its second period in office. These four themes can be identified as: globalisation as New Times; globalisation as constraint; globalisation as opportunity; and globalisation as solidarity.

Globalisation as New Times

As noted, the policy reviews of the 1980s, and the elaboration of the Third Way in the 1990s, were premised on the argument that intensifying globalisation compromised traditional forms of social democracy. In essence economic globalisation was associated with an irresistible structural transformation in the organisation and dynamics of capitalism: the growth of global markets, the dynamics of a real-time global financial system, the emergence of the knowledge economy, significant shifts in the organisation and location of production induced by greater capital mobility, and the consequent intensification of worldwide competition.[10] Castells refers to this constellation of factors as 'the new global informational capitalism'.[11] Combined with the supply-side revolution of the 1980s some considered this 'global informational capitalism' as ushering in a new economic paradigm in which the 'boom and slump' logic of capitalism was being replaced by a revolution in productivity.[12] Managing the economy to ensure the conditions for continued prosperity principally required financial stability and labour market flexibility.

This 'New Economy', it was argued, inevitably imposed constraints upon the autonomy of states, but most especially upon governments pursuing traditional social democratic programmes of redistribution and Keynesian counter-cyclical fiscal policies. As Blair put it: 'in a global economy the old ways [of social democracy] won't do'.[13] The reasoning was fairly obvious: the 'old' tax and spend strategy would be punished by global financial markets, whilst the mobility of capital and intensified global trade competition reduced the capacity of governments to finance generous welfare states. In Blair's words, under conditions of globalisation, modern social democracy had to operate within 'an open economy working with the grain of global change: disciplined in macro-economic and fiscal policy'.[14] 'The Third Way', according to Giddens, constituted a radical renewal of social democracy to fit the terms of this 'new economy' by advocating a progressive political programme which offered a realistic alternative to both discredited statist social democracy and the dystopia of the unfettered market of the neo-liberal ideologues.[15]

Of course the 'Third Way', as Giddens carefully explained, was not purely a response to the transformations in capitalism, crucial as that was.[16] Rather it spoke to other transformations which further reinforced the secular logic of 'New Times', from pervasive social changes, such as the rise of individualism, to the popular loss of faith in big government, the global hegemony of capitalism in the wake of the collapse of state socialism, and the emergence of new political agendas and allegiances which transcended traditional party politics.[17] As Blair explained, 'What globalisation is doing is bringing in its wake profound economic and social changes, economic change rendering all jobs in industry, sometimes new jobs in new industries, redundant overnight and social change that is a change to culture, to life-style, to the family, to established patterns of community life'.[18] Accordingly the 'Third Way' represented a philosophy, and 'New Labour' a programme, of progressive governance designed to 'help citizens pilot their way through the major revolutions of our time'.[19] For Blair and the advocates of the 'Third Way' what was clear was that 'Now with globalisation, a new era has begun.'[20]

Globalisation as challenge

Globalisation, and 'New Times', thereby were constructed as presenting social democrats especially with significant political challenges and choices. As Blair observed on entering government, 'Our task today is not to fight old battles but to show that there is a Third Way, a way of marrying together an open, competitive and successful economy with a just, decent and humane society'.[21] The challenges encompassed both the renewal of the social democratic project and the modernisation of Labour as a party of government. In key respects, as Callaghan notes, much of the work of sweeping away the legacy of Old Labour, from corporatism to interventionism, was completed in the policy reviews of the 1980s before 'the globalisation mantra was adopted'.[22] By the 1990s the imperatives of globalisation, however, invested both the renewal and modernisation agendas with a greater impetus. As Hay and others have argued, the intensification of globalisation was invoked as a process of inevitable change which necessitated a process of fundamental social and political adjustment.[23] There were no alternatives, noted Blair, but to 'accept globalisation and work with it'.[24]

Ideological renewal was necessary, as noted, both to distance 'New Labour' from the failed policies of Old Labour and to distinguish it from the Conservative's neo-liberal agenda. This ideological renewal, in the guise of the Third Way, however, was only tenuously related to the modernisation programme which dominated the shift from Old to 'New Labour'. It lent credence to the notions of an active – not an interventionary – state, to combining economic efficiency with social justice, financial prudence with social investment, and patriotism with international solidarity. Beyond this task of ideological renewal, of reconstructing the ideals of social democracy for the twenty-first century, the modernisation programme came to be defined, in several critical respects, as a response to the imperatives and constraints of globalisation. In effect globalisation acquired the role of a modernising force, one to be welcomed, despite its challenges. By comparison with the Conservatives whose ' … pro-globalisation discourse … followed from [Thatcher's] ideologically grounded, neo-liberal justification for change, Blair's pro-globalisation discourse has presented globalisation as the primary rationale for neo-liberal reform'.[25]

Accommodating the imperatives of globalisation required re-engineering the state's strategic role in the economy away from intervention to regulation. Modernisation involved accepting a more limited role for the state in managing capitalism within a globalising world economy. Limited, in the sense of recognising the constraints imposed on governments by the operation of global financial markets, global economic competition, the mobility of productive capital, and systems of global economic governance. These, it was argued, operated together to restrict government's economic autonomy in areas from fiscal to industrial and labour market policies. Global financial markets respected fiscal prudence and macro-economic stability whilst greater capital mobility put downward pressure on corporate taxation and increased competition for corporate investment. Likewise, increased openness to trade, and the liberalisation of markets, magnified the domestic consequences of global competition for regional policies, jobs and local communities. Working with the 'grain of globalisation' meant adjusting to these new realities by pursuing policies of fiscal prudence, macroeconomic stability, flexible labour markets, and enhancing the global competitiveness of British business. Modernisation therefore required a significant erosion – some might say abandonment – of the market logic of the social democratic state replaced by the market enhancing role of the state. As Stephen Byers, when Secretary of State for Trade and Industry, explained this shift, 'there is a role for an active as opposed to an interventionist government. Our role should be to lead people through this process of [global] change.'[26]

Such a manifest shift in the state's strategic role, under conditions of globalisation, was accompanied by advocacy of the modernisation of the Welfare State. Since global bond markets, fiscal and economic competition, amongst other factors, restricted the scope for growth in government spending, the reform of welfare became a high priority. Modernisation implied a shift from the traditional Welfare State to the 'social investment state', namely from full employment to flexible employment. In short, from the 'handout' state to the 'enabling' state. Social exclusion and poverty were to be addressed through measures, from education to tax credits, to increase employability and integration into the labour market rather than simply through income replacement.[27] Wider reform of welfare structures too, from the delivery of education to the provision of health, was conditioned by the logic of globalisation. For Blair the modernising consequences of globalisation were clear, 'Out goes the Big State.

In comes the Enabling State. Out goes a culture of benefits and entitlements. In comes a partnership of rights and responsibilities.'[28] Globalisation is therefore associated with a shift from government to governance: a process in which the state's primary role becomes the strategic coordination of a multiplicity of agencies, public and private, beyond, below and astride the state to achieve collective political goals and the delivery of services.[29]

Globalisation as opportunity

Although in New Labour thinking globalisation was more often than not conceived as a straitjacket, it was, as Friedmann points out, a 'Golden Straitjacket'.[30] With allusion to the Golden Age of welfare capitalism Friedmann considers globalisation as potentially creating an epoch of unprecedented opportunity and prosperity, most especially for the West. Underlying this view is a notion of globalisation as a virtuous circle, with liberalisation bringing economic growth and prosperity reinforcing global integration and stability in turn enhancing world peace and security. Not surprisingly, given its roots in eighteenth and nineteenth-century liberal thinking, the virtuous circle has been rediscovered by many of the advocates of market-driven globalisation. Aspects of such thinking, in modified form, can be identified in New Labour's globalisation discourse. Stephen Byers, when Trade and Industry Secretary, explained New Labour's embrace of globalisation in the following terms,

> If we turn our backs on globalisation then we will end up retreating into nationalism and protectionism ... Free trade causes and boosts economic growth. It is about economic competition which weakens the power of vested interests. It provides greater opportunities and improved standards of living for millions rather than providing privileges for the few.[31]

This advocacy of globalisation was associated with the belief that it constituted a process of benign social change. Unlike many previous Labour Governments, and many on the left of the Party, who considered globalisation to be the problem not the cure, 'New Labour' offered a different diagnosis. If globalisation was inevitable it was no longer to be resisted but to be positively embraced. Even former radicals, such as Robin Cook, espoused this position noting, 'We don't want to be Little England. We want to build a Global Britain. A country which accepts globalisation as an opportunity to be seized, not a threat to be resisted.'[32] Giddens too, in elaborating 'Third Way' politics, advocated that social democrats should 'take a positive attitude towards globalisation'.[33] However, this 'positive attitude' was tempered by a recognition that globalisation had to be regulated, to varying degrees, to advance the goals of social justice. This required more robust and effective forms of regional and global governance not only to enable globalisation but also to curb the worst excesses of global markets and to confront the host of transnational problems which it brought in its wake. Working within and through, rather than against, existing multilateral institutions of global and regional governance, from the WTO to the EU, was considered to be the most effective strategy for simultaneously advancing the dynamic of globalisation and the pursuit of social justice. Managing globalisation, rather than crudely resisting its imperatives, became an increasingly salient phrase in the lexicon of 'New Labour'.

Globalisation as solidarity

Benign as it was generally assumed to be, globalisation was also identified in 'New Labour' thinking as a source of significant insecurities and inequalities. In elaborating the 'Third Way', Giddens made much of its inherent risks and exclusions.[34] These new risks and insecurities were interpreted as reinforcing the case for the renewal and modernisation of the social democratic project. Addressing the Labour Party Conference in October 2002, Tony Blair commenced by reminding his audience that 'Globalisation and technology open up vast new opportunities but also cause massive insecurity. The values of progressive politics – solidarity, justice for all – have never been more relevant; and their application never more in need of modernisation.'[35] Solidarity in the face of globalisation and solidarity through globalisation have been significant themes in the language of 'New Labour'.

Cultivating the traditional internationalism of the left, around the twin themes of solidarity and justice, was associated with considerable enthusiasm for the EU, and for multilateral institutions, as mechanisms for managing and mediating the insecurities and risks produced by globalisation. This solidarity ethic was expressed in the language of global responsibility and economic security most vociferously articulated by Gordon Brown and Clare Short amongst others. In advancing the cause of global solidarity and justice Clare Short carefully constructed the aspirations of 'New Labour' as a return to the traditional internationalist values of Old Labour:

> the management of this globalised world is the most important challenge facing our Party and political tradition in the early years of the twenty-first century. Our Party has always been internationalist – but we have in the past seen it as our primary duty to create the conditions that would honour these values in our own country. But growing interdependence means that we cannot have economic security and social justice at home without an end to poverty, conflict and oppression across the world. Globalisation makes this task more urgent and progress more feasible. But it requires a strengthening not a weakening of our global institutions and a stronger commitment to development and the reduction of poverty.[36]

In a world in which globalisation is fuelling a growing gap between rich and poor, confronting the problem of global inequality is conceived not only as an ethical challenge but also ultimately as a threat to the security and prosperity of the West. Making globalisation work for the poor thus acquired a significant presence in the rhetoric of 'New Labour' but, for the most part, expressed as the progressive governance, rather than radical transformation, of the structures of global capitalism.

This commitment to global justice was borne of a cosmopolitan ethic which articulated a sense of responsibility for the plight of distant others. Solidarity, in this respect, was strongly associated with liberal humanitarianism. However, what distinguished 'New Labour', from its post-war heritage was a belief that in protecting and advancing universal principles of justice the claims of national sovereignty could not automatically take precedence. In effect, duties transcend borders and states had a responsibility to act to prevent humanitarian catastrophes, even if this ultimately required military intervention. This doctrine of humanitarian intervention was most clearly articulated by Blair in the wake of the 11 September 2001 tragedy:

> we are realising how fragile are our frontiers in the face of the world's new challenges ... Today conflicts rarely stay within national boundaries ... Today the threat is chaos; because for people with work to do, family life to balance, mortgages to pay, careers to further, pensions to provide, the yearning is for order and stability and if it doesn't exist elsewhere, it is unlikely to exist here ... I have long believed this interdependence defines the new world we live in .... when Milosevic embarked on the ethnic cleansing of Muslims in Kosovo, we acted ... we won, the refugees went home, the policies of ethnic cleansing were reversed and one of the great dictators of the last century will see justice in this century. And I tell you if Rwanda happened again today as it did in 1993, when a million people were slaughtered in cold blood, we would have a moral duty to act there also.[37]

For some on the left of the Party this 'liberal cosmopolitanism' harbours the danger of a new imperialism whilst on the right it represents a dangerous reversion to inter-war utopianism. Underlying this 'New Labour' internationalism is the foundational belief that globalisation is transforming the conditions of global stability and order and with this the mechanisms and prospects for realising solidarity and justice.

These four strands to 'New Labour's' globalisation discourse – New Times, challenge, opportunity and solidarity – present a rather more nuanced depiction than many contemporary analyses. It is evident, however, that for much of the public – and the Party too – the dominant strands have been those of New Times and challenge. This should be unsurprising in that, as Hay, amongst others, observes, in the construction of 'New Labour' the discourse of globalisation operated by 'rendering the contingent necessary'.[38] Whether this instrumentalist account is ultimately persuasive, however, remains to be judged.

Instrumentalism

What are we to make of this New Labour globalisation discourse? Why did the idea of globalisation come to play such a foundational role in the New Labour project? Does 'Third Way' politics represent the ultimate triumph of the neo-liberal agenda, or its nadir? How, if at all, have the policy priorities and programmes of New Labour in government been informed by this globalisation discourse? These questions have been central to contemporary assessments of New Labour. Amongst the most rigorous and critical assessments of the New Labour globalisation discourse is that arising on the left, articulated most systematically in the work of Callaghan, Coates, Hay, Hirst and Thompson amongst others.[39] Although significant differences exist between these accounts, both in relation to many of their specific claims and in their substantive focus, they tend to share certain assumptions and arguments in common. In particular, they share a profound scepticism towards: the globalisation thesis (its extent, significance and implications) considering it to be highly exaggerated; the presumption that it defines New Times and new constraints upon the social democratic state; the political conclusions drawn from this, namely that modernisation is the only viable political strategy for parties of the left; and the project and programme of New Labour which is conceived, at best, as a pragmatic accommodation with Thatcherism, and at worst, as a capitulation to the neo-liberal agenda. This reasoned scepticism advances what might be referred to as a broadly instrumentalist account of the globalisation discourse in the construction of New Labour.[40] Thus, in explaining the primacy of globalisation in New Labour rhetoric and thinking, Hay observes that 'The discourse of globalisation has been appropriated in order to render economically "necessary" the politically contingent logic of neo-liberal convergence.'[41]

Globalisation, according to this instrumentalist interpretation, played a – if not the – crucial role in rationalising, advancing and legitimating New Labour. It rendered, in Hay and Watson's phrase, 'the contingent necessary' since it denied the possibility and plausibility of political alternatives other than an adjustment to the realities of these globalised 'New Times'.[42] It functioned to suture together new social and political coalitions as well as to promote a new consensus around the politics of renewal and the Third Way. Yet it was the idea, much more than the facts, of globalisation which, according to this instrumentalist view, captured Labour's political imagination. As discussed previously, it was portrayed in Labour's internal and public discourse as a secular process of global economic and technological change which produced an imperative to political accommodation with the irresistible forces of the global marketplace. Globalisation eroded the autonomy of states, while the growing power of global markets and competition undermined the basis of social democracy: a strong, interventionist, redistributionist state with a capacity to transform capitalism to advance human welfare, social equality and solidarity. In these circumstances New Labour's political strategy was to advance the 'Third Way' as the only plausible alternative to the utopianism of 'social democracy in one country' and the failures of neo-liberal orthodoxy. However, for many on the left, the 'ideological battering ram of globalisation' was subject to much exaggeration and hyperbole.

According to Hirst and Thompson, the extent and intensity of economic globalisation have been significantly exaggerated.[43] Compared to the early twentieth century, the world of the 1990s, they argue, was much less politically and economically integrated such that they ' ... register a certain scepticism over whether we have entered a radically new phase in the internationalisation of economic activity'.[44] Even in the specific case of Britain the economy was much more open in the 'Belle Époque' of the 1890s, than it was in the early 1990s. These were not 'New Times' nor, as many argued, had the essential boom and bust logic of capitalism been replaced by the shift to a post-industrial order.[45] Globalisation was much more of a popular myth than a really existing condition.[46] If the extent of globalisation was exaggerated, so too, in particular, were its implications for the state and social democracy.[47] As Hay and Watson conclude, the constraints of the global economy on state autonomy and welfare expenditure were far less restrictive than the advocates of the Third Way made out.[48] Global financial markets did not prevent, nor necessarily punish, governments of the left for expansionary and intervention economic policies. Nor did global competition necessarily lead to a 'race to the bottom' in respect of social protection and labour market regulation. Economic globalisation therefore did not preordain the 'end of social democracy',[49] as Gray once commented, but on the contrary, 'the scope for negotiated social governance remains substantial'.[50] The evidence for this was to be found in the healthy state of social democracy and the success of progressive welfare reform, involving the preservation of generous welfare regimes, in Sweden, Denmark, Holland and other small but advanced industrial states.[51] Such cases were interpreted as validating the critics' argument that progressive alternatives to Third Way politics were not only plausible but were under construction in Europe.

Despite such arguments and evidence New Labour in government has pursued its programme of modernisation and renewal in the face of fluctuating internal and public opposition. In doing so the dictates of globalisation have been instrumental in advocating and legitimising everything from the reform of education to the pursuit of macroeconomic stability. For many on the left – and even the Old Right – modernisation and renewal in practice represent little more than a fundamental accommodation to neo-liberalism and a consequential dilution, if not abandonment, of the redistributionist social democratic programme – Thatcherite rather than Labour classic.[52] Along with other centre-left parties in Europe, New Labour

> ... spoke a deradicalised centrist version of social democracy. This was entirely uninterested in revolution, accepting of capitalism, even enthusiastic about the market ... Its socialism seemed increasingly residual, based in programmes of social justice and the defense of what remained of the welfare state.[53]

New Labour's record in office has tended to reinforce this conclusion.

Its zealous commitment to macro-economic stability and financial prudence was demonstrated by granting the Bank of England independence – almost the first act of government in 1997 – and limiting public expenditure growth to that which is sustainable over the economic cycle. Combined with the promotion – both at home and within the EU – of greater competition, liberalisation, flexible labour markets and welfare reform, Labour's policies have been interpreted as confirming a discrete break with its Croslandite and more radical political heritage. Rather than the social democratic state, New Labour has advocated the enabling state presiding over what, on the left, is perceived as the retrenchment, rather than the renewal, of the Welfare State. New Labour's globalisation discourse has been instrumental in persuading and cajoling the public, and its supporters alike, of the country's inescapable accommodation with 'the triumph of the market'. It has functioned, according to one critic, to facilitate New Labour ' … finding new ways of using the state to impose the discipline of the market on its population – from the cradle to the grave'.[54]

This instrumentalist account of globalisation and New Labour relies very much on the explanatory power of ideas or discourse.[55] In effect, the idea of globalisation, more so than its material manifestations, operates as an over-arching intellectual framework through which the New Labour project is articulated, coordinated and communicated within and outside the Party.[56] It has functioned too in a disciplinary mode negating political alternatives and encouraging ideological conformity. However, convincing as it is at one level, this instrumentalist reading provides surprisingly little illumination of the interests, motivations and politics which might be considered equally relevant to a cogent explanation and robust interpretation of the rise of New Labour.

Neo-revisionism

Certain ambiguities pervade the otherwise elegant instrumentalist account of New Labour's encounter with globalisation. Motivations and interests appear somewhat elusive. Electoral imperatives, combined with the drive for modernisation, may explain the significance New Labour attached to glob-alisation – as an 'ideological battering ram' – but the interests served by its Damascene conversion to neo-liberalism remain obscure. Curiously too, the discourse of globalisation is portrayed in largely monolithic terms – as the logic of constraint – whilst, as indicated above, it has been more diverse and nuanced. This suggests that although the invocation of globalisation clearly reinforced the dynamic of modernisation this cannot, by itself, fully account for why the modernisation programme acquired the form that it did. (There is a significant distinction to be made here between process and content.) Why, given that globalisation was so exaggerated and progressive political alternatives existed, did New Labour apparently embrace neo-liberalism? Was New Labour simply a collection of historical dupes or were its adherents so convinced of the necessity of modernisation that its political form was secondary? How far, in other words, can the discourse of globalisation, by itself, explain New Labour's apparent conversion (or capitulation) to neo-liberal modernisation? Did the apparent conversion to neo-liberalism follow from the discourse of globalisation or vice versa? Such questions caution against an uncritical acceptance of the instrumentalist account.

Some answers to these questions are discernible in what has been referred to as the neo-revisionist account of New Labour.[57] Contrary to the instrumentalist account of New Labour, which tends to accept uncritically the rhetoric of the Third Way as denoting a fundamental ideological and political break with the past, the neo-revisionist account conceives it as harbouring elements of both continuity and change. New Labour is thereby located in that tradition of social democratic renewal which Crosland, in the early post-war period, advocated as a response to radically changed domestic and global circumstances. For Crosland, as for many Labour centrists, post-war capitalism was conceived as having been 'reformed almost out of recognition' while the Cold War global order secured social democratic 'managed capitalism' as the sole alternative to either state socialism or liberal capitalism – a Third Way.[58] If, as Eley amongst others have argued, 'International factors secured social democratic success', in the form of this post-war 'managed capitalism', so global conditions too have been profoundly implicated in its subsequent crises and reconstructions.[59] As Fielding comments, 'It would be wrong to think "New Labour" unique in imagining Britain had to take account of the world economy. … Every post-war government (irrespective of its affiliation) has been acutely aware of external forces'.[60] Historically, however, Labour's engagement with 'external forces', as articulated in its protean attitudes towards Europe, often has proved highly controversial, internally divisive and punctuated by episodic crises.

As with the instrumentalist account of New Labour, this neo-revisionist account takes globalisation seriously but as a historical process rather than principally a discourse to be deconstructed.[61] Its essential thesis is that Britain's uniquely dense enmeshment in the world order makes it particularly vulnerable to the vagaries of global forces and conditions. However, it is the articulation of these vulnerabilities and sensitivities with domestic, social, institutional and political factors which, at crucial junctures, has fostered domestic processes of political adjustment, realignment and transformation.[62] Rather than prefiguring the end of social democracy, as many on the neo-liberal right and radical left proclaim, the contemporary phase of globalisation has been accompanied by its political revival and renewal. This has taken different forms in different states, reflecting the distinctive configu-rations and dynamics of political, institutional and social forces. In this respect, globalisation is associated with processes of both convergence and divergence: broad convergence in respect of macroeconomic strategies but significant divergence in terms of welfare regimes.[63] Nowhere has it involved, as the hyperglobalisers on both left and right assert, a simple capitulation to the forces of neo-liberalism and global capital. In Britain, the unique conjunction of intensifying globalisation, economic and social transformation, and

Labour's successive electoral defeats reinforced the process of modernisation which culminated in the 'New Labour' project. This 'Third Way' politics reflects the Party's pragmatic, much more than its programmatic, tradition in both its dismissal of ideology and its technocratic and managerialist impulses.[64] It represents, in other words, a distinctly British resolution of the political dilemmas consequent upon 'making social democracy safe' for a globalising era.

This neo-revisionist account of globalisation and the rise of New Labour challenges alternative interpretations. In particular, it takes issue with the instrumentalist account on the grounds that, amongst other things, it: exaggerates the 'myth' of globalisation; presents a one-dimensional ideational explanation of political and institutional change; downplays the disciplines of global capital markets; and misconstrues New Labour's (alleged) conversion to neo-liberalism. By contrast, the arguments of hyperglobalisers, whether on the left or right, are more readily dismissed as being overly structuralist and determinist, in conceiving the rise of New Labour as epiphenomenal: as simply making the world safe for global capitalism. Such criticisms arise out of the substantive analysis which informs the neo-revisionist interpretation.

Even amongst those sceptical of the globalisation thesis there is recognition that the position of the UK is distinctive amongst OECD states and that this matters politically. As Hirst and Thompson acknowledge, 'There is a very good reason why the UK is one of the centres of globalisation – talk; it is a far more internationalised country than its G7 counterparts'.[65] Moreover, as Schmidt argues, this greater openness is historically rooted and institutionalised:

> Britain's economy has long been more liberal and open than most of its Continental European counterparts, given its nineteenth century history of Empire which established the pound sterling as an international currency and ensured that British business would be among the most internationalised and outward looking.[66]

Indeed it was essentially the globalisation of the British economy which had given rise to Labour's Alternative Economic Strategy in the 1970s which sought to secure 'democratic socialism' by insulating the UK from the vulnerabilities and constraints of global economic forces and Europeanisation.[67] This apprehensiveness, if not antipathy, towards globalisation, in part, was borne of Labour's traumatic experiences of devaluation, financial crises and deeply rooted suspicion of multinational capital. If globalisation was too often constructed as a constraint in the lexicon of New Labour, this reflected the Party's political experience in government as much as a crude instrumentalism.

By the 1990s, Labour confronted an economy which, partly as the consequence of Conservative liberalisation measures, had become even more intensely globalised (and Europeanised). In finance, the UK's exposure to global markets, on almost every measure from the City's enmeshment in foreign exchange markets to foreign holdings of government debt and the internationalisation of the stock market, had increased dramatically.[68] A similar pattern existed in terms of trade, with exports at record post-war levels, and hugely expanded foreign investment flows (both inward and outward). Indeed, by the early 1990s, trade accounted for more than a quarter of economic output (compared to around 12 per cent in 1973) while the UK had become the principal destination for foreign investment outside the US, with foreign-owned companies responsible for some 20 per cent of employment and 30 per cent of sales in manufacturing.[69] Beyond the purely economic too, from the cultural to the political domain, a broadly comparable pattern was emerging, as Hirst and Thompson put it, of 'globalisation in one country' – from both within and without.[70] Of course, what matters here is how these trends came to be interpreted and understood, for they do not, by themselves, disclose any singular political logic.

For Labour the significant reshaping of the British social and political landscape, which accelerated in the 1980s, not to mention the collapse of the Cold War international order (which had underwritten post-war British social democracy), coalesced with intensifying globalisation to produce a new political conjuncture. As Eley observes, 'During 1970–1990, the bases for socialist movements of the classical kind dissolved in Europe.'[71] In Britain de-industrialisation brought dramatic shifts in employment patterns as some 2.2 million industrial jobs were lost between 1971 and 1983, with manufacturing jobs declining from 32 per cent to 18 per cent of total employment, and those in services increasing from 18 per cent to 58 per cent.[72] As the post-industrial economic order matured it created new challenges and opportunities for the social democratic project, as Robert Reich and others argued.[73] Significant attitudinal and social changes occurred too as individualism and consumerism eroded – although they did not displace – collectivism, while growing disenchantment with traditional party politics was accompanied by the rise of social movements and the 'politics of recognition'. Politically, Thatcher proceeded to dismantle the structures of the corporatist state and post-war social democratic covenant as the neo-liberal tide of privatisation, deregulation and liberalisation acquired hegemony.[74] Throughout this period Labour suffered electoral defeats, despite its continued modernisation involving an accommodation with the market in the form of 'supply-side socialism'.[75] However exaggerated the notion of 'New Times', as many on the left and neo-liberal right perceived this period, it articulated a sense that centre-left politics was on the defensive, confronting a novel historical conjuncture which demanded the rehabilitation, not simply the restatement, of the social democratic creed.

Globalisation played a significant role in this rehabilitation. Against the rising tide of opinion, on both left and right, which, in the aftermath of the collapse of state socialism considered that globalisation prefigured the end of social democracy, New Labour's modernisation programme sought to defend it. In key respects the Third Way represented a defence of social democracy against the hyperglobalist orthodoxy which argued that, under conditions of contemporary globalisation, states would increasingly converge upon the neo-liberal residual welfare model – the competition state.[76]

Amongst its advocates, the Third Way constituted not simply a defence of social democracy but an argument as to why globalisation made it increasingly indispensable – in order to mediate the social consequences of global change – and how a renewed social democracy could flourish in a world of capital mobility, real-time global financial markets, transnational production and global competition.[77] Granted, this ruled out more radical alternatives, including a return to the corporatist state and the insularity of the Alternative Economic Strategy, but these were barely credible, not principally because of the 'ideological battering ram' of globalisation but because of the transformed domestic political and social context in which Labour operated.[78]

Contrary to instrumentalist accounts, New Labour's reading of globalisation cannot be so readily dismissed as opportunism or hyperbole. That its rhetoric may have been exaggerated does not by itself invalidate either the logic of the underlying analysis nor the political conclusions drawn from it. Even amongst sceptics the assumption that economic globalisation entails domestic adjustments and constraints on state action is not in dispute. At issue are two related matters: the extent and significance of these adjustments and constraints; and the necessity, under conditions of globalisation, for the renewal of social democracy. Instrumentalist accounts are sceptical on both counts but only in large part as a consequence of discounting contrary analyses.

From the late 1980s onwards, many substantial studies highlighted the unique implications for social democratic governments of the disciplines of intensifying financial globalisation, capital mobility, trade competition and the diffusion of technology.[79] Subsequent studies have demonstrated that, in general, national vulnerabilities to economic globalisation vary according to both the profile of national enmeshment and the mediating role of domestic institutional and political arrangements.[80] High levels of enmeshment, as in the case of the UK, are associated with ' … more vulnerability to globalisation pressures'.[81] The debacle of Black Wednesday in September 1992, when the credibility of the Major Government's management of the economy was shattered by the speculative activities of traders on the global foreign exchange markets, is a point of instance. These pressures or tendencies alter the strategic calculus of social democratic governments in several ways: through markets imposing financial penalties on governments with (perceived) unsustainable levels of deficit-financed public expenditure, thus heightening the need for macro-economic stability and fiscal prudence; through the greater structural opportunities for capital to relocate production and employment-enhancing the need to cultivate business interests and promote market-enhancing fiscal and welfare policies; and through the significant redistributive consequences of trade liberalisation and global competition which, in the context of multilateral trade management, are more politically difficult and costly to address by resort to unilateral protectionist measures.[82] Given Britain's unique profile of dense enmeshment in the world economy, the electoral credibility of Labour depended, in part, on demonstrating that it could manage convincingly the political and economic consequences of this altered political calculus.

Labour politicians were acutely aware of the capacity of global financial markets to disrupt, if not derail, government economic strategy. Recent European history, from the debacle of 'Black Wednesday', by way of the collapse of Mitterrand's socialist experiment in 1981 and Sweden's austerity policies in the 1990s, reinforced this belief. Little wonder then that New Labour's first major initiative after the 1997 election landslide was to grant the Bank of England independence in order to ' ... overcome the ingrained scepticism of those running the international financial markets about any type of Labour government'.[83] This act, as Mosley suggests, 'had a more pronounced effect on market sentiment than the outcome of the general election' and was crucial in assuaging the 'nervous sensibilities' of global financial markets which, New Labour's leadership recognised, ' ... could determine the success or failure of any economic strategy'.[84] Such sensibilities, given the volatility of global financial markets in the 1990s and the dismal record of governments subject to speculative attacks, not to mention Britain's unique openness to the world economy, were certainly not misplaced nor unfounded. In Eatwell's view, 'Faced with an overwhelming scale of potential capital flows, governments must today as never before attempt to maintain market "credibility"'.[85] Caution became the rule since the stakes were perceived as momentous: if New Labour's credibility for economic management was compromised, so too would be its political project. Modernisation, at least initially, was therefore subordinate to economic credibility, generating tensions within New Labour. In this respect, New Labour's construction of globalisation as a constraint was not without foundation, but nor did it translate into a conversion to neo-liberal virtues or the minimalist state.

In advocating modernisation New Labour was ever careful to distance itself from the hyper-globalist view which considered globalisation as disabling the state or prefiguring convergence upon the neo-liberal competition state model.[86] Far from globalisation being conceived as eroding the power and autonomy of government it was understood, contrary to Thatcherism, as reinforcing the need for effective and active government.[87] In this respect, the 'Third Way' recognised the 'constraints' of globalisation, using Mosley's language, as being 'strong but narrow', thereby leaving considerable scope for progressive governance.[88] Subsequent studies have reinforced this supposition for the recent historical record, as Mosley concludes, and demonstrated that 'There is a good deal left – for the left, centre, or right – in domestic politics' in so far as governments ' ... that conform to capital market pressures in select macroeconomic areas, such as overall government budget deficits and rates of inflation, are relatively unconstrained in supply side and microeconomic policy areas'.[89] For New Labour, the 'social investment state' endorsed the strategic role of government in managing the 'new mixed economy' under conditions of globalisation.[90]

Presented as a rejection of the 'command and control state' the 'social investment state' reflected a recognition that governing Britain, or any advanced society, had become an increasingly complex process as globalisation, Europeanisation, marketisation, managerialism and informationalism transformed the conditions of government.[91] Governing became governance: a process which involved government in the strategic coordination of a multiplicity of agencies, public and private, beyond, below and astride the state to achieve collective political goals.[92] For many critics of New Labour this is simply the language of capitulation to the dictates of the market: neo-liberalism with a social democratic veneer.[93] Rather than the limp 'social investment state' they pointed to the existence of progressive political alternatives in Europe: from the 'social governance' of Danish social democracy to the 'negotiated governance' of Swedish social democracy.[94] If such small states could sustain a generous welfare model in the face of globalisation and Europeanisation then, so the argument went, so could the UK. However, this was to overlook the many special conditions – from solidaristic societies to unique political structures – which made such strategies feasible, not to mention that they largely appeared so generous because of the historically low levels of British welfare benefits. In this latter regard, critiques of modernisation have often drawn unconsciously upon 'myths' about the Golden Age of social democracy and Labour's past record on, and commitment to, redistribution.[95] By pursuing modernisation over other progressive alternatives, whether the stakeholder or the Danish model, New Labour demonstrated it was very much in keeping with the Party's historical caution in pursuing redistribution. Moreover, the actual record of continental social democracy, as a successful model for managing and mediating the combined forces of globalisation and European integration, remains far more ambiguous than its advocates have been wont to recognise.[96]

In office New Labour's record has proved much more enigmatic than either its supporters or its critics care to admit. It parallels, in many respects, the ambiguities of the 'Third Way'.[97] Rather than globalisation 'making the contingent necessary', it has been associated with a political pragmatism. Building the new mixed economy, through, amongst other policies, Bank of England independence, macroeconomic stability, fiscal prudence, public/private partnerships, and supply-side measures has been accompanied by the cultivation of the public sector through significant increases in public sector employment and spending, fiscal deficits, a higher tax burden, and expanded regulation and re-regulation. Promoting competition through, amongst other initiatives, welfare reform, labour market flexibility, and fiscal policy liberalisation in Europe and beyond, has been accompanied by the promotion of social justice through redistributive fiscal policies, endorsing the European social chapter, fairness at work, and significant human capital investment. Advancing Britain in the world by, amongst other things, asserting the national interest, combating terrorism, projecting military power, promoting globalisation and celebrating the nation has been accompanied by the fostering of international solidarity through significant redistributive efforts (increases in foreign aid, debt relief, etc.), the cultivation of multilateralism and multilateral regulation of the global economy, embracing Europe, and much more controversially engaging in humanitarian intervention. New Labour's record in government discloses a pattern of political pragmatism much more than it epitomises either a simple ideological conversion to neo-liberalism or a clean break with 'old social democracy'.[98]

Globalisation did not so much 'make the contingent necessary' as make 'pragmatism a political virtue' for New Labour. Advanced as a rational response to the prodigious task of governing complex and rapidly changing societies, made even more intractable by the dynamics of globalisation, pragmatism has acquired the mantle of 'political common sense'. For New Labour, pragmatism expresses the rejection of both the failed dogmas of neo-liberalism and state socialism, and the divisive prescriptions of ideological politics, whether neo-conservatism or religious fundamentalism, as credible or viable responses to the contemporary political condition. 'What counts is what works', not ideological purity, such that New Labour draws on an eclectic ideological heritage: neo-liberalism, Christian socialism, communitarianism and the new managerialism. As such it has never been a programmatic but always a pragmatic project in so far as the Third Way has never sought to provide ' ... a clear basis for policy choices and the foundation of a distinctive approach to governance'.[99] Indeed the significant ambiguities of Third Way politics are testament to New Labour's essentially pragmatic impulses. Such pragmatism, however, is far from novel but has its roots in the historical, as opposed to mythical, record of Old Labour in government.[100] Shonfield's classic study of 'managed capitalism' declared that 'Old' Labour's ' ... whole operation of ... planning, when it worked at all, was directed to short-term objectives' whilst even critics such as Callaghan acknowledge that 'social democracy's achievements were real but limited'.[101] New Labour is neither all that 'new', nor as Fielding somewhat controversially concludes, does it represent, as its many critics proclaim, the abandonment of social democracy: ' ... Blair remained remarkably faithful to Labour's past. The Party at the start of the twenty-first century may be a highly cautious social democratic organisation; but recognizably social democratic it remains'.[102] It is located firmly, according to Fielding, in the tradition of Labour revisionism.[103] Globalisation has been central to this neo-revisionism, not so much as an 'ideological battering ram' (important as that is) but, on the contrary, as a set of tendencies which reinforced New Labour's initially cautious strategy and gave credence to its particular brand of political pragmatism. Newman, however, doubts this Third Way pragmatism constitutes a secure political settlement since it is essentially ' ... an unstable alliance between different political groupings based on the juxtaposition of disparate ideologies and values'.[104] Paradoxically, some of the more potent challenges to its sustained political viability arise from the convergent forces of globalisation and European integration.

Dilemmas

Globalisation, understood both as unifying discourse and worldwide interconnectedness, has been fundamental to the constitution and legitimation of the New Labour project. Although complicit in dissolving the social basis of the post-war social democratic settlement, globalisation nevertheless gave rise to its own social divisions and alignments which New Labour – as with the New Democrats in the US – has successfully woven, with its traditional social bases of support, into a distinctive – and winning – progressive political coalition.[105] In seeking to transcend the orthodox left–right divide in British politics New Labour's centrist political strategy melded together a coalition of ideologically and socially diverse forces and constituencies with somewhat antagonistic interests and preferences. It embraced, amongst others, the advanced guard of global corporate capitalism alongside the social casualties of global competition; the 'symbolic analysts' of the 'new economy' alongside the steel workers of the industrial economy; and the 'aspirational voters' of Middle England alongside the 'loyal voters' of the Labour heartlands.[106] Ideologically too New Labour's coalition draws on a contentious mix of political philosophies. Yet this was hardly a unique predicament for Labour or any political party seeking office. However, the fragility of the New Labour coalition, both beyond and within Westminster, remains a consistent source of anxiety for the party's political leadership.

Many factors continue to fuel this anxiety. Globalisation and European integration, however, combine to present New Labour with significant political dilemmas which, depending upon attendant responses, may further de-stabilise its already fragile political coalition. As Rodrik points out, economic globalisation places strains on social cohesion by engendering divisions

> … between those who prosper in the globalized economy and those who do not, between those who shape its values and those who would rather not, and between those who can diversify away its risks and those who cannot.[107]

In prosperous times social cohesion may be more readily cultivated than in an economic downturn. As economic globalisation moderates, maintaining social cohesion may be inordinately more difficult as growing discontent turns into a political backlash.[108] In the current context of shrinking economic globalisation the challenges for New Labour in sustaining its unstable coalition under the divergent pressures of economic adjustment should not be underestimated. Nor, given limits to deficit spending, can the discontents be readily assuaged by greater social protection without a redistribution of the fiscal burden which that implies, thereby endangering another fissure in the coalition. To the extent that it can buck global financial markets and insulate the economy from external pressures, it potentially jeopardises the support of progressive big-business interests whilst enhancing the position of those traditionalist and radical factions which advance an alternative 'social governance' agenda.

If economic globalisation has slowed in recent years, the globalisation of conflict has accelerated. Even before the global war on terror the rationale for humanitarian intervention in Bosnia and Kosovo had rested, in some degree, upon appeals to the moral consequences of globalisation expressed in the principle of duties beyond borders. In the aftermath of 11 September and the subsequent war on 'global terrorism', national security, as in the Cold War era, has re-acquired a significant global dimension. For New Labour, the globalisation of national security has proved a highly divisive and contentious matter brought to a head by the war against Iraq in 2003. What to some appears as New Labour's moral crusade, a return to liberal imperialism, is perceived by others as the exercise of its cosmopolitan duties. This reassertion of 'might is right', however, is not what most advocates of the Third Way understood by redefining Britain's global role and identity. Far from 'cool Britannia', it appears to some as 'imperial Britannia'. To the extent that the globalisation of security involves Britain in a continued global policing role, the politically divisive consequences for New Labour will be magnified. Thus far, the political fractures in New Labour's coalition, arising from the war in Iraq, have proved enduring and are unlikely to be repaired by the perpetuation of New Labour's 'moral crusade'.

Although Robert Kagan's analysis of the growing divergence between the US and Europe presents a somewhat false dichotomy between 'paradise and power', nevertheless it is a felicitous allegory of the contemporary global predicament.[109] What is at issue today is the constitution of the twenty-first-century world order: crudely, whether global unilateralism or global multilateralism should be the dominant regulative principle. How New Labour negotiates this contest of principles will have significant implications, not only for its progressive credentials but also for the consolidation of its domestic political settlement. For that domestic political settlement depends, in part, upon the maintenance of an open but regulated global economic order. Regulating globalisation to moderate its adverse domestic and international impacts upon communities and the environment will be central to addressing the concerns of globalisation's discontents whilst neutralising the rise of protectionism and reactionary politics. But New Labour has yet to define a coherent and robust strategy for making globalisation work with 'the grain of social and environmental justice', not to mention a progressive vision for the twenty-first-century world order and Britain's role in its construction. Therein lie hugely difficult dilemmas for a political leadership which seeks to transcend the Atlanticist–European divide and placate the globalisers and anti-globalisers, both amongst its supporters and in the country at large. Nor can these choices be avoided since the exigencies of global politics are rarely synchronised with the rhythm of domestic politics.

Finally, the logic of European integration will impose its own distinctive strains upon the New Labour coalition. Beyond the fairly immediate and controversial matters of Euro membership, the Union's constitutional settlement and (post-Iraq) the common defence and foreign policy, lie equally crucial but strategic questions concerning the extended Union's 'identity and purpose'. Far from being addressed within the framework of the Constitutional Convention, politicians have procrastinated on these issues since they divide Europeans. Despite New Labour's assertive pro-European rhetoric, the future of the Union, in the context of a (militarily) unipolar world order, is as potentially divisive as it is unifying. For there are differences of view as to whether the Union should be: a building block of, or a defensive barrier against, the global market; a bandwagon or a balancer to American power; and a social market more than a free market. Such differences are overlaid and complicated by the more fundamental divisions between Atlanticists and Europeanists. As an extended Europe embarks on a further stage of political integration, New Labour's pro-European convictions and coalition will be seriously tested. Of course, none of these political dilemmas is insuperable, nor together do they prefigure the disintegration of the New Labour coalition and its modernising project. Indeed New Labour's pragmatism may be its crucial safeguard. Nevertheless, in their articulation with the fickleness of domestic politics, these tendencies have the potential to render problematic the consolidation of the New Labour political settlement. For the critics of New Labour this would surely represent 'the revenge of globalisation'.

Conclusions

As this chapter has argued, New Labour is somewhat 'soft on globalisation, soft on the causes of globalisation', but for good reason. Globalisation has never simply been just an 'ideological battering ram' for change; New Labour's preoccupation with globalisation is not purely instrumental. On the contrary, globalisation is constitutive of the British political economy: it is shorthand for the unique profile of the UK's integration with the global and European economies, its vulnerabilities to world markets, distant events and political developments. For its advocates, the 'Third Way' represents a genuine attempt to reconstruct social democracy to fit with the conditions of really existing globalisation. But the ambiguities of the Third Way have opened New Labour to the charge that it is simply a continuation of the Thatcherite project. However, as the chapter has argued, New Labour's record in office is evidence of both continuity and change. It is very much located within Labour's revisionist tradition. Globalisation has reinforced this revisionism but, as the chapter concludes, it also presents a challenge to the consolidation of New Labour's political settlement. As such the contradictions of globalisation find significant expression in the contradictions of the New Labour project.

Notes

1   Cook, R., *The Challenges of Globalisation* – Address to IISS, London, 9 March 2001, www.fco.gov.uk/servlet.
2   Blair, T., in Newman, J., *Modernising Governance – New Labour Policy and Society*, (Sage, London, 2001), p. 48.
3   Giddens, A., *The Third Way*, (Polity Press, Cambridge, 1999), p. 64.
4   Hay, C., 'Globalisation, Economic Change and the Welfare State' in Sykes, R., Palier, B. and Prior, P. (eds), *Globalisation and European Welfare States*, (Palgrave, Basingstoke, 2001), pp. 38–58; and Schmidt, V., *The Futures of European Capitalism*, (OUP, Oxford, 2002).

5   Garrett, G., Lange, P., 'Political responses to interdependence: What's 'Left' for the Left?' *International Organisation* 45(4): pp. 539–65, 1991; Callaghan, J., *The Retreat of Social Democracy*, (Manchester University Press, Manchester, 2000); Hay, C., 'The Invocation of External Economic Constraint: A Genealogy of the Concept of Globalisation in the Political Economy of the British Labour Party 1973–2000', *The European Legacy* 6 (2): pp. 233–49, 2001; and Eley, G., *Forging Democracy – The History of the Left in Europe: 1850–2000*, (OUP, Oxford, 2002).

6   Callaghan, J., *The Retreat of Social Democracy*, p. 120.

7   Coates, D., Hay, C., *The Internal and External Face of New Labour's Political Economy*, (Mimeo, 2000); Hay, C., Watson, M., *Globalisation and the British Political Economy*, (Mimeo, 2000); and Hay, C., 'The Invocation of External Economic Constraint: A Genealogy of the Concept of Globalisation in the Political Economy of the British Labour Party 1973–2000.'

8   Schmidt, V., *The Futures of European Capitalism*.

9   Fielding, S., *The Labour Party – Continuity and Change in the Making of New Labour*, (Palgrave, London, 2003).

10 Reich, R., *The Work of Nations*, (Simon and Schuster, New York, 1991).

11 Castells, M., *The Rise of the Network Society*, (Blackwells, Oxford, 1996).

12 Leadbeater, C., *Living on Thin Air – The New Economy*, (Penguin Books, London, 1999); and Friedmann, T., *The Lexus and the Olive Tree*, (Basic Books, New York, 2000).

13 Callaghan, J., *The Retreat of Social Democracy*, p. 162.

14 *Ibid.*

15 Giddens, A., *The Third Way*.

16 *Ibid.*

17 *Ibid.*

18 Newman, J., *Modernising Governance – New Labour Policy and Society*, p. 48.

19 Giddens, A., *The Third Way*, p. 64.

20 Blair, T., *Speech to the Labour Party Conference*, 2002, *Guardian Unlimited*, 2003.

21 Newman, J., *Modernising Governance – New Labour Policy and So*ciety, p. 42.

22 Callaghan, J., *The Retreat of Social* Democracy, p. 161.

23 Coates, D., Hay, C., *The Internal and External Face of New Labour's Political Economy*; Hay, C., 'Globalisation, Economic Change and the Welfare State' in Sykes, R., Palier, B. and Prior, P. (eds), *Globalisation and European Welfare States*; and Newman, J., *Modernising Governance – New Labour Policy and Society*.

24 Holden, C., 'Globalisation, Social Exclusion and Labour's New Work Ethic' 19(4): *Critical Social Policy* pp. 529–38, 1999.

25 Schmidt, V., *The Futures of European Capitalism*, p. 268.

26 Byers, S., *Globalisation and Free Trade*, (Department of Trade and Industry, London, 2002).

27 Holden, C., 'Globalisation, Social Exclusion and Labour's New Work Ethic'.

28 Blair, T., *Speech to the Labour Party Conference*, 2002.

29 Pierre, J., Peters, B.G., *Governance, Politics and the State*, (Palgrave, London, 2000).

30 Friedmann, T., *The Lexus and the Olive Tree*, p. 410.

31 Byers, S., *Globalisation and Free Trade*.

32 Cook, R., *The Challenges of Globalisation*.

33 Giddens, A., *The Third Way*, p. 64.

34 Giddens, A., *The Third Way* and Giddens, A., *The Global Third Way Debate*, (Polity Press, Cambridge, 2001).

35 Blair, T., *Speech to the Labour Party Conference*, 2002.

36 Short, C., *Speech to the Labour Party Conference*, 2001.

37 Blair, T., *Speech to the Labour Party Conference*, 2001.

38 Hay, C., Watson, M., *Rendering the Contingent Necessary: New Labour's Neo-Liberal Conversion and the Discourse of Globalisation*, (Harvard University Press, Cambridge, 1998).

39 Hirst, P., Thompson, G., *Globalisation in One Country?: The Peculiarities of the British*, (Open University Faculty of Social Sciences, Buckingham, 1999) Hirst, P., Thompson, G., *Globalisation in Question*, (Polity Press, Cambridge, 1999), Callaghan, J., *The Retreat of Social Democracy*; Coates, D., Hay, C., '*The Internal and External Face of New Labour's Political Economy*'; Hay, C., Watson, M., *Globalisation and the British Political Economy*; Hay, C., 'Globalisation, Economic Change and the Welfare State'.

40 Instrumentalist, as used here, in the sense of utilising a means–ends logic to explain a social activity or phenomenon. Thus the ascendance of the globalisation discourse (the means) within New Labour is explained principally by reference to its function in rationalising and legitimating the process of modernisation and renewal (the ends).

41 Hay, C., Watson, M., *Globalisation and the British Political Economy*.

42 Hay, C., Watson, M., *Rendering the Contingent Necessary: New Labour's Neo-Liberal Conversion and the Discourse of Globalisation*.

43 Hirst, P., Thompson, G., *Globalisation in Question*, (Polity Press, Cambridge, 1996).

44 *Ibid.*, p. xxx.

45 Gordon, D., 'The global economy: new edifice or crumbling foundations?' *New Left Review*, (168): 24–65, 1988; Hoogvelt, A., *Globalisation and the Postcolonial World – The New Political Economy of Development* (Macmillan, London, 1997), Thompson, G., 'International Competitiveness and Globalisation', in Baker, T., Kohler, J. (eds), *International Competitiveness and Environmental Policies*, (Edward Elgar, Brighton, 1998); Rugman, A., *The End of Globalisation*, (Random House, New York, 2000); and Callinicos, A., *Against the Third Way*, (Polity Press, Cambridge, 2001).

46 Hirst, P., 'The Global Economy – Myths and Realities', *International Affairs* 73 (3) July: pp. 409–26, 1997.

47 Weiss, L., 'Globalisation and the Myth of the Powerless State', *New Left Review* 225: pp. 3–28, 1997.

48 Hay, C., Watson, M., *Globalisation and the British Political Economy*.

49 Gray, J., *False Dawn*, (Granta, London, 1998).

50 Hirst, P., 'Has Globalisation Killed Social Democracy?', *Political Quarterly* (3): pp. 84–96, 1999.

51 Garrett, G., 'Global markets and national politics', *International Organisation* 52(1), 1998, Hirst, P., 'Has Globalisation Killed Social Democracy?'; Hay, C., 'Globalisation, Economic Change and the Welfare State'; Leys, C., *Market Driven Politics – Neo-liberal Democracy and the Public Interest* (Verso, London, 2001); and Thompson, G., *Can the Welfare State survive Globalisation?*, (Mimeo, 2001).

52 Callaghan, J., *The Retreat of Social Democracy*; Callinicos, A., *Against the Third Way*; Leys, C., *Market Driven Politic – Neo-liberal Democracy and the Public Interest*; and Eley, G., *Forging Democracy – The History of the Left in Europe: 1850–2000*.

53 Eley, G., *Forging Democracy – The History of the Left in Europe: 1850–2000*, p. 490.

54 Holden, C., 'Globalisation, Social Exclusion and Labour's New Work Ethic'.

55 For an excellent discussion of the 'causal' role of ideas in generating political and institutional change see Blyth, 2002.

56 Schmidt, V., *The Future of European Capitalism*.

57 Gamble, A., Kelly, G., 'New Labour's economics', in Ludlam, S., Smith, M.J. (eds), *New Labour in Government*, (Macmillan, London, 2001); and Fielding, S., *The Labour Party – Continuity and Change in the Making of New Labour*.

58 Padgett, S., Paterson, W.E., *A History of Social Democracy in Postwar Europe*, (Longman, London, 1991), p. 23; Black, L., 'The Bitterest of Enemies: Labour Revisionists,

Atlanticism and the Cold War', *Contemporary British History*, 15(3): pp. 26–62, 2001; Eley, G., *Forging Democracy – The History of the Left in Europe: 1850–2000*.

59 Ruggie, J.G., 'International Regimes, Transactions, and Change: Embedded Liberalism in the Postwar Economic Order', in Krasner, S.D., (ed.), *International Regimes*, (Cornell University Press, Ithaca, 1983), pp. 195–231; and Eley, G., *Forging Democracy – The History of the Left in Europe: 1850–2000*, p. 314.

60 Fielding, S., *The Labour Party – Continuity and Change in the Making of New Labour*, p. 150.

61 Held, D., McGrew, A., (eds), *Global Transformations: Politics, Economics and Culture*, (Polity Press, Cambridge, 1999), and Held, D., McGrew, A., *Globalisation / AntiGlobalisation*, (Polity Press, Cambridge, 2002).

62 Garrett, G., Lange, P., 'Internationalisation, Institutions,and Political Change', in Keohane, R.O., Milner, H.V. (eds), *Internationalisation and Domestic Politics*, (CUP, Cambridge, 1996), p. 48–78 Keohane, R.O., Milner, H.V. (eds), *Internationalisation and Domestic Politics*, (CUP, Cambridge, 1996; Schmidt, V., *The Futures of European Capitalism*.

63 Schmidt, V., *The Futures of European Capitalism*; and Mosley, L., *Global Capital and National Governments*, (CUP, Cambridge, 2003).

64 Shonfield, A., *Modern Capitalism*, (OUP, Oxford, 1969); and Overbeek, H., *Global Capitalism and National Decline*, (Unwin Hyman, London, 1990).

65 Hirst, P., Thompson, G., *Globalisation in One Country?: The peculiarities of the British*.

66 Schmidt, V., *The Futures of European Capitalism*, p. 148.

67 Overbeek, H., *Global Capitalism and National Decline*; and Callaghan, J., *The Retreat of Social* Democracy.

68 Held, D., McGrew, A., (eds), *Global Transformations: Politics, Economics and Culture*; and Hirst, P., Thompson, G., *Globalisation in One Country?: The peculiarities of the British*.

69 *Ibid*.

70 *Ibid*.

71 Eley, G., *Forging Democracy – The History of the Left in Europe: 1850–2000*, p. 405.

72 *Ibid*., p. 386; and Fielding, S., *The Labour Party – Continuity and Change in the Making of New Labour*, p. 6.

73 Reich, R., *The Work of Nations*.

74 Overbeek, H., *Global Capitalism and National Decline*.

75 Callaghan, J., *The Retreat of Social Democracy*, p. 121.

76 Cerny, P., *The Changing Architecture of the State*, (Sage, London, 1990); Ohmae, K., *The Borderless World*, (Collins, London, 1990); Ohmae, K., *The End of the Nation State*, (Free Press, New York, 1995).

77 Reich, R., *The Work of Nations*; Rodrik, D., *Has Globalisation gone too far?*, (Institute for International Economics, Washington D.C., 1997); Giddens, A., *The Third Way*.

78 Fielding, S., *The Labour Party – Continuity and Change in the Making of New Labour*.

79 Gourevitch, P., *Politics in Hard Times*, (Cornell University Press, New York, 1986); Julius, D., *Global Companies*, (Pinter, London, 1990); Frieden, J., 'Invested interests: the politics of national economic policies in a world of global finance,' *International Organisation* 45(4): 425–53, 1991; Garrett, G., Lange, P., 'Political responses to interdependence: what's 'left' for the left?'; Scharpf, F., *Crisis and Choice in European Social Democracy*, (Cornell University Press, New York, 1991; O'Brien, R., *The End of Geography: Global Financial Integration*, (Pinter, London, 1992).; Moses, J. W., 'Abdication from national policy autonomy: What's left to leave?', *Politics and Society*, 22(2): pp. 125–38, 1994; Wood, A., *North-South Trade, Employment and Inequality*, (OUP, Oxford, 1994).

80 Garrett, G., *Partisan Politics in the Global Economy*, (CUP, Cambridge, 1998 Mosley, L., 'International Financial Markets and National Welfare States', *International Organisation* 54(4), pp. 737–74, 2000; Swank, D., *Global Capital, Political Institutions*,

and Policy Change in Developed Welfare States, (CUP, Cambridge, 2002); and Mosley, L., *Global Capital and National Governments*, (CUP, Cambridge, 2003).

81 Schmidt, V., *The Futures of European Capitalism*, p. 24.
82 Garrett, G., *Partisan Politics in the Global Economy*; Held, D., McGrew, A., (eds), *Global Transformations*: Politics, *Economics and Culture*; Jessop, B., *The Future of the Capitalist State*, (Polity Press, Cambridge, 2002); Schmidt, V., The *Futures of European Capitalism*; Swank, D., 'Tax Policy in an Era of Internationalisation', Conference on Interdependence, Diffusion, and Sovereignty, Yale University, May 10–11, 2002, and the Annual Meetings of the American Political Science Association, August 29 to September 1, 2002, Boston, MA; Devereux, M., Lockwood, B., *et al.* 'Capital Account Liberalisation and Corporate Taxes', www.warwick. ac.uk/csgir/; Mosley, L., *Global Capital and National Governments*.
83 Fielding, S., *The Labour Party – Continuity and Change in the Making of New Labour*, p. 147.
84 *Ibid.*, and Mosley, L., *Global Capital and National Governments*, p. 64.
85 Eatwell, J., Taylor, L., *Global Finance at Risk*, (Polity Press, Cambridge, 2000), p. 52.
86 Giddens, A., *The Third Way*.
87 Gamble, A., Kelly, G., 'New Labour's economics', in Ludlam, S., Smith, M.J., (eds), *New Labour in Government*.
88 Mosley, L., *Global Capital and National Governments*.
89 Garrett, G., *Partisan Politics in the Global Economy*; Mosley, L., *Global Capital and National Governments*, p. 69 and p. 3.
90 Giddens, A., *The Third Way*.
91 Rhodes, R.A.W., *Understanding Governance: Policy Networks, Governance, Reflexivity, and Accountability*, (Open University Press, Buckingham, 1997); Pierre, J., Peters, B.G., *Governance, Politics and the State*, (Palgrave, London, 2000); and Newman, J., *Modernising Governance – New Labour Policy and Society*.
92 Pierre, J., Peters, B.G., *The New Governance: States, Markets, and Networks*, (Macmillan, London, 2000).
93 Leys, C., *Market Driven Politics – Neoliberal Democracy and the Public Interest*.
94 Hirst, P., 'Has Globalisation Killed Social Democracy?'.
95 Bevir, M., 'New Labour: A Study in Ideology', *British Journal of Politics and International Relations*, 3(2), 2000; and Fielding, S., *The Labour Party – Continuity and Change in the Making of New Labour*.
96 Gourevitch, P., *Politics in Hard Times*; Eley, G., *Forging Democracy – The History of the Left in Europe: 1850–2000*; Schmidt, V., *The Futures of European Capitalism*.
97 White, S., 'The Ambiguities of the Third Way', in White, S. (ed.), *New Labour: The Progressive Future?*, (Palgrave, London, 2001).
98 Temple, M., 'New Labour's Third Way: pragmatism and governance', *British Journal of Politics and International Relations* 2(3): pp. 302–325, 2000; and Fielding, S., *The Labour Party – Continuity and Change in the Making of New Labour*.
99 Newman, J., *Modernising Governance – New Labour Policy and Society*, p. 173; and White, S., 'The Ambiguities of the Third Way'.
100 Fielding, S., *The Labour Party – Continuity and Change in the Making of New Labour*.
101 Shonfield, A., *Modern Capitalism*, p. 89; and Callaghan, J., *The Retreat of Social Democracy*, p. 1.
102 Fielding, S., *The Labour Party – Continuity and Change in the Making of New Labour*, p. 217.
103 *Ibid.*, p. 80.
104 Newman, J., *Modernising Governance – New Labour Policy and Society*, p. 173.
105 Reich, R., *The Work of Nations*; Rodrik, D., *Has Globalisation gone too far?*; Callaghan, J., *The Retreat of Social Democracy*; Fielding, S., *The Labour Party – Continuity and Change in the Making of New Labour*.

106 Fielding, S., *The Labour Party – Continuity and Change in the Making of New Labour.*
107 Rodrik, D., *Has Globalisation gone too far?*, p. 6.
108 James, H., *The End of Globalisation*, (Princeton University Press, Princeton, 2001).
109 Kagan, R., *Paradise and Power: America and Europe in the New World Order*, (Atlantic Books, London, 2003).

9 Ownership, Planning and Markets

Stuart Holland

In the 'No' Lobby of the House of Commons, shortly after I had been elected to Parliament in 1979, Jim Callaghan led me to one side and said: 'Stuart, you may not believe this but, if we had been re-elected, I would have introduced Planning Agreements. I became increasingly convinced during the last government that we need them to deal with multinational companies.'[1]

This was some recognition. Planning Agreements had been stigmatised as outdated central planning, civil servants running industry and a variant on Gosplan. Meanwhile, some of those who first endorsed them, and the parallel case for public shareholdings in industry, later denounced them as outdated nationalisation or models from Mussolini's industry. A broad range of those who had initially agreed and supported the policies disavowed them when others did so.

What had gone wrong? For one thing, there was the deep division between the left and right of the Labour Party which later was to lead to the defection of two of the key supporters of the policies – Bill Rodgers and Roy Jenkins – to the SDP.

As Mike Hatfield well put it: 'When the pro European Right of the Party found that the Left were in favour of the new economic policy they abandoned it.'[2]

The fault line over Europe divided the Party on economic policy. Roy Jenkins was to resign from the Deputy Leadership on the issue. Also, when Tony Benn later implausibly claimed that the policies – modelled on European experience – were incompatible with membership of the Common Market, he lost both the national referendum on Europe, and the industrial policy.

The case for selective state shareholdings

In 1972, after I had presented a paper on state holding companies and planning to a conference of the 'moderate' Labour journal *Socialist Commentary*, Bill Rodgers invited me to be a Specialist Adviser to the Trade and Industry Sub-Committee of the Commons Expenditure Committee, which he chaired. My report on *European Para-Governmental Agencies* focused on the case for a major state holding company – or companies – modelled on the Italian Industrial Reconstruction Institute (IRI) and the Italian State Hydrocarbons Agency (ENI).[3]

The case I made for a state holding company in the report ran as follows: (1) the location of soundly based and competitive modern companies in less developed regions; (2) the channelling of government expenditure into directly productive activity as a growth promotion or counter-recession instrument; (3) the supplementing of macro-economic trade and exchange rate policies on a permanent and anticipatory basis through investment which is import-substituting or export-promoting; (4) the reinforcing of competition through State firms which can restrain price increases through their own competitive pricing in sectors which are not wholly exposed to foreign competition; (5) the undertaking of investment which private industry either is not willing to commit or unwilling to make on a scale or time horizon sufficient to meet long-term growth requirements; (6) the provision of an instrument which can cope with the major problems posed for national or regional enterprise by multinational companies.

Shortly afterwards I made exactly the same six-point case for State shareholding in what proved to be a key paper to the Industrial Policy Committee of the Labour Party.[4]

A central point about state shareholding on the IRI model was that, while the main holding company would be 100 per cent owned, the state's holdings in individual companies could be much less and even in a minority. The vital factor was to gain value and leverage for public money in the private sector. Thus a 15 per cent or 20 per cent shareholding could be on condition that the company located new plants in the regions; or it could fund a modernising long-term investment programme of a kind which private investors or financial institutions would not, or finance an innovation programme in products which the company otherwise might license to companies in other countries, or ensure a new long-term research and development programme.

This case for competitive public holdings in this sense was working with rather than against markets – including firms which could not gain stock market finance for long-term investment (British Leyland), could not afford to innovate their own technical breakthroughs rather than license them abroad (Ferranti), or hoarded cash mountains just to defend themselves against hostile takeovers (GEC). It was the more compelling at the time in view of already available figures on the marked trend to concentration in British industry. The top 100 companies had increased their share of manufacturing output from 20 per cent in 1950 to over 40 per cent by 1970 and their share of manufacturing employment to a third.[5] The top 30 firms accounted for a third of total UK visible export trade, the top 75 for nearly half such trade.[6] The fabric of small firms presumed by the competitive market model had given way to the dominance of two, three or four firms in any single market. In the promotion of mergers between British firms on the largely misplaced grounds of gaining economies of scale, the former Labour Government's Industrial Reorganisation Corporation actually had concentrated rather than countervailed such producer power.

State holding companies also could increase competition in sectors where a few firms were oligopolistic price-makers rather than price-takers, or oligopsonists – so dominant as buyers that they could squeeze the profit margins of suppliers.[7] Such dominance of markets by a few firms could and did qualify consumer sovereignty.[8] Consumers paid the prices set by big business. Their increasing market share crushed and still crushes smaller micro suppliers, not least in retailing.[9] Consumer sovereignty already had been compromised. Mainstream micro-economics admitted oligopoly but as an exception rather than the rule. Yet by the 1970s it already was the rule not the exception.

So were multinational companies. Virtually all of these giant firms were multinational in two senses: either they were controlled from abroad or had invested abroad on a scale which tended to substitute for exports. Unlike Germany or Japan at the time, whose value of production from subsidiaries abroad was only two fifths of their national exports, the value of production by British firms outside Britain was more than double total UK visible export trade. Foreign production on such a scale tended to substitute for exports, with loss of multiplier effects and growth in the domestic economy, as Japan has more recently found to its cost.[10] Price-making power by a handful of such multi-national oligopolies in each of the main sectors of industry was reinforced by their ability to understate exports or overstate imports in transfer pricing between domestic or foreign subsidiaries in such a way as to inflate nominal costs, reduce registered profits and avoid corporation tax.

This qualified the presumption dating from Ricardo that trade was between different firms in different countries rather than by the same firms in such countries. It also qualified the argument made by Harold Wilson after the 1967 devaluation when he declared: 'What an opportunity our exporters have now.' In a Ricardian world they could have sold at lower prices in foreign markets while gaining the same receipts in sterling. But 'our' multinationals would have been competing against themselves abroad had they done so. This misguided assumption that 'our' firms needed backing abroad also underlay the unwillingness of the government to tax them effectively. For instance, nominal corporation tax in 1975 was still 52 per cent of profits, but effective tax after Denis Healey's introduction of tax relief on stock appreciation reduced the tax paid by most big business to as little as 5 per cent. Under such conditions it was hardly surprising that the 1974–9 Labour Government found it hard to finance the health service or increase the pay of public sector workers.

Transfer pricing not only was evident to me by the early 1970s from research into the electronics industry by one of my doctoral students at Sussex,[11] but also later from Monopolies Commission reports and learning from workers in key sectors such as the oil industry. When I alerted Shirley Williams at Health that the Monopolies Commission had revealed that Hoffman–La Roche was selling Librium and Valium to the NHS at £370 and £922 per kilo while an Italian company was selling them on the market for £9 and £27, she suggested negotiating a price halving, which only half-addressed the problem.[12] Again, it was price-making power by multinationals rather than wage-making power by trades unions which was soaring the costs of the National Health Service.

In government, when he was Secretary of State for Energy, I alerted Tony Benn at Energy to the fact that a white-collar Scottish trade unionist had told me at a conference that he now understood why the prices of components from the US parent company for an oil rig being constructed on Clydeside were being inflated hand over fist every month, and that he anticipated that the company would claim the yard was unprofitable and either tell the government it had to buy and shelve the rig, or close it. Tony did nothing. The company then told him that it would have to buy the rig or it would close the yard. Tony knew of the problem of transfer pricing but lacked the powers to do anything about it, other than buy the rig. The issue, by the mid-1970s, therefore was frustrating both the right and left of the Labour Government, not least since transfer pricing, by inflating subsidiary component prices, reduced declared profits and tax. This may well have informed Jim Callaghan's conviction by the 1979 election that a Labour government needed Planning Agreements to deal with multinational companies.

The dominance of most markets by a handful of giant multinational firms meant that the conventional micro–macro distinction in economic theory and government thinking was outdated. National Plans meant little or nothing to the chief executives of such companies other than that by sitting on their sector working parties they could gain themselves a place in the honours list. This was not necessarily a conspiracy against the public interest of the kind against which Adam Smith had warned. Such companies simply could not afford to allow their global investment decisions and market strategy to be influenced by one government in one country. Globalisation already dictated that they should do so globally. They dominated a new meso-economic sector *in between* the market of many micro firms struggling for survival and the national and global macro-economy.[13] In turn, their global reach already had undermined the effectiveness of the principal Keynesian demand policies, which were premised on perfect or imperfect competition on the supply side of a national economy. National fiscal and exchange rate policy was already profoundly compromised.

It was on such grounds[14] that I argued the six-point case for competitive public enterprise in my 1972 report on *European Para-Governmental Agencies* to the Expenditure Committee. The State could not countervail oligopoly power unless it itself became an entrepreneur. The cross party committee both accepted my report and then visited IRI and its affiliate companies, as well as leading private sector companies such as FIAT and Pirelli in Italy. In its own report, the committee recommended the establishment of a British State Holding Company on the lines I had advocated.[15]

Earlier, knowing of my forthcoming edited study of IRI,[16] and also my research on regional policy, Roy Jenkins asked me whether I would draft the case for a British state holding company. He also asked how big it would have to be to register real change in the regions. I stressed that to do so it would need to be able to promote a 'broad wave'[17] of new investment by firms in the UK, otherwise there would be no investment in entirely new plants for the regions. He asked me to analyse and spell out the sectors. I did so, by an analysis of the regionally mobile or 'footloose' sectors of industry which were not location-specific or capital-intensive. This excluded most of the nationalised industries which were either highly capital intensive, or geologically specific, such as coal, or distribution specific, such as rail, the post, gas and electricity. I told him I was not sure he needed to cite all, rather than an illustrative handful, of them, but he both used my arguments for a state holding company and spelled out key sectors in the first of a series of speeches which then were published by Fontana under the title *What Matters Now*.[18]

As Roy put it, the State Holding Company should be represented in:

> the manufacturing industries which have a high proportion of labour in relation to their output (including) the whole wide range of the engineering and motor vehicle industries, together with hosiery and other clothing, pottery and glass, furniture, pharmaceuticals and one or two others.[19]

And:

> the State Holding Company would have to grow steadily from the base provided by existing holdings in private industry. Its scarcest resource is likely to be the supply of experienced yet adventurous management. It is this which is likely to set a limit to its rate of growth. But there already is a solid base, we own 49 per cent of BP, now the largest and among the most profitable of British companies. We own Rolls Royce, we have a stake in a number of other companies. These, supplemented by a limited amount of selected nationalisation, should provide a good base from which to diversify into the labour-using industries which the regions require.

Also:

> to embark on its extensive programme of acquisition and diversification the State Holding Company would require finance. This should come partly from its own profits, partly from Government grants, and partly from the capital market.[20]

Roy's case, as thus published, was more radical in scope – 'the whole wide range of engineering' and 'its extensive programme of acquisition and diversification', plus only a management constraint on its rate of growth – than the NEC Green Paper on The National Enterprise Board, which limited its build-up over time to shareholdings in 20–25 companies.[21] It required selective amnesia, or failure to read it first, for Jenkins to condemn the Green Paper as 'outdated nationalisation dogma' and actually contrast it with his case for state shareholdings in his *What Matters Now*. He had missed the chance to claim that the Left on the NEC actually was recommending no more, if not less, than he already had done. Lauded as a historian, but a selective autobiographer, Roy does not refer at all in his memoirs to this public advocacy of a major state holding company, nor to its parallel with the case for the NEB, nor to the implications of his attack for dividing rather than uniting the Party on what amounted to the central area of its economic policy.[22]

The damage to the Labour Party – and the lost opportunity for himself – was considerable. He could have claimed that the 'Old' Left on the NEC actually was following his lead towards a new mixed economy rather than its previous commitment to 'outright nationalisation'. Given that the case for it had the unanimous support of every major trades union, Roy also could have shown Harold Wilson's attempted 1973 'veto' of the Green Paper on the NEB to be both uninformed and out of touch with the Labour movement. Had he stressed publicly that he would use his weight in Cabinet to ensure that the holding would realise the 'extensive programme of acquisition and diversification' he had advocated, and exploited the fact that the models for state shareholding and planning in the NEC's Green Paper were European, he also could have isolated the 'Old' Left on its claim that Europe was not anti-public ownership or anti-planning. Had he wished, given the coincidence between The Green Paper and his own chapter in *What Matters Now*, he could have claimed that the NEC had *de facto* re-written Clause IV on his own blueprint.

Was this design, or simply default? Had Roy even read the Green Paper before he denounced it the day it was published? If not, he lost his main chance for the Labour leadership by default, while also splitting the Party. If not, also, it seems that he was not alone. A few days after his own denunciation, when challenged to confirm it at a press conference, Harold Wilson asked the assembled journalists whether they actually had read it, and volunteered that it was not as bad as it seemed at first sight. Yet he had turned down the chance to gain its first real sight when both Judith Hart and I wrote to him before its publication to advise that it would represent a major change in Party thinking and policy and that we would like to discuss it with him in advance. Again, by default, Harold failed to unite the Party on the policy.

With such misjudgement by its parliamentary leaders, how did the Industrial Policy Committee of the Party therefore manage to gain virtual consensus on the case for a state holding company from 1972, not least since it was chaired by a notably 'moderate' trade unionist, John Chalmers?

The committee at that time was composed of several members of the previous Labour Cabinet, several of the next, the assistant general secretaries of the major trade unions, and some key members of the NEC itself. The paper which I wrote criticising the framework and nature of The National Plan argued the case for state holding companies and 'Planning Agreements'[23] with leading companies on similar lines to that which had convinced the cross-party Expenditure Committee. John Chalmers moved a vote of thanks and was about to move on to the agenda for the next meeting when Ian Mikardo intervened and said:

> I don't think we can just thank Mr Holland for his paper. He has criticised the whole basis of The National Plan and the IRC[24] and argued for a major change of direction. I don't know if he is right or wrong. But if he is right then we need to re-think and re-write our whole economic policy.

He then proposed that I should be able to present the ideas for scrutiny to two new sub-committees of the Executive: one for Planning and the other for Public Enterprise. Both were to be chaired by Judith Hart. Their secretary was a young researcher at Transport House, known at that time as Margaret Jackson and later as Margaret Beckett. Another member of the committee was Tony Banks, then head of research for the AEUW.

The case for Planning Agreements

The public enterprise working group reported regularly to the Industrial Policy Committee. At one of these meetings, John Chalmers asked me the same question as Roy Jenkins – how big would a State Holding Company need to be to do its job? I replied in the same vein as I had to Roy about the need for a broad wave of industrial investment, plus the need to be represented in each of the main sectors of industry and to be able to know the basis of costs and pricing – including transfer pricing – by multinational companies. Drawing on the analysis which I had already made for Roy, I said that it could in due course be represented on a majority or minority basis in from 20 to 25 main sectors of activity.

Chalmers then said that we ought to name names. I was against this on both political and pragmatic grounds, not least, if individual companies were prepared to enter into Planning Agreements in return for public money in the private sector, including revelation of their actual cost and pricing structures.

I had modelled the case for Planning Agreements at this stage on French, Italian and Belgian experience. The French case was especially compelling and almost entirely unknown in the UK at the time. The presumption of the main architect of the National Plan, Wilson's then economic adviser Thomas Balogh, had been that French planning worked through sectoral 'modernisation committees'. This had been plain to the Conservatives before 1964, who had introduced the National Economic Development Committees or NEDCs on this model. But by 1964 the French had moved deeper than discussion by sector working parties into directly negotiated agreements with companies – in the first instance *Contrats de Stabilité* or stability agreements, and by 1966 into *Contrats de Programme* or Planning Agreements.

I had learned this in January 1966 from Jean Saingeour, then Director of Planning at the French Ministry of Finance and Economy. I had walked into his office with a copy of Francois Perroux's *Techniques Quantitatives de la Planification*[25] which I had been reading. Perroux's case was that the modernisation committees were talkshops, and that what planning in a market economy needed was a workshop style agreement with *firmes motrices* or leading firms. In an increasingly concentrated oligopolistic economy, it was they who decided what was done, where, when and how. Saingeour stressed that Perroux's approach had been very influential with the Ministry.

It had. In introducing stability agreements with leading firms, the Ministry of Finance and Economy had allowed that they could change any prices they wished for any product, provided that their overall turnover-price ratio averaged a given rate consistent with the national target for inflation – at the time some 3.5 per cent. The aim was a macro policy outcome, i.e., if the price leaders kept to the target, the national inflation target was more likely to be met in macro-economic terms.

Yet within two years the Ministry realised that they had no proper knowledge of the basis on which firms were declaring costs, not least through internal and international transfer pricing. In other words, leading firms allowed their different subsidiaries to charge 'costs' to other subsidiaries or the parent company which inflated their cost base and understated real overall profits. This included research and development (R&D) costs which the Ministry had no way of evaluating at arms length, and also import costs from subsidiaries abroad. To respond to this the Ministry introduced *Contrats de Programme* or Planning Agreements. This much tougher scrutiny meant that the companies had to submit information on the whole range of their costs and pricing framework on their national and international operations. The Ministry also decided to use *Contrats de Programme* to lever other outcomes from leading firms in both the private and public sectors including more investment in less-developed regions and greater commitment to innovation and long-term investment projects. If firms cooperated they gained approval for public grants, public loans and public purchasing contracts.

The scale of this operation within the Finance and Economy Ministry was striking. Half of its senior staff was engaged in these Planning Agreements. The outcome in France today and the contrast with the UK is evident. They have a public high-speed TGV rail system for which they produce all the rolling stock and equipment. We do not. They still have French-controlled companies in vehi-cles and trucks, tyres, electrical and mechanical engineering, chemicals, electronics and computers. We do not.[26] Their nuclear power generation industry works well, however controversially. Ours does not. They have launchers which can put a satellite into space. We do not. They have avoided de-industrialisation. We have not. While we have a civilian aircraft industry it was due to their insistence on our not backing out of Concorde, and thus preserving the technology and skills vital for the later creation of Airbus Industrie. The French then thought and still think long-term. We do not. They still plan. We do not. They are a modern industrial nation. We are not.

I used the example of the French – and parallel Belgian and Italian – Planning Agreements in the paper which I had written for the Trade and Industry Sub-Committee of the Expenditure Committee, and also in the first paper which I submitted to the Industrial Policy Committee of the Labour Party.[27] But I had also given translations of their texts, and advocated their adoption, to Harold Wilson when working for him through Thomas Balogh in the Cabinet Office,[28] and later directly when in 1967 Wilson brought me into the Political Office in No.10. I argued that this approach was a way to re-launch The National Plan, which had collapsed with the deflationary package of July the previous year. I also argued that since the French themselves had found the need to move beyond the sector talkshops of the Modernisation Committees to direct negotiation with firms we could legitimate a re-launch of The National Plan on the same basis. He declared himself impressed, and may have raised the case with Peter Shore, who had succeeded George Brown at the Department of Economic Affairs, but it resulted in nothing. This was one of several reasons for my decision to resign from No.10 in 1968. I did not anticipate at the time that I would return with Planning Agreements backed by the NEC, every major trade union and the Party Conference in 1973. But the fact that one-to-one advocacy inside No.10 on the basis of precedent and detailed argument had been ineffective with Wilson certainly influenced the vigour with which I later pursued the Planning Agreements case through the Industrial Policy Committee of the Party.

The case for Planning Agreements as a means to gain more investment and employment in the regions had been reinforced meanwhile by the second report from the Trade and Industry Sub-Committee of the Expenditure Committee which followed their recommendation of a major British State Holding Company in *Public Money in the Private Sector*. The committee had been considering evaluation of the effectiveness of agricultural price support. But I persuaded its chair, Bill Rodgers, and he the committee, that the scope and limits of this were well known, while the value of public money in regional development grants – then running at 40 per cent subsidy for any investment in scheduled development regions – was not. My judgement was that companies going to the regions did so for availability of labour and would have gone there irrespective of government subsidy at such a high rate. The committee then took evidence from some 75 of the top companies in the UK. Not one of them was prepared to claim that government grants had been the decisive factor in its decision to locate new plants in the regions rather than labour availability. In this regard, we were not using public money for a public purpose but giving it, needlessly and with no return, to some of the richest companies in the country.

The report from the Expenditure Committee confirming this[29] powerfully reinforced the case for Planning Agreements as the basis on which leading companies would be obliged to trade returns in kind – whether regional investment, or more R&D in the UK, or long-term innovative investment – in return for public grants or public purchasing or, less typically, but ruled out, public loans.

Not least, I knew, and had documentation about, both the form of Planning Agreements – their templates – as introduced in France, Italy and Belgium, and which leading companies which had accepted them in these countries. These were the documents which I had translated and made available with supporting arguments for the re-launch of The National Plan to Harold Wilson in 1966, and which I now made available to the Inflation Sub-Committee of the Industrial Policy Committee of the National Executive in February 1973, with a similar cover note of half a dozen pages placing them in the context of how French planning had shifted from modernisation committees to direct negotiations with firms.[30] In the Belgian case I also made available summaries of actual Progress Agreements signed with leading companies such as Siemens. The Siemens agreement included commitment to a four-year programme which would more than treble its investment and quadruple its employment in Belgium and open entirely new plants in the country's scheduled Development Areas. With trade union support, Siemens also committed itself to a programme for new methods of work organisation.[31]

Such evidence legitimated the case for Planning Agreements as an indirect complement to direct action through the state holding company which the Labour Party was about to endorse and introduce in the National Enterprise Board. The NEB companies also should be obliged to prepare corporate plans reflecting key roles from the six designated for them, as outlined in the initial papers for the Expenditure Committee and the Party's Industrial Policy Committee,[32] and negotiate these also through Planning Agreements.

I elaborated the case in a series of papers for the Public Sector and Planning sub-committees of the NEC Industrial Policy Committee and also a longer 'New Priorities' paper for a two-day meeting in January 1974 which related the case for planning through leading firms to the impact of the autumn 1973 oil price hike by OPEC.[33] This, like the first paper which I had submitted to the Industrial Policy Committee of the Party in 1972, argued the case for flexible Planning Agreements as a means to influence change in sector outcomes, and medium-term planning targets adjusted on an annual basis rather than the implausible fixed medium-term targets of The National Plan.

The 'New Priorities' paper of January 1974 also made the case that we should use the NEB and Planning Agreements to ensure that companies invested their way out of the impending recession threatened by the OPEC oil price of the autumn of 1973, to which most governments were reacting defensively with expenditure cuts. This was the same 'broad wave' of innovating investment which I had recommended earlier to Roy Jenkins. Although at the time I did not know it, it was also the strategy which the Japanese took in response to the 1973 'oil shock'. Their Ministry of International Trade and Industry entered dialogue with and offered incentives to leading firms to bring forward their R&D projects into new product innovation and bargained with them on diversifying from the basic sectors of steel and shipbuilding into high technology sectors.[34] These products now succeed throughout the world economy, not least cars, engines,[35] machinery and components for industry, electrical power units, household electrical goods, electronics, television and sound systems, mobile phones and personal computers.

Democratising markets

The 'New Priorities' paper also outlined how trade unions should be invited, if they chose, to enter the negotiation of a planning agreement with management and the government. This tri-partism was aimed to be creative and consensual rather than confrontational. Michael Cooley and the Lucas Aerospace trade union combine committee at the time were showing the immense creativity in terms of entirely new products which could be unlocked by asking workers what they could do with their current skills and the company's current equipment. In the Lucas case this led to prototyping the first portable kidney machine, a road–rail vehicle, and a 'mountain bike'-style low-emission truck with multiple gears to gain momentum with a constant-speed motor. The Lucas workers were designers, engineers and computer programmers with a high level of professional qualification. The Lucas management were mainly school-leavers who had gone straight into business. Rejecting the idea that workers could join in product planning, they turned down the 100-plus proposals from the workers, several of which were then licensed by them to leading companies such as General Motors. Yet Lucas Aerospace itself was 100 per cent dependent on government defence contracts. With any creative intelligence on its part, the government could have obliged the company to enter a tri-partite planning agreement and ensured that at least some of the product suggestions were produced in the UK.

There were more fundamental reasons also for democratising markets through tri-partite planning in companies which either benefited from government grants – such as for regional location – or public purchasing. Trade unions then and now were limited to virtually one role: bargaining on wages and working conditions. To justify itself a union had to be tough on both. This gave little scope for cooperation with, rather than opposition to, management, including demarcation and innovation in work practices. Such cooperation – including also profit sharing – was the basis on which leading Japanese companies at the time were achieving 'continuous improvement' in both products and the labour process. At the time at which Lucas was rejecting its trade unions' proposals outright, Toyota was gaining some 1,300 proposals for new products or new methods of production from workers, of which it adopted up to 600 each year.[36]

Industrial democracy through tri-partite negotiation of Planning Agreements clearly challenged conventional management prerogatives. But they were welcomed by serious commentators. Thus the 'moderate' Labour, Economic, Finance and Taxation Association LEFTA commented in a pre-Thatcher era that 'Government and trades union involvement in the planning of industry's future is here to stay. The Planning Agreements system provides a framework which can make this participation effective.'[37] Likewise, the Business Graduates' Association got the main point concerning trade union involvement in its assessment that

> Planning Agreements may work as a vehicle for change in the organisation of trades unions, and have an effect in promoting amalgamations or improving *ad hoc* arrangements between unions in the same plant. On a wider scale, it could also cause unions, like management, to seek consent from a wider constituency than they traditionally have. And possibly the fact that employee representatives are expected to talk about the strategic long-term issues affecting the company will of itself lead to more people within

each factory considering these issues and discussing them among themselves. This would be of benefit to British industry.[38]

Some trade unions, otherwise renowned for their 'militancy' in bargaining on pay and conditions, also came out clearly in support, such as ASTMS, which published its own draft planning agreement template.[39]

Democratisation of markets through Planning Agreements also had a wider public in France and Belgium, as I argued in the 'New Priorities' and other papers to the Industry Policy Committee and its sub-committees. For instance, the Belgian state railway had recognised the need to modernise its rolling stock and rail infrastructure and had submitted bids from the three national companies producing them. None could offer supply at prices competitive with Swedish or German companies. The government then got the companies together through a joint planning agreement procedure or 'Progress Agreement' and convinced them that they should each specialise, one in track and signalling equipment, another in engines and the third in passenger and freight carriages. By so doing they were able to reduce unit costs and prices to levels only marginally higher than their Swedish and German counterparts, with the difference offset by government regional development grants. The process of this planning agreement-style bargaining was reported in the media and open to public consultation. The outcome became so well known, and so popular, that the government hired key advertising sites for a poster which showed a new electric engine pulling a train and simply said: 'SNCFB – Progress Agreement'. The Planning Agreements for French Railways were similarly open to public discussion and advertised by a simple and by then well understood slogan: 'L'État'.

Further, in terms of democratisation, I had argued from my first paper to the NEC Industrial Policy Committee that there should a new rolling medium-term national plan which should be debated annually by Parliament. This could avoid unrealistic four- or five-year targets which easily could be undermined by changes in the economic environment. It also would include reports on the functioning of the NEB, the British National Oil Corporation (BNOC), the nationalised industries and Planning Agreements. Unlike the sectoral talkshops of the National Economic Development Committees, Planning Agreements would enable the government to negotiate specific outcomes with leading firms including investment, employment, export and import trade and prices, including transfer pricing.

Tony Crosland and 'The birth' of the social contract

Tony Crosland had been the guru of social democracy since his classic *The Future of Socialism*, published in 1956.[40] We shared a similar academic background, an unwillingness to let a non-conformist upbringing inhibit enjoyment of life, and a similar intellectual arrogance. For precisely those reasons I liked him. I therefore was glad when he sat beside me at the meeting of the Industrial Policy Committee at which I was to present my first paper on the case for a new economic strategy.[41]

Tony stubbed out his cigar, opened his briefcase, pulled out the paper, turned to me and said: 'Good God. This is single-spaced and over twenty pages long. I hope we are not supposed to have read it?' I said that I would rather he had since I wrote it, but would be glad if he could do so after the meeting. I intended no put-down. I wanted him to read it when he could. But in practice it debarred Tony from making any critique of the paper during the meeting. He chafed a bit, but offered no direct criticism.

Tony Crosland attended the next major meeting of the committee in the Commons on 28 November 1972 and promptly went into attack mode. After some preliminaries to the effect that there was nothing fundamentally wrong with the National Plan except the exchange rate, John Chalmers advised him that there already was wide support on the committee for the proposals and queried why he had not challenged them earlier. Crosland expostulated 'Dammit, we can't go into the next election offering more nationalisation and no incomes policy'. Chalmers, by now into his stride, replied: 'Dammit Tony. If that is all you can offer you shouldn't have been in the last Cabinet and don't deserve to be in the next. There is no way the unions are going to accept another incomes policy without a trade-off on investment and jobs.' He then asked me to speak.

I started by saying that I was surprised that Tony should claim that the proposals for a state holding company were 'nationalisation' and that in fact he could claim if he chose to have authored the case for it by arguing in *The Future of Socialism* for more competitive public enterprise rather than more national- isation.[42] 'No,' he replied, 'this is not at all what I had in mind.' I answered that surely it was, with the key difference that concentration in British industry had doubled since the last industrial census available to him when he wrote the case for it, which was why the state holding company – or companies – needed to be wider-ranging. I also claimed that one of the key limits of a standard fixed-wage incomes policy was that it allowed no incentive for productivity increases of the kind which Planning Agreements did. He answered, 'So why not call it an incomes policy?' I replied by agreeing with John Chalmers that the unions would not accept either the same policy or the same name. 'So what would you call it?' he asked.

I had never considered the issue. But his provocation brought it to me, helped by the fact that I had read and taught Rousseau at Oxford. 'A Social Contract', I answered. 'Meaning what?' he growled. I then ran at some length through the case that Rousseau's social contract was a written agreement, pre-agreed by all members of society. Rousseau's society had to be small. Everyone was supposed to know each other. This was why he had stressed that it could not apply to big countries. But in a real sense what we were doing in the committee in preparing a written programme for the Party was similar to his exercise in preparing a written Social Contract. The basis of Labour's contract would be that, in return for a given degree of wage restraint, the trade unions would gain a commitment from a Labour government to aim to fulfil Labour's programme and extend trade union rights. Also, as with Rousseau, if there were to be a change to the contract, it should be argued out by those who agreed it and seek consent rather than be decided and imposed by an individual or a government. Unlike a fixed-rate incomes policy, it could be flexible, allowing for higher pay with productivity increases. It also could be revised and take account of circumstances beyond the government's own control. I did not realise how relevant this was in relation to the oil shock of the autumn of the next year.

Tony sensed the support from the rest of the committee and relapsed into silence. I was glad to win the exchange, but would have preferred him to accept the open suggestion that the state holdings argument was consistent with his own case for competitive public enterprise, and for him at least to enter discussion of a Social Contract. He not only chose not to do so but thereafter gained the consent of Tony Howard for his later FCO adviser Wilfrid Beckerman to launch a three-page assault on me in the *New Statesman*. Margaret Beckett rang to ask whether I had seen it, saying 'You must reply. It is an open attempt at character assassination'. Tony Howard offered me a 400-word letter in reply. I threatened the Press Council and gained a column and a bit. Beckerman replied, I answered and Mike Hatfield declared that we were quits in terms of mutual vituperation. But another chance for consensus had been lost. And, thereafter, with Crosland having lost the battle, but grasping an ally on their side, the social democrats went to war against the programme.[43]

The term 'Social Contract' none the less survived. It took some time to gain common usage. 'Social Compact' was preferred for some time by some trade union leaders. Nor had I been alone in arguing a similar case. The NEC, PLP and TUC Liaison Committee already had gone a long way on this basis[44]. But the intellectual case for it had been stated openly in the presence of key future members of the Cabinet and the NEC and the assistant general secretaries of the main national trade unions.

The problem, again, was that Harold Wilson did not concur or, at worst, simply did not grasp the case. He used the term Social Contract simply as a re-branding of his former incomes policy, i.e. a fixed increase for all workers. It was Jack Jones who brilliantly translated this into the £6 a week upper limit to increases, which at least was redistributive in favour of lower-paid workers. The contract worked until the winter of discontent in 1978. But many workers by then had accepted a decline in real incomes without the trade-off in the range of social policies which had been agreed by the NEC, PLP and TUC Liaison Committee in the early 1970s. Such a 'Contract' also suffered the same inflexibility as the earlier incomes policy which meant, in particular, that more skilled and white-collar workers lost out. Unsurprisingly, swathes of them voted for Margaret Thatcher in 1979.

The NEC Green Paper on the National Enterprise Board

The event which made a Labour government possible in 1974 was Edward Heath's decision during the miners' strike to call an election in the spring of that year on the misguided slogan 'Who Governs?' For a government with a year and half to run, it was a calculated error. It happened also to pre-empt the publication that spring of the Labour Party Green Paper on Planning Agreements which had been intended to complement its earlier publication of the Green Paper on The National Enterprise Board.[45] While the two issues may appear incommensurate, this played a key role in the reluctance of some trade unions, notably the Transport and General Workers Union, to throw their weight behind union participation in Planning Agreements despite the fact that this had been agreed earlier by the Industrial Policy Committee of the NEC on which the TGWU was represented, with strong support from the assistant general secretaries of other key unions such as the AEUW, TASS and ASTMS.

The National Enterprise Board Green Paper reflected the concern of John Chalmers that the Party should spell out just how big the NEB would need to be to register the leverage on macro policy which I had outlined in the initial paper for the NEC on Planning and Policy Coordination.[46] I argued that we should make plain that it would need to be represented in each main sector of activity if we were to be able to gain information on costs and tax avoidance through transfer pricing[47] and promote a broad wave of regenerative investment; i.e. the same point as I had made to, and had been explicitly accepted by, Roy Jenkins in his case for a holding across 'the whole wide range of engineering' with an 'extensive programme of acquisition and diversification.' But I also argued, unlike Jenkins, that we should have more than one holding company to avoid a monolithic structure; for instance, a holding in oil and hydrocarbons similar to the Italian ENI – already being advocated by Thomas Balogh – another in manufacturing, and another in banking and insurance etc., as was the case for the sub-holdings of IRI in Italy where it in fact controlled three of the major banks. I also made and gained acceptance of the case that there should be development agencies and regional enterprise boards. The latter should offer venture capital to smaller firms and on occasion for larger local firms to work through joint ventures with the NEB, which also would give a more plural and less monolithic structure. I also had made the case that a re-introduced Industrial Re-organisation Corporation should be remitted to re-organise firms in difficulties, leaving the NEB to reinforce and promote success.

The NEB Green Paper stressed that it already was the policy of the Party that, whenever the state puts public money into private industry, it should take shares in return and must have either a total holding or at least a controlling interest. But, as I had stressed throughout to the NEC committees, a small minority shareholding could give effective control because of the dispersal of ownership and the interest of most shareholders in dividend income rather than influencing management decisions. Exceptions were when pension funds would indicate that they would reconsider their holdings unless there were changes in management, but these were relatively rare for 'blue chip' leading firms. This was not a new argument. It had been recognised since the pioneering study of Berle and Means in 1932 on the difference between formal 51 per cent control and effective control.[48] Moreover, of some relevance to a later stage of the debate, this point and the Berle and Means argument had been supported in making the same case for competitive public enterprise on the basis of minority holdings by Tony Crosland in his *Future of Socialism*.[49] The figures on companies were concerned to influence – and facilitate – their long-term investment and regional development location so to gain sufficient labour for entirely new plants and not proposals for 100 per cent ownership. The distinctions appeared lost to key political players, and was universally lost to the press.

New Left, Old Left and New Labour

So how new was the 'New Left' case for selective public shareholding, Planning Agreements and the social contract, and how does it compare with the 'Old Left' or New Labour's economic policies?

1   On ownership, the case was for selective shareholdings, not nationalisation in the sense of outright ownership and control of an entire sector. As already stressed, minority holdings of as little as 10 per cent or 15 per cent could give control and thereby finance long-term innovating investment when the stock market would not. Where 100 per cent ownership occurred it was of a company, not a sector, as where the NEB took over an already 100 per cent publicly-owned company, such as International Computers Ltd, then a major player in the national and international markets.[50]

2   Unlike nationalisation, the case for shareholdings through a state holding company or companies was competitive not monopolistic. It was to introduce competition into oligopolistic sectors and especially to ensure that prices reflected costs, rather than fictitious transfer pricing. The case differed from the 1972 Common Programme of the Left in France, which recommended nationalisation of – as it happens – 25 firms, but on a rigid sectoral model which did not allow the kind of flexibility open to state holdings to diversify into entirely new sectors of activity.

3   It was a formula for reinforcing and promoting commercial success in what would remain companies with private shareholdings, rather than a formula for underwriting failure, as had been the case in Ted Heath's one-clause bill nationalising Rolls Royce after its costly experimentation with carbon fibre blades for aero engines, or the failure of the pre-war mines and railways to modernise under private ownership. This still is relevant to the failure to gain private finance for long-term modernisation of railways or the London Underground in Britain today.

4   It was for a plural mixed economy formula with a variable ownership stake in individual companies, rather than the Old Labour dual mixed economy of nationalised sectors on the one hand and private companies on the other. Companies would not be obliged to enter into such agreements if they did not need or wish to be beneficiaries of public money and public purchasing. In this sense, as I stressed to the NEC from the outset, such intervention would be 'more than indicative but less than imperative.'[51]

5   Joint public and private shareholding in companies was not dissimilar to the principle of joint Private Finance Initiative (PFI), but with the difference that the government could gain immediate value for public money invested in the private sector rather than borrow from it now and pay several times as much years later. It also had wider social gains inasmuch as such shareholdings, with public purchasing, and loans to companies – rather than the reverse as in the PFI – would not only be financial but, through Planning Agreements – should gain real economy trade-offs such as new investment and jobs, not least in the regions.

6   Neither the case for state shareholdings nor that for Planning Agreements was anti-profit. Both the new state holding companies and companies entering Planning Agreements – unlike nationalised sectors – would continue to be listed on the stock market and be able to buy or sell shares. The private shareholdings in state holding or other companies could be enhanced by higher growth and a fuller declaration of profits than was the case with understated profits through transfer-pricing. This could enhance shareholder value, subject to the degree of re-investment of profits negotiated through Planning Agreements, which would be subject to debate in Parliament within the new rolling planning framework. But it was a formula for socially accountable profits in senses: the financial reporting of real costs and profits, and the economic and social – or externalities – case that companies gaining public money or public purchasing would need to enter negotiation of Planning Agreements.[52]

7   Planning Agreements were not 'rigid' top-down central planning, as most of the press and several social democrats claimed after their adoption by the Left-controlled NEC, and provoked by Tony Benn's eccentric and unwarranted use of the term 'compulsory Planning Agreements with the top 100 companies'. They were devolved meso-level planning with macro implications. Unlike the National Plan's rigid and unrealistic sector targets, Planning Agreements were to be customised to where companies were at and take account of what they already were doing well but with specific meso outcomes changing macro-economic performance.

8   The case did not imply the State taking over management with 'civil servants running industry'. Rather than civil servants running industry, managers would continue to manage the companies, and be free to draw on their managerial experience of what was feasible in terms of changed parameters for performance in Planning Agreements, as in the above-cited case of Siemens and others with the Belgian or French governments. They concerned only a minor fraction of 1 per cent of all companies, while the rest could be assisted generally by regional or other grants, regional enterprise boards and development agencies.

9   The case was neither backward-looking to 'Old Labour' nor nationalist. It brought the national ownership and planning debate up-to-date with

changes in continental experience, and not least the adoption since the 1960s by governments in France, Belgium, Germany, Sweden and elsewhere of agencies modelled on the IRI state shareholding experience. It also was the first time a political party had sought to countervail the globalisation of capital and trade with national policy instruments. But it also recognised the need for its companies to act globally. One of the NEB's early decisions was to fund the inventor Clive Sinclair setting up two companies in the United States – Inmos and Nexos – so that they could be closer to the 'Silicon Valley' innovation frontier in computers and related electronics. One of the best decisions concerning British Leyland, brought into the NEB, was to form a joint venture with Honda, which enabled it to learn and adapt Japanese methods of work organisation ahead of most US and European vehicles producers.

10   Like New Labour, the case was not anti-market but aimed to socialise market outcomes. Where it differed from some aspects of New Labour was in not sharing the presumption that 'markets always knew best' or that commercial values should dominate criteria for the use of public contracts or public investment. Rather, Planning Agreements should oblige big business to give 'social externalities' or public value trade-offs for public money in the private sector, such as more R&D and innovation, new investment and jobs, especially in the regions, greater transparency in costs, pricing and thus profits and tax etc.

Afterwards

So what happened to this 'New Left' case for a differently mixed economy?

Immediately it was nearly wrecked in practice by the nationalism of Tony Benn. At a meeting at his home after the policy had passed the 1973 Labour Conference he insisted that the Party should recognise that the programme was fundamentally incompatible with membership of the Common Market and call for a referendum on Europe. I made two points. First, that this was absurd when we had legitimated the policies on the basis of continental European models. Second, that if he claimed this in a referendum he could lose it and thereby the industrial strategy. He did, and Eric Varley was moved into Industry to assure the markets that neither public shareholdings nor Planning Agreements would be anything but voluntary.

None the less, shortly after the February 1974 election, Tony Benn co-opted me onto the committee drafting the Industry Bill. The committee produced the draft in record time. This meant that there still was a National Enterprise Board and new Scottish, Welsh and Northern Ireland Development Agencies.

Such were the needs of modern and advanced British industry for long-term public finance that by 1979 the National Enterprise Board employed nearly a million people in companies in which it took an outright or partial shareholding. Since abolition of the NEB by Margaret Thatcher, most of them either no longer exist or survive as shadows of their former selves. The Scottish, Welsh and Northern Ireland Development Agencies have survived and in the main flourished. Regional Planning Agreements and enterprise boards, modelled on the case as made to the NEC and in Labour's Programme 1973, were adopted in the West Midlands Enterprise Board and in the Greater London Enterprise Board. Regional development agencies have now been introduced to England, some 25 years since John Prescott asked me to help rework them as Labour Party policy for all the UK. In such a sense, the strategy was short-lived nationally but long-lived in the regions.

It also went abroad. In France, the case I made in *The Socialist Challenge*[53] influenced the adoption of *Contrats de Region*, or regional Planning Agreements, which have been an outstanding success. As *Programmatiki Sinfonias* they are the basis of regional planning in Greece. The Italians adapted their own 'programme agreements' in a more focused form or planning agreement, or *Accordi di Piano*.

Most of the new mixed economy case and its implied shift in the imbalance of public and private power was adopted in the Out of Crisis Project which I initiated in 1981 with the support of Jacques Delors, then finance minister of France. This brought together 25 personalities of the European Left, several of whom later were ministers and one of whom, Enrique Baron, later became President of the European Parliament. Notably it endorsed the plural mixed economy case written Europe-wide rather than the nationalisation case of the Common Programme of the Left in France. The Out of Crisis report became the basis of the manifesto of the Confederation of European Socialist Parties – forerunners of the Party of European Socialists (PES) – for the next two European elections.[54] Its non-Brussels case for recovering growth through public investment, restructuring power between the public and private sectors through Planning Agreements, and redistributing income from growth was drawn to the attention of Neil Kinnock by Charles Clarke, then his chief of staff. It also supported his initiative, on becoming Leader of the Labour Party the same year, in shifting it from ritual opposition to the Common Market to a party committed to Europe.[55]

Out of Crisis, the same year, persuaded Andreas Papandreou, leader of the Greek Socialist Party, and the first socialist prime minister of Greece, to do the same for PASOK (the Panhellenic Socialist Movement). Papandreou invited me to bring together several of the Out of Crisis team to prepare the first Greek European Council with his key ministers. Out of this, on the same agenda, came his call for a New Messina Conference in December 1983, echoed by François Mitterrand in the Presidency Conclusions of the French European Council in June the following year.[56] The outcome was the Single European Act with its 'twin pillars' of the single market and economic and social cohesion.

More followed when in 1989 I accepted the invitation of Jacques Delors to help him make a reality of the cohesion pillar of the Single European Act, and left Parliament to do so. Other than Neil Kinnock and Charles Clarke, then his chief of staff, who knew why I was going, only Ian Gow, in the debate on my applying to take the Chiltern Hundreds, got the point that I had not given up on

Labour but was going to help Delors to write an agenda to 'socialise' Europe. The report which I did for Delors[57] became the basis for his 1993 White Paper on Growth, Competitiveness, Employment.[58] This gave the rationale for the first employment target set by the Union – 15 million jobs to be created by a combination of long-term social investment and increased labour intensity in the social sphere – more teachers and smaller class sizes in education, and more health and social workers – which later was endorsed by the Essen European Council, as well as social negotiation of reduced working time, later on the agenda of German companies and the Jospin socialist government in France.

It also included a key 'mixed economy' case which I had made in the 1972 Planning and Coordination paper to the NEC that only public intervention would assure long-term social investment. This included the recommendation that the European Union should issue its own bonds. As Union rather than national borrowing, like US Treasury bonds, these need not count on national debt nor therefore condemn member states to the monetarist national debt provisions for a single currency in the Treaty of Maastricht.[59] Thanks to advocacy by Antonio Guterres, and other Left prime ministers and finance ministers who had been part of the 'Out of Crisis' initiative of 1981–3, including Paul Nyrup Rasmussen, Costas Simitis and Dominique Strass-Kahn, both the bonds and the focus for their investment in health, education and urban environment were called for by the European Council as the Amsterdam Special Action Programme and endorsed at Luxembourg in 1997. The European Investment Bank (EIB) now issues these Euro Bonds and on-lending for up to 30 years in these areas at Libor plus a small administrative charge. Thirteen of the fifteen member states do not count borrowing from the Bank against national debt,[60] and the potential to avoid deflationary pressures by a social investment-led recovery programme financed by the EIB is vast.[61]

Another recommendation to Delors was for a new European Investment Fund on the same principle as that which I had advocated for regional enterprise boards – public venture capital for Small and Medium-sized Enterprises (SMEs). Such capital now is being guaranteed by the Fund throughout the EU and is especially relevant to the Accession countries where entrepreneurship abounds but venture capital has been lacking. Regional Planning Agreements resurfaced as the Union's Local or Territorial Employment Pacts. I also gained the right for trade union involvement in extending skills to new product areas, which then became the EU's ADAPT programme. My case to Delors that we should shift regional development from investment in infrastructure to investment in people, plus my co-option onto the drafting committee of the Fourth Framework Programme, had two outcomes. The first was the new human resources Objective 4 (now Objective 3) of the Structural Funds. The second was that all Framework Programmes should be networked to include an Objective 1 or least developed regions, thereby giving people and institutions in these regions the chance of learning from innovation and best practice in the more developed and assisting smaller firms to gain some of the features of larger multinationals without needing comparable size.

Trade union involvement in democratising the market also was the basis on which, on the invitation of Antonio Guterres, I drafted the Innovation Agreements policy adopted by the Feira and Lisbon European Councils. Like the original proposal of Planning Agreements, these imply social dialogue and trade-off – flexible production, new methods of work organisation and competitiveness by consent, in return for skills extension plus, in the Lisbon Council Presidency Conclusions, the right to negotiate the balance of working and non-work time. Thanks to Delors, their adoption as EU Framework Agreements depends on the initiative of the Social Partners themselves, rather than the Commission or the Council, again pluralising power.

In effect, the 'New Left' case in Britain in the 1970s has gone European and has reinforced a Europe-wide social agenda. The model of Europe as a social market economy offers an alternative to the US for developing countries which has been well grasped by the Socialist International, still the largest political organisation in the world.[62] The outcome of a Social Europe confirmed Labour as a European Party and split the Tories from the mainstream of the European Centre Right. Delors was reviled by the *Sun* newspaper and much of the British Right for this reason, but remains an inspiration for much of the present generation of European leaders in demonstrating that the EU can and should aspire to being more than a free trade area with reduced social rights.

The British footnote is less positive. According to Patrick Cosgrave, at her first shadow cabinet meeting after succeeding Ted Heath, Margaret Thatcher asserted: 'Labour knows what they want. We don't. I need an economic programme.' Keith Joseph and Enoch Powell obliged with pamphlets published by the Institute of Economic Affairs re-cycling the anti-planning and anti-public intervention arguments of Friedrich von Hayek and Milton Friedman. The fate of Clive Sinclair was symptomatic of what was to come. Thatcher recommended him for a knighthood, but abolished the NEB and cut his financial support. Within a year he was out of business. So, not long afterwards, was much of the rest of British industry. Whether it can regenerate through Europe remains to be seen.

Notes

1   Jim also asked whether I would prepare material concerning the activities of multi-nationals for a speech he was to give shortly on the subject, which I duly did.
2   Hatfield, M., *The House the Left Built* (Gollancz, London, 1978).
3   Memorandum on European Para-Governmental Agencies, in Sixth Report from the Expenditure Committee: Public Money in the Private Sector, Vol. III, pp. 740–53.
4   Holland, S., 'Planning and Policy Coordination', Paper to the Industrial Policy Committee of the Labour Party, RD 315, March 1972.
5   See further *The Annual Census of Production* and Prais, S.J., *The Evolution of Giant Firms in Britain*, (CUP, Cambridge, 1976). Professor Prais had kindly made the key figures of his study available to me for use before publication.
6   See further The Department of Trade's Annual Overseas Transactions Enquiry, HMSO. The top 75 firms reached the 50 per cent share of visible export trade in 1975.

7 Tony Blair recently has commented on the 'armlock' of the major supermarkets on small farmers. Twenty years ago the top three supermarkets already accounted for 40 per cent of packaged grocery sales. Cf. Monopolies and Mergers Commission Report, 1985.

8 None of this would have surprised Adam Smith, who wrote in the *Wealth of Nations* that nothing is more certain when two or three producers gather together than that 'they will conspire against the public interest by a contrivance to raise prices.'

9 The number of firms in the UK representing the upper half of all retail sales fell from 4,750 in 1950 to 350 by 1976 and less than a 100 by the later 1980s. Source: Department of Trade and Industry.

10 Bertil Ohlin gained the Nobel Prize for Economics for the work in which he pointed this out, although the point thereafter was lost to most theorists of international trade. Cf. Ohlin, B., *Interregional and International Trade*, (Harvard University Press, Cambridge, 1933). I had first been alerted to the role of multinationals in this regard by Robin Murray who pioneered analysis of their macro significance in the UK.

11 Scribberas, E., *Multinational Electronics Companies and National Economic Policies*, (JAI Press, Greenwich CT, 1977).

12 Hoffman–La Roche was quick to point out that the Italian company had disregarded its patents, and claim that the price difference reflected its R&D costs, which appears to have stalled Shirley in following through. Had the NEB already been based in a pharmaceuticals company it could have known the real scale of such R&D and informed her judgement, as the establishment of the British National Oil Corporation – Labour's ENI-modelled holding – was able to inform ministers on real drilling costs, which resulted in more realistic bids by multinationals for North Sea Oil franchises.

13 Greek: *mesos* – intermediate. See further Holland, S., *The Socialist Challenge*, (Quartet Books, London, 1975) and Holland, S., *The Market Economy and The Global Economy*, (Weidenfeld and Nicolson, London, 1967).

14 See *inter alia* my contribution to Kennet, W., Whitty, L. and Holland, S., *Sovereignty and Multinational Companies*, Fabian Tract 409, July 1971, and in particular Part 4 on Effects on National Demand Management and the Balance of Payments.

15 Memorandum on the Visit of the Trade and Industry Sub-Committee to Italy, April 1972, in *Sixth Report from the Expenditure Committee: Public Money in the Private Sector*, Vol. III, pp. 753–73.

16 Holland, S. (ed.) *The State as Entrepreneur: the IRI State Shareholding Formula*, (Weidenfeld and Nicolson, London, 1972).

17 This 'broad wave' approach had been advocated by Ragnar Nurkse and Paul Rosenstein-Rodan. Their case, however, had been for broad-ranging infrastructure in countries which lacked it, rather than through companies.

18 Jenkins, R., *What Matters Now*, (Fontana Paperback, London, 1972).

19 *Ibid.*, p. 35. 'Hosiery and other clothing' was his idea, not mine. Later, the Greater London Enterprise Board, modelled on the NEB, did intervene in the declining London furniture industry.

20 *Ibid.*, pp. 35–6.

21 The Labour Party, 'The National Enterprise Board', Opposition Green Paper, London, April 1973.

22 Jenkins, R., *A Life at the Centre*, (Macmillan, London, 1991).

23 At that time unfelicitously known as 'Programme Contracts' which was their name in their respective Italian, French and Belgian versions.

24 The Industrial Reconstruction Corporation introduced by the previous Labour Government whose aim was to promote mergers as the basis of restructuring the competitiveness of British industry.

25 Perroux, F., *Les Techniques Quantitatives de la Planification*, (Presses Universitaires de France, Paris, 1965).

26 Even our long-standing major companies such as GEC in electrical and mechanical engineering and ICI in chemicals have been stripped down or hollowed out. We still have a significant aerospace sector, but in large part due to the French government consistently backing the Airbus project through Aérospatiale.

27 The Italian versions of Planning Agreements or Programmazione Contrattata were mainly concerned with gaining regional investment by private companies in Southern Italy. The Belgian versions in the form of *Contrats de Programme* were mainly concerned with the first pre-occupation of the French government – counter-inflation.

28 Paper on French Incomes and Prices Policy, Cabinet Office, 2 December 1966.

29 Second Report from the Expenditure Committee, Session 1973–4, *Regional Development Incentives*, HMSO December 1973.

30 Holland, S., *Inflation and Price Control: Note on French Programme Contracts*, Labour Party Working Group on Inflation, RD 605, February 1973. The paper also included text of Stability Contracts and the reason why the government had seen the need to gain more direct information from firms on their cost structures through Programme Contracts.

31 Employment was to increase from 1,100 to 4,100 jobs in electronics and computers, telecommunications and medical equipment. In return for this and the commitment that the new plant would be located in specified development areas, the Belgian government guaranteed specified public purchasing of a range of the goods concerned 'on condition that the prices were not higher than those charged by Siemens on the Belgian market to other purchasers and were competitive with prices elsewhere on the European market'. Contrat de Progrès Entre l'Etat Belge et S.A. Siemens, ST. no. 265/8.5. 1970.

32 See the opening of this chapter, para. 3.

33 'New Priorities for the Public Sector', Paper for the LP NEC Public Sector Group, 5–6 January 1974.

34 Cf. Johnson, C., *MITI and the Japanese Miracle*, (Stanford University Press, Los Angeles, 1982).

35 Honda extended its core competence – engines – from motor bikes to cars, and now is the biggest engine producer in the world, selling double the total of GM and Ford combined, and for a wide range of industrial uses other than vehicles. Kawasaki Steel diversified through joint ventures into electronics etc.

36 Womack J., Jones D.T. and Roos, D., *The Machine that Changed the World*. (Macmillan, Basingstoke, 1990).

37 Labour Economic, Finance and Taxation Association, *Planning Agreements in Practice*, 1975.

38 The Business Graduate Association, *Planning agreements? – Practical Considerations*, March 1975.

39 ASTMS, The Crisis in British Planning and a Draft Planning Agreement: A Discussion Paper, 1975.

40 Crosland, C.A.R., *The Future of Socialism*, (Jonathan Cape, London, 1956).

41 'Planning and Policy Coordination', The Labour Party, 1972.

42 I thoroughly agreed with his case. I never advocated more 'nationalisation' in any of the papers I wrote in the early 1970s for the NEC, nor in any of my books or articles published thereafter. I was not against the earlier nationalisation of basic industry and services such as coal, steel, rail, gas, electricity, post or telecommunications. Richard Pryke, a key member of the various NEC committees, had just published an impressive analysis which demonstrated that productivity – and thus efficiency – on a range of measures had been higher for a decade in the nationalised industries than in the private sector. Cf. Pryke, R., *Public Enterprise in Practice: the British Experience of Nationalisation over Two Decades*, (MacGibbon and Kee, London 1971). Richard had been one of the first to advocate a state holding company for the UK but, as he later volunteered, as an institutional means of managing disparate public holdings rather than a means of harnessing or countervailing oligopoly power.

43   Roy Jenkins was to come out against the proposals – identical in substance, since I had drafted both, to his own in *What Matters Now* – as dogmatic nationalisation. Bill Rodgers later was to refer to them as modelled on 'Mussolini's Italy'. Hitherto-supporting social democrats such as Edmond Dell also moved to the attack. See further, Hatfield, M., *The House the Left Built*, (Gollancz, London, 1978).

44   See further in detail the Appendix to Michael Hatfield, *The House the Left Built*.

45   The National Enterprise Board etc.

46   'Planning and Policy Coordination', The Labour Party, 1972.

47   As especially important in the activities of the British National Oil Corporation.

48   Berle, A. and Means, G., *The Modern Corporation and Private Property*, (Harcourt Brace, New York 1932).

49   Crosland, *The Future of Socialism*.

50   Later taken over by Fujitsu, as the General Electric Corporation's rail coach-making was by the French company Altom and then, in 2003, closed.

51   The perception – and the phrase – was Andrew Shonfield's in relation to the first French Plan directed by Jean Monnet. Shonfield, A., *Modern Capitalism* (Oxford University Press, Oxford, 1965).

52   State holding companies in Italy were listed on the stock market.

53   Holland, *The Socialist Challenge*.

54   Holland, S. (ed.) *Out of Crisis*. (Spokesman Books, Nottingham, 1983).

55   See further Kinnock, N., 'A New Deal for Europe', *New Socialist*, Spring 1984.

56   The Messina Conference of 1956 led to the Rome Treaty the following year. But Messina was much more positive in its call for industrial, social and regional policy than the Rome Treaty.

57   Holland, S., *The European Imperative: Economic and Social Cohesion in the 1990s* (Spokesman Books, Nottingham, 1993)

58   European Commission, *Growth, Competitiveness, Employment*, (Brussels, December, 1993).

59   Holland, *The European Imperative*.

60   The exceptions at the time of going to press are the UK and the Netherlands.

61   At more than €40 billion EIB lending already is bigger than that of the World Bank, comparable with all spending through the CAP and, since expanding, approaching half of Union 'own resources' financed from national tax by member states. Much of this increase in investment is in the Amsterdam Council areas of health, education and urban renewal.

62   The main arguments of my second report to Delors, published as *Towards a New Bretton Woods*, (Spokesman, Nottingham, 1994), were supported by Antonio Guterres, then chair of the SI economic and environment committee, and now the SI president, and were the basis of the World Economy resolution at its 1996 New York convention. This remains the official policy of the Socialist International.

10 Labourism

Eric Shaw

What is 'Labourism'?

Labourism is an elusive concept and though frequently used lacks any agreed definition. However, all the various usages agree that it refers to the nexus ('interdependence of two elements': Penguin English Dictionary) between the trade unions and the Labour Party and the way this has conferred upon the latter a distinctive outlook, organisational design and way of operating. For McLean, 'labourism is a name one might give to the view that more energetic steps should be taken towards working-class representation in Parliament in order to redress working-class grievances.'[1] Similarly Morgan defined labourism as 'an economic creed of support for the working class rather than a doctrine for the conquest and mobilisation of power.'[2] However, the term has come to be most closely associated with critiques of the Labour Party from two opposing political quarters, the Marxist and (what we shall call) the 'proto-New Labour'. Both argue that Labour's political outlook and *modus operandi* owe a heavy debt to its trade union founders and both agree that, whatever the short-term advantages, this imposed upon the Party heavy long-term costs – though they differ sharply on how they construe these costs.

'Labourism' was first deployed as an explanatory concept by John Saville in a seminal essay. He defined it as:

> a theory and practice which accepted the possibility of social change within the existing framework of society … and which increasingly recognised the working of political democracy of the parliamentary variety as the practicable means of achieving its own aims and objectives.[3]

Thereafter the concept occupied a central place in the Marxist critique of the Labour Party. Its influence, once profound in scholarly quarters, has now abated and the eventual fate of the concept may have that of a minor contribution to the historiography of the labour movement. But it has been unearthed, rehabilitated and given a different twist by commentators from a quite different intellectual tradition. In 1991 David Marquand presented an analysis and interpretation of labourism that was to exert a formative impact on New Labour strategic thinking.

This chapter begins with a sketch of the Marxist interpretation of New Labour and then outlines the 'proto-New Labour' alternative in a little more detail. The rest of the chapter explores the extent to which this second theory of labourism has generated valid and insightful propositions about the nature of the Labour Party.

Marxism, 'Proto-New Labour' and 'Labourism'

Labourism, for its Marxist interpreters, was the Labour Party's vapid substitute for a genuine socialist doctrine. Its adoption reflected the particular experiences of the British labour movement as it had evolved over the course of the nineteenth century. By the end of that century it had acquired a mentality 'already profoundly adapted to the conditions of bourgeois society and imbued with its conservatism'.[4] Trade unionism lacked the intellectual tools and the political confidence to engage in a critical analysis of capitalist society because – in contrast to continental movements – it had no Marxist theory upon which to draw. In consequence, labourism was an ideology 'inflected and conditioned by bourgeois thought'.[5] This was the legacy bequeathed to the Labour Party founded in 1900. Its *raison d'être* was to promote the 'concrete demands of immediate advantage to the working class and organised labour': to this extent it was a 'class party'. But these demands were disconnected from any strategy 'for the creation of a fundamentally different kind of society', and its ambitions were 'narrowly bound by the capitalist environment' which was accepted as given.[6]

Labourism was also defined by its unswerving loyalty to British constitutional conventions and a staunch faith in British Parliamentary institutions as the ultimate repositories of political virtue and wisdom: 'the Labour Party has not only been a parliamentary party; it has been a party deeply imbued by parliamentarianism'.[7] This involved abjuring any action – notably extra-parliamentary mobilisation – that could be construed as in any way inconsistent with British constitutional doctrine. 'Because of the wholesale integration of the theory and practice of the Party into the national cultural formation,' it failed to envisage the working class as a maker of its own destiny.[8] Thus Labour's programme was geared to affording the working class protection against unemployment, insecurity, sickness and poverty through a range of ameliatory measures but not to overthrowing the system which (in Marxist eyes) gave rise to these maladies. Far from seeking to create a classless society, the object was the incorporation of the working class into the existing social order – which meant the working class accommodating to its subordinate role.[9] Thus 'a "labourist" reading of working class political interests emphasises their discrete and limited nature, their attainability within capitalism, and their capacity for realisation through parliamentary channels.'[10]

The Marxist analysis of labourism contains insights into Labour's character and pattern of development: that it was steadfast and unshakeable in its adherence to established parliamentary conventions; that though it was a class party it was so in a narrow and limited sense; that it believed that though the interests of classes often diverged from each other, ultimately they could be reconciled. However, its plausibility as an explanation of the dynamics of Labour politics is contingent upon the validity of key Marxist theorems: that the social order is fundamentally fissured; that the interests of capital and labour cannot be accommodated; that the needs of the latter can only be fully realised by a fundamental transformation of social relations and the production system; and that, finally, this aim could only be achieved by a left-wing party equipped with the correct (Marxist) intellectual tools.

Marquand's concept of labourism drew upon the Marxist usage of the term but turned it in a quite different direction. All industrial societies, he wrote, 'have to solve the problem of how the "labour interest" immanent in the very structure of modern industry, is to express itself in politics'. The solution of the American New Deal was to incorporate it into a 'broad-based, cross-class coalition'; that of Scandinavia and central European social democratic parties closely associated with, but organisationally separate from, centralised trade unions. The British solution, 'the exception – and a very rare exception at that', was 'Labourism', whereby the labour interest has been 'sustained by, and embodied in, a Labour Party'.[11] Unlike its continental counterparts, the Party – established not by committed socialists but by trade unions – 'deliberately chose to identify itself as the instrument of the labour interest rather than as the vehicle for any ideology'. In a sense not true of its social democratic sister parties, it 'has been a trade union party, created, financed and, in the last analysis, controlled by a highly decentralised trade union movement, which was already in existence before it came into being'. This union influence has permeated all aspects of the Party. 'Above all, its ethos – the symbols, rituals, shared memories and unwritten understandings which have shaped the life of the party and given it its unmistakable style – has been saturated with the ethos of trade unionism.'[12]

Though the Party was (after 1918) ostensibly committed to radical socialist change, this ethos was essentially a cautious, defensive one, 'an ethos of resistance, not of attack; of the objects of history, not of the subjects.' Here Labour reflected its roots for 'the labour movement was a product of the world of "us" against "them", but it existed to protect "us" against the injustices perpetrated by "them", not to enable "us" to join "them", and still less to replace "them" by "us".'[13] It replicated the consciousness of those from amongst whom it sprang, a resilience in adversity, a stolidity in defending established rights but also a pinched and rigid mentality which seriously curtailed its ability to renew itself.

The Party's labourist character meant that it would be, above all, a party of the working class, 'bound by its very nature to stress class identities and appeal to class loyalties'. Class divisions were regarded as 'somehow fundamental or superordinate ... other social divisions were trivial in comparison' and, because politics were class politics 'working-class interests had a special legitimacy denied to other class interests. Labour's class appeal has always been fundamental to it.'[14] On the one hand, this secured for Labour the allegiance of those working-class voters for whom class was their primary form of identification but, on the other, alienated those, irrespective of class for whom it was not. Many working-class members 'obstinately refused to give primacy to the class dimension of their lives' and many others, in other social classes, 'could not see why the working class, as a class, had any moral claim on anyone else'.[15] The Party locked itself into narrow social confines thereby ensuring that its tenure in government would always be unsteady and intermittent. This was a serious problem, but not a fatal one, when the working class comprised over two-thirds of the electorate. But when that percentage remorselessly shrank, episodic success at the polls was replaced by outright and total failure. The social transformation of Britain in the last generation, the reduction of the working class to the status of shrinking minority, the attrition of class identity, the blurring of class boundaries and the rise of consumerism and individualism meant that as a class-based 'labourist' party Labour would be consigned to permanent opposition. Rooted as it was so fixedly 'in the labour interest and the ethos of Labourism' the Party could not 'transcend these without betraying its vocation and dishonouring its origins'.[16] The narrowness and, in the final analysis, sterility of its genetic inheritance flung Labour by the 1980s into a crisis which it was unable, without a metamorphosis, to surmount.

This analysis was to prove very influential when a new, young generation of Labour politicians and their advisers in the early 1990s pondered the causes and the resolution of the Party's electoral woes. All social democratic parties, Tony Blair's principal political strategist Philip Gould wrote, increasingly faced perplexing and thorny problems as they sought to adapt to a rapidly changing world, but few failed as dismally as Labour. It stubbornly remained the party of 'failed solutions ... trade union domination and state control'. By the 1980s 'Labour had not merely stopped listening or lost touch: it had declared political war on the values, instincts and ethics of the great majority of decent, hard-working voters.'[17] It inevitably paid a desperately heavy electoral price. But why this uniquely 'stubborn refusal to modernise?' The answer lay 'buried deep in [the Labour Party's] character, its ethos, implicit in its founding moments'[18] – in short, in its labourism.

What is the nature of this diagnosis? How valid is it? This chapter will seek to answer these questions by exploring three interconnected issues: first, the character, scale and legitimacy of trade union involvement in the Labour Party; second, the Party's identity, its understanding of itself as part of a wider labour movement; third, the nature and effects of Labour's status as a class party.

Labourism, the unions and power in the Party

Since the Party's formation, the (affiliated) trade unions have played a crucial role in all aspects of its internal life. Thus the unions until recently commanded up to 90 per cent of votes in the Party's sovereign decision-making body, its annual conference, elected two-thirds of the members of its (once) powerful National Executive Committee, were strongly entrenched at constituency and regional level, sponsored (and helped finance the expenses of) a large block of Labour MPs, possessed a major say in the selection of parliamentary candidates and, above all, supplied the bulk of the Party's funding. The result, theorists of labourism have argued, is that the unions have a preponderant influence over the fashioning of Party policy 'the ultimate casualty' of which was Labour's capacity to modernise itself.[19] By the late 1970s, not only was the sight of over-weening union power repelling millions of voters but the tight grip of union leaders rigidified the policy process and entrenched unpopular and obsolete poli-cies. Gould records that the message of his focus groups in the mid-1990s was unequivocal: voters demanded reassurance that the unions no longer ruled the roost: 'New Labour is defined for most voters by Tony Blair's willingness to take on and master the unions.'[20] As a result, a *leitmotiv* of New Labour's attitude to the unions was 'fairness, not favours'. As Blair put it in the run-up to the 1997 election, 'we will not be held to ransom by the unions ... We will stand up to strikes. We will not cave into unrealistic pay demands by anyone ... Unions ... get no special favours in a Labour Government.'[21] For this reason, a distancing of the Party from the unions was deemed essential, culminating in, it was hoped – when new sources of funding allowed it, an end to the Party–union link.

He who pays the piper calls the tune; he who commands the votes makes the decisions: two propositions which, as Minkin demonstrates with a wealth of detail, are in fact false. Why is this? They presuppose an instrumental view of power which asserts, first, that key actors are motivated primarily by the desire to maximise their own goals and, second, that their success in so doing depends principally on the amount of power resources (e.g. votes, money) they control. The problem with this view as applied to the Labour Party, as Minkin amply demonstrates, is that by focusing on the resources available to power-holders it ignores the factors which constrain their use. Labour is not simply a *congerie* of ambitions and interests but a social organisation that is an intricate fabric of roles, rules and relationships. Senior actors are not only goal-seeking individuals but also role-occupants whose freedom to pursue their objectives is heavily restrained by the responsibilities and expectations attached to their roles. Minkin contends that 'it is impossible to understand the trade union–Labour Party rela-tionship (and much else about the Labour Movement) without understanding the powerful and long-lasting restraints produced by adherence to [the] "rules".'[22] The 'rules' are norms and conventions which set roles and stipulate appropriate and acceptable behaviour. They had a profound impact upon the exercise of power in the Party since 'they acted as boundaries producing inhibitions which prevented the absolute supremacy of leadership groups in either wing of the relationship.' In short, power relations between the unions and the Party 'cannot be fully understood without appreciating the inhibitions, restrictions and constraints that the "rules" produced'.[23] To take one example: did he who paid the piper call the tune? No, for throughout the Party's history there existed 'unwritten prohibitions against open threats of financial sanctions, and ... inhibi-tions and constraints which limit the implementation of such sanctions.'[24] Equally, it is inaccurate to claim that union block votes have determined the Party's programme and policies. Not only because the unions very rarely voted as a block – indeed Minkin could find 'no single issue where they united in direct

opposition to the position of the Parliamentary leadership'[25] – but, more fundamentally, because the role of the unions was always more constrained, and that
of the leadership (except for rare internals) much more authoritative than the
claim suggests.[26] Only on matters which they regarded as impinging upon their
core function as wage bargainers did they flex their muscles – notably income
determination and the rules governing labour relations – though it is true these
were important issues. Elsewhere they regarded policy development as the functional responsibility of the leadership and were generally content to follow where
it led.

> Within the union–Labour Party relationship, the role-playing, the 'rules'
> and protocol which went with them produced a syndrome of inhibition and
> self-control which was the most remarkable feature of a relationship in
> which all the initial levers of power appeared to lie in the hands of the
> unions.[27]

None of this is to gainsay the real and, in some areas, formidable power of
the unions. The size of the union vote at Conference – now reduced to 50 per
cent – and the extent of its representation on the NEC (now also cut) provoked
considerable resentment amongst the rank and file of the Party as well as the
Parliamentary Party and leadership: though whose complaints were loudest
depended upon the balance of advantage between left and right at any one time.
More to the point (for the purposes of this chapter) the unions, at least when
they acted in concerted fashion, could in matters which they considered of high
priority considerably limit leadership discretion. As Minkin notes, the 'rules'
provided 'a network of *mutual* restraint specifying obligations which were a duty
on both sides of the relationship.'[28] However, the issue for the proto-New
Labour theory of labourism was not simply, not even principally, the *scale* of
union power but its *legitimacy*. Was it right and proper that the unions wielded a
major say in party decision-making and *a fortiori* enjoyed a special relationship
with Labour governments? Until quite recently, whilst Party and unions might
disagree, sometimes vehemently, over policy, 'the legitimacy, centrality and natu-
ralness of the relationship were rarely brought into question.'[29] Virtually all
sections of the Party concurred in this.

> Treasuring that linkage, even while occasionally acknowledging its costs,
> meant that left, right and center in the party all bought into the idea that
> 'this great movement of ours,' as the phrase, went, clearly transcended the
> normal definition of a political party and gave it a different imperative.[30]

But this is precisely what the thesis of labourism challenged. Britain's 'exception-
alism' had cost the party dear. 'The culture of Labourism' – 'the notion that
there is one party, one history and one future'[31] – hamstrung its ability to
compete in the electoral market-place by tying it to one interest, one view of the
world and one class.

For New Labour, however, it was essential that the Party be 'normalised': that it be understood (to borrow Burke's definition) as 'a body of men united for promoting by their joint endeavours the national interest, upon some particular principle in which they are all agreed.' It should be beholden to no 'special interests', for this sullied its claim to promote 'the national interest'. The Blairites wished in short to transform Labour from a class-bound, trade-union-tilting party into a 'national' one, by which they meant one with an encompassing appeal to all social strata and all interests. In short, New Labour challenged the whole notion of 'this great movement of ours' – the labour movement.

The Labour movement

The Party–union relationship, Minkin observes, 'was defined in terms of a common loyalty and a deeply felt commitment to a wider entity and purpose – the Labour Movement.'[32] 'This great movement of ours' (TIGMOO to the *afficianados*) was more than a self-interested alliance between Party and unions, it was the 'spearhead of the aspirations and the repository of the loyalty of an economic and social class'.[33] The concept of a movement articulated a range of sentiments. The first was the indissolubility of the Party–union link. Declamations at Party conference that the Party was nothing without the unions and insistence upon 'solidarity' between the two wings of the movement reflected the degree to which 'the spirit of the Party; its traditions, its habits, its feel' were all largely a product of its ties with trade unions. 'The party is unthinkable without the unions.'[34] The metaphor 'movement' connoted not only a permanent alliance, rooted in solidarity and shared interest, between the industrial and political wings 'What constituted Labour as a *movement* was the belief that each struggle was, or could be, linked into a larger social purpose'[35] – or a 'shared historical project'.[36] None of this, of course, prevented recurrent disagreements – sometimes intense – between the leaderships of the 'two wings of the movement'. But, however volatile and stressful the relationship, few envisaged its termination. As former Labour Prime Minister Jim Callaghan declared in 1996, the Party–union alliance 'is part of our heritage and it is instinctive in our party and movement that we should keep the link. Anyone who doesn't believe that doesn't understand our history or the natural foundation of our party.'[37]

To the theory of labourism this notion of a 'shared historical project' was misplaced – indeed was exploited to legitimise, according to the unions, both in the Party and (when Labour was in office) in government undue preferment. Thus much-needed reforms were delayed and too many concessions were made to placate the producer interests of the unions. From this perspective, the concept of a labour movement – with its implication of the need to countervail the power of business – is irrelevant, dated and counterproductive. It has been enthusiastically endorsed by New Labour. Blair, it has been noted, has 'no sympathy, enthusiasm or concern for the collective values of trade unionism such as solidarity and feels no need to identify himself with them'.[38] What was, in the traditional labourist discourse, seen as a natural partnership between the 'two wings of the movement' is now perceived as the improper exercise of influence – 'favours, not fairness'. In effect, 'New Labour has repositioned the trade unions as one pressure group among many, with no special claim on government attention, sympathy or support.'[39] Such claims reflected 'the old form of corporatism' whilst – Blair declared – what was called for was 'a real sense of shared national purpose' in which business and government would work together in 'a genuine partnership'.[40] Such a partnership the Labour Government has endeavoured to forge. In contrast, as John Monks, TUC General Secretary, put it, the unions often felt they were treated like 'embarrassing elderly relatives at a family get-together'.[41]

Labourism and class

As is well known, the Labour Party was formed to give 'the labour interest' and the working class in general a direct voice in the deliberations of government from which previously it had been effectively excluded. It was a class party in the sense that the bulk of its voters were working-class and, in the decisive phase of its growth and consolidation, much of its electoral effort was devoted to its mobilisation. But theorists of labourism go further. They contend that it has been a party not only *of* but primarily – if not exclusively – *for* the working class. This class is seen to be morally more worthy, its claims meriting privileged treatment even when these jarred with national needs and the class divide seen as pre-eminent. As a result, Labour's electoral strategy and platform were primarily targeted at those amongst the working class for whom class was the principal source of allegiance.

Such an approach unnecessarily confined the Party's appeal, a serious handicap but one which became fatal when the proportion of voters who were working-class began to dwindle fast. The Party gradually shrank to 'a very narrow coalition ... defined by reference to trade unions, the public sector and not much else.'[42] According to the New Labourite strategist, Philip Gould, by the 1990s over 60 per cent of people have come to regard themselves as middle-class – including many who are in skilled manual occupations. The class strategy was now completely defunct. 'Mass Politics is becoming middle-class politics. Winning the century means winning middle-class support.'[43]

By the same token, labourism's class exclusivity contributed to rupturing the 'progressive alliance'. Whilst for Marxists Labour faltered from birth due to its inability to break with the mental universe of bourgeois society, for Marquand (and New Labour commentators) its failure lay in precisely the opposite direction: in its separatism, its insistence upon a rigorously independent party of the working class. This required a sharp demarcation from liberalism. 'In establishing itself as a socialist party immutably linked to trade unionism, Labour broke with Liberalism and cut itself off from the other great radical movement in British politics.'[44] The effect of this (combined with other factors) – so the argument runs – was to split the promising 'progressive alliance' of Liberals and Labour which had emerged after the latter's great electoral triumph in 1906. This had two, mutually reinforcing, consequences. First, given the first-past-the-post electoral system the splintering of the left led to the Conservatives' dominance in government. Second, severed from the Liberal tradition 'Labour's intellectual compass became unbalanced, tilting too far towards the state, away from the individual.'[45] The labourist insistence upon the primacy of the class divide, the irrevocability of the trade union link coupled with the 'Clause IV' dedication to public ownership fractured the progressive majority, tarnished the appeal Labour might otherwise have had to Liberal voters and guaranteed the twentieth century would became the age of Conservative hegemony.[46]

This line of reasoning advances three propositions: first, that Labour (wrongly) perceived class divisions and identities as fundamental to society; second, that its electoral appeal was directed more or less solely to working-class voters; and, third, that this class strategy demolished a progressive alliance that would otherwise have been the ruling political formation in twentieth-century British politics. How valid are they?

The first proposition essentially raises the issue of whether the notion of a class-divided society is a relevant one. Where a class system can be said to exist depends, Labour's most influential post-war theorist wrote, on whether the various disparities in the distribution of social goods took the form of 'a few broad and deep incisions into the social body, as opposed to innumerable shallow cuts; and how far these deep incisions coincide to form a single set of national divisions.' In Britain there was clear evidence that the hierarchies of education, occupational prestige and style of life all show pronounced and visible breaks; and these breaks broadly coincide.[47] This represented the main-stream Labour viewpoint. It was committed to replacing large and unmerited class-based inequalities in the distribution of rewards and life-chances by a fairer and more equitable system of resource-allocation. To the extent that 'pronounced inequalities in access to social resources' were seen as the outcome of a class-grounded pattern 'of deep, cumulative and reinforcing social disparities' Labour did indeed regard class divisions as more fundamental than others.[48] There was assumed to be a differentiation in the interests between labour and capital, between those who own industrial property and those who do not, between those who occupy positions of power and prestige and can command high emoluments in the major institutional hierarchies and those who fill more subordinate roles and live on modest incomes. In political terms, it was a divide between who stood to benefit from a more equal society, with generously-funded public services based on need rather than the ability to pay financed by a progressive high tax regime, and those who did not. 'We regard as unjust', the Labour leader Hugh Gaitskell declared, 'a class structure, in which a person's income, way of living, education, status and opportunities in life depend upon the class into which he is born.'[49] Furthermore different classes were seen to have divergent interests.

They must compete over the distribution of class privileges, and each has a direct interest in preserving or improving its superior or inferior position. The consequence is a real class rivalry, either manifest or latent according to historical circumstances. This rivalry is normally articulated in the political system.[50]

It did not follow, of course, that Labour subscribed in any way to Marxist notions of class struggle. Conceptions of a party's representational role spring from images of the social order. Political formations differ in their ideological orientations, Panitch contended, according to whether they construe the social order 'as either basically unified or basically fissured'.[51] He argues that the Labour Party adhered to an integrationist ideology, whose concern is

> ultimately with unifying the society by developing a policy of national and party interest which will be acceptable to a broad range of sectional organisations ... its role as a party, and especially as a government, is to facilitate compromise among the conflicting interests by means of a policy 'in the national interest'.[52]

The Party's greatest ideological debt was to Fabian socialism. This supplied 'the basic intellectual ingredients for the labour movement after 1900 and in so doing reinforced the fundamental assumptions of the labourist ideology' furnishing labourism with 'an intellectual rationale for evolutionary and reformist practices.'[53] Fabianism neatly meshed with labourism in its contentions, first, that social change emerged as an evolutionary process in which conflicts could be subsumed in a national recognition of the public good and, second, in its insistence that the state (as already constituted) was the appropriate agency of progressive social reform. The Fabians applauded the 'inevitability of gradualness', that process by which enlightened opinion would invariably come to recognise that social maladies, such as poverty, ignorance and disease, could be most effectively cured by collectivist means. As Blackwell and Seabrook comment, 'labourism never moved beyond the bounds set by Sidney Webb' who, in his Fabian Essays, wrote that:

> no philosopher now looks for anything but the gradual evolution of the new order from the old, without breach of continuity or abrupt change of the entire social tissue at any point during the process. The new becomes itself old, often before it is consciously recognized as new; and history shows us no example of the sudden substitutions of Utopian and revolutionary romance ... Advocates of social reconstruction have learnt the lesson of democracy, and know that it is through the slow and gradual turning of the popular mind to new principles that social reorganisation bit by bit comes.[54]

Labour politicians were:

> not concerned with fighting the class war, or creating social revolution and abolishing capitalism, but with creating the conditions for gradual, peaceful

reform by winning over the middle classes and the ruling class through the moral force and economic sense of their arguments.[55]

Industrial militancy and industrial strife were regarded with disapproval – as action to be deplored and problems to be resolved.

> Neither trade union leaders steeped in labourism … nor certainly Labour's political leaders thought of society as a battlefield upon which the working class was engaged in a permanent and irrevocable struggle against domination and exploitation … But for the most part they thought of 'society' as presented with 'problems' whose solution mainly required the kind of good will, intelligence, knowledge and compassion that their Conservative opponents somehow lacked.[56]

This reflected the belief that, although the interests of capital and labour did in certain respects come into contention with each other, they could be conciliated by negotiation and compromise.

It is worth noting that the whole notion of class structure and inequality has vanished from New Labour's discourse, dismissed as obsolescent. Indeed the conception of a social order composed of structurally-differentiated social positions to which correspond markedly disparate life-chances cannot be easily reconciled with the image of a fluid and individualistic society based on free and voluntary transactions which permeates New Labour thinking. This view marks a very substantial change from traditional 'labourist' thinking. The scale, basis and intensity of class-based differences and the most appropriate means of compressing them have long been debated within the Labour Party but with the common presumption that such differences exist, are inequitable and should be narrowed. New Labour does not recognise this distributional divide. 'We must never', Brown warned, 'return to a situation here in Britain where, unlike in America and most of Europe, one party is seen as pro-business and the other anti-business.'[57] Since the welfare of society is contingent on business prosperity, there can be no opposition between the private interest of business and the public good. Distributional conflict – and this assumption underpins the 'proto-New Labour' theory of labourism – is seen to arise from a malfunctioning of the system, or short-sighted, self-interested behaviour by 'producer interests'. Since society as a whole benefits from a dynamic and competitive market economy, New Labour holds, it follows that there is a broad correspondence between the needs of investors and those of entrepreneurs in the market and society at large – a natural convergence of interest. This stance was articulated by Blair in a speech to American financiers in New York in April 1998 which marks a sharp break from earlier Labour patterns of thought:

> the new Labour Government attaches enormous importance to its relations with business both here and in the UK and abroad. The importance we attach not just to developing close links with British business but also with

business abroad is demonstrated by the degree with which we want to go out and have a proper dialogue with business and *be the natural party of business*. We believe that is what we should be. The days when business and government had a difficult relationship are largely over, but we want to build now a relationship for the long term that really works.[58]

In effect, New Labour adheres to a broadly unitary frame of reference, which replaces the notion of distributional conflict with the presumption of an underlying harmony of interest amongst all social groups. It discerns no structured conflicts of interest over the distribution of material resources, status or power, either at workplace or at societal level, between capital and labour, employers and employees. 'All too often,' Tony Blair averred, 'we were concerned with the distribution of the national cake between profits and wages, and too little concerned with increasing the size of the cake itself ... Penal rates of taxation' – Blair is here referring to the tax system prior to the Thatcherite reforms – do not 'make economic or political sense ... I want a tax regime where, through hard work, risk and success, people can become wealthy.'[59]

What of Labour's class-based electoral strategy? It was a class party in the sense that, for its first two generations or so, the bulk of its vote was from the working class and much of its appeal was concentrated on maximising that support. Furthermore, as Beer points out, for socialists, the basic unit of representation was not individual or groups but classes. However, precisely what was meant by the working class, and how the relationship between its interests was seen to relate to other classes, could vary, though it was never exclusive.[60] The formulation used in Labour's constitution – 'workers by hand or brain' – 'implied a wider constituency than the manual working class' although just how wide was never clear, though 'the clerical workers, professionals and small traders' were all 'targeted as part of Labour's appeal to rational progressive forces.'[61] The Webbs in 1920 believed that there was a solidarity of interest ... amongst the great mass of wage-earning folk' including some white collar workers, and expressed their conviction that 'the aspirations and desires of the wage-earners and salariat can be formulated in a programme for legislation ... that will command their general assent.'[62]

As early as 1926 the major policy document *Labour and the Nation* affirmed that the Party 'speaks not as the agent of this class or that, but as the political organ created to express the needs and voice the aspirations of all those who share in Labour which is the lot of mankind'. It appealed to 'men and women of good-will of all classes of the community to aid it to accomplish [its] indispensable task.'[63]

Nor, equally, did Labour rely mainly on the language of class in framing its electoral programme. It often deployed the older radical terminology of 'the interests' versus 'the people'.[64] As Minkin comments, 'although Labour had its special class appeal it had a wider terminology which was often used to enlarge its appeal to the electorate'. The terms 'the Community', 'the People' and 'the Nation' were all frequently used.[65] The 1950 manifesto closed with a rallying call:

> to manual workers – skilled, semi-skilled and so-called unskilled; farmers and agricultural workers; active and able managers and administrators in industry and the public services; professional workers, technicians and scientists.[66]

The interests of the working class were furthermore equated with those of the community as a whole. The 1950 manifesto explicitly made the point that:

> social legislation has benefited *all* sections of the community, including members of the middle classes. Hundreds of thousands of middle class and professional families have been relieved of one of their worst anxieties – the fear of the sudden illness, the expensive operation, the doctors' crippling bills.[67]

Indeed, Labour's leaders became increasingly uneasy with the language of class as their main point of reference came to be 'the nation'. In government, 'far from proclaiming any special concern with the interests of the working classes', the sociologist and historian Alan Fox wrote, they contended that Labour's status as a national party required that all must make sacrifices to meet its objectives – including such 'non-class' ones as defence of the pound, reassuring markets and restoring profitability. 'Class and class interests are felt to be embarrassing concepts left over from a less sophisticated era and rarely mentioned.'[68]

A linked 'labourist' proposition is that Labour's ethos was so saturated by the traditions, discourse and rituals of trade unionism as to alienate those from middle-class backgrounds. The ethos of the movement was manifested 'in the style and atmosphere of the Party's annual conference; in the very language of "our people" which Labour politicians used almost without realising what they were doing.'[69] How valid is this proposition? Here, in the absence of much research, generalisation must be tentative. However, the evidence does indicate that, first, the cultural configurations of different levels of the Party – the affiliated unions, the PLP, the constituency parties – have historically all tended to vary. Second, and more significantly, from the late 1960s an influx of young, often university-educated, white-collar public-sector employees – teachers, social workers, local government officers and so forth – joined Labour's ranks and sharply altered constituency culture in many parts of the country. In a sample survey of 1978 constituency Conference delegates, Whitely found that 70 per cent were white-collar, of whom 57 per cent were in professional occupations, 60 per cent were employed in the public sector and 27 per cent were university graduates[70] (a high figure given the modest proportion of the population who then received university education). In the first systematic survey of Labour's membership conducted in 1989 Seyd and Whiteley estab-lished that 49 per cent of members were in the salariat (professional middle class) and the rest were divided equally between lower-middle-class and working-class. School teachers comprised the largest occupational group.[71]

This inevitably affected cultural patterns. Party members inhabited 'two distinct universes … exemplified by their newspaper-reading habits', that of the *Guardian* and that of the *Daily Mirror*, of which the former was the pre-eminent: Seyd and Whiteley's research confirmed 'a common journalistic assumption that middle-class, public sector professionals predominate among Labour Party members'.[72] This is even more the case amongst those who actively participate in the work of constituency parties, thereby setting the tone and tenor of local party culture.[73] In fact, many of the battles in the 1970s and early 1980s – espe-cially in London, but also in several other large urban centres, were between the new cohorts of the young, white-collar and university educated seeking to pry control over constituency party machines from older, more working-class members. For most active party members the ambience of the Party was a heavily middle-class one.[74]

The third 'labourist' proposition is that 'labourism' (coupled here with Clause IV socialism) demolished the emergent progressive alliance of Labour and the Liberals, sundered the ranks of the left and thereby guaranteed that the twen-tieth would be the Conservative century. It meant that any hopes of building 'one united progressive party, similar to the broader coalitions in the United States and Scandinavia' were dashed.[75] The labourist ethos bred insularity, a sense of moral superiority and a lack of tolerance towards other political tradi-tions which estranged potential sympathies. Thus the New Labourite cabinet minister Patricia Hewitt deplored 'the culture of "Labourism"' with its 'tendency, in its extreme form, to trust too little and put tribalism before core values': an unwillingness to recognise and honour 'other voices and the legiti-macy of other centres of power, and realise that difference is not always threatening'.[76]

In fact, the thesis of the progressive alliance aborted by 'labourism' is a myth. It rests on assumptions which cannot be substantiated. The first is the depiction of the Liberal Party as a party of the left, or centre-left, with the corollary that Liberal politicians and voters (an important distinction generally ignored) had a greater affinity for Labour and the left than for the Conservatives and the right. Historical evidence suggests otherwise. In the crucial interwar years the Liberal Party fragmented three ways, with one group transferring their allegiance to Labour, a second (including an organised section, the National Liberals of the 1930s) joining the Conservatives and a third remaining independent. Although Gould claims that 'the schism also cut Labour off from a body of ideas which would have broadened its base and widened its appeal',[77] in fact most of the radical intelligentsia deserted to Labour.[78] At the local level the pattern was more clear-cut. 'The Liberal Party showed increased willingness to mask its decline by participating in anti-socialists pacts with Conservatives at both local and parliamentary levels.'[79]

Second, the purportedly left-inclined preferences of Liberal voters. In the absence of systematic electoral research we know little of the Liberal vote prior to the 1960s. However, the two elections of 1950 and 1951 offer one interesting piece of evidence. In the former year the Liberals sported 475 candidates, winning 9.1 per cent of the vote. The following years, with money desperately short, they offered only 109 candidates, gaining a mere 2.6 per cent of the vote. Labour added about 700,000 votes, the Tories over 1,100,000. Labour election organiser Len Williams calculated that the withdrawal of Liberal candidates disproportionately benefited the Tories, perhaps costing 17 of the 22 seats lost. He estimated that in these constituencies the Liberal vote transferred to the Conservatives in preference to Labour in the ratio of three to one.[80]

Third, the assumption that a progressive alliance between a social democratic and a liberal party is a natural development inhibited solely in Britain by Labour's 'labourism'. In fact, in no country in Western Europe did such a party emerge – least of all in Sweden with the most electorally successful party of the left in the world.[81] The precise relationship between liberalism and social democracy varied according to characteristics of the Party and electoral systems but in not one country did a broad 'progressive' bloc on the pattern envisaged by New Labourites emerge.

Conclusion

Why, then, has the theory of labourism given rise to over-simplified, over-generalised and in some cases simply erroneous views about the Labour Party? The major reason would appear to lie in the concept itself, and the interpretative style it articulates. By postulating some overarching structure of meaning held to be constitutive of Labour it facilitates grand explanatory propositions that the use of more precise and empirically-grounded concepts might hamper, and therein lies its weakness. To David Coates, the concept of labourism 'is meant to capture the dominant definitions of "the political" enshrined in the political philosophy and practice of the Labour Party since 1900.' It has been and remains – Coates is here writing in 1980 – 'the dominant political perspective amongst large sections of the British labour movement.'[82] From a different vantage point, Cronin agrees that 'for those trying to make sense of the Labour Party's long-run project, the term "Labourism" has proven especially useful in describing the package of ideas, attitudes and predispositions that seems to hold it all together.'[83] This use of the term reflects what Freeden sees as 'a preoccupation among students of ideologies with coherent a priori models of the great "isms" and a concomitant assumption that they, rather than *some* of their components, shape acts of public policy.'[84] By stipulating what is taken as the essence of Labour thought and practice, theorists of labourism exhibit a propensity to treat Labour's history in a static and deterministic manner, to assume that the elements that composed it in its earlier years have persisted, and have continued (until the advent of 'New Labour') to govern its collective mind. To take one example, the proposition that the culture of the Labour Party has been suffused by the labourist ethos fails to explain how that ethos (borne of working-class experience) has survived two decades or more of a membership composed largely of teachers and other middle-class, public-sector employees. It ignores the fact that identities are fluid, constantly being refashioned, and not fixed and immutable. 'Violence is done to the real diversity of ideas', Greenleaf points out, 'if these are pressed into the nice conformity of an unchanging system.'[85] 'Ism' reasoning distorts what it seeks to clarify by *imposing an explanatory dynamic* by definitional fiat *rather* than uncovering that dynamic through methodical empirical investigation.

Our conclusion would be, then, that in so far as it pertains to a creed, doctrine or ethos, the concept of labourism has little explanatory value. In so far as it is desegregated into discrete components which bear upon the Party-union nexus – for instance the idea of a 'labour movement' or a conception of Labour's representational role as the promoter of working-class interests – then the concept has more analytic use. Defined in such a way, its empirical significance, however, is diminishing. The notion of the labour movement – 'this great movement of ours' – as the ultimate repository of loyalty is rapidly fading and is becoming little more than a rhetorical device. Equally, with the size, nature and social and political orientation of the working class having altered so drastically, and with New Labour repositioning itself in the electoral market-place, doubts must attach to the extent to which working-class representation can any longer be seen as a primary function of the Party. To this extent, the age of 'labourism' would appear to be passing.

Notes

1 McLean, I., *Keir Hardie* (Allen Lane, London, 1975), p. 20.
2 Morgan, K.O., *Callaghan: A Life* (OUP, Oxford, 1997), p. 708.
3 Saville, J., 'The Ideology of Labourism', in Benewick, R. Berki, R.N. and Parekh, B. (eds) *Knowledge and Belief in Politics – The Problem of Ideology* (Allen & Unwin, London, 1973), p. 215.
4 Nairn, T., 'The Nature of the Labour Party', in Anderson, P. and Blackburn, R. (eds.) *Towards Socialism* (Fontana, London, 1965), p. 172.
5 Marriott, J., *The Culture of Labourism* (Edinburgh University Press, Edinburgh, 1991), p. 5.
6 Quoted in Coates, D. and Panitch, L. 'The Miliband School of Labour Scholarship: an Internal Retrospective', Past Paper presented to the Labour Movements Group of the Political Studies Association, University of Salford, July 2001, p. 4
7 Miliband, R., *Parliamentary Socialism* (Allen & Unwin, London, 1961), p. 61.
8 Marriot, J., *The Culture of Labourism*, p. 4.
9 Saville, J., 'The Ideology of Labourism', p. 222.
10 Coates, D., *The Crisis of Labour* (Philip Allan Publishers, London, 1989), p. 36.
11 Marquand, D., *The Progressive Dilemma* (Heinemann, London, 1991), pp. 16–17.
12 *Ibid.*, pp. 16–17.
13 *Ibid.*, pp. 21–2.
14 *Ibid.*, p. 23.
15 *Ibid.*, p. 25.
16 *Ibid.*, p. 23.

17 Gould, P., *The Unfinished Revolution* (Abacus, London, 1998), p. 19. He adds:
To millions of voters Labour became a shiver of fear in the night, something unsafe, buried deep in the psyche ... One woman said to me just weeks before the 1997 election, 'When I was a child there was a wardrobe in my bedroom. I was always scared that one night, out of the blackness, a monster would emerge. That is how I think of the Labour Party'. (p. 21.)

18 *Ibid.*, p. 23.

19 *Ibid.*, p. 26.

20 *Ibid.*, pp. 257–8.

21 Quoted in Ludlam, S., 'New Labour and the Unions: The End of the Contentious Alliance?' in Ludlam, S. and Smith, M.J. (eds.) *New Labour in Government* (Macmillan, London, 2000), p. 115.

22 Minkin, L., *The Contentious Alliance* (Edinburgh University Press, Edinburgh, 1991), p. 27.

23 *Ibid.*, p. xiv, p. 45.

24 *Ibid.*, pp. 626–7.

25 *Ibid.*, p. 456.

26 See *ibid.* and Minkin, L., *The Labour Party Conference*, for a huge amount of evidence.

27 Minkin, L., *The Contentious Alliance*, p. 27.

28 *Ibid.*

29 Ludlam, S., Bodah, M. and Coates, D., 'Trajectories of Solidarity: Changing Union-Party Linkages in The UK and The USA', *British Journal of Politics & International Relations*, Vol. 4: Issue 2, 2002, p. 224.

30 Cronin, J., 'New Labour's Pasts', Paper presented to the Labour Movements Group of the Political Studies Association, Bristol, July 4–5, 2002.

31 Neal Lawson and Neil Sherlock in the *Guardian*, 22 June 2001.

32 Minkin, L., *The Contentious Alliance*, p. 4.

33 Panitch, L., 'Ideology and Integration: The Case of the British Labour Party', in Panitch, L. (ed.) *Working Class Politics in Crisis* (Verso, London, 1986), p. 61.

34 Drucker, H., 'The Influence of the Trade Unions on the Ethos of the Labour Party', in Pimlott, B. and Cook, C. (eds) *Trade Unions in British Politics*, (Longman, London, 1991), p. 244.

35 Hinton, J., *Labour and Socialism: A History of the British Labour Movement, 1867–1974*, (University of Massachusetts Press, USA, 1983), p. viii.

36 Minkin, L., *The Contentious Alliance*, pp. 4–5.

37 Quoted in Morgan, K.O., *Callaghan: A Life*, p. 745.

38 Taylor, R., 'Economic Reform and New Industrial Relations' 2000 http://www.europaprogrammet.no/sider/4_publikasjoner/4_bokerhefter/hefter/9 8_5/taylor.html.

39 Blair, Tony, Prime Minister's speech at the CBI Annual Dinner, 17 May 2000, in Ludlam, S., Bodah, M. and Coates, D. 'Trajectories of Solidarity', p. 229.

40 *Ibid.*

41 *Observer*, 20 June 1999.

42 Blair, T., *Observer*, 27 April 1997.

43 Gould, P., *The Unfinished Revolution*, p. 396.

44 *Ibid.*, p. 27.

45 *Ibid.*

46 *Ibid.*, p. 39.

47 Crosland, C.A.R., *The Future of Socialism* (Jonathan Cape, London, 1956), p. 118.

48 *Ibid.*, p. 120.

49 Gaitskell, H., *Socialism and Nationalisation* (Fabian Society, London, 1956), p. 3.

50 Crosland, C.A.R., *The Future of Socialism*, p. 119.

51 Panitch , L. (ed.) *Working Class Politics in Crisis*, p. 62, 58.

52 *Ibid.*, p. 57.

53 Saville, J., 'The Ideology of Labourism', p. 224.

54 Blackwell, T. and Seabrook, J., *A World Still to Win: The Reconstruction of the Post-War Working Class,* (Faber & Faber, London, 1985), p. 80.

55 Forrester, T., *The Labour Party and the Working Class* (Heinemann, London, 1975), p. 40.

56 Miliband, quoted in Coates, D. and Panitch, L. 'The Miliband School of Labour Scholarship', p. 4.

57 *Electronic Telegraph,* 11 November 1996.

58 Quoted in Grant, W., 'Globalisation, Big Business and the Blair Government', Paper for the *Political Studies Association, UK* 50th Annual Conference 10–13 April 2000, London. (Grant's emphasis.)

59 *Electronic Telegraph,* 17 September 1996; 14 November 1995.

60 Beer, S.H., *Modern British Politics* (Faber, London, 1969), p. 83.

61 Minkin, L., *The Contentious Alliance,* p. 17.

62 Beer, S.H., *Modern British Politics,* p. 83.

63 Panitch, L. (ed.) *Working Class Politics in Crisis,* p. 67.

64 For example, the 1945 and 1950 election manifestos champion 'the people' and 'the nation' against 'the interests' and 'big business'. Craig, F.W.S., *British General Election Manifestos* (Political Reference Publications, Chichester, 1970), pp. 97–105, pp. 126–35.

65 Minkin, L., *The Contentious Alliance,* p. 17.

66 Craig, F.W.S., *British General Election Manifestos,* p. 135.

67 *Ibid.*, p. 132.

68 Fox, A., *Shop Floor Power Today,* Fabian Research Series, 338, 1978, p. 6.

69 Marquand, D., *The Progressive* Dilemma, p. 24.

70 Whitely, P., 'Who are the Labour Activists?' *Political Quarterly,* Vol. 52, 1981, pp. 162–3.

71 Seyd, P. and Whiteley, P., *Labour's Grassroots: the Politics of Party Membership,* (Clarendon Press, Oxford, 1992), pp. 33–4.

72 *Ibid.*, p. 36.

73 *Ibid.*, pp. 98–9.

74 It remains true that representatives of the affiliated unions, at Conference, at regional and at constituency level, were much more working-class in orientation. But even here we must be cautious. Throughout the 1980s and 1990s, for a range of reasons, the social and occupational composition of the union movement as a whole was being transformed. By the end of the 1990s union members were *more white-collar* than the workforce as a whole.

75 Gould, P., *The Unfinished Revolution,* p. 27.

76 Hewitt, P., 'The Principled Society: Reforming Public Services', *Renewal,* Vol. 9 Nos. 2 and 3, 2001.

77 Gould, P., *The Unfinished Revolution,* p. 397.

78 Joyce, P., *Realignment of the Left?* (Macmillan, Basingstoke, 1999), p. 58

79 *Ibid.*, p. 58.

80 *Ibid.*, p. 106.

81 Misgeld, K., Molin, K. and Amark, K., *Creating Social Democracy* (Penn State Press, Philadelphia, 1992). In Sweden the Liberals are placed in the so-called 'bourgeois' bloc along with the Conservative and agrarian Centre Party compared to the left bloc now composed of Social Democrats, left social democrats and Greens.

82 Coates, D., *The Crisis of Labour,* p. 36; and Coates, D., *Labour in Power* (Longman, London, 1980), p. 271.

83 Cronin, J. 'New Labour's Past', p. 6. See also Marquand, D., *The Progressive Dilemma* and Gould, P., *The Unfinished Revolution.*

84 Freeden, M., 'The Stranger at the Feast: Ideology and Public Policy in Twentieth Century Britain', *Twentieth Century British History*, 1 (1), 1990, p. 11.
85 Greenleaf, W.H., *The British Political Tradition, Vol. 2, The Ideological Inheritance* (Routledge, London, 1983), p. 10.

11 Constitutional Reform

Dilys M. Hill

Introduction

> I do not regard changing the way we are governed as an afterthought, a detailed
> fragment of our programme – I regard it as an essential part of the new Britain,
> of us becoming a young confident country again.[1]

New Labour has been praised for 'the most extensive programme of constitutional modernisation for more than a century – indeed, since the Great Reform Act of 1832.'[2] Some commentators, however, point to the lack of a coherent rationale for the reforms or their final destination,[3] viewing Labour's pragmatism as deriving from its lack of a coherent philosophy of the state.[4]

Traditionally, Labour supported the constitutional status quo. From the early Fabians onwards, Labour believed that the state was the only agency which could control market forces and deliver social justice, and rejected any calls from the left for syndicalist or guild socialist alternatives. After 1945, democratic socialism remained firmly tied to the Westminster model. By the 1990s, however, many in the Labour Party were becoming active in the constitutional reform movement, Charter 88.[5] New Labour's position is to reject 'statist' solutions in favour of a more participative and pluralist political system,[6] and denies there is opposition between state and market.

This chapter considers Labour and the constitution in the light of these traditions. It covers seven areas: devolution; parliament; human rights; freedom of information; parties and elections; the issue of Europe; and changes in the modern state.

Devolution

From the 1880s onwards Labour supported 'home rule all round', but had abandoned this position by the mid-1920s. For many, nationalism was a distraction from class politics and the use of state planning to achieve socialist objectives. After 1945, with nationalism dormant as Scotland's economy improved in the Welfare State, Labour's interest in it waned. In 1956 Gaitskell said that Labour was against Home Rule and in 1959 the Scottish Labour Conference withdrew support for devolution.[7] In November 1967, however, the nationalist threat re-emerged with Winifred Ewing's victory for the Scottish National Party (SNP) at the Hamilton by-election.[8]

In Wales, Labour traditionally fought as a socialist party speaking as one for England and Wales. In 1946 Aneurin Bevan described devolution as 'Not Socialism … [but] escapism',[9] and resisted any calls for a separate Welsh or Scottish health service. Attlee dismissed the demand for a separate Secretary of State for Wales, while Herbert Morrison claimed that the best future was for both Wales and Scotland to 'form part of a single economic plan for the whole country'.[10] In the 1960s, nationalism (Plaid Cymru won the Carmarthen by-election in July 1966) changed this perspective. Prime Minister Wilson appointed the first Secretary of State for Wales in 1964 and the Welsh Language Act was passed in 1967.

In the late 1960s, nationalism was re-emerging as an electoral threat but Wilson compromised by establishing the Crowther/Kilbrandon Royal Commission on the Constitution in 1969.[11] In February 1974 (despite having fought the election on a platform opposed to devolution), Wilson promised discussions on the 1973 Kilbrandon Report, followed by specific proposals. The White Paper, 'Devolution in the UK – Some Alternatives for Discussion' of May 1974, set out five options but these were rejected by Labour's Scottish executive. The Cabinet, fearing the revival of nationalism, was determined to go ahead. After bitter debate at a special conference of the Party in August 1974, the trade union block vote, from the right, was used to push through a motion in favour of devolution.[12] A further White Paper in November 1975 offered a directly elected Assembly in Scotland with legislative powers, but that in Wales had executive powers only. The suggestion for regions in England was dropped. The Government's small majority, its internal divisions and its reliance on the Lib-Lab pact, stalled action.

The Callaghan Government was equally constrained by its small majority. The single Scotland and Wales Bill passed its second reading in the House of Commons in December 1976 but was defeated in February 1977. In November 1977 separate bills were introduced, to become law in July 1978 subject to favourable votes in referenda in the two countries. After acrimonious debate in the House of Commons, the compromise required a favourable vote from 40 per cent of the registered electorate in both referenda. The referenda were held on 1 March 1979. That in Wales was defeated outright, while in Scotland the proposal was lost on the percentage of the electorate voting, though 52 per cent of those who did vote were in favour.

Michael Foot, leader of the Party from 1980 to 1983, remained a socialist with a UK remit in the Bevan mould. His successor Neil Kinnock, reversing his opposition of the 1970s, supported devolution in the 1987 and 1992 general elections. A major factor was the changing situation in Scotland. In 1988 the Campaign for a Scottish Assembly appointed a Constitutional Steering Committee which produced a Claim of Right for Scotland. This declared that Scottish sovereignty resided not in the UK Parliament but in the Scottish people. The Scottish Constitutional Convention, established in 1989, was dominated by Labour and the Liberal Democrats, with the SNP and the Conservatives refusing to take part. In 1995 its final report advocated a devolved government and Assembly for Scotland but within the United Kingdom. In Wales, there was no comparable constitutional convention or any Claim of Right, and the issue remained divisive.

By the beginning of the 1990s Labour's views on devolution had changed significantly. This was not due to pragmatic considerations alone. John Smith, elected party leader in July 1992, was a conviction supporter of devolution.[13] Prime Minister Blair, while dismissing the 'narrow politics of identity', broadly followed the Convention proposals in respect of Scotland, including elections to the Parliament by the additional member system of proportional representation. But, mindful of the events of 1979, Blair insisted on prior referenda to elicit support for the devolved parliament/Assembly. In Scotland voters would also be asked if the parliament should have tax-raising powers. The Referendums (Scotland and Wales) Act 1997 was New Labour's first bill in government; the Scottish referendum was held on 11 September 1997 and that for Wales two weeks later.

The separate bills for Scotland and Wales defined the powers and functions of the Parliament and Assembly, and their mode of election.[14] The Government of Wales Act did not, unlike that in Scotland, provide for the future reduction of the numbers of Welsh MPs at Westminster.[15] But the future for both Scotland and Wales remains problematic. For the present, the Labour/Liberal Democrat alliance in the Scottish executive precludes moves to independence.[16] In Wales, the Assembly has called for powers closer to those of the Scottish Parliament. A Commission on Assembly Powers, chaired by Lord Richard, the former Labour leader of the House of Lords, has been established, and is due to report after the Assembly's 2003 elections. The Labour Party remains divided over granting more powers to the Assembly.

New Labour's devolution reforms, building on John Smith's commitment, have been a major constitutional success. Nevertheless a question mark over Westminster sovereignty, which the devolution legislation preserves, remains. In 1999 a *Memorandum of Understanding and Supplementary Agreements* between the British, Scottish and Welsh administrations was published.[17] Although the Scotland Act lays down that devolution does not affect Westminster's power to make laws for Scotland, the Memorandum of Understanding states that the UK government would not normally legislate on devolved matters except with the agreement of the devolved legislature.[18] But as Bogdanor says: 'Power devolved, far from being power retained, as implied by constitutional theory, will be power transferred, as dictated by political reality …'[19] The division of powers between the different bodies will be adjudicated by the Judicial Committee of the Privy Council, 'which will come to assume the role of a constitutional court on devolution matters'.[20]

Northern Ireland has always operated within a different constitutional and value framework, following the establishment of the Irish Free State in 1921.[21]

In the Stormont years the relation between Northern Ireland and the rest of the UK had many quasi-federal characteristics.[22] The Stormont parliament was abolished in 1973. In 1974 the Northern Ireland Act, passed by the Labour Government, restored direct rule.

In 1997, Labour extended John Major's reforms. The Good Friday Agreement of April 1998 provided for devolved government in Northern Ireland and for cross-border, all-Ireland bodies. Following endorsement in the referenda held simultaneously in both parts of Ireland in May 1998, the Northern Ireland Act 1998 replaced the former Anglo-Irish Agreement with a British–Irish Agreement. The 1998 Act devolved a wide range of executive and legislative powers to an Assembly, elected by the Single Transferable Vote proportional system, and an Executive. A new North–South ministerial council, and a British–Irish Council (the Council of the Isles, including the Isle of Man and the Channel Islands) were established. The powers of the Assembly are similar to those of the Scottish Parliament. But the cabinet (the Executive Committee) will, unlike the provisions laid down for Scotland, always contain ministers representing the minority community. Similarly, the members and chairs of Assembly Committees are proportionately allocated. In addition, the application of the 1998 Human Rights Act to Northern Ireland set up a Northern Ireland Human Rights Commission and an Equality Commission.

The question of how England fits into the constitutional settlement of the UK has been the subject of uneasy neglect. New Labour, like the Callaghan Government before it, has rejected the claim for an English Parliament.[23] The case for devolved regions within England, however, has appeared to shift between disquiet and approval. In 1991 the Party statement, 'Devolution and Democracy', made a case for regional government. The manifesto of 1992 promised a tier of regional administrative bodies in England which would eventually form the basis of elected regional government.

In 1982, John Prescott, a long-standing advocate of regionalism, published his *Alternative Regional Strategy*. In 1994 he set up a regional policy commission under Bruce Millan to develop the policy. Labour's 1997 General Election Manifesto pledged to introduce 'directly elected regional government, where residents vote for it and where people decide in a referendum to support it and where predominantly unitary local government is established.' The 1998 Regional Development Agencies Act set up an RDA in each of the eight English Regions together with advisory regional chambers composed of local councillors and members of the voluntary and business communities.

Prescott's White Paper of 2002, 'Your Region, Your Choice: Revitalising the English Regions',[24] promised elected assemblies, but only where voters had expressed an interest and had demonstrated this in a referendum. The paving bill (the Regional Assemblies [Preparations] Bill) of November 2002, which came into law in May 2003, allowed for referenda, the first of which will go ahead in the north-east, the north-west and Yorkshire and the Humber regions. By that time the Government will have published a draft bill setting out the powers of the 25 to 35 member assemblies, including oversight of the Regional

Development Agencies and responsibility for planning, housing, transport, culture and tourism, environmental protection and the ability to frame health improvement strategies. The regional assemblies broadly resemble the Greater London Authority and will be funded by a similar system of a block grant with power to precept on the local council tax in their areas. Members will be elected under the additional member system of proportional representation used by the Scottish Parliament and the Welsh Assembly and with a leader and cabinet chosen by the assembly. The Boundary Committee for England will review local government in the three regions, providing at least two options for a unitary system of local authorities to submit to the voters. If the referenda produce a 'Yes' vote, then the first assembly elections could take place in the spring of 2006.

These moves, which offer the regions a potentially powerful lobbying role *vis-à-vis* Westminster and Brussels, imply a major constitutional shift. In 2001, Peter Mandelson, the former Northern Ireland Secretary, emerged as a self-appointed champion of the regions:

> I believe if a second term Labour government fails to act on a regional devolution it will leave the constitutional settlement enacted by New Labour dangerously unbalanced. Indeed, it might lead some to question the legitimacy of those constitutional changes.[25]

Prescott himself sees English assemblies as unfinished constitutional business, 'putting in place the last piece of the framework for a new constitutional settlement for the whole of the UK.'[26] To critics, however, the proposed powers are strategic and limited; the result is neither real decentralisation nor the basis for viable democratic renewal.[27]

The Greater London Authority (GLA) offers an interesting contrast. Following the 1998 referendum, the Greater London Act 1999 provided for a directly elected Mayor and Assembly (elected on a form of proportional representation). Elections took place in May 2000 and the GLA came into operation in July 2000. The Government intended the GLA to be an upper tier of local government. But it is beginning to see itself as England's first regional government. In opposition Labour had been committed, following the abolition of the Greater London Authority in 1986, to bringing in a London-wide body. The Blair Government, however, saw the new authority as having a co-ordinating and strategic role rather than an executive one, and feared a possible future challenger to the centre (as indeed GLC leader Ken Livingstone had been to the Thatcher Government in the 1980s).

In the case of local government as a whole, Labour has shifted its position over time. In its early years, the case for municipal socialism, and the enthusiasm of the Webbs, and of Herbert Morrison[28] as leader of the London County Council in the 1930s, promoted vigorous local government. At the end of the Second World War, however, the Labour Government had to move swiftly: services were taken away from local councils as utilities were nationalised and a

National Health Service set up. In the Welfare State, Labour ideology stressed services for all, regardless of territorial differences, and set to national standards.

In the 1980s, the Thatcher Government's outsourcing (privatisation) of services and increased central control brought vocal criticism from the left. But Prime Minister Blair's 'Third Way' stance of 'what matters is what works', demonstrates an agnosticism towards local government and a dislike of what are seen as outmoded and potentially obstructive local interests.

New Labour has given little consideration to the constitutional position of local government in a political system based on parliamentary sovereignty. As Rhodes has put it, if before 1972 local government could be described as part of the constitution, no such claim would be made today in these centralising times.[29] In 2000 the Government asserted that it was promoting a more vigorous local democracy in its White Paper, 'Local Leadership, Local Choice', and the Local Government Act. This established a choice of new forms of governance, including directly elected mayors, which Blair favoured. In practice, however, the Government has concentrated on service delivery. The emphasis now is on decentralisation to front-line services rather than to elected local councils.

The Government continues, however, to assert that it is committed to greater local freedoms. The White Paper, 'Strong Local Leadership – Quality Public Services' (Cm 5237), and the Local Government Bill of 2002, promised to relax borrowing constraints, and give greater financial freedom to the top-achieving local councils. But debate on the constitutional role of local government, the relations between the several countries of the UK, the regions, local councils and Westminster, remains not only unresolved but largely unexpressed.

Parliament and the monarchy

The House of Lords

Historically, the Labour Party saw the House of Lords as a barrier to socialist objectives and favoured abolition. The Parliament Act of 1911, which removed the Lords' power of veto, did not wholly remove Labour's hostility.[30] In 1922 the Party rejected any restoration of the Lords' powers; for the rest of that decade its election manifestos made no mention of the upper chamber. In 1934 the Labour Party Conference again committed the Party to total abolition.

After 1945, Attlee had no interest in revising the composition of the House of Lords but made some reduction of its powers. The Government saw Conservative opposition to Iron and Steel nationalisation as a defiance of the spirit of the Salisbury convention which held that the Lords should not challenge at Second Reading any measure set out in the 1945 General Election Manifesto. The Government responded by passing the 1949 Parliament Act which cut the Lords' delaying power from two years, spread over three parliamentary sessions, to one year spread over two sessions. In 1958 Labour opposed the Life Peerage Act because it feared that it would strengthen the legitimacy of an unelected second chamber,[31] with Aneurin Bevan being particularly scathing. By the late

1960s, though the left continued to call for abolition, the centre and right view was, in Richard Crossman's words, 'that an indefensible anachronism is preferable to a second Chamber with any real authority'.[32]

Under the Wilson Government, the 1968 Parliament (No. 2) Bill sought to reduce the total number of peers and attacked the hereditary principle. But opposition from the left, and the Labour–Conservative blocking movement in the House of Commons led by Michael Foot (an abolitionist) and Enoch Powell (who favoured the status quo), effectively killed the Bill, and Wilson abandoned it in 1969. The 1970 election Manifesto still proposed a reduction in the Lords' powers, but this was missing from both the February and the October 1974 General Election Manifestos. In 1977 the Party Conference voted for a unicameral parliament but Callaghan struck the proposal from the 1979 election Manifesto. The left, angry at this move, fought for its reinstatement and the 1983 Manifesto committed the Party to the abolition of the Lords. But that of 1987 omitted the pledge and Kinnock's 1989 Policy Review 'Meet the Challenge, Make the Change' rejected abolition for an elected second chamber, in large part due to the Lords' role in opposing legislation of the Thatcher Government. The 1992 manifesto proposed an elected upper House with reduced delaying powers. And although the 1994 Labour Party Conference called for abolition, by 1996 Blair was stressing that: 'We have always favoured an elected second chamber'[33] – a position which he himself appeared to reject in 2003.

New Labour has reversed the Party's former support of a democratically elected Upper House in favour of the more ambiguous goal, as Morrison puts it, of modernising it.[34] The 1997 Party Manifesto proposed the removal of the hereditary peers' right to sit and vote as a first stage in making the House of Lords more democratic and representative, though with its legislative powers unaltered.

The 1999 House of Lords Act reduced the numbers of hereditary peers from 759 to 92 (elected by their colleagues); the number of Life Peers increased from 482 to 533 and the overall proportion of non-hereditaries rose from 41 to 87 per cent. The legacy of the 1968 failed Bill made New Labour determined to reform the Lords by stages, and in 1999 a Royal Commission on the Reform of the House of Lords, chaired by the Conservative peer Lord Wakeham, was set up to make recommendations for Stage Two (rather than a Joint Committee of the two Houses as proposed in Labour's Manifesto). Its terms of reference emphasised 'the need to maintain the House of Commons as the pre-eminent Chamber of Parliament', and to take 'particular account of the nature of the constitutional settlement'.[35] The Wakeham Commission recommended a reformed House of Lords of about 550 members, mainly appointed but with a 'significant minimum' elected from the regions and nations of the UK.

The General Election Manifesto of 2001 promised completion of the reforms. The 2001 White Paper proposed a composition of some 600 members (332 recommended by party leaders; 120 directly elected by proportional representation for a term of 15 years or less, to represent the nations and regions of the UK; 120 appointed by the statutory Appointments Commission; 16 Bishops and around 12 Law Lords). The remaining hereditary peers would be removed, but existing Life Peers could continue until they died or chose to retire.[36] In May 2002, in the face of continued divisions, the Government stepped back from its reform proposals and agreed to the setting up of a Joint Committee of the two Houses, and a free vote in the Commons. In December 2002 the joint report suggested seven options: a fully appointed House; a fully elected House; 80 per cent appointed, 20 per cent elected; 20 per cent appointed, 80 per cent elected; 60 to 40 appointed/elected; 60 to 40 elected/appointed; 50 to 50 appointed/elected. Lord Irvine feared that the deadlock over composition between the two houses would make a consensus solution impossible.[37] In the January 2003 debate, splits emerged in the Parliamentary Labour Party between the centre and right supporting an overwhelmingly appointed Lords (as do some ministers and most peers including Lord Irvine) and the left backing total abolition.[38] In an extraordinary move, and following a passionate speech by Cook calling for reform, on 4 February MPs rejected all the options (the Lords voted overwhelmingly for an appointed chamber). All the parties were split on the issue and, a week before the vote, Blair (reputedly persuaded by Lord Irvine) had called for an appointed second chamber to avoid 'rivalry' between the two chambers. Twenty-five Commons ministers, including four Cabinet ministers, and left-leaning Labour MPs voted against the Blair option.[39] The issue was returned to the Joint Committee – and reform was lost. In September 2003 the Government announced a limited package of measures that removed the remaining 92 hereditary peers. The House of Lords would become a wholly nominated body (with no limit on its size) in which the Government would have more seats than the main opposition, but with the Prime Minister's powers of patronage transferred to an independent eight-person appointments commission. The move did not satisfy those whose criticised the Government reneging on its previous reform commitments, even though Lord Falconer's foreword to the White Paper promised that it marked the next, 'but not the final, stage of Lords' reform'.

The Monarchy

Labour's 1997 General Election Manifesto declared there were 'no plans to replace the monarchy'. There has been no debate on the monarchy at Labour Party conferences since the early 1920s; in the post-war period, Herbert Morrison's *Government and Parliament* (1954) praised the institution. From the left, Tony Benn's Commonwealth of Britain Bill of 1991 advocated that the monarch as head of state be replaced by a President elected by a two-thirds majority in the two houses of the commonwealth parliament, for a three-year term which would be renewable once. The prerogative powers of the Crown would pass to this elected President.

Tony Blair, like Prime Ministers before him, jealously guards the use of the prerogative powers (see below). But he has gone further, defending the monarchy and denying that there is any contradiction between this position and House of

Lords' reform. It has been suggested that New Labour's constitutional reforms stop short of the monarchy because removing our status as subjects of the Queen and the Crown's role as the prosecuting authority of the legal system would raise awkward questions about the weakness of British democracy and of the overweening powers of the prime minister.[40] A number of issues, however, remain, notably the provisions preventing the heir to the throne marrying a Roman Catholic, and the future position of the monarchy in Australia and New Zealand if republican support there grows. The role of the monarch as head of the Church of England, and the disestablishment of the Church of England, remain off the agenda.

House of Commons

Debate here centres on two concerns: 'modernisation', and the relations between government and parliament. Reforms, from Attlee onwards, have provided for some increased scrutiny of the executive, including Richard Crossman's (Leader of the House in the Wilson Government) Select Committees on Agriculture and on Science and Technology, and the Select Committee on Expenditure of the Callaghan administration. But reforms have been procedural and limited, and stressed 'efficiency' goals.

The Manifesto commitment of 1997 set out modest reforms. In June 1997 a Modernisation Select Committee, chaired by Leader of the House Anne Taylor, was set up. That July, its first report advocated publication of government bills in draft, greater use of Special Standing Committees and a shift of Second Reading debates from the floor of the House to Second Reading Committees. Blair himself changed Prime Minister's Question Time from two quarter-hour weekly sessions to one half-hour. In addition, Westminster Hall was used as a more informal setting for debates on public issues and on Select Committee reports.

When Robin Cook became Leader of the House of Commons in 2001, hopes were raised for further reforms, though the Cabinet was reported as split on the issue.[41] Tension still exists, as shown by the conflict over the power of the Party whips to control membership – and chairmanships – of the Select Committees. Cook linked reform to the Prime Minister's decision to give evidence twice a year to a televised session of the Commons Liaison Committee of senior backbenchers. Peter Hennessy saw this as an important constitutional move to narrow the accountability gap by exposing the most powerful figure in the executive to select committee scrutiny.[42] Cook proposed revision of the working hours to allow morning sittings of the Commons together with a shorter working week overall, proposals which divided MPs across party and gender lines and passed the House in October 2002 only on a very narrow majority. The new timetable came into force in January 2003, and some MPs continued to express disquiet. The Modernisation Committee also recommended a carry-over of legislation from one parliamentary session to another, more pre-legislative scrutiny through the publication of draft bills, and the limitation of back-

benchers' speeches to ten minutes. Uncertainties remain following the resignation of Robin Cook over the Iraq war and his replacement first by John Reid
(viewed as less interested in further reform) and then in June 2003 by Peter Hain.
Hain seems likely to continue the modernising approach. In September 2003 he
advocated continued discussion on reform, including prior scrutiny of proposed
legislation and greater support for Select Committees. The essential dilemma is
that modernisation has two meanings – to facilitate the working of the House, or
to make its scrutiny of the executive more effective – and it is the former which
has predominated.

Human rights

New Labour's reform of the human rights regime is a major constitutional
achievement. Traditionally, Labour rejected a Bill of Rights, pursuing socialist
objectives through class and group (trade union) rights, not individual rights. Sir
Stafford Cripps, Chancellor of the Exchequer in the Attlee Government, also
opposed ratification of the European Convention of Human Rights, fearing that
it would obstruct Labour's nationalisation plans. But in March 1951 the UK was
the first to ratify the Convention. It did not, however, become part of UK
domestic law and cases could only be brought in Strasbourg after going through
the UK courts.

In the 1980s Tony Benn called for the reform of the Prime Minister's powers
of patronage, freedom of information and other proposals, on the grounds that
they represented the rights of the people against the powerful. But they were not
couched in terms of individual rights per se.[43] And the Labour Party's Policy
Review of the late 1980s again rejected suggestions for a Bill of Rights on the
grounds that it took power from parliament and gave it to unelected judges.

In the early 1990s, part of the John Smith legacy was his commitment to the
incorporation of the European Convention on Human Rights (ECHR) into UK
law and the establishment of an independent Human Rights Commission. New
Labour's position had evolved out of the dissatisfaction of jurists and others with
the situation in the Thatcher years, the length of time it took for UK cases to go
through the European Court, and the embarrassing number of government
defeats sustained at Strasbourg.[44] But, while the National Executive Committee
(NEC) of the Labour Party's 1993 statement 'A New Agenda for Democracy'
included an entrenched Bill of Rights, this idea was dropped after John Smith's
death in favour of the more limited ECHR incorporation. Nor did the Party's
1997 Manifesto section 'Real rights for citizens', or the subsequent White Paper
of July 1997, 'Rights Brought Home', or the Bill, include a Human Rights
Commission. Instead, a Joint Human Rights Committee of both Houses of
Parliament was substituted, and was established in January 2001.

There are interesting variations within the UK as the result of devolution.
The devolution legislation bound the Scottish Parliament and the Welsh
Assembly, and their Executives and law officers, to act in accordance with the
European Convention on Human Rights. As a result there could develop a

distinctive Scottish human rights regime.[45] In Northern Ireland, the Belfast Agreement promised a Human Rights Commission and this was appointed in January 1999.

The Labour Government stressed that incorporation would not affect parliamentary sovereignty. The Human Rights Act 1998 empowers courts to issue a 'declaration of incompatibility' of legislation with ECHR and it is then the Government's responsibility to take remedial action. The judges' power to issue declarations of incompatibility, however, means that the political executive will no longer be above the judiciary as the doctrine of parliamentary sovereignty holds. King has also argued that judicial power will grow as the courts challenge the acts of the Executive and judicial review increases.[46] A contrary view is taken by Leigh, who suggests that the tradition of judicial deference to the legislature and the executive will persist. The catch then would be that if domestic judges remained deferential, those in Strasbourg would not be so reticent.[47]

Freedom of information

Openness and transparency have been major themes for both old and new Labour. Every election manifesto since 1974 has committed Labour to a Freedom of Information Bill. From the left, Tony Benn's Commonwealth of Britain Bill of 1991 proposed that all official information should be published, subject to specific exceptions. After Labour's defeat in 1992, however, the Party downgraded the priority. But it was taken up again by John Smith, and Blair's commitment to freedom of information was also very strong, as part of the programme of comprehensive constitutional reform.[48]

In December 1997 the Government's White Paper, 'Your Right to Know: the Government's Proposals for a Freedom of Information Act' (Cm 3818) proposed a right of access to documents or information from a wide range of public bodies. Exemptions would be subject to the high threshold of a 'substantial harm test', and enforcement would lie with an Information Commissioner with powers to order disclosure. It was not until May 1999, however, that the Consultation Paper, which included a draft Bill (Cm 4355), was published, and the Bill itself appeared in November 1999. To the disquiet of jurists and others, the Bill differed from the White Paper, increasing the list of defined exemptions. Ministers argued that freedom of information must allow for 'the efficient and effective conduct of public affairs', with policy advice being 'exempt information'.[49] The Bill gave ministers, not the Information Commissioner, a veto over final decisions on disclosure.

The Bill's passage was protracted and contentious, but the Government gave little ground, and it became law in November 2000. The Act will not be implemented by government departments until January 2005. The legislation did provide for channels of compliance and appeals, setting up a new office of Information Commissioner (absorbing the functions of the Data Protection Registrar) with appeals to an Information Tribunal (absorbing the Data Protection Tribunal) and appeals on points of law to the courts. But the veto remains with ministers, who can override the Commissioner.

Notably, as a result of devolution, freedom of information in Scotland is now wider than that in England and Wales. The Scottish 'substantial prejudice' test is a tougher test than the simple 'prejudice' test and requires Scottish authorities to operate more openly. The Scottish Information Commissioner, who enforces the Freedom of Information (Scotland) Act, has greater powers than the Commissioner under the UK Act. The Act, however, contains similar provisions for the exemption of information relating to the formulation of government policy to those in the UK legislation.

Parties and elections

Labour, while traditionally constitutionally conservative, has been divided over voting systems. Ramsey MacDonald and the Fabians opposed proportional representation, but in 1931 the Labour Government advocated, unsuccessfully, the alternative vote system. In 1945, the priority was to maintain a strong executive rather than reform the rules of the game. Limited changes were made, with the Representation of the People Act 1948 abolishing the university and business votes, and the Redistribution of Seats Act 1949 removing the dual-Member constituencies. In 1969, the Wilson Government's reduction of the voting age from 21 to 18 was seen less as a principled commitment to wider participation than a belief that young people were more likely to vote Labour than Conservative.

New Labour's push for improved democratic processes was also a pragmatic response to its long period out of power and uncertainties over its electoral strength. In 1990 a working party on electoral systems under Raymond Plant was set up. But recommending changes for House of Commons elections proved problematic; Plant switched support from the Additional Member System (AMS) to the non-proportional supplementary vote system. The proposals were not followed up, though John Smith did support a referendum on electoral reform. Blair saw debate on electoral reform as a distraction from the main problem of internal reform of the Labour Party.[50] Before the 1997 General Election, the Report of the Joint Consultative Committee on Constitutional Reform (jointly chaired by Robin Cook, Labour, and Robert Maclennan, Liberal Democrat) said that a referendum on PR should not offer a range of alternatives but a choice between First Past The Post (FPTP) and a single proportional alternative. Any impetus for reform waned, however, as Labour's massive majority removed the need for alliances with the Liberal Democrats.

The Independent Commission on the Voting System, set up in December 1997 and chaired by Liberal Democrat peer Roy Jenkins, arose out of the Government's reluctance to honour its promise to make a time-specific commitment to a referendum on proportional representation for House of Commons elections (see below). Jenkins proposed a mixed electoral system of constituency representatives based on the Alternative Vote (which is not proportional per se) and list MPs drawn from open top-up lists. But the Commission's report of October 1998, like the Plant report, languished.

Different electoral systems, however, were accepted for the rest of the UK. Elections to the new Northern Ireland Assembly of June 1998 were by the Single Transferable Vote (STV) system of proportional representation. AMS is used for elections to the Scottish Parliament, the Welsh Assembly and the Greater London Assembly. It is based on single-member constituencies. Each elector has two votes: one to elect a constituency representative by FPTP, and a second vote to choose the party list (the AMS system) in order to add 'top-up' members to the parliament or assembly to ensure overall proportionality between the parties. The London Mayor is elected by the supplementary vote system (a version of the Alternative Vote System, and a variant on the simple plurality system rather than a proportional one). The elections to the European Parliament are based on a proportional list system, where the regional lists are closed lists drawn up by the political parties.

The Political Parties, Elections and Referendums Act 2000 (PPERA), while not concerned with voting systems as such, gave, for the first time, statutory recognition to political parties. Limits were set on campaign finance, and disclosure of donations was tightened. The Act also established an Electoral Commission, which in 2005 will take over the work of the former Parliamentary and Local Government Boundary Commissions, and a Commons body, the Speaker's Committee, to oversee the Electoral Commission's work. In part the motivation behind these changes was the Labour Party's concern, in opposition, over 'sleaze', and the need to re-examine the legislation consequent on the different electoral systems being introduced for elections to the European Parliament and to the Scottish, Welsh and Greater London bodies.

New Labour's constitutional modernisation has made notable use of referenda. The Wilson Government's 1975 referendum, which sought support for continued membership of the European Economic Community (EEC) while allowing Ministers to oppose it – the 'agreement to differ' – appeared to challenge two constitutional conventions: parliamentary sovereignty and cabinet collective responsibility. Attlee, in 1945, said referenda were 'alien to all our traditions', and the belief that referenda were unconstitutional was widely held within the Party up to the 1970s. In 1979 Callaghan resorted to the use of a referendum to determine support for devolution. But, like Wilson's usage in 1975, this was an occasion when the Party was deeply divided.

Just before the 1997 General Election the Joint Labour–Liberal Democrat Consultative Committee on Constitutional Reform called for a referendum on elections to the House of Commons, to be held in the first term of a new parliament. At this point Blair promised four referenda: on the electoral system; one each on Scottish and Welsh devolution; and on the creation of the Greater London Authority and its directly elected Mayor. In government, two further referenda were promised: on the acceptance of the Good Friday settlement for Northern Ireland and on the entry of Britain into the Euro currency. Four of the six have taken place; that on the electoral system was sidestepped when Labour won office with a massive majority, and that on the Euro deferred. Further referenda will now go forward in those regions of England where elected Regional

Assemblies are proposed. In the summer of 2003, there was heated political conflict over the proposed new Constitution of the European Union, with the Government resisting vociferous Opposition demands that a referendum should be held on the issue. The PPERA, for its part, included a general provision for referenda in the UK, but specific primary legislation would be required for a particular case. The position now seems to be that popular referenda have become part of the British constitution – but we are a long way from a general doctrine on when referenda should or should not be held.[51]

The issue of Europe

New Labour faces the challenge – as did its predecessors – of how, and to what extent, parliamentary sovereignty has been eroded. While politicians, and Westminster procedures, still endorse parliamentary sovereignty, the lack of a written constitution poses real difficulties in squaring parliamentary supremacy with the realities of power sharing with Brussels.[52]

Europe has been a divisive issue for the Labour Party. In the 1960s the left of the Party was opposed to entry to the EEC, as were Wilson and Crossman. Gaitskell, on the right, played a waiting game. When the terms were announced Gaitskell was shocked, and attacked Premier Macmillan's attempts to gain entry in 1962.[53] In 1966 Wilson himself changed his position to endorse entry – but knowing that de Gaulle was still likely to veto Britain's application.

After Britain's entry in January 1973, Labour remained bitterly divided, with Benn emerging as the left's leading opponent. Interestingly, it was the alliance between the Labour left and the Tory right which stressed that the fundamental issue was the constitution, defending parliamentary sovereignty. The pro-Europe Labour right, though a minority, was a strong one, led by Roy Jenkins, David Owen and Shirley Williams. Divisions within the Party induced Wilson to use the constitutional innovation of the referendum – in fact at Benn's suggestion – to 'renegotiate' the terms of entry.[54] Labour's views on Europe changed during the Thatcher years, when government attacks on Welfare State provision and the unions meant that Europe's social policy stance looked much closer to Labour's, and the trade unions', interests. Labour's 1987 General Election Manifesto, 'Labour Will Win', dropped the commitment made in 1983 to withdraw from the EEC.

Prime Minister Blair promised a referendum on entry into the Euro zone – something which has been repeatedly delayed – and tied it to Chancellor Gordon Brown's 'five economic tests'. Economic, not constitutional or political criteria, are promoted as the essence of the problem. On the other hand, Blair is opposed to any increases in the powers of the European Parliament, and to some of the proposals for a future European constitution. In addition, the Government has been ambivalent over proposals for a European Charter of Fundamental Rights which are legally enforceable; the matter is due to be resolved in 2004. Overall, the Government, while continuing to back its preferred option of informal co-operation between leaders at the European

Council summits, now supports the creation of a permanent President of the European Council while insisting that taxation and foreign policy will not become subject to EU majority voting. In June 2003 Foreign Secretary Jack Straw defended the draft constitution, which is to be finalised during an inter-governmental conference over 2003–4, in the face of growing Conservative Party opposition, and denied that it created a substantial expansion of EU powers or a radical overhaul of its existing treaties and competencies. It seems likely that debate on the constitutional issues involved, which has hitherto been muted in the UK compared with Europe, will become more heated.[55]

Changes in the modern state

From subject to citizen: New Labour and the debate on citizenship

Debate on the relationship between the citizen and the state is difficult in the UK which lacks a formal written constitution and where individuals are subjects of the Queen. The situation is changing, however, with the introduction of the Human Rights Act 2000, which construes the individual 'as a citizen in the full sense of the term'. Trevor Smith also argues that the Northern Ireland Act 1998 has widened the rights of citizens there compared with the rest of the UK.[56]

Labour's traditional lack of interest changed in the 1980s as concern grew over a range of constitutional issues. New Labour endorsed John Smith's advocacy of a shift in the balance of power between the citizen and the state. In 1993 the NEC statement 'A New Agenda for Democracy' called for modernisation of the constitution, including citizenship based on a Bill of Rights. In 1999 the then Home Secretary Jack Straw's emphasis was different, calling for a new constitutional relationship between the citizen and the state, in which rights were balanced by responsibilities. Such a 'balance' echoed Tony Blair's 'Third Way' references to the 'rights and duties of citizenship'.[57] This is a communitarian model, with an emphasis on mutually beneficial contractarian relations between the state and the individual.[58]

Changes to the central state

Tony Blair presented constitutional reform as a 'modernisation' project, part of a vigorous 'New Britain'. These included reforms of parliament, devolution, the legal system, the core executive and the civil service, and the independence of the Bank of England which, through its Monetary Committee, is now responsible for the setting of interest rates. At the centre, the Cabinet Office has been strengthened and new units have proliferated inside No. 10, which has virtually become a Prime Minister's Department. The changes have inevitably led to charges of increased centralisation in the system.[59]

Changes to the core executive have brought concerns over the role of Special Advisers. Outside advisers have existed since the Wilson Governments; by 2001 there 78 Special Advisers, of whom 38 worked in No. 10. The Sixth

Report of the Committee on Standards in Public Life (Cm 4557, 2000) recommended that there should be a separate Code of Conduct for Special Advisers and that the total number be capped; both suggestions to be covered by the proposed Civil Service Act. The Act is still awaited (it did not appear in the 2001 Manifesto, and in June 2003 the Public Administration Select Committee itself proposed to produce a bill), but after the 2001 General Election the Government did agree to the Select Committee on Public Administration's report (HC 253, 2000–1) calling for more rigorous methods of appointment and for a Code of Conduct, which was eventually promulgated in July 2001.[60] The Civil Service Code itself, which was brought into force by Order in Council in 1996, awaits the Civil Service Bill to give it statutory backing. Questions arise not over the impartiality of civil servants but over their role in policy *vis-à-vis* the Special Advisers. There are also issues of how the Government's emphasis on bringing in outside personnel relates to the constitutional context of the public service. Such appointments could, argues Bogdanor, 'undermine the constitutional foundations on which our civil service has for so long been based'.[61]

An equally problematic area is use of the prerogative powers of the Crown. The prerogative powers, which cover such areas as the creation and abolition of central government departments, also include sensitive issues: the power to make and accede to international treaties and the power to deploy military resources and declare war, the appointments of bishops, peers and members of the senior judiciary and military. None of these prerogatives have a statutory base and the Prime Minister, in the name of the Crown, can exercise them without parliamentary approval. The Privy Council, whose remit covers a wide range of bodies including the universities, the medical and professional councils, and the BBC, also operates under the prerogative powers.

Tony Benn has been a long-standing critic of the use of prerogative powers. In the 1980s he attacked prime ministerial patronage and the unrestrained power of the executive,[62] and called for the strengthening of the Parliamentary Labour Party (PLP) to include the election of cabinet ministers.[63] His 1991 Commonwealth of Britain Bill proposed the transfer of the royal prerogative powers to a President, elected by a two-thirds majority in the two Houses of the Commonwealth Parliament, who would act on the advice of the Prime Minister or on a resolution of the Commons.[64]

In 1992, Labour promised to end the misuse of prerogative powers to bypass parliament. Reform of the royal prerogative was also a part of the 1993 NEC statement 'A New Agenda for Democracy'. Plans to reform the powers, however, were dropped after Tony Blair succeeded John Smith as leader of the Party.

Labour and the trade unions

As Madgwick and Woodhouse put it, the balance of interests is a major task of governments committed to pluralism and to constitutional procedures.[65] The Labour Party has had a complex relationship with the trade unions. For the leadership, the General Strike of 1922 was a disaster, threatening Labour's claim to be a constitutional party governing in the name of all citizens. From the late 1920s onwards, Labour was a statist party, rejecting alternatives such as syndicalism, guild socialism or workers' control. This emphasis was reinforced by the experience of the Second World War. By the end of the 1960s, friction between Labour and the unions grew as Barbara Castle published the 1969 industrial relations White Paper, *In Place of Strife*, which envisaged major changes in the relations between trade unions and the state, including increased power for the Secretary of State and penal sanctions. But acrimony over the proposals led to the Bill being dropped in favour of a face-saving undertaking by the TUC that member unions would observe the TUC's own guidelines – an undertaking it could not deliver.

In the 1970s, Tony Benn advocated wider industrial democracy and workers' co-operatives – but at the same time called for greater state power over the economy. These Bennite views, popular on the left in the early 1980s, were dropped after Labour lost the 1983 General Election and abandoned its commitment to the Alternative Economic Strategy.

Currently, New Labour does not recognise a role for the trade unions in economic governance of the country or consult them over increased private sector involvement in public service delivery which unions challenge. On the other hand, on the policies of the minimum wage and union recognition rights, the Government has been more proactive than its Labour predecessors. And in February 2003, in a notable decision, the Labour Government reversed the Thatcherite 'contracting-out' cuts in wages and conditions. Now, people working for a contracted-out public service will have 'no less favourable' terms and conditions than those employed by public services. But there are still tensions. The unions are re-examining the terms on which they provide financial support for the Party, and have expressed fears about state funding for political parties as a threat to their influence.

Conclusion

The constitutional changes of the first two Blair administrations are the most radical of New Labour's reforms. The Labour Government introduced change with panache, with the 1997–8 parliamentary session dealing with 11 constitutional bills, covering devolution to Scotland, Wales and Northern Ireland, an elected Mayor for London, development agencies for the English regions, human rights, electoral reform (for European Parliament elections), the implementation of the Amsterdam Treaty, and the independence of the Bank of England. But in large part Blair has been seen as the inheritor of John Smith's agenda[66] and, at least in the first term, it was the driving oversight of Lord Irvine which produced the human rights enshrinement, the actual devolution settlement (as Chair of the cabinet committee) and the freedom of information legislation (however limited). And Blair's position on the House of Lords changed from his Opposition support for an elected chamber to a positive rejection of that option.

After the General Election of 2001, all the constitutional responsibilities of the Home Office (the Crown, Church and State, human rights, freedom of information) were transferred to the Lord Chancellor's department, in effect making the Lord Chancellor the 'Minister for Justice and the Constitution'.[67] This position, however, was radically altered in June 2003 on the occasion of the retirement of Lord Irvine and the establishment of a Department of Constitutional Affairs. The announcement gave rise to outcry at Prime Minister Blair's unilateral action in announcing major constitutional changes without prior consultation and seemingly as part of a Cabinet reshuffle.[68] The departure of Lord Irvine, it was reputed, was in part due to the clashes with Home Secretary David Blunkett over suggestions for a re-examination of functions between his and the Lord Chancellor's Office. Both Blunkett and Irvine opposed suggestions for a Ministry of Justice, the former over loss of Home Office functions, and the latter in opposition to any division of his own roles encompassing executive, judicial and legislative powers. In the House of Lords, concern was expressed over potential revisions to the self-regulation of their working practices.[69]

Prime Minister Blair presented the reforms as part of the Government's ongoing modernisation of the constitution. The new Department for Constitutional Affairs, with its first Secretary of State Lord Falconer, would put the relationship between executive, legislature and judiciary on a modern footing. The Lord Chancellor's roles as judge and Speaker of the House of Lords would end and a new independent Judicial Appointments Commission[70] to recommend candidates for appointment as judges would be set up. A new Supreme Court would replace the Law Lords operating as an appellate committee of the House of Lords. A new post of Speaker of the House of Lords, a non-ministerial position, would be established. In the transition period Lord Falconer would exercise the functions of Lord Chancellor, including the Speakership, but would not sit as a judge in the House of Lords.

Such reforms will receive a broad welcome from the legal profession and others concerned with the Lord Chancellor's tripartite role and with the need to make appointments of judges both more transparent and to diversify the judiciary. Criticism that responsibility of the new Department for Constitutional Affairs should lie with the Commons rather than the Lords has been challenged: Hazell argues that it is not unusual for second chambers to have such powers.[71] The proposal for the Supreme Court (long campaigned for by senior law lord Lord Bingham) is interesting. Such a body, it is argued, has seemed inevitable once the Human Rights Act 2000, with its guarantee of a hearing by 'an independent and impartial tribunal', came into effect. But it may be at least three years before it is operational.

The Prime Minister, however, met further criticism over proposals to deal with the residual functions of the Scotland Office and Wales Office. While sensibly pragmatic in the light of the devolution settlement, the actual provisions appear chaotic. The Secretary of State for Constitutional Affairs would assume responsibilities for the residual functions of the two bodies, and for the Parliamentary

Under-Secretaries of State for the two countries. But at Cabinet level, responsibility for Scottish and Welsh business would lie with Alistair Darling (the Transport Secretary; member for Edinburgh Central) and with Peter Hain (formerly Welsh Secretary and currently Leader of the House of Commons; member for Neath).

The new constitutional arrangements will take time to be enacted. Discussion papers were promised for July 2003 on: the creation of the Supreme Court; the establishment of the Judicial Appointments Commission; the future of the rank of Queen's Counsel.

A number of questions remain. While there is now a Department of Constitutional Affairs, there is no formal constitution. Relatedly, there is no fundamental questioning of the exercise of the prerogative powers by the Prime Minister, the position of the monarchy, and the relation between church and state. The reforms still appear to lack an overall philosophy. 'Modernisation' has never been defined as a theory – except as 'not Old Labour'. The original New Labour emphasis on the need for greater democratisation of the British constitution has given way to the more ambiguous 'modernisation', with uncertain outcomes.

For the Blairite centre, the constitutional changes are an invigorating move to a more open democracy and a more decentralised system of power. While the old right saw constitutional reform as a distraction, the new right has largely accepted the changes, though further possible moves – greater divergence in Scotland and Wales as the result of devolution, proportional representation and state funding of political parties – raise concern. For the old left, Welfare State socialism – coherent state solutions to economic and social problems – has been undermined by the constitutional reforms of devolution. The new left also echoes some of the old left's concern over Labour–trade union relations, the role of the market in public service delivery, and the increased power of the executive and its operation inside No. 10.

New Labour sees the state as but one actor among many, with globalisation setting limits to what national governments can do. The nation state has, according to Bobbitt, become the market state, in which the state's role is to maximise opportunity for (global) market forces.[72] New Labour's constitutional modernisation, particularly its decentralising aspects, reflects this reality and makes the British state more effective and efficient. This decentralisation has been achieved by devolution within the continuing UK framework. But the asymmetrical, quasi-federal nature of devolution has given rise to potential intergovernmental tensions, divergence and continuing demands for increased powers. Relatedly, there is concern over the future role of local government, given New Labour's position that public service values, not the public sector per se, are the objectives of modernisation. And there is still unfinished business, including the use of the prerogative powers, the triple role of the Lord Chancellor, the absence of a proper Supreme Court, and an independent system for appointing judges.

New Labour's new constitutional balance has produced a quasi-federal, more rights-based and more open system of government, with power shifting from

Westminster and Whitehall to other political bodies, to the judiciary and to the individual. But this has also been seen as incompatible with the overarching goals of socialism, and as more Gladstonian liberalism than social democracy.[73] Others commend the steps taken but see further change as essential – true democratisation not just 'modernisation' – if New Labour is to fulfil its promise that constitutional reform would be the key to a new framework for the state and its relations with its citizens.

Notes

1 Blair, T., '1996 John Smith Memorial Lecture', quoted in Bogdanor, V., *Power and the People* (Victor Gollanz, London, 1997), p. 14.

2 Mandelson, P., *The Blair Revolution Revisited* (Politico's, London, 2002), p xxii.

3 Morrison, J., *Reforming Britain: New Labour, New Constitution?* (Reuters/Pearson Education, London, 2001).

4 Jones, B. and Keating, M., *Labour and the British State* (OUP, Oxford, 1985), p. 53.

5 The document called Charter 88 was published at the end of 1988. It called for a new constitutional settlement, including a Bill of Rights. The original impetus came from people associated with the former Alliance parties.

6 Freeden, M., 'True Blood or False Geneology: New Labour and British Social Democratic Thought', in Gamble, A. and Wright, T. (eds) *The New Social Democracy* (Blackwell/Political Quarterly, Oxford, 1999), p.164.

7 Devine, T.M., *The Scottish Nation: 1700–2000*, (Allen Lane, and the Penguin Press, London, 1999).

8 It is interesting to note that the then Opposition leader Edward Heath's 1968 Perth Declaration (at the Scottish Party Conference) committed the Conservatives to a devolved Scottish Assembly and thereby reversed a century of consistent opposition to Home Rule (T.M. Devine, *The Scottish Nation: 1700–2000*, p. 575). His successor Margaret Thatcher remained resolutely in favour of the Union.

9 Bogdanor, V., *Devolution in the United Kingdom* (OUP, Oxford, 1999), p. 152.

10 Morgan, K.O., *Rebirth of a Nation: Wales 1880–1980* (Clarendon Press, Oxford, 1981), p. 377.

11 The Royal Commission on the Constitution, *Report*, Cmnd 5460, 1973. The Commission was appointed in 1969 under the chairmanship of Geoffrey Crowther. Its remit was to examine all aspects of the constitution in the UK, with particular regard to nationalism in Scotland and Wales. After Crowther's death, the chairmanship was taken by Lord Kilbrandon. The Report of October 1973 recommended that Scotland and Wales should each have a legislative Assembly with its own budget, tax-raising powers and responsibility for a wide range of functions.

12 The Scottish Trade Union Congress having become 'an enthusiastic convert to Home Rule'. (T. M. Devine, *The Scottish Nation: 1700–2000*, p. 576).

13 In the Callaghan government John Smith had been given responsibility for the legislative process for devolution; this came to an end with the defeat in the referenda in 1979.

14 The Scotland Act 1998 does not specify the powers devolved to the Scottish Parliament, but lists those reserved to Westminster – constitutional matters; foreign policy; defence and national security; immigration and nationality; macro-economic, monetary and fiscal policy; the regulation of markets; employment and social security; and transport safety and regulation – with all the rest devolved to Edinburgh. The Wales Act 1998 provides for an assembly with executive power and powers of secondary legislation, within a framework of primary legislation laid down by Westminster.

15 In February 2002 the Boundary Commission for Scotland proposed that the number of Scottish seats in the Commons should be cut from 72 to 59.

16 Following the Scottish Parliament elections of May 2003 the Lib-Lab pact was renewed for a further four years.

17 Most Whitehall departments now have Devolution or Constitution Units to handle relations with the new devolved administrations. In 1999 the first four written agreements, called Concordats, were published between the UK, Scottish and Welsh administrations. In addition, there is an External Relations Division in the Scottish Executive and a Cabinet and Constitution Unit in the Welsh Assembly.

18 Cm. 4806, *Memorandum of Understanding and Supplementary Agreements*, London, HMSO, 2000.

19 Bogdanor, V., 'Devolution: Decentralisation or Disintegration?', *Political Quarterly*, Vol. 70, 1999, p. 187.

20 *Ibid.*, p. 188.

21 The name for southern Ireland from 1921, when it gained dominion status on the partition of Ireland, until 1937 when it became the sovereign state of Eire.

22 Forman, F.N., *Constitutional Change in the United Kingdom* (Routledge, London, 2002), p. 64.

23 Blair criticised the ideas for 'English votes on English laws' put forward by the then Conservative Party leader William Hague in 1998 and 1999; F.N. Forman, *Constitutional Change in the United Kingdom*, p. 123; p. 135.

24 Cm 5511, *Your Region, Your Choice: Revitalising the English Regions*, (HMSO, London, 2002).

25 Hetherington, P., ' "Power for the regions" warning to Blair', *Guardian*, 22 June 2001.

26 Hetherington, P., 'Prescott to push English devolution', *Guardian*, 6 May 2002.

27 Jones, G. and Stewart, J., 'Toothless wonder', *Local Government Chronicle*, 5 July 2002, p. 13.

28 Herbert Morrison was Mayor of Hackney 1920–21. He became a member of the London County Council (LCC) in 1922 and, although elected to Parliament in 1923, he continued his LCC membership and became its Leader in 1934. His outstanding London achievement was the establishment of London Transport.

29 Rhodes, R.A.W., 'New Labour's Civil Service: Summing-up Joining-up', *Political Quarterly*, Vol. 71, 2000, pp. 151–66.

30 Sidney and Beatrice Webb's 1920 *A Constitution for a Social Constitution of Great Britain* called for the abolition of the hereditary House of Lords and the creation of two independent, co-equal assemblies, a political one and a social one, both popularly elected from territorial constituencies.

31 In 1964 the incoming Prime Minister Harold Wilson announced that he would not be recommending any hereditary honours. No new hereditary peerages were thereafter awarded for almost 20 years, until the advent of the Thatcher Government.

32 Bogdanor, V., 'Constitutional Reform', in Seldon, A., (ed.), *The Blair Effect: The Blair Government 1997–2001* (Little, Brown & Co., London, 2001), p. 142.

33 In the John Smith Memorial Lecture, 1996. Shell, D., 'Labour and the House of Lords: A Case Study in Constitutional Reform', *Parliamentary Affairs*, Vol. 53, 2000, p. 295.

34 Morrison, J., *Reforming Britain: New Labour, New Constitution?*, p. 151.

35 The Royal Commission on the Reform of the House of Lords (the Wakeham Commission), Cmd 4534, *A House for the Future*, (HMSO, London, 2000).

36 White Paper, 'The House of Lords: Completing the Reform', Cmd 5291, (HMSO, London, 2001).

37 Perkins, A., 'Irvine gloom on Lords reform', *Guardian*, 8 January 2003.

38 White, M. and Perkins, A., 'MPs and peers remain split on Lords reform', *Guardian*, 22 January 2003.

39 But the majority against was a slender 179:173. The defeat of the favourite 60 to 40 per cent elected/non-elected option was attributed to some 20 ostensibly pro-election Conservatives who switched sides in a tactical move to embarrass the Prime Minister. It has also been argued that a rearguard action by Old Labour MPs achieved a three-way split and thus defeated reform. Cf: Michael White and Patrick Wintour, 'MPs reject all options for Lords', *Guardian*, 5 February 2003.

40 Ashley, J., 'The Queen comes through for Blair every single day', *Guardian*, 6 November 2002.

41 Grice, A., 'Cabinet split over reform of Commons', *Independent*, 19 July 2002.

42 Perkins, A., 'Blair agrees to scrutiny by MPs', *Guardian*, 27 April 2002.

43 Benn, T., *Arguments for Democracy*, (Cape, London, 1981).

44 Morrison believes that as a result of these embarrassing defeats, an incoming Labour government had little choice but to incorporate ECHR. Morrison, J., *Reforming Britain: New Labour, New Constitution?*, p. 348.

45 Hazell, R. *et al.*, 'The British Constitution in 1998–99: The Continuing Revolution', *Parliamentary Affairs*, Vol. 53, 2000, p. 254.

46 King, A., *Does the United Kingdom still have a constitution?* The Hamlyn Lectures (Sweet and Maxwell/The Hamlyn Trust, London, 2001), p.72.

47 Leigh, I., 'Taking Rights Proportionately: Judicial Review, the Human Rights Act and Strasbourg', *Public Law*, Summer 2002, pp. 265–87.

48 'My commitment ... Extracts from a speech by Tony Blair on March 25 1996 before he became Prime Minister' *Guardian*, 22 June 1999; at *Guardian Unlimited*, www.guardian.co.uk/freedom, 29 November 2002.

49 Forman, F.N., *Constitutional Change in the United Kingdom*, p. 294.

50 Blackburn, R. and Plant, R. (eds) *Constitutional Reform: The Labour Government's Constitutional Reform Agenda* (Longman, London, 1999), p. 71.

51 Blackburn, R. and Plant, R., (eds.), 1999, *Constitutional Reform: The Labour Government's Constitutional Reform Agenda*, p. 81.

52 Morrison, J., *Reforming Britain: New Labour, New Constitution?*, p. 13; p. 15.

53 Gaitskell died in January 1963, the same month that de Gaulle vetoed Britain's entry.

54 The decision to hold a referendum led to Roy Jenkins resigning from the deputy leadership (though he rejoined the Shadow Cabinet in October 1973).

55 Morrison, J., *Reforming Britain: New Labour, New Constitution?*, pp. 489–90.

56 Smith, T., 'How Citizenship got on to the Political Agenda', *Parliamentary Affairs*, Vol. 55, July 2002, p. 483; p. 484.

57 Blair, T., *The Third Way: New Politics for the New Century*, Fabian Pamplet 588, London, the Fabian Society, 1998. Cf. especially section 4, 'Strong Civil Society: Rights and Responsibilities'.

58 Freeden, M., 'The Ideology of New Labour', *Political Quarterly*, Vol.71, 2000, p. 48.

59 Holliday, I., 'Is the British State Hollowing Out?', *Political Quarterly*, Vol. 71, 2000, p. 173.

60 Gray, A. and Jenkins, B., 'Government and Administration: Reasserting Public Services and their Consumers', *Parliamentary Affairs*, Vol. 55, 2002, p. 238. For the efficacy of the Code of Conduct, see: Terence Daintith, 'Analysis: "A very good day to get out anything we want to bury"', *Public Law*, Spring 2002, pp. 13–21.

61 Bogdanor, V., 'Come back, Sir Humphrey', *Guardian*, 9 April 2002.

62 Benn, T., *Arguments for Democracy*.

63 Benn, T., 'The Case for a Constitutional Premiership', *Parliamentary Affairs*, Vol. 33, 1980, pp. 7–22.

64 Oliver, D., 'Written Constitutions: Principles and Problems', *Parliamentary Affairs*, Vol. 45, 1992, pp. 173–87.

65 Madgwick, P. and Woodhouse, D., *The Law and Politics of the Constitution* (Harvester Wheatsheaf, Hemel Hempstead, 1995), p. 259.

66 Though arguably an increasingly reluctant one, conceding reform for Scotland, Wales and London but seeming to undermine it by trying to impose his own candidates for the lead positions.

67 Hazell, R. *et al.*, J., 'The Constitution: Coming in from the Cold', *Parliamentary Affairs*, Vol. 55, 2002, p. 219.

68 Following representation by Leader of the Opposition Iain Duncan Smith to the Speaker, the Prime Minister was forced to make an unprecedented statement to the House. See: Press release, 'PM statement on reshuffle', http://www.number-10. gov.uk, 18 June 2003.

69 Unlike the Speaker in the House of Commons, the Lord Chancellor presides over Lords' debates without responsibility for calling to order or choosing speakers. He is appointed by the Prime Minister rather than elected by the members of the House, as is the case in the Commons.

70 Scotland already has a ten-member Judicial Appointments Commission, with a majority of non-lawyers and chaired by a lay person. It remains unclear whether the proposed Judicial Appointments Commission for England and Wales will appoint the most senior judges or whether these will remain appointed by the Queen on the advice of the Prime Minister.

71 Hazell, R., 'Orphan adopted', *Guardian*, 14 June 2003. The House of Lords already has a select committee on the constitution (though potential rivalry exists with the more recent House of Commons Select Committee on the Lord Chancellor's Department, chaired by Liberal Democrat MP Alan Beith).

72 Bobbitt, P., 'Blair, the pioneer of a new order', *New Statesman*, 30 September 2002, pp. 26–8; and cf: Bobbitt, P., *The Shield of Achilles: War, Peace and the Course of History* (Allen Lane, London, 2002).

73 Bogdanor, V., 'Constitutional Reform', in Seldon, A. (ed.), *The Blair Effect: The Blair Government 1997–2001*, p. 154.

12 Internationalism

Brian Brivati

The key question about the Labour Party's international and defence policy over the course of its history is the question of a 'socialist' Britain's role in the world. When is it right for a democracy to intervene in the affairs of other states? What circumstances need to exist for that democracy to agree with or participate in the use of force in other sovereign states or against international groups? What relationship should Britain have with organisations of states? The second set of questions concerns Labour as a socialist party: What is the nature of the leadership that Britain should take? Can we separate a capitalist war from a democratic war? What is the connection between pacifism and socialism? All of these questions cut to the core of the dilemma faced by a party with a strongly utopian element in its founding ideology and an almost entirely practical orientation in its operation in practice. This chapter will attempt to explore the way in which Labour grappled with this question through an analysis of Labour's construction of Britain's place in the world.

The basis of the political economy that Labour adopted at its foundation, and confirmed and extended in its 1918 constitution, was intervention. It was a belief in the state and state action. From the ownership of industry, through the use of direct taxation, to the legal representation of trade unionism, the principle was that the existing structures of the British State would be used to represent the interests of the working class. Eventually, this political economy evolved into something that was both distinctive and recognisably connected to ideas of socialism. Taking the Parliamentary road obviously produced many difficulties and challenges but the foundational assumptions about state action and intervention remained intact down to the 1980s. To an extent of course, they still remain. The central focus on public service echoes the notion that collective action remains the feature that separates Labour from the other parties, but the Blair–Thatcher consensus on the ownership of industry and the role of the market economy has concentrated state activism in highly defined ways.

However, the Labour Party, at its foundation, found it possible to be a distinctive presence in domestic policy. Though struggling for a time with the 'Lib-Lab' label, the role of the trade unions and strong component of intellectual socialism allowed a series of discrete policy positions to evolve. The problem for the Party from its inception was what view could it develop on foreign and defence questions that made sense in a similarly distinctive way? The basis of its domestic policy was state action: a domestic 'forward' policy. How could this be applied to foreign and defence policy? How was Labour to apply this sense of action and intervention to foreign and defence policy? The problem was acute because the basis of the socialist critique of Salisbury and the Imperialists was that it was time for the British state to come home, to deliver the fruits of the industrial revolution and the benefits of progress, to the toilers in the 'dark satanic mills'. No longer on the condescending basis of Tory Democracy, but structurally and as of right. If the British state was to come home, how could it be active abroad?

For early socialists like Ramsey MacDonald the ethical basis of policy in these areas was therefore inaction and withdrawal. The ideas of pacifism and anti-imperialism, in so far as they informed policy debate in Labour Party circles before the First World War, were actually in tune with old-fashioned Gladstonian liberalism. But in the same way that the grand old man's morality clashed with his domesticity, so for Labour the notion of leadership in a global sense clashed directly with the idea of isolationism. Socialism was an international movement. The Communist class analysis was very much a working assumption in the parliamentary socialist parties before the First World War. When war broke out, MacDonald, in his opposition, was being consistent in his analysis of the conflict as a class-based one and a product of imperialism. In this instance leaders like MacDonald put the idea of class solidarity above that of democracy or self-determination. This was a clash of Empires and therefore inaction, opposition to the conflict, was both consistent and complementary of socialist ideals. That other sections of the Party took a different view exposed the centrality of the division that has plagued the Party down to the present. The phases in the evolution of this central dilemma mirror the unfolding century.

What was at stake in the decisions made by the Parliamentary Party in 1914 were to be repeated over the Spanish Civil War, the question of the Popular Front, Appeasement, the future of Europe in the post-war world, CND, Vietnam, the Pol Pot regime and so on. In the clash between action and inaction, between class and state responsibilities and between forms of leadership, Labour has tried and largely failed for nearly a century to find a basis for its foreign policy that is not case by case. Since 1997, that basis has evolved and is being applied but it has caused significant divisions in the Party. It is a forward policy of moral and political leadership that sacrifices potential collective positions with the European Union in favour of an Atlanticist-based multilateralism. In a sense it is the embracing of the defence of Belgium against the definition of class interest, re-written for a new century. It is a new Imperialism in the sense that it is a forward policy that seeks to remake the world in the image of liberal democracy and capitalism. As such it is consistent with some elements of Labour's history on these questions and inconsistent with others; what it does not allow for is indifference.

The factional reading of the history of the Party implicit in the suggested structures for the chapters in this book does not apply neatly to foreign and defence questions. The terms New and Old Left, or New and Old Right, do not catch the way in which the Party split and reconfigured itself around these issues. For example, almost all the leading lights of New Labour were once passionate advocates of unilateral nuclear disarmament, almost all the key ministers in MacDonald's breakaway national government had opposed the First World War. Ernest Bevin, the 'Old Right' trade unionist, was a leading opponent of neutrality towards the Spanish Civil War and the main architect of the North Atlantic Treaty Organisation. Hugh Gaitskell was the emotional opponent of the EEC and a passionate multilateralist. Nye Bevan as the personification of the left was also a multilateralist, and so on.

Patrick Seyd[1] has suggested that the division in the Party between socialists and social democrats can be summed up thus: 'Socialists are committed to the transformation of property relationships and social democrats are committed to the modification of property relationships, "Managing Capitalism set against replacing Capitalism"'. This is a clear and useful differentiation between the two main brands of Labour Party ideology: what underlies both is a vision of Britain that emphasises the backward, the unequal and the poor. The vision of the problem is more or less the same: the prescription for type of treatment needed is very different. I will adopt this distinction for the purposes of this chapter. It has very important implications because it is a much wider definition than can be encompassed by a fundamentalist versus revisionist divide, or the moderniser versus traditionalist (New Labour vs. Old Labour) divide so popular today. Both of these divisions are based on the presumption of managed capitalism and are thus divisions between kinds of social democrats. With this definition the group within the Party which we might call socialist is tiny.

The majority of the Labour Party for the bulk of the post-war period has been social democratic. The Labour Party in power is a social democratic party. Social Democrats have different policy orientations through time and follow different routes, but their objective has been to manage change, and manage capitalism in such a way as to reach a fully modern society. The definition of what constitutes the modern society may change but it was usually represented by something foreign and or new. The differentiation between the modern and the new in social democratic philosophy is often ambiguous. This may stem from the need to manage what they perceive to be the chaos of the market. Markets do not achieve the redistribution objectives that social democrats feel as necessary to bring equality to an unequal but increasingly affluent society. Left to the market Britain would continue to divide between the rich and the poor and continue to be a pre-modern society.

To bring a rational organisation to the chaos of the market it was necessary to use planning. The problem was that after the Attlee Governments of 1945–51 there was very little intellectual capital left among the social democrats. They could not find a plan, a blueprint with which to carry on the work of reconstruction. They therefore looked abroad. Tony Crosland looked abroad and saw America: he saw the management structure of the 'new' forms of capitalism. America became Modernity. Other social democrats also looked abroad. They saw the economic miracle of the six, the reconstruction of Germany on a largely social democratic state model. They adopted this as their model of modernisation. Federal Republic became Modernity. Others looked abroad and saw Scandinavia and advocated adopting this as a model. Sweden became Modernity. Yet others looked East and with an at times uncritical acceptance of the Soviet's self image, adopted the idea of the command economy as the model for modernisation – not the creation of a fully planned economy but the extension of social ownership to the commanding heights of the economy leaving a small private sector. The Soviet Union became Modernity. Those who adopted the idea of the fully planned economy, following the logic of Seyd's distinction, are the tiny socialist minority, among them the Communist and Trotskyist fellow travellers. And yet, paradoxically, for all their enthusiasm as intellectual wholesalers, they still felt that British social democracy could lead the world.

This contradiction holds for the relationship between British social democracy and the EC, and on the debate on Britain's possession of nuclear weapons – it does not, and is not intended as, a model for all areas of policy because there are exceptions, like decolonisation.

The social democrats' main image of Britain was of a decaying and backward state and society in need of reform by the adoption of a model for modernisation. This diagnosis directly contradicted the social democrats' notion of Britain in relation to the world, which was of a state capable of playing a leading role. The nature of the leading role that Britain could play was different at different times for different social democrats. Some felt that Britain could lead only by trying to keep up with the Americans, a belief which I characterise as political leadership. Others felt that it was only by offering an alternative to the superpowers, through for example unilateralism, that Britain would keep its place in the world. This I characterise as moral leadership. What is striking is the regularity with which the underlying assumption was that Britain would naturally assume a position of leadership. The social democratic image of Britain is infused with a sense of patriotism. The British would assume a position of leadership because of their special characteristics as a people. At times this became chauvinism tinged with a radical social agenda.

There was a rapid recognition in the Labour Party that in the post-Second World War world Britain would need to make a huge effort just to stand still in terms of its international position. Anne Deighton has made the case clearly: the Labour Government's foreign policy objective in the immediate post-war period was to maintain an independent role in foreign affairs. 'To assert Britain's own great power status and restore a favourable balance of power in Europe'[2], and,

> With the same determination that welfare and nationalisation measures were introduced during this period of financial stringency, the Government sought to try and sustain Britain's status as a great power with an independent role to play as the United States' partner in European recovery.'[3]

Or as Bevin summed it up on the British bomb: 'we've got to have the bloody union jack on it'.[4]

The chief topic of foreign and defence policy debates within the Labour Party was over the nature of the relationship between a social democratic Britain and the individual states, and collections of states, which came to dominate the post-war world. In these debates one can detect the main signposts on the road to the schism and electoral oblivion of the early 1980s – the Cold War, unilateralism, the EEC. In turn the place of intervention in these debates becomes clouded as Britain's international role, in the pre-Falklands War period, gradually moves away from activism towards passivity. There are four general stages of the debates.

The first is concerned with the conflict between political leadership and moral leadership – and is generally dominated by ideas of political leadership. The second is coming to terms with Europe and the period of dominance of moral leadership. The third period, after 1983, saw the implementation of Kinnock's Policy Review which reduced the emphasis on moral leadership and slowly, especially after the defeat of 1987, the European Social Democratic agenda came to dominate. The fourth is the transcendence of that social demo-cratic agenda by a forward policy based on global intervention in conflict situations with the intention of defending human rights and in some instances imposing regime change. In the first three stages the Labour Party, following the lead of Ernest Bevin in the inter-war period and the post-war Attlee Governments, has been motivated by a highly developed notion of patriotism, often indistinguishable from chauvinism. Indeed, you could go so far as to say that the siege economy and neutralist foreign policy, which became the election Manifesto of 1983, were at heart an expression of a radically informed chau-vinism – the level of superiority assumed goes beyond the merely patriotic and is founded on the triumph of prejudice over what any reasonable observer with the benefit of hindsight would describe as reality. In the fourth stage, that chau-vinism is informed by a paradoxical combination of the triumphalism of democracy and capitalism after the collapse of the Soviet Union and insecurity bred by the events of September 11.

The first major division in the Labour Party on foreign and defence policy was concerned with the response of the Party to the outbreak of the First World War and developed through the inter-war period with the rise of the European dictators, the policy of appeasement and the fighting of the Second World War, and then the possibility and reality of the Cold War. There were three positions. First, what we might call 'The Popular Front' position that the First World War was a capitalist war which should not include the parties of the working class, that the inter-war dictators could only be fought by a united working class and then that a second front needed to be opened to help Russia. This evolved into a 'left can talk to left' mentality. The second was a straightforward pacifism in the face of the First World War and the deepening crisis of the 1930s. The third was personified by Ernest Bevin: the fight was to save not capitalism but socialism and democracy. In these pre-war debates we can begin to see the shape of the main positions on Labour's view of Britain's place in the world but the arguments are brought together most clearly in the responses within the Party to the Cold War.

As the world situation stabilised after the fighting ended in 1945, the choices Labour faced quickly crystallised. Was Britain to fight the Cold War and thereby keep a leading place at the head of the global table, or was the Labour Government to try and diffuse the Cold War by offering a distinctive third force position by developing an alternative power block? This debate resulted in confrontation between Gaitskell and Bevan on Korean rearmament, and was followed by arguments on German rearmament and on the place of the UK in the nuclear arms race. Was Britain to have nuclear weapons and, if so, would they be made by Britain or purchased from the Americans? Those who advocated fighting the Cold War through the Atlantic Alliance and the United Nations and who supported Korean rearmament, those who supported German rearmament and the British procession of the bomb preferably made in Britain, believed that Britain could play the part of a political leader of the free world. The dominant image that Bevin, Gaitskell, Patrick Gordon Walker *et al.* carried around in their heads was an image of Britain as a great power – as a partner and not a client of the United States: an image of global political leadership on one side of a profound ideological struggle.

It is vitally important to put the Cold War at the centre of any analysis of the social democrats' image of Britain in the post-war period. The underlying policy assumption of the political leadership wing of the Party was that Britain had to play a leading role in the Cold War as a part of the Atlantic Alliance. The great conflict and challenge to this mandate to implement US policy was the transitional period between the old and the new worlds. It was Macmillan's bid for entry to the EEC, more than any other event, which challenged the unity of the social democrats' worldview. It was the European question – more than others – that crystallised the conflicts and contradictions in the social democrats' image of Britain. Without the challenge of the idea of a unifying western Europe, the rest of the policy priorities of the United States could have been pursued with little difficulty. In the EEC the contradictions between an adherence to the UK's role as a world leader of some kind and the United States' policy of supporting European unity – clashed fatally. The clearest illustration of this was in the process of Hugh Gaitskell making his mind up on the European issue. The actual issue of the Community was part of the on-going Party political discourse, both inside the Labour Party and between Government and Opposition. Gaitskell partly accepted the view that it was an issue that transcended Party politics – but only partly. It was also, clearly, an issue on which he could unite the Party in opposition to the Macmillan Government. The key passage in his conference speech of 1962 in which he rejected the Community in favour of the Commonwealth and EFTA was a series of ifs: if the Commonwealth could be safeguarded; if the EFTA countries could be brought in, and implicitly if it could be an inter-governmental organisation. If, in other words, the Community were a different entity and could be proved to be a different entity, then Gaitskell was prepared to believe in it. By the same token his objection was based not on the principle of entry but on the particular terms secured by the Conservative Government. It was a political choice, made to unite the Party mid-way through a parliament against a government that was increasingly in trouble and had staked much of its reputation on the possibility of joining the Community. But it was also a political choice about leadership and a choice that illustrated a set of assumptions about Britain's role in the world.

Behind the rhetoric of the conference speech and behind the political expediency, there was a core of ambivalence towards the process of European unity and a core of commitment to the Commonwealth. Gaitskell was not alone in this ambivalence to the process of European integration:

> Wilson was always mildly anti-European, in the sense that he seemed not to like continental Europeans, their style of life or their politics. He was basically a north of England, non-conformist puritan, with all the virtues and the inhibitions of that background. The continental Europeans, especially from France and southern Europe, were alien to him ... Despite this background, Harold Wilson decided from October 1974 that a 'yes' position was the most practical choice. As a statesman – which was part, but only part of his complex personality and always was – he knew that Britain must be centrally placed in Europe's future. As a party leader, he saw it as the best way to hold Labour together – because the antis would not leave the Party over Europe, but the pros would. As a shrewd politician, he saw the pro position as the most likely winning one ... Mr Heath had taken the British Establishment into Europe. Harold Wilson took in the British people.[5]

Twelve years earlier, when Gaitskell came out against the EEC, he did so for political reasons, his judgement was expedient and politically practical but the conflicts that lay behind that judgement are indicative of the wider ideological malaise that Labour was plunged into by the Macmillan bid. It is worth re-reading the famous passage:

> We must be clear about this: it does mean, if this is the idea, the end of Britain as an independent European state. I make no apology for repeating it. It means the end of a thousand years of history. You may say, 'Let it end,' but my goodness, it is a decision that needs a little care and thought. And it does mean the end of the Commonwealth. How can one seriously suppose that if the mother country, the centre of the Commonwealth, is a province of Europe (which is what Federation means) it could continue to exist as the mother country of a series of independent nations? It is sheer nonsense.
>
> (Hugh Gaitskell, Labour Party Conference, 1962.[6])

Gaitskell's patriotism in this passage is intermingled with images of Britain as the mother country and not merely a province of Europe. This is a telling phrase. Other European countries can become provinces, but Britain has greater responsibilities and needs to be aware of them. Britain is not merely a European province – it has a role to play in the political leadership of the world through the Commonwealth.

The opposing strands of political and moral leadership, the images of Britain as global player by power or by example and influence, began to unravel in the late 1950s and early 1960s as the debate on Europe intensified. The emphasis began to switch between the Atlantic–rearmament–disarmament–third-force axis of debate, to become increasingly, although often simultaneously, concerned with debates about Britain *vis-à-vis* the EEC–the Commonwealth–decolonisation.

Over these issues the divisions became more complex, the nature of the opposing ideas more confused and the images of Britain which they conveyed in their rhetoric more blurred. It would be neat and convenient if those who had previously been advocating moral leadership had also advocated decolonisation through a genuinely altruistic desire to free people, supported interventions against totalitarian regimes to spread freedom and argued for a reorientation towards Europe, and that those who argued for the maintained global role through political leadership were now advocating a global free trade common-wealth tied up with EFTA. In fact, many of the old advocates of moral leadership became keen on decolonisation as the only means of maintaining Britain's influence in the world, and as a means of exporting British social democracy and the Westminster model, and they opposed the Common Market on the grounds that it was little more than a capitalist club.

As the Wilson Governments progressed the moral leadership wing of the Party became increasingly disillusioned with the direction of foreign policy. This developed, once the Party was in opposition, into a set of policies advocating opting out of the EEC, condemning any intervention by any power (if it was the USA) in any conflict situation as being by necessity merely a form of imperi-alism, creating a siege economy and providing moral leadership to the world by unilateral nuclear disarmament, withdrawal from NATO and the closing of US bases. Their image of Britain became that of an aircraft carrier for Uncle Sam and the tool of US and European multinationals.

As this wing of the Party hardened its resolve against the Community there was a smaller group left sitting unhappily in its midst. They too had rejected the EEC, mainly because of their faith in free trade, and while they supported opting out of the Community they did not favour opting out of the late 20th century altogether. The best example of this anti-European flotsam was Peter Shore who found himself in increasingly bizarre company as he consistently opposed the EEC. Others began to work out schemes for a global free trade area, most notably Douglas Jay, while others developed either an on/off attitude, like Denis Healey, or cultivated a studied boredom with the subject (itself a symptom of intellectual arrogance if not chauvinism), like Tony Crosland. At the heart of their opposition was an image of Britain as something greater than other European states, and of the potential of a social democratic Albion rising to lead the world by example. The desire to de-fuse the Cold War and offer a third way for civilisation did not die with Nye Bevan.

For those from both the earlier groupings not impeccably opposed to the Community, life became even more complicated. For those who became Euro-fanatic, life became incredibly easy – if rather lonely at times if they were at the top of the Labour Party. In the special relationship Britain could no longer be a Greek state to the American Rome, but in the EEC it could be a Prussia among the German states. Britain would enter to lead, because leadership was the natural role for the British. For them the Community became the central issue in politics because the Community was the future. It was the defining policy issue of the 1970s and 1980s and, when the radical chauvinist wing of the Labour Party took over and the Labour Party adopted anti-Community manifestos, the Euro-fanatics split and formed the SDP. After the split, three groups of social democrats occupied the political space of the left. The electoral repercussions of this crowded scene were four electoral victories for the Conservative Party.

But the schism was not simply about Europe. For some of the SDP founders the role of political leadership included the possession of the bomb as a matter of principle, for others it was a matter of tactics, but this was an important subsidiary issue for them all. Those who opposed the political leadership wing of the Party on the issue of nuclear weapons did so on the basis of a profoundly different reading of the dynamics of the Cold War. They no less believed in Britain's great role than did their opponents, they had no less of a patriotic vision than did the Bevanite or the Gaitskellite advocates of political leadership. If anything they had an even greater belief that their country, or perhaps just the Labour movement, invariably this great Party of theirs, had the ability and the duty to offer the world leadership, their brand of leadership was somewhat different, they were offering moral leadership. The best expression of this desire was made, in 1951, almost inadvertently by Nye Bevan:

> This great nation has a message for the world which is distinct from that of America or that of the Soviet Union. Ever since 1945 we have been engaged in this country in the most remarkable piece of social reconstruction the world has seen. By the end of 1950 we had assumed the moral leadership of the world. [interruption] It is no use Hon. Members opposite sneering, because when they come to the end of the road it will not be a sneer which will be upon their faces. There is only one hope for mankind, and that hope still remains in this little Island. It is from here that we tell the world where to go and how to go there ... there is only one hope for mankind – and that is democratic socialism. There is only one party in Great Britain which can do it – and that is the Labour Party.[7]

But the real high point of the cult of moral leadership was the first flowering of CND, and its high priest was Bevan's acolyte Michael Foot in his pre-1980 incarnation.

The debates on Britain's role as a world leader were of profound importance to those taking part. One should never underestimate the self-importance of politicians, and quite how profound and far reaching some of their arguments could be – at least to themselves. Moreover as there is individual self-importance, so there is collective self-importance, and the relationship between the two is not always clear. The politicians' self images and the collective loyalty they have to their political party infect the way in which they think about policy questions, especially foreign and defence policy questions. This raises the question: is a belief that it is worth serving your nation-state simply a component part of being a politician, or is there a significant difference in the way Labour politicians deployed patriotism? In a sense, did they feel a need to be even more patriotic at times than the Conservatives because of the perception of the political content of their positions on key issues?

I do not want to go too far down the road of analysing language but I would like to take one example from the moral leadership wing of the Part, a fairly typical example of a Michael Foot unilateralist speech from the 1950s:

> We were told of one of the most disgraceful incidents in British History, when an American Secretary of State in Paris, at a critical moment in world affairs was willing to give orders about planes flying over these Islands without consulting the British Prime Minister. We all might have been blown up to pieces by that monumental folly.

Foot was only warming up, and he went on:

> Is there any lady, mother or grandmother who can step to this microphone, who can take part on the platform, who can listen peacefully in the galleries and not be fully conscious that when the die is cast today, irrespective of whether we have a Labour Government within the next four years or not, human destiny is being decided?[8]

Did Foot, I wonder, really believe that human destiny was being decided on what was a dreary October day in Scarborough? It is also necessary to be wary of the way the Cold War intrudes. Take Wilson's 'white heat of technology' speech. What was this a response to? Primarily it was to sentiments like those expressed by Michael Foot after the 1959 election: 'While placards on every hoarding were prophesying the doom which nationalisation would bring, while Labour leaders were lisping their much too mild peeps in favour of the principle of public ownership, a nationalised rocket hit the moon and another circled it.'

Thus the context of the white heat speech is important:

> For those of us who have studied the formidable Soviet challenge in the education of scientists and technologists, and above all, in the ruthless application of scientific techniques in Soviet industry, know that our future lies not in military strength alone but in the efforts, the sacrifices, and above all the energies which a free people can mobilize for the future greatness of our country.
>
> (Harold Wilson, Labour Party Conference, 1963.[9])

The paradox of these debates is that those who responded from the political leadership side of the Party did so in ways that undermined their own belief in the residual importance of Britain. The argument from Bevan in 1957 to Healey and Gaitskell in 1960 and beyond was simple: if Britain gives the moral lead who will follow? The political leadership wing could not of course follow through the logic of this argument which was that if the ownership or otherwise of the British bomb actually made no difference to anyone, – the implication of saying no one will notice if we give it away – then why does it make a difference having it?

Their response, cogently argued by Healey in among other places the Godkin lectures which he wrote for Gaitskell, was that by having the bomb one was playing a part in the Atlantic Alliance. It was in essence all about keeping our end up with the Americans. There were profound arguments on these points and often-bitter disputes. But underlying both positions was the desire to keep Britain in the game.

One small caveat should be entered here. It is important to differentiate between the idea of secular moral leadership, which might well be pragmatic, and the ethical/Christian idea of moral leadership. The basis of pacifism among opponents of the First World War, 1930s rearmament and the founders of CND was not consistent; indeed it was often at root contradictory. Foot and other Labour politicians who supported CND in the first phase did so because they saw it as a way of increasing Britain's global standing. Anyone who thinks that Foot was pacifist in an ethical/Christian sense need only read his part of the Falklands debate. Foot is a patriot.

CND in its second manifestation is rather different. As the system of democratic centralism, so brilliantly analysed by Eric Shaw in his book *Discipline and Discord*, became undermined by the Bennite agenda of democratising the Party, so membership of and support for organisations like CND became more of a political necessity for Labour MPs. It is difficult to try and tease out the meaning of the second flowering of CND because of these politically important organisational changes. The paths and strands intermingled and conflicted on the road that lead to 1983. The image of Britain put before the electorate by the Labour Party in that election came closer than anything else in summing up the contradictions at the heart of the social democrats' image of the UK.

All was backward and needing reform – yet all was forward and offering the moral leadership of the world. As Budge[10] has argued in the context of the decline debate, and Rubinstein[11] in a slightly different way, politics almost necessitates images of backwardness that need change for advance. The method of advance can be constructed from images of a nation-state's own history, i.e. back to the future; or one can look abroad to discover in the way others do things the method of advance, i.e. abroad to the future.

One of the least-heralded victims of the Cold War was the concept of social democracy as a label which could be used to differentiate between left wingers who were genuinely anti-communist and those who were at times equivocal towards other openly fellow travellers. The Labour Party is made up of social democrats today, not because of a response to the agenda of Thatcherism, or even a modified response that came from a set of debates within the Party, as Martin Smith argues in *The Changing Labour Party*,[12] but because the Cold War is over. There is no external threat from the super-power world, or internal threat from subversion: therefore social democratic images of Britain as a leader in this conflict are redundant. In one sense, the Labour Party is united in its vision of Britain – it merely squabbles over the details.

The process of reaching this accord on the agenda of European Social Democracy has been long and acrimonious. At the heart of the debate has been the notion of patriotism. When social democrats considered Britain in relation to the world then they were patriotic in both a positive and a negative sense. A dictionary definition of patriotism would be the belief in the unique virtue of the national and other characteristics of the people of a nation-state. As J.C.D. Clark has persuasively argued, this can be the ability of these people to defy oppression or their ability to oppress. In the History Workshop debate on the content of history in the National Curriculum, Clark asked:

> ... what form the patriotism should take: should it be a story of achievement, advance, enlightenment? Or should it emphasise a dark side – exploitation, suffering, poverty? Nothing in the methods of scholarship can answer this question: it is essentially political ... Patriotic history is not a series of sentimental anecdotes of Drake, Nelson or the Battle of Britain, though these can still evoke it. Patriotism is essentially the idea that we are related to 'our' history by something more than contingency; that both the sins and the success of the fathers are visited upon the children unto the third and fourth generation; that we are part of our past, inhabitants not tourists.[13]

If we accept Clark's view that there can be both positive and negative patriotism, then how does this fit into the argument that patriotism, at times boarding on chauvinism, is central to understanding social democratic images of Britain?

Dan Keohane usefully quotes Attlee on the subject. Speaking in 1937 Attlee said, 'There is a deep difference of opinion between the Labour Party and the Capitalist parties on foreign affairs as well as on home policy, because the two cannot be separated. The foreign policy of a government is the reflection of its internal policy.'

Keohane contrasts this with Attlee's later statement that ... it is desirable, wherever possible, that, in foreign affairs particularly, Government policy should have the support of all. It strengthens us in giving what I believe is a necessary lead in international affairs.'[14]

For Keohane this is an acute example of the impact of the war on Attlee's perception of international relations. Which is of course true, but it is also a reflection of the way in which the patriotism of Attlee has been subtly altered from negative to positive. From the struggle to achieve power by the party of the working class to the achievements of the first majority Labour Government, it is a manifestation of the responsibilities of power. It reflects what the Attlee Government did to the Labour Party; to the solid base of the negative patriotism of the struggle was added an infusion of patriotism and pride in the achievement of the Labour Governments. These quotes also reflect Attlee's abiding belief that the natural role of the British in world affairs is one of leadership – even if this was only in terms of helping to create a world government. The Attlee of 1937 and the Attlee of 1953 are at one in the conviction that what actually matters is Britain. They are at one because they believe that there are certain national characteristics that make the British special; and that the British have a responsibility because of their 'specialness' to play a role in world affairs. This holds for all the great social democrats: for Bevin in the 1940s, for Gaitskell in the 1960s, for Wilson in the 1970s, for Owen in the 1980s, and for Tony Blair today. Of course politicians believe that their country matters. They would not be in politics if they did not believe that in some sense their country counted for something; what is striking is the presumption of leadership. This informs the rhetoric of these people and has been the primary concern of social democratic politicians in the post-war period. But they have, until Blair, failed in the main to follow through on the logic of their position when it comes up against the need for intervention, for the actual exercise of leadership.

Quoting Attlee is useful but it raises certain dangers. So much, of such quality, has been written about the Attlee Governments that we are in danger of somehow putting the years 1945–51 on so high a pedestal that it will be difficult, if not impossible, to actually see them. The process of analysis has separated the Attlee Governments from the rest of Labour history – all that came before was a preparation for that day in July 1945 when Labour became the British nation and there was nothing that the country could do about it; all that came after has been a long and steady unravelling of all those achieve-ments, a long anti-climax, with only a pause in the glory of 1966. In all this time, it sometimes seems as if all the Labour Party has been doing is searching in vain for that unity of purpose, sense of ideological direction and coherent identity that characterised those governments: for much of time and throughout on the main policy issues.

The Government that was in power between 1945 and 1951 was a Labour Government – the men and women who ran the Government were, to use Ken Morgan's phrase, Labour people. Their vision of Britain and its place in the world was the Labour Party's vision of Britain, and it was a vision that domi-nated the Labour Party for a generation. It was a vision that laid the foundations for British perception of its place in the world through the post-war period. And further, that because it was a Labour Government that achieved a great deal it changed the way in which social democrats thought about Britain: their innate patriotism became a positive feature. It was the achievements of this Government, from the NHS to social cohesion, to myths of crime-free streets and ideas of collectivism, that they returned to again and again, culminating in the Bennite rhetoric of the late 1970s and early 1980s which became a form of radical chauvinism. No other period of Labour Government had similar impact. The paradox is that the right took the lessons of government differently.

The logic of radical chauvinism was that Labour had failed in power between 1966 and 1970 because of external pressures. To prevent this occurring again the Labour Party had to recreate the spirit of the 1940s and tap into the patriotism that had been the foundation of the first Attlee Governments. The siege economy, the withdrawal from NATO and the rest was in essence an attempt to go back to the high point of collectivism as though nothing had happened in the interim. In contrast, the right, adopting similar kinds of positive and negative patriotism, concluded that Britain as a nation-state was finished. One could not go backwards to the future, but instead had to latch onto the process of European integration. What this analysis lacked in chauvinist belief in the potential of the British to put the clock back, it more than made up for in an unthinking faith in the technocrats of the Community.

To understand the social democrats' image of Britain in the world it is necessary to understand that the social democrats in the period 1945 through to the mid-1960s were not trying to find a way forward from the perceptions of Britain that had dominated the Attlee Governments, but trying to get back to a situation in which that vision could be realised. Now I do not claim that this was so for all the members of the Labour Party, or even all the social democrats, for all of the period, although I would argue that patriotism was at the heart of all the brands of Labourism, socialism, democratic socialism, social democracy, that cohabited in the Labour Party during this period, and that without understanding the nature of patriotism in the politics of the Labour Party it is very difficult to get to grips with people like Attlee, Bevin, Gaitskell or Wilson, or indeed Bevan, Foot, Mikardo, Castle and Benn.

As Labour developed its thinking on Britain's place in the world over the post-war period, the debate unfolded in a series of key arguments. In the first the disagreement was about how best to achieve a leading position in a bi-polar world by supporting the USA – an image of Britain sitting at the global head table – the conflict about the form of leadership that would achieve that place: political or moral. The second phase is characterised by the gradual readjustment, the extremely slow readjustment, to Britain's reduced status. Conflict centres on how best to respond to the simultaneous pressures of EEC, decolonisation and the US. This phase is the longest and most complex. It was only resolved after years of schism and four electoral defeats by the adoption of European Social Democracy and the ending of the Cold War. The third phase is the post-Cold War phase in which the issue of unilateralism is removed and the question becomes centred on the role of the European Union in maintaining Britain's global position.

New Labour's foreign and defence policy can therefore be understood as the culmination of a series of significant disagreements and a fusion of the moral and political strands of Labour's perception of Britain's leading role in the world. From the moral leadership strand comes the commitment from Gordon Brown and Clare Short to tackle third-world debt, increase spending on aid and use the European Union as an instrument of poverty reduction as much as wealth creation. From the political leadership strand comes the Atlanticist and interventionist policy of Tony Blair and Jack Straw in a succession of cases – Kosovo, Afghanistan and Iraq. Disarmament as a form of moral leadership and unilateral intervention as a form of political leadership have disappeared, patriotism and the centrality of Britain's right and potential as a world leader are at the forefront. In essence the balance in Labour's political thought on Britain's position in the world has been entirely inverted since the Party's foundation. The activist and interventionist state has been largely banished from domestic policy but dominates foreign and defence policy. The forward policy that some have characterised as a new imperialism sits alongside a humanitarian instinct. Lord Salisbury would have had problems understanding the latter but would have been reasonably comfortable with the former.

Notes

1 Seyd, P., *The Rise and Fall of the Labour Left*, (Macmillan, Basingstoke, 1987) p. 22. The distinction between Social Democrats and Democratic Socialists is more difficult to make. The essence here is of self-image. Democratic Socialism is a powerful self-image in the Labour Party: before 1980 it differentiates the Party from European social democratic parties, after 1980 from the SDP. It is also an internal Party label that might just be used to differentiate a more interventionist domestic policy, but the difference is very marginal and the deploying of the term so widespread as to make it meaningless. I accept that more people in the Labour Party described themselves as Democratic Socialists than as Social Democrats, but in a comparative context I think it is more useful to call a social democrat a Social Democrat. Socialist in this context is a different creature and describes, if you accept my argument, policies which are outside the political reality of the Labour Party in this period.

2 Deighton, A., 'Towards a "Western Strategy": The Making of British Policy Towards Germany, 1945–46', in Deighton, A. (ed.) *Britain and the First Cold War*, (Macmillan, London, 1990) p. 67.

3 *Ibid.*, p. 54.

4 Hennessy, P., *Whitehall*, (Fontana, London, 1990) p. 713.

5 Donoughue, B., 'Renegotiation of the EEC terms: A witness account,' in Brivati, B. and Jones, H. (eds), *From Reconstruction to Integration, Britain and Europe since 1945*, (Leicester University Press, Leicester, 1993) pp. 204–5.

6 LPACR 1962 p. 159.

7 Aneurin Bevan, House of Commons, 21 April 1951.

8 LPACR 1960, p. 189.

9 *Ibid.*

10 Budge, I., 'Relative Decline as a Political Issue: Ideological motivations of the Politico-Economic Debate in Post-war Britain', *Contemporary Record*, Vol. 7, No. 1, 1993.

11 Rubinstein, W.H., *Capitalism, Culture and Decline in Britain*, (Macmillan, London, 1992).

12 Smith, M.J., 'A Return to Revisionism? The Labour Party's Policy Review', in Smith, M.J. and Spear, J. (eds), *The Changing Labour Party*, (Routledge, London, 1992); and Sasson, D., 'Reflections on the Labour Party's Programme for the 1990s', *Political Quarterly*, Vol. 62, No. 3, July–September, 1991.

13 *Special Feature: History, the Nation and the Schools, History Workshop Journal*, issue 29, Spring 1990, Introduction, Anna Davin, pp. 92–4.

14 The quote is from *The Labour Party in Perspective* (Gollancz, London, 1937), pp. 226–7; quoted in Keohane, D., *Labour Party Defence Policy since 1945*, (Leicester University Press, Leicester, 1993) p.1.

Part III

Commentaries

13 The Old Left

Tam Dalyell

I was elected to the House of Commons in May 1962. From January 1963 until 1972, when in London, Mondays to Fridays I had a room at the top of Dick Crossman's house at number 9 Vincent Square, and used to make his breakfast downstairs three or four mornings a week. I tell you this, because his sitting room on the ground floor was the weekly lunchtime haunt of the Bevanites – where the plots were hatched, or, certainly, where the right of the Parliamentary Labour Party imagined them to be hatched. If those walls could speak, they would record the impassioned argument of Aneurin Bevan and his wife Jennie Lee, Fenner Brockway, Barbara Castle, Dick Clements, G.D.H. Cole, Desmond Donnelly, Tom Driberg, Michael Foot, John Freeman, Victor Gollancz, Tony Greenwood, Leslie Hale, Judith Hart, Clive Jenkins, Elwyn Jones, Jack Jones, Nicholas Kaldor, Fred Lee, Harold Lever, Ian Mikardo, Dick Mitchison, Jo Richardson, Sidney Silverman, Donald Soper, John Strachey, Richard Titmuss, George Wigg, Harold Wilson, Woodrow Wyatt, Michael Young and Konni Zilliacus.

Some, like Donnelly and Wyatt, drifted to the (far) right. Others were less than regular attenders. But this was the amorphous core of the 'Old Left', the Bevanites, of the 1950s. My only credentials for writing about them half a century later is that I was imbued by Crossman and Mikardo with their beliefs: my own arrival in the Commons coincided with the fag-end of the 'Old Left'.

The dominant issue was the rearmament of Germany. On this, the 'Old Left' was as united as they were on any single issue: they were against such a move. Some, like the fluent Russian speaker and son of a Finno-Swedish writer Konni Zilliacus, advocated close relations with Russia. Zilly had been an official in the Information Section of the League of Nations Secretariat, and worked closely with Arthur Henderson, with whom he had drafted the Geneva Protocol of 1924. In the 1930s he wrote an influential memorandum on war and peace, which was adopted by both the TUC and the Labour Conference in 1934. He was the ring-leader of those who criticised those who risked war, and who remained pro-Soviet during the Cold War.

The majority of the 'Old Left' were more circumspect. They were genuinely concerned with a resurgence of militarism in Germany, and were not unhappy that the country should be divided between East and West Germany. They were concerned that Germany, rising from the ashes, without the burden of a huge armaments budget, would threaten British trade and exports. The answer of some of the 'Old Left' was to demand reparations from Germany, which could be used by the victors, and some of which could be siphoned off to tropical countries. Terms such as the 'Third' World and the Developing World had not, at that time, been invented. German speakers, prominent among them Crossman and the publisher Victor Gollancz, were noted for establishing links with post-war Germany. Out of the contacts between the left and the energetic German, Lito Milsack, was born the Königswinter Conferences, which did so much to heal post-war divisions.

The second foreign policy cause of the 'Old Left' was support for the State of Israel. And on this, the intense sustained interest of two leaders of the 'Old Left' coincided. Dick Crossman had been appointed by Attlee to be a Gentile member of the Anglo-American Palestine Commission in 1946. He returned, to an extent that his colleagues had by no means anticipated, a fervent supporter of the Jews and a Jewish State. On his return, he demanded to see the Prime Minister and was given a quarter of an hour of his time. As befitted the ex-philosophy tutor of New College, Oxford, he harangued Mr Attlee for fourteen minutes, and then waited for a response. All he got was, 'Dick, how's your mother?' The Chancery Lawyer Judge, Mr Justice Crossman, was a Tory friend of the Attlees. Crossman organised an amendment to the 1946 King's Speech and was never ever to be forgiven by Ernest Bevin, the Foreign Secretary.

If Crossman was the intellect of the 'Old Left', then Ian Mikardo, above all, was its arch-manoeuvrer. He was the most subtle political tactician I ever saw in action. Both of Mikardo's parents came to Britain in the massive Jewish exodus from the Tsarist Empire in the last decades of the nineteenth century, and the first of the twentieth. His mother, Bluma, came from a village called Yampol, in the western Ukraine. His father, Morris, anglicised from Moshe, arrived at the time of the Boer War from Kutno, a textile manufacturing town to the west of Warsaw. When Morris disembarked in London, his total possessions were the clothes he stood up in, a little bag containing a change of shirt and underclothes, his accessories for prayer, and one rouble. They went to the East End of London, which their son was to represent in Parliament with such distinction from 1964 to 1987. Ian's parents left the East End and set up home in Portsmouth in 1907. Mikardo was born a year later. He recalled that the language of the family in those days was Yiddish. When Mikardo went to school at the age of three, he had only a few words of English, and that put him at a disadvantage in relation to his classmates. He used to tell his many friends in the House of Commons how, when he became Member of Parliament for Reading, containing many Indian sub-continent families whose young children had only a few words of English, and saw them harmed by having to study the usual range of school subjects whilst they were unfamiliar with the language of their teachers and text-books, he well understood what they were up against. In 1930 he met Mary Rosette, who was to be his life-long partner for over 60 years. He joined the

Labour Party and at the same time Poale Zion, the Zionist Worker's Movement, which was affiliated to the Labour Party. Thus began a life-long commitment to Israel, a cause shared by those with similar stories to tell, such as Sidney Silverman and Harold Lever.

Another of the 'Old Left', Fenner Brockway, founded the Movement for Colonial Freedom in 1954, which championed the independence of Ghana, Kenya, Cyprus, British Guyana and many other lands. They prevailed, perhaps because the Labour Party put the view that once we had left the Indian sub-continent in 1948, there was not much point in fighting to hold on to what John Strachey memorably called 'The End of Empire'.

In spite of a lot of concerted work by Crossman in the late 1950s and early 1960s on pension proposals, geared to rising earnings, and made inflation proof, it is my impression that the 'Old Left' rested on the laurels of Nye Bevan's Health Service; perhaps ideas were kept pickled in aspic.

Their campaigning ardour on the Home Front was less on the bread-and-butter issues of education, health, housing and transport, but more on various libertarian causes such as modernising the indecency laws. Tom Driberg never held ministerial office, blaming 'deeply prejudiced puritans' such as Clem Attlee and Harold Wilson for keeping him out on account of his homosexuality. But Driberg was the superb Chairman of my first Labour Party Conference at Scarborough in 1957–8. He became, like Michael Foot, a friend of Beaverbrook, and wrote for the Express. Michael Foot's tribute to Beelzebub, Lord Beaverbrook, is one of the most eloquent essays ever penned. Often some bons viveurs of the 'Old Left' have had no qualms about using the capitalist press!

The 'Old Left's' greatest triumph must surely be the abolition of the death penalty. Had it not been for their passionate principled support of Sidney Silverman, I do not believe that abolition would have been achieved for another decade and a half.

What would the 'Old Left' be doing today? Truthfully, one can but specu-late, as 50 years has passed since their heyday. My hunch is that they would be challenging American hegemony. Their cause – with the probable exceptions of Crossman and Wigg – would have been United Nations control of any mili-tary operations, not unilateral decision-making by the United States. Certainly, they would have been active about not allowing the Americans the use of Fylingdales and Henwith Hill for Star Wars or, as it is politely known, National Missile Defense. Certainly, they would have questioned the bombing of the infrastructure of Serbia, such as the bridges at Novi Sad, the centre of Belgrade, the chemical complex at Pancevo, and the Yugo car factory at Zastava. Certainly, they would have been protesting at the very idea of bombing Iraq, in the absence of the clearest and most current of mandates from the United Nations. With their wartime experience, probably they would have advocated an intelligence response, laced with bribery, as a response to Al-Qaida in Afghanistan.

About the home policy causes of the 'Old Left', I am less certain. I think they would be calling for the re-nationalisation of the railways. Curiously, guided by

Nye Bevan, they would have recognised that the expectations made possible by modern medicine, such as transplant of organs, had to be met by new developments, some of them unpalatable at first sight to socialists. On Education and Crime, I suspect they would have been reconciled to the Government policies. They would have resisted any privatisation of Air Traffic Control and Water. Of one thing I am absolutely sure, they would have resisted, to their last breath, any Presidential tendencies of the Prime Minister!

Whatever their shortcomings, the 'Old Left' were issue politicians, entertaining passionate views. I wish today's politicians were equally immersed in issues, and less concerned with 'careers'. Warts and all, they could do with a transfusion of red blood from the 'Old Left'.

14 The New Left

Frances Morrell

Introduction

In 1970 after the defeat of the Labour Party in the General Elections I was invited by Tom Ponsonby, then General Secretary of the Fabian Society, to work with him in a voluntary capacity. Tom wanted the Society to act as a ginger group in enabling the Party to rebuild and revitalise itself. My job would be to support him in achieving that goal. With Tom I attended that autumn a weekend gathering of the Shadow Cabinet plus key advisers that was held at Buscot Park, the country seat of Lord Faringdon. The purpose of the gathering was to ask what went wrong. One critical, albeit unsurprising, conclusion was that the delaying of devaluation had had devastating consequences for the Labour government's economic strategy. The significance of this – which I did not realise for some time – lay in the implication that the effectiveness of Labour's economic strategy was not in doubt. Problems had arisen from ineffective implementation.

Economic policy

In 1971, the Fabian Society published a pamphlet by Tony Crosland entitled *A Social Democratic Britain*. Because I was involved in the arrangements for publication, I read it with exceptional care. It was – is – an inspiring piece of work, egalitarian and humane in spirit, and rigorous in argument. In particular it re-affirmed Tony Crosland's commitment to the mixed economy, his view of public ownership, as one of several possible instruments to deal with excessive monopoly power or consistent underinvestment, and his emphasis on the importance of public expenditure: 'I did not anticipate that successive governments would be so eccentric as to use periodic bouts of deflation – that is deliberate reductions in growth – as almost their only means of regulating the economy.'

When Labour unexpectedly was elected to power in 1974, Tony Benn became Secretary of State for Industry. I was appointed as one of Tony Benn's two policy advisers. The other was the Cambridge economist Francis Cripps. Thus I was present in government when, in December 1976, the visit to London took place of representatives of the International Monetary Fund (IMF) to discuss the terms under which they would lend money to the British Government to avert further sterling crises.

When the pound had begun to fall in value in 1976 several different proposals were put forward to the Cabinet. On the left, Tony Benn argued for the rejection of the IMF loan and the maintenance of existing levels of public spending. His alternative economic strategy based on import controls had been presented to the Cabinet a year earlier in a paper written by Francis Cripps and myself in response to an earlier round of spending cuts. Tony Crosland, then Foreign Secretary, advocated the minimum level of spending cuts necessary to satisfy the IMF and currency speculators, and the maintenance of the strategy at a more constrained level. Prime Minister James Callaghan, supported by his Chancellor Denis Healey, demanded and got Cabinet support for a substantial programme of spending cuts.

It is not my intention to revisit that fraught decision-making process with the benefit of hindsight. It was an impossible situation for all concerned. It is not obvious that there was a right answer. What was clear was that the decision that was finally taken had enormous implications for the Labour Party.

After the fall of the Labour Government in 1979, Francis Cripps and I contributed an article to a publication by Spokesman Books entitled 'What Went Wrong'. In it we argued that, following Crosland, Labour leaders had for years believed that they had the formula for full employment – namely high spending (public or private) within Britain combined with devaluation to promote exports and prevent imports, and incomes policy to control inflation. Labour's contribution consisted of choosing high *public* spending and *redistributive* taxation within that formula. Social democrats and socialists who upheld diametrically opposed political objectives had been able to compromise and work together on the basis of the formula for full employment and high public spending. This in turn enabled the building over time of a more egalitarian society.

Public spending was the fulcrum of this strategy. Sustained reductions in public spending were tantamount to the abandonment of the strategy as a whole. That was in fact what happened. A part of the reason for the intense frustration, despair and bitterness of Party members expressed in the aftermath of Labour's election defeat in 1979 derived from a sense that Labour had in some mysterious way lost its soul. There were of course other conflicts. None in my opinion threatened the Labour Party's basic *raison d'être* in the same way as the loss of the guiding Croslandite vision, strategy and plan.

Other conflicts

The terms right and left in the Labour Party tended at that time to refer to factions in the Parliamentary Party. These were the groups of MPs who led and articulated the various conflicts. There were three main areas of dispute. Each reflected an aspect of the intellectual crisis for the Labour left's particular brand of one-nation socialism posed by the altering world order.

The Atlanticist strategy had long had powerful supporters within the Parliamentary Party and in the Labour movement as a whole. This strategy gave absolute priority to Britain's relationship with the United States and held that so far as possible the organisation of our defence system should integrate it with that of the Americans. The traditional opponents of this perspective were to be found in the Campaign for Nuclear Disarmament (CND), which was founded in 1958, and which enjoyed the support of distinguished left-wingers such as Michael Foot and his colleagues in the Tribune Group. I was never a member of CND nor did I attend its meetings and rallies. I admired the commitment of those involved, while never expecting to see unilateral disarmament nor withdrawal from NATO become the official policy of the Labour Party.

To this traditional fissure amongst Labour's elected representatives and their supporters now had to be added another. A large group of MPs believed that Britain's membership of the European Economic Community was an absolute policy priority transcending, if it came to it, a three-line whip in the House of Commons. This commitment to the EEC foreshadowed conflicts with supporters of the Atlanticist perspective. In the early seventies the division lay between supporters and opponents of Britain's continued membership of the Community. The Labour Common Market Safeguards Committee, established under this name in 1975, led the opposition, and numbered several cabinet ministers amongst its supporters. Prime Minister Harold Wilson set himself the task of 'renegotiating' the terms of British membership. The implication was that the decision about whether Britain should continue to be a member would be taken on purely pragmatic grounds.

As a policy adviser to Tony Benn, in his capacity as Secretary of State for Industry, I was one of the support team which worked for the Dissenting Ministers – i.e. those who opposed Britain's continued membership – in the referendum campaign in 1975. From my perspective the referendum originally proposed by Tony Benn was an outstanding success. Entirely properly, the people decided on this great strategic question. For some the referendum defeat was a setback, which made no difference to their basic analysis. For others – such as myself – the referendum settled the issue of principle regarding membership of the EEC. Barbara Castle, at that time a Cabinet Minister and one of the Dissenting Ministers, went on to become a Member of the European Parliament.

A third area of conflict concerned industrial policy. The contribution of Stuart Holland, a prophet of globalisation before his time, has been well documented. Stuart produced a range of publications for institutions as diverse as the Fabian Society and the Institute of Workers' Control and its publishing arm Spokesman Books. He argued that multinational companies had expanded their international production and trade to such an extent that effectively we lived in a borderless world. Governments in this analysis had lost the power to regulate their own countries' industries.

Tony Benn, then Shadow Secretary of State for Industry and also Chairman of the Labour Party in 1971–2, worked with Geoff Bish, head of research at the Labour Party, to respond to this analysis. His proposal involved the establishment of a National Enterprise Board, which would be an instrument for taking a stake in or even acquiring leading companies. The NEB's work would be supplemented by a regime of planning agreements with the top hundred companies. The policy was of course contested. The right of the Party stood for the maintenance of the existing distribution of power between the government, nationalised industries, multinationals, smaller companies and trade unions. This policy threatened that settlement.

In the event, the Labour Government passed a very much weaker version of the policy into legislation. It was never quite clear to me how much support such an ambitious industrial policy had enjoyed at leadership level amongst trade unionists, or even at grass roots level in the Party. Part of the reason for the founding of the Labour Co-ordinating Committee by a group of people including MPs Michael Meacher and Audrey Wise, active and influential party members such as Chris Mullin and Tony Banks as well as myself and my colleague Francis Cripps, was a sense that party members were not well informed about its policy-making processes and therefore found it difficult to make a contribution to the debate.

Pressure for constitutional change within the Party

The three broad areas of conflict referred to above had two things in common. First, they were about policy. Second, they were top-down, in the sense that the conflicts were organised along traditional lines. Different groups of MPs both led and articulated the campaigns, supported by Party members and trade unionists.

The emergence of the grass roots organisation Campaign for Labour Party Democracy, (CLPD) on whose Executive I served for a period during the late 1970s introduced a different kind of conflict. First, CLPD did not stand for any particular policy – and this was both a matter of principle and the practical day-to-day reality. It was therefore able to draw wide support from local parties and Party members. Second, though it was supported with varying degrees of enthusiasm by a few MPs, it was not led or directed by members of the Parliamentary Party. CLPD was autonomous and energetically guarded its independence. The fissure that opened up lay in broad terms between Party members on the one hand and members of the Parliamentary Party on the other.

CLPD was formed in 1973 by a group of Party members, with support from about ten Labour MPs. The first President was Frank Allaun. The main motivation for the Campaign was the record of the Labour governments in the 1960s and the way that – from CLPD's perspective – Annual Conference decisions were continually ignored on key domestic and international issues.

When the Labour government fell in 1979, it was after a second period in office beset by economic crises and conflict with the trade unions. The disillusionment that had been building up amongst Party members since 1970 was extreme. The anger, frustration and despair poured into the campaign to achieve changes to the constitution of the Labour Party.

CLPD campaigned for mandatory reselection of MPs so that they would be under pressure to carry out Conference policies. This proposal was accepted in 1979–80. CLPD also sought to make the Leader of the Party accountable through election by an electoral college involving MPs, CLPs and TUs. Hitherto Labour leaders had been elected by MPs alone. This proposal was approved by Conference in January 1981.

There was of course division and debate within this movement. In October 1979 Brian Sedgemore and I published an article in the *Guardian* in which we placed on record our support for the selection of local parliamentary candidates by all members of the Party rather than the general management committee. We pointed out that

> left wingers who oppose the theory of representative democracy as expounded by Dick Taverne and Reg Prentice are beginning to argue that members of local management committees have superior capacities to those of the ordinary party member.

It is perhaps indicative of the spirit of the times that this was regarded by some as a great betrayal. I and others continued to argue the case for this point of view within CLPD. We remained in a minority, albeit a not insignificant one.

CLPD also promoted a range of reforms to give Labour women and black and ethnic minority members greater representation within the Party. This campaign was far from acceptable to male comrades on the left. 'We want socialists, not women', they regularly explained.

I was involved in the establishment of the Women's Action Committee (WAC) in 1979. We put on a series of satirical shows in the 1980s with titles such as *Natural Selection: The Story of Why Men Run the Labour Party*. These shows played to packed audiences at Labour Party Conferences. One performance took place at the Almeida Theatre in London. At the time that I was involved, WAC drew support from across the Party. Glenys Kinnock, Brenda Dean and leading women from the trade unions joined women Party members acting and performing in this show. The main demand for a woman on every parliamentary shortlist was achieved over the period 1986–8.

The Old Left network described by Tam Dalyell met in Vincent Square and those present included leading members of the Tribune Group of MPs, and left intellectuals of distinction. CLPD gathered between official meetings at a house in Golders Green, full of telephones and Gestetners and envelopes waiting to be packed and taken to the post. This was the home of CLPD's Secretary Vladimir Derer and his wife Vera. He was a strategist and tactician of outstanding ability. In addition he and Vera, aided by volunteers, provided the administrative support to this extraordinarily disciplined grass roots organisation. If any single individual was responsible for the changes to the Party constitution that were agreed in the period after Labour left office, then it was undoubtedly Vladimir Derer.

Relevance today

Of what relevance are the struggles of the 1970s to government and party today? The message is mixed.

The changes to the constitution of the Labour Party have had an impact. The election of the party leader by the whole movement created a stable and secure leadership. Reading accounts of the premiership of Harold Wilson it is impossible not to be struck by the insecurity with which he viewed his own position. The election of the leader by the whole movement, for better or for worse, placed the leader beyond the possibility of intrigues and coups from within the Parliamentary Labour Party. This change was a necessity for the survival of the Labour Party.

The struggle for the mandatory reselection of MPs did have the effect of focusing all Members of Parliament on the need to be regularly in touch both with the constituency parties and their constituencies as a whole. There are now many more women MPs and also MPs from black and ethnic minorities. In this sense the Labour Party is today more unified and the Parliamentary Party is more representative of society as a whole. Other expectations have been disappointed.

The strategic conflicts between the Atlanticist, pro-European and one-nation socialist perspectives respectively remain unresolved. These have been played out in a number of policy areas from disputes about the future of the BBC to the decision about whether to go to war with Iraq. CND and the Labour Euro-Safeguards Committee – as it is now called – are still leading oppositional players in this debate. Indeed the secretary of the Safeguards Committee, John Mills, has held his post continuously since 1975.

Post-privatisation, the mixed economy in the form identified and supported by Tony Crosland no longer exists. The activity of wealth creation and the relationship between managers, workers and consumers are subject to the rules of the economic community. There is no public-sector industrial base. Industrial planning 1970s-style, whether as envisaged by Ted Heath or by Tony Benn is, by definition, no longer a task of central government.

Finally and of enormous significance is the disappearance of the egalitarian dream. 'Socialism is about equality', argued Crosland. Over the last two decades the scope, role, finance, management and accountability of the public services have – in some ways perfectly properly – been contested. In the course of that debate and the interminable policy initiatives from central government that have flowed from it there is a sense that the right-wing Conservative agenda of the 1970s and 1980s has triumphed. Credit must be given for pioneering policies aimed at promoting social inclusion. But English society and the distribution of life chances within it remain preposterously linked to social class. The generation of Labour leaders that gathered at Buscot Park in 1970 accepted and articulated this perspective in a way that is no longer part of the political agenda.

15 The Centre

Joe Haines

Marshal Ferdinand Foch's gleeful summary of his desperate position – 'my centre is giving way, my right is in retreat; situation excellent. I shall attack' – may have rallied an army *in extremis* but as a strategem it would never do for a political party, except, perhaps, a Marxist-Leninist one. Without a solid, un-wavering centre, occasionally defended by the right from left-wing theologians, and saved by the left from right-wing revisionists, any party, particularly a demo-cratic socialist one, faces catastrophe. It was the Foch-like weakening of Labour's centre which courted the Party's extinction in the early 1980s. The centre then, including many of the former Callaghan Government cabinet members, faltered in the face of hostility from the rampant and Militant left and desertion from a spiritless right. Certain of being booed if they approached the rostrum at Party Conferences – had they been so lucky as to catch the eye of the partisan chairmen of those days – they regrettably ducked below the parapet and betrayed their purpose in politics. It was the high-water mark of the centre's cowardice, demonstrating the peril when it does collapse. The right, meanwhile, with few exceptions, was in headlong retreat and actively in search of a different home. The result was that Labour's position swiftly became more hazardous than at any time since 1931, culminating in the fiasco of 1983, a general election fought on a manifesto aptly described by Gerald Kaufman as the longest suicide note in history. Before the last gasp, however, the centre regained its nerve, and its resurgence – surprisingly if inevitably led by a former left-winger, Neil Kinnock – made Labour electable again, though it took 14 years after the depar-ture of Michael Foot from the leadership for the Party to return to government.

But what is the centre? Where are its roots? What is its philosophy? For a start, its political position cannot be fixed geographically, unlike the wings. As the extremes move, so must the centre, sometimes inclining mildly to the right, sometimes leaning slightly to the left, always acting as the moderating force. It was because both extremes were moving farther out and concerned only with their own rectitude during the early 1980s that the centre weakened. Its roots are firmly planted in the commonsense of Labour's core working-class support, which has never agonised over the academic theorising of left and right, though it has become far less homogenous than it once was. As for philosophy, the centre has no philosophy, other than reason, rationality and a concern for what works.

It understands, instinctively, what voters want. It knows which way the tide is flowing, which includes knowing when the tide cannot be stopped flowing against it. Above all, it has values – of social justice, equality and all the other clichés of democratic socialism – which it is realistic to expect might, from time to time, capture the loyalty of the voters. It is not glamorous, romantic or flamboyant. It does not glorify the workers' struggles nor idealise them. It knows that syndicalism is as great a nonsense as fascism is a menace, that the unions while being a 'good thing' can often be a bad thing, and vice versa for capitalism. It seeks a realisable better life, not a theoretical Utopia.

Of all the Labour leaders (most of whom, except perhaps Hugh Gaitskell, started on the left and moved sharply on election to the top post), Harold Wilson epitomised the centre. He was pragmatism personified. He popularised the word in relation to politics and he made a rough and ready philosophy of it. His overwhelming purpose was to keep a naturally fissiparous party united. To that end, he would duck and weave, often bewilderingly and at a cost to his reputation as a politician of principle, if he ever had one. He was pre-eminently and always a man of the Labour centre. If he appeared otherwise it was because it served his purpose to retain the loyalty and sympathy of the Bevanite and wider left who believed, despite the evidence, that he was one of them. Aneurin Bevan knew differently. Indeed, Wilson more than once claimed to me that Bevan's celebrated denunciation of Hugh Gaitskell as a 'desiccated calculating machine' was, in fact, a reference to him (Bevan named no names). Though he had values, he had little ideology; when asked, as he frequently was by students seeking their Politics, Philosophy and Economics, to define what socialism meant to him, he would pass the request to me to answer on his behalf.

Making Labour the natural party of government – an ambition which had only brief success until Tony Blair's administrations, more pragmatic and successful in electoral terms than Wilson could usually contemplate – was enough in itself. But that ambition in itself makes it impossible for high principles and raging passion to thrive. Britain is not a country of permanent revolution. The illusion that Wilson was of the left was heightened by the fact that the closest of his few real friends in politics, such as Barbara Castle, were firmly entrenched there, but his reputation as a youthful left-winger forced by circumstances or experience to move to the middle ground was false, aided by his detestation of colleagues such as the pro-Arab Ernest Bevin and the devious Herbert Morrison; but their place on the right of the Party was coincidental to his dislike of them, not consequential. His antipathy to them, and his admiration for Sir Stafford Cripps, reinforced his early standing among the left, which in the immediate post-war years was heavily pro-Israel and sympathetic to the Soviet Union, which Cripps had once been. But, again, Wilson's regard for Cripps was personal and more to do with respect for his austere character rather than sympathy with his erratic political views, particularly those which had earned him such notoriety in the pre-war years. Wilson's political placement, as a centrist's position always is, was determined by the need to win general elections. He regarded the elevation of principles above the need for power as the politics of the dilettante. Without power, politics had no purpose. If Bevin, who brought to foreign affairs the brutality he honed as a big-booted trade union leader, was of the right, then Wilson's private but widely-known antagonism to Labour's first post-war Foreign Secretary automatically labelled him as of the left. It was overlooked that the centre can occasionally have its hatreds, too. 'The only good thing I ever heard about Bevin was when they told me he was dead,' Wilson said to me, an unusually vituperative private remark for a man who kept vituperation for public speeches about the Tories.

The truth is that a party which professed to laud principles above personalities but which habitually indulged in personalities at the expense of principles could only be led from the centre where the principles of left and right could be sensibly modified and kept under control. Wilson regarded the nationalisation of Britain's 25 top companies to be as nonsensical as privatisation of the already-nationalised industries, and remained an opponent of both. On the other hand, he would have been open to conviction on the latter because he saw nationalisation as a means to an industrially effective end, not an end in itself. If he had believed privatisation would work, he would have advocated it, always provided he could have carried a pusillanimous Cabinet with him. That was not an heroic attitude, but, then, the centre does not throw up heroic figures. It does not cut a dash, because that would not be natural to it. It does not tempt the emotions because it is not its purpose to inflame. What is pragmatic and practical rarely does. However, Wilson did sense a sea-change in Labour's traditional loyalties, a crumbling of the core, and attempted to push his Government into a substantial programme of council house sales, to keep up with and ahead of the thinking of the times. That was a decision reached on pragmatic political grounds, to buttress the council house vote and to enable tenants to share in the boom in house values, not on grounds of principle. (Ironically, it was the right-wing intellectual, Anthony Crosland, who scuppered both the 25 companies proposal – 'bringing Marks and Spencer up to the level of the Co-op' – and the sale of council houses – 'our councillors won't like it'.)

Gaitskell was, perhaps, the most passionate and intellectual leader the Labour Party has ever had, but he led from the right. Michael Foot was almost equally endowed with passion and principle, but he led from the left. Callaghan ought to have been of the centre, but until the final disillusionment of 1978–9 was of the trade union right and deferred too often to it little good though it did him in the event. If they all failed, as they did, it might have been that they shouldn't have started from where they were in the first place.

Labour's attempt to join the Common Market after the 1966 general election was classic Wilson centrism. He wanted Britain to join because he was convinced that it made economic sense, and not for any mystical belief that it was the way to end the fear of future Franco-German war in Europe. He thought, and rightly, that NATO and the nuclear bomb had ended that particular possibility for good. In the beginning of course, there were many on the left who agreed with him, including, for example, Tony Benn and Eric Heffer, but eventually ideology compelled their U-turns into the anti-Europe camp. The right, led by Roy Jenkins on this issue, didn't trust him because they continued to believe that he was of the left. It was their greatest unshakeable mistake, right from the beginning of his leadership campaign when they pressed the claims of the appalling George Brown instead. They were just as ideological as those of the left and dashed helter-skelter to form the SDP at the first opportunity that electoral defeat presented. Between them, they almost paralysed the centre. In the end, of course, the two wings of the Party over-reached themselves. The left grew arrogant with their apparent assumption of power; winning votes at conferences and in caucuses was more important to it than regaining office. The right despaired and departed and those who remained were ineffectual. Kinnock's revival of the centre, marginally assisted by Roy Hattersley from the right, opened the path to Labour's return to being a formidable political force and to Tony Blair's eventual success.

It is a sad fact that no leader of the Labour Party would ever choose as his epitaph that 'He was a Man of the Centre'. History, or, more accurately, the historian, doesn't deal kindly with boring politicians. It prefers a Robespierre to a Reynaud, a Churchill to a Baldwin and a hare to a tortoise. But all politicians ought to ask themselves why they are in politics and what politics is for. If they are in politics for reasons of self-advancement, vanity and the ego, then it matters little on which wing of the Party they end up, though the House of Lords will beckon to them in old age. 'Those are my principles and if you don't like them, I'll change them' is still the motive force of too many would-be statesmen on both sides of the Atlantic. If, on the other hand, they believe that politics is for the realisation of Marxist, Maoist or totally unfettered free-market philosophies then the eventual failure will only add to the belief that all political life ends in such. But the majority will, in the end, gravitate towards the centre, not so much because that is where the wisdom lies, but because it is where the road to power lies. The few who grow more extreme in their middle and late years fit Wilson's description of Tony Benn: that he immatured with age. The centre is very British, very unspectacular, but it works. That is its justification.

16 The Old Right

Austin Mitchell

Labour has never been an ideological party. Being a coalition it lacked an over-arching system of thought. Seeking power in a nation which wouldn't recognise an ideology if it drove over them in a tank, it eschewed ideological clobber. What it has had are instincts and conditionings called 'Labourism' and plans for the 'good' society called ideology. Today it isn't left with much of either because the galloping inferiority complex developed in the last two decades of the century led it to stop thinking and concentrate on marketing.

Both have been the subject of a battle, which has gone on as long as the party, between left and right; shorthand categories which cover overlapping sets of attitudes struggling for power within the Party. Now that struggle too is over. Neither side has won. Both have been blandised out. The Party has moved onto another dimension where both left and right are relegated to the museum of 'Old Labour', and debate is replaced by a low-intensity muttering among Old Fartonians who remember the battles of yesteryear but are ignored by the bland majority. They wear 'New' badges on smart suits and wait to be told what they think, while viewing left and right as creatures from a primordial past, irrelevant to a new party which began on 1 May 1997 and has expelled ideas, ideology, any over-arching philosophy or even thought from its smiling head. Only winning and holding power count now.

Still called 'Socialist', but only by its critics, Labour has disassociated from Socialism, its mild dilution, Social Democracy, indeed any ideology at all. Herbert Morrison's dictum 'Socialism is what Labour governments do' has become what they don't do. The Party has become 'New Labour', like any product in decline, though New Daz doesn't tell the world that Old Daz was crap. Labour has moved so far to the right that it is now off the old scales. Indeed, as the last surviving Gaitskellite, once on the right, I am now left because that party has moved so far right behind me. Only Tony Benn, Roy Hattersley and Dennis Skinner lie in the left wasteland beyond me. Marketing rules. We're all Modernisers now. Our ideology 'Modernisation' is the mission statement of those without a mission. Very few now have an ideological route map, except a swampy third way which is essentially a continuous re-triangulation between an assumed Labour past and a quixotic Tory present. Few have an ideological picture in their heads, merely an empty canvas with a few 'post-it' notes stuck on at random, mostly so lightly they can be easily removed on any prospect of promotion.

The long conflict between left and right, usually a creative tension, occasionally civil war, was waged between hedgehogs on the right, foxes on the left, conservative caution against radical impulses, trade union instincts against ideological restlessness, slower versus faster, less against more, all fought within Labour and its conditioning, that set of attitudes and reflexes instilled by the working-class and trade-union backgrounds from which most MPs, but not most leaders (for they were solidly middle-class) sprang. The basic argument was over the post-war settlement of which Labour was so proud, which was not an ideological structure, more a mixture of war-time management co-operation, a tilting of structures and balances to the masses, all topped off by the Welfare State.

Labour's left–right battles have always been bigger and noisier in opposition than in power and dominated by reactions to its record. So in the 1950s the core of the argument was the post-war settlement and whether to change, extend, strengthen or prune it. The side fights were over defence, nuclear or not, foreign policy, pro-American or pro-Soviet, redistribution, more or less, and public ownership, another dimension of the American versus Soviet argument. At times all this became a pitched battle between two blocks, left and right, ideologies against the cautious instincts of those to whom power was more important than perfection.

The great Labour government of 1945–51 had built a new post-war settlement which the Tories broadly accepted as it ran out of steam. That exhausted both party and programme but in the 1950s a new programme and a new ideology, for the right at least, was supplied by Tony Crosland's *Future of Socialism* in 1956. Crosland's task was to adjust 'socialism' to the realities of an affluent society. He discounted the state and public ownership as means to an end, not purposes in themselves. The end – Socialism – was a more equal society enriched by a dynamic mixed economy for which Crosland looked not to the Soviet Union, which the left admired, but to the dynamism of the American economy. Socialism was to be advanced by economic growth, raising all boats and allowing painless redistribution through public spending, and the right's position was now clearly defined as Keynesian economic management, equality, more public spending generated by growth, a better public sector, and a mixed economy with full employment.

This programme was approved and shared by Hugh Gaitskell. With it Labour could drop the nationalisation albatross and chime in with the new Britain by pointing the way to a better society enriched by growth and redeemed by greater equality and better public spending. Labour could widen its appeal to the growing middle class, ease its dependence on the industrial working class and its unions and offer them the thing every sector was coming to want in the affluent society, or admass as Priestly called it: more.

The prescription was daring and, therefore, radical but it gave the right the intellectual credibility it needed. The left dismissed it as unsocialist, unideological and a betrayal. They never really defined socialism but knew instinctively that

Crosland's version wasn't it. Nevertheless, from now on the left were the conservatives swimming against the tide as Cold War heightened in the 1960s and 1980s, looking to a working class which was shrinking and to unions which were divided and becoming unpopular, as was socialism and ideology. Britain was becoming more conservative as it became more middle-class. Working-class communities were being pulled down, industries closed, the old ethos shattered, the class war abating.

In Labour's 50 years war, both sides struggled for control of the Party and its programme rather than for its soul. Both failed because Labour itself failed in power. In the 1960s and 1970s, the two decades in which the Party came nearest to dominance and turning into the natural party of government Harold Wilson wanted it to be, Labour failed to deliver because it didn't get the economic growth it needed. The public voted for well-being, a better public sector with better services, improvement and betterment. They didn't get it. That failure re-ignited the internal war, relegated Labour to the angry impatience of opposition and invalidated the prescriptions of both left and right.

Crosland had assumed that growth would go on more or less automatically as it had in the 1950s. He provided no prescription for it but by the 1960s the British economy was lagging badly in a harder, more competitive world and when it came to power in 1964 Labour had to face hard choices between growth boosted by devaluation and carrying on conventional conservative policies. Harold Wilson, ever conventional, doggedly defended the existing exchange rate and always balancing between the conservative left, broadly opposed to devaluation, and the radical right who were for it, rejected it, breaking his government in the process. Everything Labour had promised was predicated on growth. That wasn't forthcoming and the devaluation which would have produced it was painful, humiliating and too late when forced on the government. Had Crosland's prescription delivered, the Old Left–Right argument would have been over with the right triumphant, the left reduced to a muttering resentment, and Labour enthroned in power long-term. Instead Labour was thrown out in 1970.

The next Government had to grapple with the five-fold oil price increase and the massive transfer of purchasing power to the OPEC states, making 1974–9 a long rearguard action to defend the status quo through higher taxation and incomes policy. Reactions against both brought down the Government in 1979. Labour wasn't working. Nor were the prescriptions of either right or left. With that failure went the collapse of faith in socialism, growth in one country, Labour's ability to run the economy competently and faith in Britain itself. Increasingly, the right began to look to Europe and common action there to do what they had been unable to do in Britain, the left to isolation, a siege economy and more desperate measures.

Crosland's revisionism is still relevant. It has been variously re-written, though never replaced. Yet slow, and at times negative, growth meant that the vision was never fulfilled. This was a national failure as well as a Labour failure, but it left Britain with worse education, transport, health and social conditions, an under-invested public sector and, therefore, less socialism than countries which had grown faster but would not describe themselves as socialist.

That failure was Britain's. Casting round for answers to it produced desperate solutions from a siege economy, to monetarism, to free market frenzy, breaking the power of labour and handing everything to the EU and to Euro money, all of which only made things worse. Increasingly in the 1970s and onward the right became defensive, fighting to defend the post-war settlement rather than update it, coming to see the future in Europe which it viewed as Social Democracy, market regulation and welfarism in action in a form appropriate to a modern world in which Britain was seen as incapable of achieving anything on its own.

This left the left as extremist, advocates of new policies relevant to another planet, and a resistance movement to the Common Market, which it saw as a right-wing plot. Against the defensive programme of the 1974–9 government they now moved back to basics: public ownership of the Top Fifty Companies and a siege economy. Both sides in the argument were now embarked on a struggle for control of the wreckage and both lost their lodestars and beacons as America moved to Reaganism (Thatcherism with a vacuous smile) and the Soviet Union disintegrated.

Crosland never updated his thinking. *Socialism Now* was all he wrote in the 1970s and the splits of the early 1980s were more about wrestling over his body than re-defining his legacy. Deserters to the SDP claimed that Crosland would have left with them. Loyalists, like Roy Hattersley, claimed he would have stuck with Labour through thick, and in those years, thin. His disciples were now the right of a bitterly divided party. In the outpouring of battle-books which the war produced the left offered a wide range of new/old prescriptions, from Michael Meacher's *Socialism with a Human Face* through Tony Benn's ultra democracy to the wilder shores of Marxism, and Militant's Trotskyism. The right offered only rehashed Crosland via Roy Hattersley, Bryan Gould and Raymond Plant, all of whom added large doses of John Rawls whose *Theory of Justice* defended egalitarianism by the 'difference principle': inequalities should be tolerated only to the extent that they benefited the least well-off, whose interests should be paramount unless inequalities offered benefits to them. A compelling theory but less straightforward than Crosland's simple 'socialism is about equality' because it is a calculus capable of answering the perennial question of how much equality is equality, but difficult to sell in the hurly burly of political debate.

Such were the higher levels of the battles of 1979 to 1983. In reality, books were only weapons to throw at each other in Labour's nervous breakdown. The left claimed to be 'Socialist' but was dedicated to grabbing the levers of power by controlling Conference, getting leaders elected by the outside party, and disciplining the Parliamentary Party by re-selection. The unions gave up their supervisory role as the party's men in white coats and joined the fray. The right became a resistance movement, trying to stand unshaken amidst a bursting world, and keep the electable. The outcome was a party split. The flabby right departed to form a mediagenic SDP dedicated then to destroying Labour, though several crawled back once that attempt had failed. The embattled right, essentially the core of the last government, fought back through Solidarity, a well organised rearguard action whose only real success was to manage Denis Healey's 0.4 per cent 'triumph' over Tony Benn for the Deputy Leadership, holding Labour's Stalingrad but illustrating how divided we were.

Labour had grown up in a world of class blocs but in the new consumer democracy of a pluralistic society 'us versus them' was less important than a plethora of single issues. The 'post-it' politics of feminism, animalism, internationalism, unilaterialism, peacenickery, anti-nuclearism, ethnicity and greenism took over and a hundred plants blossomed. So Labour tried to replace the dying mass party with a policy smorgasbord and a coalition of causes only to find that coalition divided because one man's cause was another woman's anathema. The result was the largest suicide note in history and the Party's greatest post-war electoral failure, in 1983.

The struggle ended only with the election of Neil Kinnock as leader on the assumption that only a man of the left could lead Labour to the right. Kinnock did that job, but far too slowly. In the process he became infected with 'Europeanism', then turning into a substitute for socialism. As Kinnock was converted, unions began to see the virtues of a Europe in which they were listened to, offered more than the cold hostility of Thatcherism, and could get union rights and social reform via European regulation and currency union. Anything to which Mrs Thatcher was hostile and which divided the Tories must be a good thing. Thus Labour, which had viewed the EEC as a capitalist plot in the 1970s, began to see it as a new religion whose priests, Smith, Mandelson, Blair, Kinnock and (then) Brown, waxed positively evangelical.

Kinnock stood down after a 1992 defeat which ended the civil war by destroying both Labour's confidence and the search for policy prescriptions. Left and right were bemused to find that the public not only failed to listen to either but was unsympathetic to views Labour had long taken for granted. Both had assumed that defeating wrong-headed policies and a crazed government would be easy. Both were disoriented when marching round the walls of Jericho and sounding the trumpets produced only a shower of bricks and abuse from the walls while party members rushed to buy up the goodies flogged off in Jericho's market. Despite two huge recessions the electorate kept on re-selecting Jericho Council. Labour discovered that it had to conform to a new world whose citizens didn't respond to the old signals in the old way.

This began the long review of policy, seen now not so much in the light of what was needed but what would sell. The galloping inferiority complex led to the chucking of all the staples of both left and right overboard. Marketing and sales became more important than ideology, instinct, conditioning or thinking. The transition was from John Smith to Paul Smith. John Smith's brief tenure of the leadership is now seen by the left as a golden age. In fact they resented him as a man of the right at the time and it was a holding period. The Party trusted John, his instincts were Labour, and he gave the Labour Party a credibility Kinnock never could attain. Yet the modernisers hated it because Smith mistrusted and disliked them. Mandelson and Phillip Gould were relegated.

Smith's death opened the cage, allowing the modernisers to take over and begin Labour's *Kristallnacht*, breaking the windows of both left and right. Modernisers, now on another dimension entirely, saw both as irrelevant nuisances. The argument about alternatives, left, right, socialist, liberal, new SDP or dusty Old Labour ended in brain death with no-one proffering any alternative to the modernisers or the Leninist coup by which they seized the Party and moved quickly by *blitzkrieg* to smash one shibboleth after another: Clause IV, the Union tie, Growth (replaced by 'stability'), economic management (replaced by the Bank of England). Having no alternative neither left nor right put up any fight. Both were banished to irrelevance.

This end to the left–right argument was the prelude to Labour's greatest electoral triumph. Not cause and effect. The nation so hated the Tories that Labour could have won under Michael Foot with the 1983 manifesto, but in fact Labour had tied its hands, renounced its policies, accepted the Tory revolution and offered only vacuous goodwill. It was elected with an indecently huge majority to do nothing very much.

Blair is the ideology but he hasn't any. Never programmed to Labour instincts, hypocrisies and sentimentalities, its egalitarianism or its trade union solidarities, he doesn't particularly like any of them. He has ideals and policies, but these keep changing as he moves from stakeholderism to communitarianism or the intellectual vacuities of the Third Way. As the 'Great Explainer' he means it – how he means it – at the time, even if the subject of his passion changes. His instinct is always to compromise, to avoid hard edges and hard policies, and his policies are not usually thought through because they are there to generate goodwill rather than be implemented. We're all conservatives now and Labour is much better at it than the Tories. Blairism is managerialism as a system of government. Its policies are developed not by debate but by focus group, its aim is to hold things together rather than build a new heaven or a new earth. Critics will question whether Labour's glass is half full or half empty. Government wants things that way. Each half is important to someone.

So the right is now less irrelevant than the left but not by much. Their historic battle is over, their groupings dissolved as both scramble on board New Labour and compete to reach its upper decks, even the bridge, for a reward in pelf and place which is granted in inverse ratio to their willingness to eat their own words, disavow their own past, and embark on the management training course.

Is ideology dead? It wasn't killed. There is no evidence of *felo de se*: though it might have succumbed to public boredom, it was not the failure of ideology or consistent ideas which meant that a government with a majority to do anything hasn't done much in contrast to the huge achievement of a 1974–9 government programmed to the ideology of the Old Right. They fought a brave and successful rearguard action to defend the post-war settlement by solidarity, equality of sacrifice, incomes policy and higher taxation to sustain public spending with no majority at all. The contrast with today's approach is total.

Yet *tout passe tout casse tout lasse*. Even New Labour, our luckiest government ever. After seven successful years government now faces real problems and hard choices. Public spending is rising but we haven't generated the economic growth to bear it. We've shown goodwill to Europe but got no reciprocal benefits, only constant demands for new concessions which Britain finds it difficult to make, on the Euro, a common foreign and defence policy and a European Constitution. Money is pouring into health, education and now transport, but without corresponding reward, and the areas into which it hasn't been put – housing, local government, care of the old – all get worse. Inflation has been broken but at the cost of undermining manufacturing and enthroning 'stability' and prudence.

As the impetus dies, the easy policies fail and real politics and difficult choices return, debate will revive. The initiative then returns not to the Old Left, whose policies are out of sync with the world and whose ageing adherents have no base because the new union leaders, however much the press portray them as the new Scargills, are really a new showbiz, but to the Old Right, now the only advocates of the polices this vacuous Government needs: Keynes, equality, redistribution, intervention, fairer taxation and a boosted public sector. Its ideas, though not now its aged figures, can give Blairism the intellectual backbone it lacks. Labour's past is no longer that of another party in another country. The experience and wisdom developed then is relevant as the 'New' is dropped and Labour comes down from a 'Mandelsonian Fairyland' to face all the old problems. As the old politics return, the ideology of Labour's Old Right becomes relevant again.

17 New Labour:

Polly Toynbee and David Walker

During Labour's conference week in October 2002, Tony Benn chose to write
a denunciation of his party's leaders in the columns of the newspaper that
published the Zinoviev letter.[1] Perhaps we should not be too hard on the
memory lapses of an ageing sansculotte; after all, the history of the left is full
of instances of true believers hating their comrades more than the class enemy.
But Benn's career is worth bearing in mind in judging how far New Labour did
adopt 'New Right' positions. The revision of Labour commitments and attitudes was carried through in the 1990s with surprisingly little reverence to
Labour's 'Old Right' associated with Anthony Crosland and the Gaitskellites
but in strongly conscious rejection of the 'New Left' which had come to the
fore without quite dominating the Labour Party in the later 1970s and the
early 1980s.

Our question is what did these 'New Right' positions mean for the practice of
government after 1979? How does New Labour appear when judged against the
'socialist' achievements of previous Labour Cabinets, such as those of which
Benn was a member (1966–70; 1974–9), ostensibly based on 'Old Labour'
commitments plus some admixture of 'Old Right'? Here is one scale: the definition of socialism provided at mid-century by the level-headed Francis Williams
advance public control of the primary source of economic power for the good.[2]
Did previous Labour Governments take discernible steps towards the creation of
socialism's 'new society'? If not, perhaps they should be scored on more down-
to-earth measures such as quantitative fairness in household incomes, income
distribution or mere advances in material prosperity for working families. On
that basis, the possibility opens that the Blair Government, for all its New Right
baggage, might paradoxically turn out to be more successful, according to those
routine measures of social democratic intent. The alternative basis for judgement is idealism. Weigh New Labour on the virtual scales of twentieth-century
socialist aspiration – never realised or even capable of realisation – and it is
bound to be found feather-light.

On most tallies, New Labour is to be placed several notches along from
1992's manifesto position let alone the touchstone statement of socialist aspiration of 1983. In its soft shoe shuffle, stage right, the Labour Party adopted tenets
of neo-liberalism and Thatcherism, though not always with attribution. In this

essay we pose two questions. One is about about the practice of government. In an interview Tony Blair said heretically 'we need entrepreneurs to be able to go out there and make money and do well, we want successful people to be well rewarded.'[3] The phraseology echoes with Reaganite trickle-down and similar neo-liberal ideas. But what if, none the less, New Labour's performance in office stands in comparison with its socialist predecessors in terms of their own hopes for greater social justice? In the same interview, Blair added 'but there is a level of inequality in parts of our country that is unacceptable.' What if in changing the relative position of poorer households in the income distribution, the Third Way works – at least as measured by Labour's previous attainments, whether Croslandite or neo-Marxist in intellectual inspiration?

Our other question requires a fine, counterfactual judgement. Has New Labour gone further right than it 'needed'? David Lipsey, with impeccable party credentials, put it like this: 'I think the Labour leadership has gone further than was absolutely necessary away from the party's traditional commitment to the collective provision of public services, and its contribution to practical equality.'[4] Put that way, we need to address the possibility (presumably to be dated some-time between 1983 and 1995) of another 'third way' opening up, that is to say a route between the failed formulae of Old Labour and the surrender of neo-liberalism by Blair–Brown. With that arrogance characteristic of the 'we understand the direction of history' Marxists, Eric Hobsbawm says that after 1992 Labour could have 'reformed' but stopped short of Blair becoming 'Thatcher in trousers'.[5] If only the reformation had stopped at Wittenberg and not moved on to Geneva. A touch of union reform perhaps, sauced with some tax restraint and a cautious, but not total, rewording of Clause IV? Somehow, to paraphrase one of the many disappointed, Labour could have retained its 'idealism' while it jettisoned the baggage of electoral failure.[6]

Alternatively, the Blair–Brown was indeed 'necessary' whether we call it market liberalism plus active government or individualism within a hesitant collectivism or, even more hoary a formula, capitalism with a human face. In 1984 John Dunn said the failures of democratic socialism in the West over the last ten years had been predominantly intellectual, 'failures in comprehension and not in intrepidity or the capacity for evocative non rational persuasion.'[7] A decade later you could have repeated the point about intellectual failure (under-standing what makes a capitalist economy tick) while noting growing incapacity for evocative non-rational persuasion, or idealism. Labour idealism had evapo-rated long before the arrival of Tony Blair. The new intellectual base for Labour 'radical but firmly in the centre ground'[8] may not involve any more profound understanding of capitalist dynamics, neo-classical endogenous growth theory included, but it did make Labour electable in 1997 – a capitalist party fit for election in a capitalist democracy. It also provided more or less of a template for governing afterwards and not just for governing but for making, with some style, the necessary compromises of holding power in a capitalist democracy and, additionally, successfully compromise to effect policies within a free market framework, specifically benefiting the disadvantaged.

New Labour borrowed the Clinton entourage's idea of 'triangulation'. This is the formula for finding a political position allowing you to criticise some members of your own party as unrealistic extremists while also criticising most members of the opposing party as dangerous extremists.[9] So, Labour had to appear to be neither Tory nor the same as the party that lost in 1992. But this triangle was not equilateral, say critics. New Labour owed more to right than left. But New Labour has made an art form of disingenuous rhetoric or 'spin', for the sake of covering tracks and muddying wells. In power it taxed by stealth and redistributed by stealth. Whether New Labour has been more tilted to right than Old Labour, according to practice in office rather than socialism's ineffable spirit, is best answered by the following short review of Blairism in action.

You do not have to go quite as far as does Richard Rose[10] to agree that, over the past six decades, it is not easy to spot the policy or fiscal consequences of electoral change or, more particularly, the effects of previous socialist government on such obvious performance indicators as the relative income of poorer households. The marked growth in inequality during the 1980s, commonly ascribed to Thatcherism, began two years before Jim Callaghan left power[11] and may have to do with the failure of his Cabinet (which of course included Tony Benn) to manage a capitalist economy or put any faith in any alternative, really existing socialism in the Soviet Union being then a decade away from implosion.

Neo-liberalism demands a smaller state. Yet direct taxation of incomes and profits under the Blair Government (37.4 per cent in 2001) is pretty much its 1948 value and several points ahead of what it was when Harold Wilson took power again in 1974. Analysts of change in the distribution of income since the 1960s note a rough and ready association between growing inequality and bursts of economic growth – and deliberate policy changes in the case of the Thatcher government.[12] There is reason to believe that Blairite measures have, to some extent, bucked this trend: the upswing from the mid-1990s has not seen a marked growth in inequality. The first Wilson Governments were effectively egalitarian. Income was more fairly distributed when Harold Wilson left office in 1970 compared to 1964. The 'main reason seems to have been increases in cash benefits' including family allowances.[13] Under Blair, at least after 1998–9, 'increased generosity of benefits came to dominate the path of social security spending'.[14] The first term saw an unambiguous transfer of spending power to the poorest households.[15] That trend continues, with the minimum pensions guarantee and tax credits. The point is not that New Labour could or should do more; it is that this Labour Government stands comparison with its predecessors and may even turn out to be 'more socialist'.

An answer to the question whether New Labour jumped too far to the right in terms of rhetoric or commitments must ultimately rest on a judgement about elections or, more specifically, the desperate search by Labour leaders for a formula that would end the drought and then, after 1997, ensconce it as – the old clichés are the best – the natural party of government. This meant, as Gordon Brown reminds us *ad infinitum*, tight spending control, debt repayment and no increase in income tax rates, together with such correlates as 'public–private partnership'.

Some on the left argue New Labour made an empirical mistake about the electorate. First, it underestimated how damaged the Major government was during the 1990s, especially after Black Wednesday 1992; there was no need to shift policy as much in order to secure a victory in 1997. Second, it failed, after 1997, to gauge the electorate's willingness to respond to 'strong', e.g. left-tending, leadership. The trouble is the first of these arguments relies heavily on wise hindsight. It also ignores how few people in politics, high or low, believed this thesis until 2 May 1997. The second is based less on evidence than on faith. The public continued to assert its confidence in aspects of the Welfare State during the Thatcher years. But that is not the same as saying the public (or at least the psephologically demonstrative bit of it) had any enthusiasm for the extension of tax, public spending or redistribution of income. There is an 'appetite for socialism' school which feeds on the fact the total votes cast for Labour at the 1951 general election exceeded the Tory total. But it was their maldistribution that was the point then, as it was after Labour lost in 1959 and Gaitskell began his campaign against Clause IV, and again in 1992. After that defeat advocates of a southern strategy became, belatedly, vocal; revisionism ensued. To win national power in UK elections means dealing with a southern, increasingly middle-class electorate with a limited appetite for statism or redistribution. There is very little evidence since 1997 that that has changed.

In 2001, turnout fell and all sorts of points can be and have been made about trust.

> At the very least, the precipitate decline in turnout in Britain's inner cities and evidence of structural disengagement from the political process by many of the country's poorest people must give pause for thought to a government that preaches the language of social cohesion.[16]

But that is no basis for an argument suggesting that had Blair–Brown been more 'socialist' between 1997 and 2001, people would have turned out in greater number.

That mention of social cohesion cues a repetition of the central argument of this essay. In power New Labour have addressed themes conventionally associated with socialism: social exclusion, child poverty, urban regeneration, the life chances of the disadvantaged, the educational attainment of children from poorer homes. And have not addressed such themes as income distribution, market-place inequalities. Has it none the less left a mark on the social order comparable with its post-Attlee predecessors?

According to Raymond Plant, a fundamental division between neo-liberalism and social democracy is whether policy should seek to improve the relative position of the poor or improve their absolute standard of life: New Labour, he argues, has been mighty reluctant to decide.[17] Yet there is reasonable evidence how during the first term policy significantly benefited the worst-off households relatively as well as absolutely. Measures since, notably the minimum pension guarantee, look likely to have similar effect.

Blair's principal offence against the socialists is thus more conceptual than actual. Wilson, Callaghan, or Attlee for that matter, had no theory of capitalist development, productivity or growth and certainly no worked-out idea of what a socialist government could do to replace the operation of private markets. They accepted capitalism – totally, in Callaghan's case – without feeling a political need or being required to alter the language or thought world of the Labour Party, including a trade union movement wedded simultaneously to free collective bargaining and statist intervention. While they were in power, the shape of society and its classes changed, along with economic geography: they made a victim of successive Labour governments.

New Labour was and remains determined not to be a victim; that required accepting market liberalism. Put at its harshest, social democratic aspiration then becomes a residual: Gordon Brown's 'enabling state'[18] and Tony Blair's mystic marriage of individualism and universal service provision.[19] In these compromises Blair (and Brown) seek an answer to the long twentieth-century question of reconciling economic performance powered by capitalist enterprise and inclusion and some mitigation of inequality. In terms of tax or social security, their compromises have not always been made explicit; they have preferred stealth. But are these compromises any less honest than the pretensions of previous Labour governments to socialist transformation, a political illusion given up in practice if not party rhetoric before the end of the first Attlee Government?

Notes

1   Benn, T., 'The Tyranny of Tony', *Daily Mail*, 1 October, 2002, p. 24.
2   Williams, F., *Fifty Years March* (Odhams Press, London, 1950), p. 377.
3   *Observer*, 29 September 2002.
4   Lipsey, D., 'Revisionists Revise', in Leonard, D. (ed.) *Crosland and New Labour* (Macmillan, London, 1999), p.15.
5   Hobsbawm, E., *Interesting Times* (Allen Lane, London, 2002), p. 276.
6   Jacobs, M., *Prospect*, September issue 2002.
7   Dunn, J., *The Politics of Socialism*, CUP, Cambridge, 1984), p.49.
8   Blair, T., Speech, 18 February 2001.
9   Morris, D., *Power Plays: Win or Lose – how History's Great Political Leaders Play the Game* (Regan Books, New York, 2002).
10 Rose, R., *Do Parties Make a Difference?* (Macmillan, London, 1984).
11 Clarke, T., 'The Limits of Social Democracy: Taxation and Spending under Labour 1974–79', Institute of Fiscal Studies working paper, W01/04, 2001.
12 Jenkins, S., 'Trends in UK Income Distribution', Institute of Social and Economic Research, Essex, www.iser.essex.ac.uk/pubs/workpaps/pdf/99–22pdf.
13 Stewart, M., 'The Distribution of Income', in Beckerman, W. (ed.) *The Labour Government's Economic Record 1964–70* (Duckworth, London, 1972), p. 110.
14 Clarke, T., Brewer, M. and Wakefield, M., 'Five Years of Social Security Reforms in the UK', Institute of Fiscal Studies working paper, W02/12, 2002.
15 Toynbee, P. and Walker, D., *Did Things Get Better?* (Penguin, London, 2001), p. 41.
16 Geddes, A.P. and Tonge J., (eds) *Labour's Second Landslide* (Manchester University Press, Manchester, 2002), pp. 5–6.

17 Plant, R., 'Crosland, Equality and New Labour', in Leonard, D. (ed.) *Crosland and New Labour*.

18 Brown, G., 17th Arnold Goodman charity lecture, 20 June 2000.

19 Blair, T., 'The Courage of our Convictions', Fabian Society, London, 2002.

Afterword

Roy Hattersley

The moral and the message of *The Struggle for Labour's Soul* is set out with disturbing clarity in the opening sentence. 'The Labour Party is a party of values, but not very often of ideas.' Impatience with 'philosophic speculation' – a feature of the Labour Representation Committee's inaugural conference in 1900 – was encouraged by the success of Mr Attlee's post-war Government, the undoubted high water mark of Labour achievement. What seemed to be a victory of pragmatism, 'doing what needed to be done', confirmed that ideology was 'best left to exponents of American free enterprise and Russian Communists.' Dick Crossman believed that, during the years of failure which followed 1951, Labour ' ... lost its way not only because it lacks a map of the new country it is crossing, but because it thinks maps unnecessary for experienced travellers.'[1]

In fact, during the 50 years which followed the Attlee Government, all sorts of attempts were made to construct new theories of socialism. Many of them (see Stuart Holland's chapter in this volume) seemed more convincing to their authors than to the general public. The most coherent were variants or adaptations of Marxism. The most famous was Aneurin Bevan's *In Place of Fear*. But that was a work of absolutely no ideological importance or philosophic originality. As contributor after contributor to this book makes clear, Tony Crosland's *The Future of Socialism* was the seminal work of the period.

Sadly there were few ministers in the Labour governments which followed its publication who were willing to prescribe its social and economic remedies. After the 1976 IMF crisis, high levels of public expenditure – an essential feature of Crosland's 'revisionism' – were accepted as incompatible with the essential maintenance of international confidence. Egalitarian socialism was being covertly rejected as impractical 20 years before Tony Blair proscribed it as a heresy against the three shibboleths of his political faith – markets, managerialism and mobility.

Neil Kinnock at least made an attempt to focus the Party's attention on philosophical principle when, in 1988, he asked me to write a new statement of *Aims and Values*. My paper was, in horse racing language, by Tony Crosland out of R.H. Tawney. It argues that greater equality, far from being the enemy of freedom, actually increases 'the sum of liberty' by extending the ability to make the choices of a free society. The Conference Arrangements Committee allocated 40 minutes to Labour's first full-scale debate on ideology since the adoption of Sidney Webb's constitution in 1918. Three delegates (all of them critical) asked to speak and the vote (carried without either dissent or enthusiasm) ended ten minutes before the allotted time was completed.

Of course the advocacy of a more equal society – the defining principle of democratic socialism – went on. But too often it was led into the intellectually sterile dispute between 'equality of opportunity' and 'equality of outcome'. That distraction remains a tedious part of the debate. A chapter heading in *The Future of Socialism* asserts 'Equality of opportunity is not enough' – something of an understatement for egalitarians since it is not equality at all. Equality of opportunity, 'the open road', promotes mobility. But mobility and the meritocracy, which is its self-justifying sophistication, produce only shifting patterns of inequality. The open road offers no adequate form of social justice unless the journey is begun on the same starting line. Even the equal start is not enough. Some travellers will fall down along the way. True egalitarians require them to be picked up and helped to complete the distance. Equality of opportunity provides no more that the scant consolation that they were given a chance but failed to take it.

Denunciations of equality of outcome are based on a (sometimes intentional) misunderstanding of what its proponents seek. They are also paradoxically utopian. We could pursue the most egalitarian policies that a democracy would allow for several centuries and society would still be so unequal that the question 'how far should equality go?' would remain to be answered. In any case, John Rawls's 'difference principle' has already proved the reply. Equality should be pursued until the ' … representative man … prefers his prospects with the inequality to his prospects without it'.[2] More important, in terms of the Labour Party debate, nobody who shares Crosland's view that the 'equality of opportunity is not enough' wants to impose a cultural, social or economic uniformity on society. Quite the opposite. Tawney described the true objective of democratic socialism. To support the definition of equality on which it is based

> … is to hold that, while natural endowments differ profoundly, it is the mark of a civilised society to aim at eliminating such inequalities as have their source, not in individual differences, but in its own organisation, and that individual differences, which are the source of social energy, are more likely to ripen and find expression if social inequalities are, as far as practicable, diminished.[3]

The achievement of that state is to some of us a moral imperative. But if it has no generalised and objective merit which can be demonstrated to open minds of other faiths, the same criticism can be levelled at marginal utility. A pound in the hands of a poor man has a great deal more practical value than a pound at the disposal of his rich neighbour. Equality has some certain economic consequences – increased velocity of circulation and the reduction in the savings ratio – which may or may not be desirable depending on the conditions of the time. But it also guarantees that the incremental pound is used to best effect.

The opponents of equality have never attacked it on its merits. Colin Hughes and Patrick Wintour claim that the most effective way of attacking Labour continued to be the insult that socialism was out of date. It has also proved to be the most effective way of shifting the Labour Party to the right. Ideas should be judged on their merits.

Of course *policies* must change with the times. It would be absurd to suggest that, despite the development of the global economy, the arrival of electronic technology and a dozen other crucial changes, which range from the break-up of the Soviet Union to the general availability of IVF, a political party should not change its programme. It is the principles on which the policies are based which should be immutable.

The implication that critics of New Labour believe in a return to exchange controls, a massive programme of public ownership and the re-creation of the ground-nut scheme as the best way of assisting the developing world is just a canard which is repeated to discredit people who reject the 'project' and its limited vision of a new society. I admit that what is left of the Croslandite left encourages one severe failing – the intellectual arrogance which makes it impossible even to counterfeit agreement with some of the sentimental nonsense on which many current policies are built. The idea that men and women of goodwill can devise policies which simultaneously benefit every section of society is clearly absurd. Rawls, hardly a Marxist, is right. In a free society, liberties collide and governments must adjudicate between conflicting claims. That is the reality, not the class war. Only synthetic absurdities like the Third Way – rightly barely rating a mention in *The Struggle for Labour's Soul* – pretend that a government does not have to look at society and decide which side it is on.

If we were tempted to believe that policies (as distinct from principles) did not have to change with a constantly changing world, a passage from *The Future of Socialism* would convince us that a constant adjustment is essential. Paradoxically it is one of the few places in the book where Crosland, although right at the time, has been overtaken by events. 'The most characteristic features of capitalism have', he claimed, 'disappeared – the absolute rule of private property, the subjection of all of life to market influences, the domination of the profit motive, the neutrality of government, typical *laissez-faire* division of income and the ideology of individual rights.'[4]

Margaret Thatcher reversed all that. And in so doing made the need for a coherent, consistent and convincing socialist alternative all the more important. In conditions of increasing prosperity – not particularly to her credit, only in Sweden during two years of Conservative government has GDP actually declined – she preached the doctrine of inequality. That made the need for an intellectually watertight alternative absolutely essential if Labour was not to fall into the trap of producing its own variation on her favourite themes – less tax, more choice and efficiency through increasingly unregulated competition.

In 1945, the need for a social revolution was obvious. The poor, unable to afford doctors' bills, lacked medical care. Thousands of families lived in slums which were inadequate houses even when they were built in the mid-nineteenth century. For millions of working men and women old age brought unavoidable poverty. Who then needed a theory to justify a new social order? Today, the argument for greater equality is less obvious. The need for a principle to live by is therefore more essential. That principle must be consistent with the modern world. But the preoccupation of the age is liberty. What Tawney, Crosland and Rawls provided was a prescription to make us all free.

The need for a principle is still misunderstood even by people of a radical disposition. Polly Toynbee and David Walker are right to point out that New Labour's fiscal policies – minimum income guarantees and tax credits – explicitly help the poor and, as those benefits are (by definition) not available to the rich, the balance between income groups was shifted. But the gap between rich and poor has widened during the six years of Labour government and the most memorable moment during the 2001 election campaign was the Prime Minister's pointed refusal to express any regret that it had happened. The more equal society cannot be created by marginal tax adjustments – important though they are. The whole economy has to be focused on that aim. Unless that greater equality is achieved, the poor are deprived of power and influence as well as wealth and we experience all the problems – crime, ignorance and racism – which follow what we now call 'exclusion'.

Ruth Lister is right to warn that redistribution by stealth carries all the dangers of doubletalk. Because tax increases were denounced as inimical to the enterprise economy, the Government was adjudged to have failed when it extended national insurance contributions, which amounted to the same thing. A party which is afraid to admit its commitment to redistribution will never redistribute enough. Ministers who either openly espouse meritocracy or attack the straw man of equality of outcome will inevitably preside over a divided society.

Yet, as Professor Arthur Lewis wrote 50 years ago, 'Socialism is about equality.'[5] It is the big idea which defines the socialist ethic and transcends all the sterile and outdated arguments about public ownership as an object in itself. Equality is the only guiding light we have to follow. Lose sight of it and we wander through governments setting our course by opinion polls, focus groups and the Prime Minister's instincts. Since consistency is an essential feature of political success, equality is necessary for good Labour governments as well as the creation of the good society.

Notes

1   Crossman, R.H.S., 'Towards A New Philosophy of Socialism', in Crossman, R.H.S. (ed.), *Planning for Freedom*, (Hamish Hamilton, London, 1965), p. 36.
2   Rawls, J., *A Theory of Justice*, (Harvard University Press, Cambridge, 1971), p. 64.
3   Tawney, R.H., *Equality*, (G. Bell & Son, London, 1931), p. 49.
4   Quoted in Hattersley, R., *Choose Freedom*, (Michael Joseph, London, 1987), p. 16.
5   *Ibid.*, p. xvii.

Bibliography

Addison, P., *The Road to 1945*, (Pimlico, London, 1994).

Anderson, P., Blackburn, R. (eds), *Towards Socialism*, (Fontana, London, 1965).

Anderson, P., Mann, N., *Safety First: The Making of New Labour*, (Granta, London, 1997).

Ashton, J., *Red Rose Blues*, (Macmillan, Basingstoke, 2000).

Baker, T., Kohler, J. (eds), *International Competitiveness and Environmental Policies*, (Edward Elgar, Brighton, 1998).

Barratt Brown, M., Holland, S., *Public Ownership and Democracy*, (IWC, Nottingham, 1973).

Beckerman, W. (ed.), *The Labour Government's Economic Record 1964–70*, (Duckworth, London, 1972).

Beer, S.H., *Modern British Politics*, (Faber, London, 1969).

Benewick, R. Berki, R.N., Parekh, B. (eds), *Knowledge and Belief in Politics – The Problem of Ideology*, (Allen & Unwin, London, 1973).

Benn, T., 'The Case for a Constitutional Premiership', *Parliamentary Affairs*, Vol. 33, 1980.

Benn, T., *Arguments for Democracy*, (Cape, London, 1981).

Benn, T., *Against the Tide*, (Hutchinson, London, 1989).

Benn, T., *End of an Era*, (Hutchinson, London, 1992).

Berle, A., Means, G., *The Modern Corporation and Private Property*, (Harcourt Brace, New York 1932).

Bernstein, E., *The Preconditions of Socialism* (edited and translated by Tudor, H., CUP, Cambridge, 1993).

Bevan, A., *In Place of Fear* (Quartet, London, 1978).

Bevir, M., 'New Labour: A Study in Ideology', *British Journal of Politics and International Relations*, 3(2).

Black, L., 'The Bitterest of Enemies: Labour Revisionists, Atlanticism and the Cold War', *Contemporary British History*, 15(3): 2001.

Blackburn, R., Plant, R. (eds) *Constitutional Reform: The Labour Government's Constitutional Reform Agenda*, (Longman, London, 1999).

Blackwell, T., Seabrook, J., *A World Still to Win: The Reconstruction of the Post-War Working Class*, (Faber & Faber, London, 1985).

Blair, T., *New Britain: My Vision Of A Young Country*, (Fourth Estate, London, 1996).

Blair, T., *The Third Way: New Politics for the New Century*, (Fabian Society, London, 1998).

Blair, T., *Prime Minister's speech at the CBI Annual Dinner*, 17 May 2000.

Blair, T., *Speech*, 18 February, 2001.

Blair, T., *Speech to the Labour Party Conference*, 2001.

Blair, T., 'The Courage of our Convictions', Fabian Society, London, 2002.

Blair, T., *Speech to the Labour Party Conference, 2002, Guardian Unlimited*. 2003.

Blyth, M., *Great Transformations: Economic Ideas and Institutional Change in the Twentieth Century*, (CUP, New York, 2002).

Brivati, B., *Hugh Gaitskell*, (Richard Cohen Books, London, 1996).

Brivati, B., Jones, H. (eds), *From Reconstruction to Integration, Britain and Europe since 1945*, (Leicester University Press, Leicester, 1993).

Bobbitt, P., *The Shield of Achilles: War, Peace and the Course of History*, (Allen Lane, London, 2002).

Bogdanor, V., *Power and the People*, (Victor Gollanz, London, 1997).

Bogdanor, V., 'Devolution: Decentralisation or Disintegration?', *Political Quarterly*, Vol. 70, 1999

Bogdanor, V., *Devolution in the United Kingdom* (OUP, Oxford, 1999).

Booth, A., 'The Keynesian revolution in economic policy-making', *Economic History Review*, 36, 1983.

Bosanquet, N., *After The New Right*, (Heinemann, London, 1983).

Boucher, D., Kelly, P. (eds), *Social Justice From Hume to Walzer*, (Routledge, London,1998).

Brooke, S., *Labour's War: The Labour Party during the Second World War*, (OUP, Oxford, 1992).

Brown, G., 17th Arnold Goodman charity lecture, 20th June 2000.

Brown, M.B., *From Labourism to Socialism: A Political Economy for Labour in the 1970s*, (Spokesman Books, Nottingham, 1972).

Budd, A., *The Politics of Economic Planning*, (Fontana, London, 1978).

Budge, I., 'Relative Decline as a Political Issue: Ideological motivations of the Politico-Economic Debate in Post-war Britain', *Contemporary Record*, Vol. 7, No. 1, 1993.

Burk, K., Cairncross, A., *'Goodbye Great Britain'. The 1976 IMF Crisis*, (Yale University Press, London and New Haven, 1992).

Byers, S., *Globalisation and Free Trade*, (Department Trade and Industry, London, 2002).

Cairncross, A., *Years of Recover: British economic policy, 1945–51*, (Methuen, London, 1985).

Callaghan, J., *The Retreat of Social Democracy*, (MUP, Manchester, 2000).

Callinicos, A., *Against the Third Way*, (Polity Press, Cambridge, 2001).

Campbell, J., *Nye Bevan: A Biography*, (Hodder & Stoughton, London, 1987).

Castells, M., *The Rise of the Network Society*, (Blackwells, Oxford, 1996).

Cerny, P., *The Changing Architecture of the State*, (Sage, London, 1990).

Clarke, P., *A Question of Leadership. Gladstone to Thatcher*, (Hamish Hamilton, London, 1991).

Coates, D., *Labour in Power* (Longman, London, 1980).

Coates, D., *The Crisis of Labour*, (Philip Allan Publishers, London, 1989).

Coates, D., Hay, C., *The Internal and External Face of New Labour's Political Economy*, (Mimeo, 2000).

Coates, D., Panitch, L., 'The Miliband School of Labour Scholarship: an Internal Retrospective', Past Paper presented to the Labour Movements Group of the Political Studies Association, University of Salford, July 2001.

Commission on Taxation and Citizenship, *Paying For Progress: A New Politics of Tax for Public Spending*, (Fabian Society, London, 2000).

Cook, R., *The Challenges of Globalisation* – Address to IISS. London. 9 March 2001, www.fco.gov.uk/servlet

Coopey, R., Fielding, S., Tiratsoo, N. (eds), *The Wilson Governments, 1964–70*, (Pinter, London, 1993).

Craig, F.W.S. (ed.), *British General Election Manifestos, 1918–1966*, (Political Reference Publications, Chichester, 1970).

Craig, F.W.S., *British General Election Manifestos,1959–87*, (Dartmouth Press, Aldershot, 3rd edition, 1990).

Cronin, J., 'New Labour's Pasts', Paper presented to the Labour Movements Group of the Political Studies Association, Bristol, July 4–5 2002.

Crosland, C.A.R., *The Future of Socialism*, (Jonathan Cape, London, 1956).

Crosland, C.A.R., *The Conservative Enemy*, (Jonathan Cape, London, 1962).

Crosland, C.A.R., *Socialism Now and Other Essays*, (Jonathan Cape, London, 1974).

Crosland, C.A.R., *Social Democracy in Europe*, Fabian Tract 438, London, 1975.

Crosland, S., *Tony Crosland*, (Jonathan Cape, London, 1982).

Crossman, R.H.S. (ed.), *New Fabian Essays*, (Turnstile Press, London, 1952).

Crossman, R.H.S., *Planning for Freedom*, (Hamish Hamilton, London, 1965).

Crossman, R.H.S., *Socialism and Planning*, Fabian Tract 375, London, 1967.

Crossman, R.H.S., *Paying for the Social Services*, Fabian Tract 399, London, 1969.

Daintith, T., 'Analysis: "A very good day to get out anything we want to bury"', *Public Law*, Spring 2002.

Dalton, H., *Practical Socialism for Britain*, (Routledge, London, 1935).

Deighton, A. (ed.), *Britain and the First Cold War*, (Macmillan, London, 1990).

Desai, R., *Intellectuals and Socialism. 'Social Democrats' and the British Labour Party*, (Lawrence and Wishart, London, 1994).

Devine, T.M., *The Scottish Nation: 1700–2000*, (Allen Lane and the Penguin Press, London, 1999).

Driver, S., Martell, L., *New Labour: Politics After Thatcherism*, (Polity Press, Cambridge, 1998).

Drucker, H.M., *Doctrine and Ethos in the Labour Party*, (Allen & Unwin, London, 1979).

Dunn, J., *The Politics of Socialism*, (CUP, Cambridge, 1984).

Durbin, E., *The Politics of Democratic Socialism*, (Routledge & Sons, London, 1940).

Durbin, E., *New Jerusalem: The Labour Party and the Economics of Democratic Socialism*, (Routledge & Kegan Paul, London, 1985).

Eatwell, J., Taylor, L., *Global Finance at Risk*, (Polity Press, Cambridge, 2000).

Eley, G., *Forging Democracy – The History of the Left in Europe: 1850–2000*, (OUP, Oxford, 2002).

Etzioni, A., *The Essential Communitarian Reader*, (Rowman & Littlefield Publishers, Oxford, 1998).

Fairclough, N., *New Labour, New Language*, (Routledge, London, 2000).

Fielding, S., *The Labour Party – Continuity and Change in the Making of New Labour*, (Palgrave, London, 2003).

Flathman, R.E. (ed.), *Concepts in Social & Political Philosophy*, (Macmillan, London, 1973).

Foot, M., *Aneurin Bevan 1945–1960*, (Paladin Books, London, 1975).

Foote, G., *The Labour Party's Political Thought*, (Macmillan, Basingstoke, 1997).

Forman, F.N., *Constitutional Change in the United Kingdom*, (Routledge, London, 2002).

Forrester, T., *The Labour Party and the Working Class*, (Heinemann, London, 1975).

Fox, A., *Shop Floor Power Today*, Fabian Research Series, 338, 1978.

Franklin, J. (ed.), *Equality*, (IPPR, London, 1997).

Freeden, M., 'The Stranger at the Feast: Ideology and Public Policy in Twentieth Century Britain', *Twentieth Century British History*, 1 (1), 1990.

Freeden, M., 'The Ideology of New Labour', *Political Quarterly*, Vol.71, 2000.

Frieden, J., 'Invested Interests: the Politics of National Economic Policies in a World of Global Finance', *International Organisation* 45(4), 1991.

Friedmann, T., *The Lexus and the Olive Tree*, (Basic Books, New York, 2000).

Gaitskell, H., *Socialism and Nationalisation*, (Fabian Society, London, 1956).

Gamble, A., Wright, T. (eds), *The New Social Democracy*, (Blackwell/Political Quarterly, Oxford, 1999).

Garrett, G., 'Global markets and national politics', *International Organisation* 52, (1), 1998.

Garrett, G., *Partisan Politics in the Global Economy*, (CUP, Cambridge, 1998).

Garrett, G., Lange, P., 'Political Responses to Interdependence: What's 'Left' for the Left?', *International Organisation* 45(4), 1991.

Geddes, A. P., Tonge J. (eds.), *Labour's Second Landslide*, (MUP, Manchester, 2002).

Giddens, A., *Modernity and Self-Identity*, (Polity Press, Cambridge, 1991).

Giddens, A., *The Third Way: The Renewal Of Social Democracy*, (Polity Press, Cambridge, 1998), p. 30.

Giddens, A., *The Third Way and Its Critics*, (Polity Press, Cambridge, 2000).

Giddens, A., *The Global Third Way Debate*, (Polity Press, Cambridge, 2001).

Goodman, A., 'Income Inequality: What has happened under New Labour?', in *New Economy* Vol. 8, No. 2, June 2001.

Gordon, D., 'The global economy: new edifice or crumbling foundations?', *New Left Review*, (168): 24–65, 1988.

Gould, P., *The Unfinished Revolution: How The Modernisers Saved The Labour Party*, (Abacus, London, 1998).

Gourevitch, P., *Politics in Hard Times*, (Cornell University Press, New York, 1986).

Grant, W., 'Globalisation, Big Business and the Blair Government', Paper for the Political Studies Association, UK 50th Annual Conference, 10–13 April 2000, London.

Gray, A., Jenkins, B., 'Government and Administration: Reasserting Public Services and their Consumers', *Parliamentary Affairs*, Vol. 55, 2002.

Gray, J., *After Social Democracy*, (Demos, London, 1996).

Gray, J., *False Dawn*, (Granta, London, 1998).

Greenleaf, W.H., *The British Political Tradition, Vol. 2: The Ideological Inheritance*, (Routledge, London, 1983).

Harris, T., 'The Effects of Taxes and Benefits on Household Income, 1997–1998', *Economic Trends*, No. 545, April 1999.

Haseler, S., *The Gaitskellites: Revisionism in the British Labour Party 1951–1964*, (Macmillan, London, 1969).

Hatfield, M., *The House the Left Built*, (Gollancz, London, 1978).

Hattersley, R., *Choose Freedom: The Politics of Democratic Socialism*, (Penguin, London, 1987).

Hay, C., 'The Invocation of External Economic Constraint: A Genealogy of the Concept of Globalisation in the Political Economy of the British Labour Party 1973–2000', *The European Legacy* 6 (2).

Hay, C., Watson, M., *Rendering the Contingent Necessary: New Labour's Neo-Liberal Conversion and the Discourse of Globalisation*, Center for European Studies Program for the Study of Germany and Europe, Working Paper 8.4 (Cambridge, Mass., Harvard University, 1998).

Hay, C., Watson, M., *Globalisation and the British Political Economy*, (Mimeo, 2000).

Hayek, F., *The Constitution of Liberty*, (Routledge and Kegan Paul, London, 1960).

Hayek, F., Law, *Legislation and Liberty Vol. II: The Mirage of Social Justice*, (Routledge and Kegan Paul, London, 1979).

Hazell, R. *et al.*, 'The British Constitution in 1998–99: The Continuing Revolution', *Parliamentary Affairs*, Vol. 53, 2000.

Hazell, R. *et al.*, 'The Constitution: Coming in from the Cold', *Parliamentary Affairs*, Vol. 55, 2002.

Heath, A., Jowell, R., Curtice, C., *The Rise of New Labour* (OUP, Oxford, 2001).

Heffer, E., *Labour's Future*, (Verso, London, 1986).

Held, D., McGrew, A., (eds), *Global Transformations: Politics, Economics and Culture*, (Polity Press, Cambridge, 1999).

Held, D., McGrew, A. *Globalisation/AntiGlobalisation*, (Polity Press, Cambridge, 2002).

Hennessy, P., *Whitehall*, (Fontana, London, 1990).

Hill, D. (ed.), *Tribune 40*, (Quartet, London, 1977).

Hinden, R. (ed.), *The Radical Tradition*, (Allen & Unwin, London, 1964).

Hinton, J., *Labour and Socialism: A History of the British Labour Movement, 1867–1974*, (University of Massachusetts Press, USA, 1983).

Hirsch, F., *Social Limits to Growth* (Routledge, London, 1977).

Hirst, P., 'The Global Economy – Myths and Realities', *International Affairs* 73 (3 July), 1997.

Hirst, P., 'Has Globalisation Killed Social Democracy?', *Political Quarterly* (3), 1999.

Hirst, P., Thompson, G., *Globalisation in One Country?: The Peculiarities of the British*, (Open University Faculty of Social Sciences, Buckingham, 1999).

Hirst, P., Thompson, G., *Globalisation in Question*, (Polity Press, Cambridge, 1999).

Hobsbawm, E., *Interesting Times*, (Allen Lane, London 2002).

Hodgson, G., *The Democratic Economy*, (Penguin, Harmondsworth, 1983).

Hoggart, S., Leigh, D., *Michael Foot: A Portrait*, (Hodder & Stoughton, London, 1981).

Holden, C., 'Globalisation, Social Exclusion and Labour's New Work Ethic', *Critical Social Policy* 19(4): 1999.

Holland, S., *The Market Economy and The Global Economy*, (Weidenfeld and Nicolson, London, 1967).

Holland, S. (ed.), *The State as Entrepreneur: the IRI State Shareholding Formula*, (Weidenfeld and Nicolson, London, 1972).

Holland, S., *The Socialist Challenge* (Quartet, London, 1975).

Holland, S., 'An Alternative Economic Strategy', *The Spokesman*, 34, Winter 1977–8.

Holland, S. (ed.), *Out of Crisis*, (Spokesman Books, Nottingham, 1983).

Holland, S., *The European Imperative: Economic and Social Cohesion in the 1990s*, (Spokesman Books, Nottingham, 1993).

Holland, S., *Towards a New Bretton Woods*, (Spokesman Books, Nottingham, 1994).

Holliday, I., 'Is the British State Hollowing Out?', *Political Quarterly*, Vol. 71, 2000.

Hoogvelt, A., *Globalisation and the Postcolonial World – The New Political Economy of Development*, (Macmillan, London, 1997).

Hoover, K., Plant, R., *Conservative Capitalism in Britain and the United States: A Critical Appraisal*, (Routledge, London, 1989).

Howard, A. (ed.), *The Crossman Diaries. Selections from the Diaries of a Cabinet Minister 1964–70*, (Hamish Hamilton, London, 1979).

Howard, A., West, R., *The Making of a Prime Minister*, (Jonathan Cape, London, 1965).

Hughes, C., Wintour, P., *Labour Rebuilt: The New Model Party*, (Fourth Estate, London, 1990).

Hutton, W., *The State We're In*, (Jonathan Cape, London, 1995).

James, H., *The End of Globalisation*, (Princeton University Press, Princeton, 2001).

Jay, D., *The Socialist Case*, (Faber, London, 1937).

Jay, D., *Change and Fortune. A Political Record*, (Hutchinson, London, 1980).

Jefferys, J., *Anthony Crosland*, (Richard Cohen, London, 1999).

Jefferys, K., *Finest and Darkest Hours. The Decisive Events in British Politic from Churchill to Blair*, (Atlantic Books, London, 2002).

Jefferys, K. (ed.), *Labour Forces. From Ernest Bevin to Gordon Brown*, (IB Tauris, London, 2002).

Jenkins, M., *Bevanism: Labour's High Tide*, (Spokesman Books, London, 1979).

Jenkins, P., *Mrs Thatcher's Revolution*, (Jonathan Cape, London, 1987).

Jenkins, P., *Anatomy of Decline*, (Cassell, London, 1995).

Jenkins, R., *What Matters Now*, (Fontana Paperback, London, 1972).

Jenkins, R., *A Life at the Centre*, (Macmillan, London, 1991).

Jessop, B., *The Future of the Capitalist State*, (Polity Press, Cambridge, 2002).

Johnson, C., *MITI and the Japanese Miracle*, (Stanford University Press, Stanford, 1982).

Jones, B., Keating, M., *Labour and the British State*, (OUP, Oxford, 1985).

Jones, M., *Michael Foot*, (Gollancz, London, 1994).

Jones, T., 'Labour Revisionism and Public Ownership 1951–63', *Contemporary Record*, 5, 3 (1991).

Jones, T., *Remaking the Labour Party. From Gaitskell to Blair*, (Routledge, London, 1996).

Joyce, P., *Realignment of the Left?* (Macmillan, Basingstoke, 1999).

Julius, D., *Global Companies*, (Pinter, London, 1990).

Kagan, R., *Paradise and Power: America and Europe in the New World Order*, (Atlantic Books, London, 2003).

Kennet, W., Whitty, L., Holland, S., *Sovereignty and Multinational Companies*, Fabian Tract 409, July 1971.

Keohane, D., *Labour Party Defence Policy since 1945*, (Leicester University Press, Leicester, 1993).

Keohane, R.O., Milner, H.V. (eds), *Internationalisation and Domestic Politics*, (Cambridge University Press, Cambridge, 1996).

Keynes, J.M., *The General Theory of Employment, Interest and Money*, (Prometheus, New York, 1997, 1st edition, 1936).

King, A., *Does the United Kingdom still have a Constitution?* The Hamlyn Lectures (Sweet and Maxwell/The Hamlyn Trust, London, 2001).

Kinnock, N., 'A New Deal for Europe', *New Socialist*, Spring 1984.

Kinnock, N., 'Reforming the Labour Party', *Contemporary Record*, 8, 3 (1994).

Krasner, S.D. (ed.), *International Regimes*, (Cornell University Press, Ithaca, 1983).

Labour Party, *Statement of Democratic Socialist Aims and Values*, (Labour Party, London, 1988).

Labour Party, *It's Time to get Britain Working again*, (Labour Party, London, 1992).

Labour Party, *New Labour, because Britain Deserves Better*, (Labour Party, London, 1997).

Labour Party, *Ambitions for Britain: Labour's Manifesto 2001*, (Labour Party, London, 2001).

Leadbeater, C., *Living on Thin Air – The New Economy*, (Penguin Books, London, 1999).

Le Grand, J., *The Strategy of Equality*, (Allen & Unwin, London, 1982).

Lee, J., *My Life with Nye*, (Penguin, London, 1981).

Leigh, I., 'Taking Rights Proportionately: Judicial Review, the Human Rights Act and Strasbourg', *Public Law*, Summer 2002.

Leonard, D. (ed.), *Crosland and New Labour*, (Macmillan, London, 1999).

Levitas, R., *The Inclusive Society? Social Exclusion and New Labour*, (Macmillan, London, 1998).

Leys, C., *Market Driven Politics – Neo-liberal Democracy and the Public Interest*, (Verso, London, 2001).

Lipsey, D., Leonard, D. (eds), *The Socialist Agenda: Crosland's Legacy*, (Jonathan Cape, London, 1981).

Lister, R., 'From Equality to Social Inclusion: New Labour and the Welfare State', *Critical Social Policy*, 55, 1998.

Lister, R., 'Doing Good by Stealth: The Politics of Poverty and Inequality under New Labour', *New Economy*, Vol. 8, No. 2, June 2001.

Livingstone, K., *If Voting Changed Anything They'd Abolish It*, (Hutchinson, London, 1987).

Ludlam, S., Bodah, M., Coates, D., 'Trajectories of Solidarity: Changing Union-party Linkages in The UK and The USA', *British Journal of Politics and International Relations*, Vol. 4, Issue 2, 2002.

Ludlam, S., Smith, M.J. (eds), *New Labour in Government*, (Macmillan, London, 2001).

Lukes, S., *Essays in Social Theory*, (Macmillan, London, 1977).

McBriar, A., *Fabian Socialism and English politics, 1884–1918*, (CUP, Cambridge, 1962).

McLean, I., *Keir Hardie*, (Allen Lane, London, 1975).

MacIntyre, D., *Mandelson and the Making of New Labour*, (Harper Collins, London, 1999).

Madgwick, P., Woodhouse, D., *The Law and Politics of the Constitution*, (Harvester Wheatsheaf, Hemel Hempstead, 1995).

Mandelson, P., *The Blair Revolution Revisited*, (Politicos, London, 2002).

Mandelson, P., Liddle, R., *The Blair Revolution: Can New Labour Deliver?*, (Faber and Faber, London, 1996).

Marquand, D., 'Inquest on a Movement', *Encounter*, July 1979.

Marquand, D., *The Unprincipled Society*, (Jonathan Cape, London, 1988).

Marquand, D., *The Progressive Dilemma: From Lloyd George to Kinnock*, (Heinemann, London, 1991).

Marquand, D., Seldon, A., *The Ideas that Shaped Postwar Britain*, (Fontana, London, 1996).

Marriott, J., *The Culture of Labourism*, (Edinburgh University Press, Edinburgh, 1991).

Marx, K., *Critique of the Gotha Programme*, in Marx and Engels, Collected Works, Vol. 24 (Lawrence and Wishart, London, 1989).

Mason, A. (ed.), *Ideals of Equality*, (Blackwell, Oxford, 1998).

Miliband, R., *Parliamentary Socialism*, (Allen & Unwin, London, 1961).

Mikardo, I., *Back-Bencher*, (Weidenfeld & Nicholson, London, 1988).

Minkin, L., *The Labour Party Conference*, (Manchester University Press, Manchester, 1978).

Minkin, L., *The Contentious Alliance*, (Edinburgh University Press, Edinburgh, 1991).

Misgeld, K., Molin, K., Amark, K., *Creating Social Democracy*, (Penn State Press, Philadelphia, 1992).

Morgan, K.O., *Rebirth of a Nation: Wales 1880–1980*, (Clarendon Press, Oxford, 1981).

Morgan, K.O., *Labour in Power 1945–1951*, (Oxford University Press, Oxford, 1985).

Morgan, K.O., *Labour People: Leaders and Lieutenants*, (OUP, Oxford, 1987).

Morgan, K.O., *Callaghan: A Life*, (OUP, Oxford, 1997).

Morris, D., *Power Plays: Win or Lose – how History's Great Political Leaders Play the Game*, (Regan Books, New York, 2002).

Morrison, J., *Reforming Britain: New Labour, New Constitution?* (Reuters/Pearson Education, London, 2001).

Moses, J. W., 'Abdication from national policy autonomy: What's left to leave?', *Politics and Society*, 22(2), 1994.

Mosley, L., 'International Financial Markets and National Welfare States', *International Organisation*, 54(4), 2000.

Mosley, L., *Global Capital and National Governments*, (CUP, Cambridge, 2003).

Mulhall, S., Swift, A., *Liberals and Communitarians*, (Blackwell, Oxford, 1996).

Mullin, C., *How to Select or Reselect your MP*, (CLPD/IWC, Nottingham, 1981).

Naughtie, J., *The Rivals: The Intimate Story of a Political Marriage*, (The Fourth Estate, London, 2001).

Newman, J., *Modernising Governance – New Labour Policy and Society*, (Sage, London, 2001).

Padgett, S., Paterson, W.E., *A History of Social Democracy in Postwar Europe*, (Longman, London, 1991).

Panitch, L. (ed.), *Working Class Politics in Crisis*, (Verso, London, 1986).

Panitch, L., Leys, C., *The End of Parliamentary Socialism*, (Verso, London, 1997).

Pelling, H., *A Short History of the Labour Party*, (Macmillan, Basingstoke, 1993, 10th edition).

Perroux, F., *Les Techniques Quantitatives de la Planification*, (Presses Universitaires de France, Paris, 1965).

Pierre, J., Peters, B.G., *Governance, Politics and the State*, (Palgrave, London, 2000).

Pierre, J., Peters, B.G., *The New Governance: States, Markets, and Networks*, (Macmillan, London, 2000).

Pimlott, B., *Hugh Dalton*, (Jonathan Cape, London, 1985).

Pimlott, B., Cook, C. (eds), *Trade Unions in British Politics*, (Longman, London, 1991).

Plant, R., *Equality, Markets and the State*, (Fabian Society, London, 1984).

Plant, R., *Citizenship, Rights and Socialism*, (Fabian Society, London, 1988).

Ponting, C., *Breach of Promise: Labour in Power, 1964–70*, (Hamish Hamilton, London, 1987).

Prais, S.J., *The Evolution of Giant Firms in Britain*, (CUP, Cambridge, 1976).

Prior, M., 'Problems in Labour Politics', Interviews, *Politics and Power 2* (1980).

Przeworski, A., *Capitalism and Social Democracy*, (CUP, Cambridge, 1985).

Przeworski, A., Sprague, J., *Paper Stones: A History of Electoral Socialism*, (University of Chicago Press, Chicago, 1986).

O'Brien, R., *The End of Geography: Global Financial Integration*, (Pinter, London, 1992).

Ohlin, B., *Interregional and International Trade*, (Harvard University Press, Cambridge, 1933).

Ohmae, K., *The Borderless World*, (Collins, London, 1990).

Ohmae, K., *The End of the Nation State*, (Free Press, New York, 1995).

Oliver, D., 'Written Constitutions: Principles and Problems', *Parliamentary Affairs*, Vol. 45, 1992.

Orwell, S., Angus, I. (eds), *The Collected Essays, Journalism and Letters of George Orwell*, (Secker & Warburg, London, 1968).

Overbeek, H., *Global Capitalism and National Decline*, (Unwin Hyman, London, 1990).

Radice, G., 'Revisionism Re-visited', *Socialist Commentary*, May 1974.

Radice, G., *Labour's Path to Power: The New Revisionism*, (Macmillan, London, 1989).

Rawls, J., *A Theory of Justice*, (Oxford University Press, Oxford, 1999).

Reich, R., *The Work of Nations*, (Simon and Schuster, New York, 1991).

Rhodes, R.A.W., *Understanding Governance: Policy Networks, Governance, Reflexivity, and Accountability*, (Open University Press, Buckingham, 1997).

Rhodes, R.A.W., 'New Labour's Civil Service: Summing-up Joining-up', *Political Quarterly*, Vol. 71, 2000.

Rodrik, D., *Has Globalisation gone too far?*, (Institute for International Economics, Washington D.C., 1997).

Rollings, N., 'British budgetary policy, 1945–55: a "Keynesian revolution"?' *Economic History Review*, 41, 1988.

Rose, R., *Do Parties Make a Difference?* (Macmillan, London, 1984).

Rosen, G. (ed.), *Dictionary of Labour Biography*, (Politicos, London, 2002).

Rubinstein, D., *Socialism and the Labour Party 1945–50*, (ILP Publications, London, 1979).

Rubinstein, W.H., *Capitalism, Culture and Decline in Britain*, (Macmillan, London, 1992).

Rugman, A., *The End of Globalisation*, (Random House, New York, 2000).

Sasson, D., 'Reflections on the Labour Party's Programme for the 1990s', *Political Quarterly*, Vol. 62, No. 3, July–September 1991.

Scharpf, F., *Crisis and Choice in European Social Democracy*, (Cornell University Press, New York, 1991).

Schmidt, V., *The Futures of European Capitalism*, (OUP, Oxford, 2002).

Schrecker, E., *The Age of McCarthyism*, (St Martin's, Bedford, 2002).

Scribberas, E., *Multinational Electronics Companies and National Economic Policies*, (JAI Press, Greenwich, Connecticut, 1977).

Seldon, A. (ed.), *The Blair Effect*, (Little Brown, London, 2001).

Seyd, P., *The Rise and Fall of the Labour Left*, (Macmillan, Basingstoke, 1987).

Seyd, P., Whiteley, P., *Labour's Grassroots: the Politics of Party Membership*, (Clarendon Press, Oxford, 1992).

Shaw, E., *Discipline and Discord*, (MUP, Manchester, 1988).

Shaw, E., *The Labour Party since 1945*, (Blackwell, Oxford, 1996).

Shaw, G.B., *The Intelligent Woman's Guide to Socialism and Capitalism*, (Constable, London, 1928).

Shell, D., 'Labour and the House of Lords: A Case Study in Constitutional Reform', *Parliamentary Affairs*, Vol. 53, 2000.

Shonfield, A., *Modern Capitalism*, (Oxford University Press, Oxford, 1965).

Short, C., *Speech to the Labour Party Conference*, 2001.

Smith, M.J., Spear, J. (eds), *The Changing Labour Party*, (Routledge, London, 1992).

Smith, T., 'How Citizenship got on to the Political Agenda', *Parliamentary Affairs*, Vol. 55, July 2002.

Stephenson, P., 'Tony Benn's guru', *Socialist Commentary*, October 1975.

Stepney, P., Ford, D. (eds), *Social Work Models, Methods and Theories: A Framework for Practice*, (Russell House, Lyme Regis, 2000).

Stone, I.F., *The Truman Era*, (Turnstile Press, London, 1953).

Strachey, J., *Contemporary Capitalism*, (Victor Gollancz, London, 1956).

Swank, D., *Global Capital, Political Institutions, and Policy Change in Developed Welfare States*, (CUP, Cambridge, 2002).

Sykes, R., Palier, B., Prior, P. (eds), *Globalisation and European Welfare States*, (Palgrave, Basingstoke, 2001).

Tanner, D., Thane, P. and Tiratsoo, N. (eds), *Labour's First Century*, (CUP, Cambridge, 2000).

Tawney, R.H., *The Acquisitive Society*, (Bell and Sons, London, 1921).

Tawney, R.H., *Equality*, (George Allen & Unwin, London, 1931).

Temple, M., 'New Labour's Third Way: Pragmatism and Governance', *British Journal of Politics and International Relations*, 2(3), 2000.

Thompson, G., *Can the Welfare State survive Globalisation?*, (Mimeo, 2001).

Thompson, N., *Political Economy and the Labour Party*, (UCL Press, London, 1996).

Thompson, N., *Left in the Wilderness. The Political Economy of British Democratic Socialism since 1979*, (Acumen, Chesham, 2002).

Thorpe, A., *A History of the British Labour Party*, (Macmillan, Basingstoke, 2001).

Tiratsoo, N. (ed.), *From Blitz to Blair*, (Phoenix, London, 1998).

Tomlinson, J., *Democratic Socialism and Economic Policy, the Attlee years, 1945–51*, (CUP, Cambridge, 1997).

Townsend, S., *The Growing Pains of Adrian Mole*, (Puffin Books, Harmondsworth, 2002).

Toynbee, P., Walker, D., *Did Things Really Get Better?*, (Penguin, London, 2001).

Vaizey, J., 'Remembering Anthony Crosland', *Encounter*, August 1977.

Walker, R. (ed.), *Ending Child Poverty: Popular Welfare for the 21st Century*, (Polity Press, Bristol, 1999).

Warde, A., *Consensus and Beyond*, (MUP, Manchester, 1982).

Weiss, L., 'Globalisation and the myth of the powerless state', *New Left Review*, 225, 1997.

White, S. (ed.), *New Labour: The Progressive Future?* (Palgrave, London, 2001).

Whitehead, P., *The Writing on the Wall*, (Michael Joseph, London, 1985).

Whitely, P., 'Who are the Labour Activists?' *Political Quarterly*, Vol. 52, 1981.

Wickham-Jones, M., *Economic Strategy and the Labour Party*, (Macmillan, Basingstoke, 1996).

Williams, F., *Fifty Years March: The Rise of the Labour Party*, (Odhams Press, London, 1950).

Williams, P. (ed.), *The Diary of Hugh Gaitskell 1945–1956*, (Jonathan Cape, London, 1983).

Womack J., Jones D.T., Roos, D., *The Machine that Changed the World*, (Macmillan, Basingstoke, 1990).

Wood, A., *North-South Trade, Employment and Inequality*, (OUP, Oxford, 1994).

Index

abolition of death penalty 249
abortion legislation 76
absolute level of poverty 90
accountability 33–4
ADAPT programme 182
Additional Members System 217–18
AES *see* Alternative Economic Strategy
AEUW 169, 177
Afghanistan 243, 249
'agreement to differ' 218
Airbus Industrie 170
Aitken, Ian 16, 41
Al-Qaida 249
Albion 236
Aldermaston 22
Alexander, A.V. 19
Allaun, Frank 254
Alternative Economic Strategy 29, 36, 39, 50, 58, 149, 151;abandonment of commitment to 222
Alternative Regional Strategy 209
Alternative Vote system 217–18
ambiguity of New Labour 99
American New Deal 189
AMS *see* Additional Members System
Amsterdam Treaty 222
Anderson, Evelyn 12
Anglo-American capitalism 51–67
Anglo-Irish Agreement 209
anti-communism 11–12, 20–21; *see also* Cold War
anti-market resonances 55
anti-poverty measures 128
anti-social behaviour 95
Appeasement 230
argument for equality 131–3, 274–7
Arguments for Socialism 30–31
Ashton, Jack 43
Asian Tiger economies 88

aspirational voters 155
assisting principles 99
ASTMS 28, 174, 177
Atlantic Alliance 234, 239
Attlee, Clement 7, 14–16, 19, 77, 242; defeat in 1951 71
Attlee Governments 7, 14, 121–2, 125, 231–3, 241–2; revisionist antecedents, 1935–55 69–72
Australia 19, 214

background to history of New Left 24–7
Bank of England 63, 147, 152–3, 220, 266; independence 147, 152, 222; Monetary Committee 220
Banks, Tony 169, 254
Barratt Brown, Michael 30–31, 37
'basic error' of Croslandism 79
BBC 221
Beckett, Margaret 30, 43, 87, 169, 176
bedrock of political economy 53
Belfast Agreement 216
Belgium 169–72, 174, 179–80, 230
Belle Epoch 146
Benn, Tony 24–5, 29–44, 86, 163, 165–6, 179, 242; critic of use of prerogative powers 221; hostility towards European Economic Community 34, 219; model of socialism 34; nationalism of 179–80
Bennism 25, 80, 87
Berlin, Isaiah 116
Bernstein, Eduard 69–70, 108–110, 116; revisionism 109; social democracy 111
Bevan, Aneurin 7, 10, 14, 16, 207, 237, 242; architect of NHS 14, 249; denunciation of Gaitskell 258; on devolution 207; fundamentalist supporters 71; on Korean rearmament

234; 'Leftwing firebrand' 16, 231;
resignation of 14
Bevanism 15–16, 20, 30–32, 34, 40, 72
Beveridge report 7–8
Bevin, Ernest 10, 19, 233, 242, 258
'Big Bang' 138
Bill of Rights 215, 220
birth of the social contract 174–6
Bish, Geoff 30, 253
Black Wednesday 82, 151–2, 271
Blair Governments 7, 43–4
Blair, Tony 18, 24–5, 44, 82–3, 93–5, 129,
139–40; abolition of House of Lords
213; belief in community 93, 95;
commitment to equality 133; election
as leader of Labour Party 86;
endorsement of trickle down theory
130; equality of opportunity 129;
freedom of information 216; on
globalisation 137; globalisation 'thesis'
87–8; interventionist policies 243;
mastery of the unions 191; prerogative
powers 213–14; Prime Minister's
powers 215; shift to centre 49;
supporter of devolution 208
blockade of Berlin 12
Blunkett, David 43, 223
boom and slump logic of capitalism 139
Bosnia 155
Boundary Committee for England 210
bourgeoisie 55
BP 167
Brains Trust 16
Bretton Woods 51, 53, 58
Britain will Win with Labour 58
British Communist Party 13, 20; exodus
from 20
British Leyland 164, 180
British National Oil Corporation 174
British 'specialness' 241
British-Irish Agreement 209
British-Irish Council 209
Brown, George 171, 260
Brown, Gordon 43, 83, 86, 117, 143, 242;
cumulative effect of budgets 127; entry
into Euro zone 219; equality of
opportunity 129
Brussels 219
Bullock report 33
Business Graduates' Association 173
Byers, Stephen 43, 141–2

Callaghan Government 68, 79, 93, 140,
207–8
Callaghan, James 68, 76–80, 145, 154,
163, 166; disintegration of social
democracy under 76–80; on the history
of the Party 193
Cambridge Economic Policy Group 29–30
Campaign for Democratic Socialism 75
Campaign for Labour Party Democracy
30–31, 40, 254
Campaign for Nuclear Disarmament
19–22, 230, 237–9, 253
Campaign for a Scottish Assembly 207–8
Campbell, John 17
Castle, Barbara 75, 126, 222, 242, 253,
258
CDS *see* Campaign for Democratic
Socialism
censorship legislation 73
central state changes 220–21
Centre 47–67, 257–60
centre of gravity 96
challenge 140–42
changes in the modern state 220–22;
changes to central state 220–21;
Labour and the trade unions 221–2;
New Labour and debate on citizenship
220
character assassination 176
character of New Left 29–31
Charter 88 206
chauvinism 236, 242
child poverty 90
Child Poverty Action Group 27
Chiltern Hundreds 181
Choose Freedom 81, 116
Christian Democrats 12
Christian socialism 93, 96, 154
Church of England 214
Churchill, Winston 7–8, 14; defeat by
Labour 8
CIA 12
citizenship 107, 220
Civil Service Act 221
Civil Service Code 221
Claim of Right 207–8
Clarke, Charles 181
class 194–201
class antagonism 36, 72–3, 123
Clause IV 18, 21, 38, 49, 74–5, 78,
109–110, 168
climax of Labourism 7
Clinton, Bill 270

CND *see* Campaign for Nuclear
    Disarmament
Co-operative Development Agency 60
Code of Conduct for Special Advisers 221
Cold War 10, 12–14, 16, 20–21, 233–4,
    242; collapse of political boundaries 88,
    150; 'managed capitalism' 139;
    national security 155–6; obsessions of
    21; pro-deterrence stance during 34;
    realignment of the Left after 127; 'Reds
    under the bed' 16, *see also* anti-
    communism
commentaries 245–77; afterword 274–7;
    the Centre 257–60; New Labour
    268–73; the New Left 251–6; the Old
    Left 247–50; the Old Right 261–7
Commission on Taxation and Citizenship 93
Committee of the One Hundred 22
Common Market *see* European Economic
    Community
Common Market Safeguards Committee
    253, 256, *see also* Labour Euro-
    Safeguards Committee
Common Programme of the Left (France)
    178
Commons Expenditure Committee 163
Commonwealth 236
Commonwealth of Britain Act 1991 213,
    216, 221
communications revolution 88
communism 10, 69
communitarian liberals 96
communitarianism 95–6, 120, 154
community 93–4, 99, 115–20, 131
competitive public enterprise 37–8
comprehensive secondary education 17
conceptions 114
Concorde 170
Confederation of European Socialist
    Parties 181
Conference Arrangements Committee
    274–5
Conference decisions 48
Conservative Enemy 75, 123
Conservative Party 8
consolidation 9, 20, 71, 74
constitutional change within the Party
    254–5
Constitutional Convention 156
constitutional reform 40, 206–228;
    changes in the modern state 220–22;
    devolution 206–211; freedom of
    information 216–17; human rights

215–16; issue of Europe 219–20;
    parliament and the Monarchy 211–15;
    parties and elections 217–19
Contemporary Capitalism 74
'contingent necessary' 144–5, 154
contracting-out 222
convergence 88
Cook, Robin 43, 87, 137, 142, 213–14,
    217; on globalisation 137; resignation
    of 214
cool Britannia 156
corporate socialist ideology 71
crime prevention 88, 95
Cripps, Francis 30, 251–2, 254
Cripps, Stafford 14, 19, 215, 258
critical mass 48
Crosland, Anthony 15–21, 27–9, 34–8, 40,
    76–80, 109–119; and America 231–2;
    birth of the social contract 174–6;
    central tenet of social democracy 90,
    174; champion of egalitarian socialism
    77, 92, 99; definition of socialism 68;
    high priest of revisionism 75, 77;
    laissez-faire capitalism 89; legacy 79;
    liberty and 96, 99; post-war capitalism
    148
Crosland Memorial Lecture 1997 129
Crossman, R.H.S. 8, 13, 15, 20–21, 72,
    125; on abolition of House of Lords
    212
Crown 213–14, 221
Crowther/Kilbrandon Royal Commission
    on the Constitution 1969 207
crypto communism 13
cynicism 86
Czechoslovakia 12

Dalton, Hugh 7, 14–15, 19, 69–72, 121
Dalyell, Tam 125, 247–50, 255
Damascene conversion 147
'dark satanic mills' 230
Darling, Alistair 224
Data Protection Registrar 216
Data Protection Tribunal 216
de Gaulle, Charles 219
death penalty 249
debate on citizenship 220
decentralisation 80
'declaration of incompatibility' 216
decolonisation 236
defection 80
defence 88
definition of labourism 187–8

definitive principles 99
deflation 27
deindustrialisation 170
Delors, Jacques 181–3
democracy 33–4, 116, 214; weakness of British 214
democratic equality 92, 126
Democratic Labour Party 78
Democratic Party 13
democratic socialism 10, 14, 28, 80–81, 120–21, 239; conditions for achievement of 138; and equality 120–21, *see also* social democracy
democratisation 225
democratising markets 172–4
Demos 131
Denmark 146, 153; social governance 153
Department of Constitutional Affairs 223–4
dependency culture 131
devaluation 76
development of New Left 27–8
devolution 116, 206–211, 218
'Devolution in the UK' White Paper 1974 207
Dewar, Donald 87
difference principle 92–3
dilemmas 154–7
dirigiste planning system 39
disabled citizens' legislation 95
discontent 8
distributional conflict 197
divorce legislation 73
Dobson, Frank 43
doubletalk 277
Douglas-Home, Alec 76
Downing Street 17, 90; Number 10 90, 170–71, 220, 224; Number 11 90
Durbin, Evan 70–72, 121

Easter Aldermaston march 22
ecology 80
economic liberalism 120
economic policy 251–2
education 75, 95, 99; private 75; state 75, 99
EEC *see* European Economic Community
efficiency 32–3
EFTA *see* European Free Trade Association
egalitarian socialism 77–8, 274
egalitarianism 75, 117–18
Egypt 19
EIB *see* European Investment Bank

11 September 144, 155, 233
Empire 230
employment 7–8, 60, 63
ends and means 105–119
enlightened managerialism 83
Enlightenment 114
entryism 80
equality 17, 32, 61, 73, 91–2, 115, 120–36; case for 131–3, 274–7; New Labour 127–31; Old Right 121–6
Equality 121
Equality Commission (Northern Ireland) 209
Essen European Council 182
ethical socialism 50, 93
EU *see* European Union
Euro 88, 156, 218
Euro Bonds 182
Euro zone 219
Europe 219–20
European Charter of Fundamental Rights 219
European Commission 78
European Convention on Human Rights 215–16
European Council 219–20
European Court 215
European Economic Community 21, 28, 34, 77, 218, 233, 236, 242; Labour's attitude towards membership of 77; New Left hostility towards 39; reform of 28
European Free Trade Association 236
European Investment Bank 182
European Investment Fund 182
European Union 88, 143, 147, 230; enthusiasm for 143
Europeanisation 149, 153, 155
Europeanism 265
Ewing, Winifred 207
'exempt information' 216
extremism 26

Fabianism 29, 51–6, 73, 108, 196; patois of 54; and voting systems 217
fairness 61
fairness of outcome 92
Falklands 233
Fascism 10, 69
faultlines 58
fellowship 93
Ferranti 164
FIAT 166

First Past The Post system 217
First World War 230–31, 239
five economic tests 219
Foot, Michael 8, 12, 20–21, 41, 80, 237–8,
    242; and abolition of House of Lords
    212; devolution 207; lack of leadership
    49, 80, 257; as unilateralist 238
Foote, Geoffrey 125
FPTP *see* First Past The Post system
France 169–71, 174, 178–82
fraternity 93, 115–19
freedom 32, 61, 80, 96–9, 114–15; neo-
    liberal 97; as a triadic relation 96
freedom of information 216–17
Freedom of Information Act 216
Freedom of Information (Scotland) Act
    217
Freeman, John 14, 16
French Revolution 114
Friedmann, Milton 142, 183
from government to governance 142, 153
from subject to citizen 220
Future of Labour 78
Future of Socialism 17, 29, 73, 75, 89, 110,
    117

G7 149
'Gaiters' 75
Gaitskell, Hugh 14–15, 20, 49, 71, 74–6,
    82, 242; on class 195; 'desiccated
    calculating machine' 258; election as
    Labour leader 72; on Korean
    rearmament 234; opponent of EEC
    231, 235; revisionism 20, 72–6, 89, 109
GDP *see* gross domestic product
GEC 164
general election 1945 7, 52, 211
general election 1950 9, 54–5, 71
general election 1951 16, 54–5; Labour
    defeat in 125
general election 1955 55, 72
general election 1959 18, 55, 74, 238, 271
general election 1964 76
general election 1966 76, 259
general election 1970 24, 27, 57, 212;
    Labour defeat in 76
general election 1974 38, 41, 58–9, 77, 212
general election 1979 68, 87, 166; Labour
    defeat in 87
general election 1983 60, 80; Labour
    defeat in 87, 222
general election 1987 87, 219
general election 1992 61, 81, 265

general election 1997 63, 87, 127, 152,
    209, 212–18
general election 2001 130, 212, 221, 223
General Motors 173
General Strike 1922 222
General Theory 52
Geneva Protocol 247
geo-political change 88
Germany 10, 17, 59, 69, 106, 165, 174,
    180–82; re-armament 17; as social
    democratic state model 232
Giddens, Anthony 131–2, 139–40, 142–3;
    and the 'Third Way' 139–40, 142–3
ginger group 251
Gini coefficient 127
Gladstonian liberalism 225, 230
global solidarity 143
global terrorism 155
globalisation 36, 61, 87–8, 119, 137–62,
    166; as challenge 140–42; dilemmas
    154–7; instrumentalism 145–7;
    introduction 137–8; neo-revisionism
    147–54; as new times 139–40; as
    opportunity 142–3; rhetoric 138–9; as
    solidarity 143–4; 'thesis' 87–8
'gnomes of Zurich' 138
golden age of social democracy 69, 153
'Golden Straightjacket' 142
Good Friday Agreement 1998 209, 218
Gosplan 163
Gotha Programme 106
Gould, Philip 26, 190, 194, 265
Government's Industrial Strategy 59
Government and Parliament 213
Government of Wales Act 208
grain of globalisation 141, 156
Great Reform Act 1832 206
Great War 51
Greater London Act 1999 210
Greater London Authority 210, 218
Greater London Enterprise Board 181
Greece 181, 237
Greek Socialist Party 181
Green movement 123
gross domestic product 54, 60, 276
'grouse-moor' Tories 76
Guild Socialism 121

H-bomb 15, 18, 239
Hain, Peter 214, 223
Hampstead Set 73
Hart, Judith 30, 35, 37, 42, 168–9
Hattersley, Roy 32, 47, 80–81, 90; citizen

empowerment 132; egalitarian socialist 92, 99; and equality 116
Healey, Denis 69, 72, 78–80, 165, 236
Heath, Edward 77, 176, 178, 256
Heffer, Eric 38, 259
Hennessy, Peter 214
Hewitt, Patricia 200
high priest of revisionism 75, 77
Hinden, Rita 74
Hitler, Adolf 15, 70
Hobsbawm, Eric 36, 269
Hoffman-La Roche 165
Holland 146
Holland, Stuart 29–44, 126, 253; 'Tony Benn's guru' 29
Home Policy Sub-Committee 20
home rule 206–7
homosexuality legislation 73, 76, 95
Honda 180
House of Commons 8, 43, 214–15
House of Lords 211–13
House of Lords Act 1999 212
Howard, Tony 176
Hughes, John 31
human rights 215–16
Human Rights Act 1998 209, 216
Human Rights Act 2000 220, 223
Human Rights Commission 215
humanitarian intervention 155, 243
Hungarian uprising 20
'hungry thirties' 69
hunting the snark 47, 49
hyperglobalisers 148–9

idealism 20
ideas 1–2
identity of ends 114–19; community, fraternity, solidarity 115–19; equality 115; freedom 114–15
ideological battering ram of globalisation 146–7, 151, 154, 157
ideological bedrock 50
IMF *see* International Monetary Fund
Immediate Programme of 1937 70
impact of New Left on New Labour 41–4
imperialism 230, 243
impotence 31
In Place of Fear 10, 16, 18
'In Place of Strife' White Paper 1969 28, 57, 222
Independent Commission on the Voting System 217
Independent Labour Publications 31

industrial democracy 33, 39, 60
Industrial Policy Committee 164, 168–70, 174
Industrial Reconstruction Institute (Italy) 163, 166, 177
Industrial Reorganisation Corporation 164, 177
Industry and Society 18
inflation 60–61, 77
Inland Revenue 93
Inmos 180
inner-city housing estates 130
Institute of Economic Affairs 183
Institute of Workers' Control 29–30, 33, 253
instrumentalism 145–7
inter-war utopianism 144
international capitalism 63
International Computers Ltd 178
International Monetary Fund 68, 79, 138, 251–2
internationalism 34–6, 39, 144, 229–44
intolerance 16
intra-regional trade liberalisation 60
Iraq 19, 156, 214, 243, 249, 256
Irish Free State 208–9
Israel 248
Italian Communist Party 12
Italian Socialist Party 12
Italy 12, 34, 58, 163, 169–71, 181
IVF 276
IWC *see* Institute of Workers' Control

Japan 7, 165, 173, 180
Jay, Douglas 70–72, 110, 121, 236
Jenkins, Peter 26, 42
Jenkins, Roy 15–16, 69, 72, 76–80, 163; pro-Europe Labour right 219; state holding companies 166–9, 172, 177
Jones, Jack 28, 176
Joseph, Keith 96, 183
justice as fairness 92

Kaufman, Gerald 60, 80, 257
Keep Left 8–9, 12
Keeping Left 12
Keynesianism 18, 27, 36–7, 40, 43, 47–67; corporatist 59; decline in operation of 87; demand management 69; economic techniques 111–12; and full employment 57; macroeconomic management 49; social democracy 50, 54–5, 57–60, 62

Kilbrandon Report 1974 207
Kinnock, Glenys 255
Kinnock, Neil 32–3, 60, 80–82, 138, 181,
    257; abolition of House of Lords 212;
    policy review 80–81, 87, 138, 140, 233;
    resignation of 81; supporter of
    devolution 207
Königswinter Conferences 248
Konzertierte Aktion 59
Korea 12–14, 234; rearmament 234
Kosovo 155, 243
Kremlin 12
Khrushchev, Nikita 19

Labour Club 69
Labour Co-ordinating Committee 31, 44
Labour, Economic, Finance and Taxation
    Association 173
Labour Euro-Safeguards Committee 256
Labour movement 193–4
Labour Way is a Better Way 59
'Labour Will Win' 219
Labour/Liberal Democrat alliance 208
labourism 187–205, 261; and class
    194–210; definition 187–8; the Labour
    movement 193–4; Marxism, Proto-New
    Labour and 188–90; unions and power
    in the Party 190–93
Labour's National Plan 27, 49, 56–7, 76,
    166, 168
Labour's Path to Power 81
Labour's Programme for Britain 1973 38, 42,
    58
Laffer Curve 121
laissez-faire capitalism 89
land nationalisation 52
Laski, Harold 69–70
Left Book Club 70
legacy of New Left 41–4
Lestor, Joan 30, 34–5
Let us Face the Future 51–2
Let us Win Through Together 54
*Let us Work Together – Labour's Way out of the
    Crisis* 58
Let's go with Labour for the New Britain 55
Lib-Lab pact 20–27, 229
liberal communitarianism 96
liberal cosmopolitanism 144
Liberal Democrats 48, 64
Liberal-SDP Alliance 80
Liberalism 194–5
libertarianism 73
liberty *see* freedom

liberty principle 92–3
Libor 182
Librium 165
Liddle, Roger 130
Life Peerage Act 211
Lister, Ruth 127, 133, 277
Little England 142
Livingstone, Ken 24, 28, 210
Local Government Act 211
Local Government Bill 2002 211
Local Government Boundary
    Commissions 218
'Local Leadership, Local Choice' White
    Paper 2000 211
London County Council 210
London Mayor 210, 218, 222
London Passenger Transport Board 71
'longest suicide note in history' 80, 265
Lord Irvine 222–3
Lord Salisbury 230, 243
love-feast 76
Lucas Aerospace 172–3

McCarthyism 15
MacDonald, Ramsay 69, 217, 230–31
Mackintosh, John 79
Maclennan, Robert 217
Macmillan Government 234
Macmillan, Harold 75–6, 219, 234–5
macroeconomic management 49, 54
macroeconomic stability 141, 146
Major Government 82, 87, 94, 271
Major, John 82, 128, 151, 209
'managed capitalism' 139, 148
managerial revolution 76
Mandelson, Peter 87, 130, 210, 265
Manifesto Group 79
mantra of globalisation 140
Margaret Jackson *see* Beckett, Margaret
market economy 98
market injustice 98
market outcomes 130–32
markets and planning 163–86
Marks & Spencer 259
Marquand, David 26, 38, 41–2, 79, 82,
    187–9; on failure of Labour Party 194
Marshall Aid Plan 12–13
Marshall Tito 21
Marx, Karl 40, 69, 74, 106–113
Marxism, Proto-New Labour and
    labourism 188–90
Marxist socialism 69, 96
maverick left 47

May Day Manifesto group 31
Meacher, Michael 30, 43, 254
means of production 106
measuring poverty 90
'Meet the Challenge, Make the Change'
  81, 212
membership of the European Economic
  Community 21, 77, 163, 180, 218, 253
Memorandum of Understanding and
  Supplementary Agreements 208
Middle England 155
middle-class support 49
midwifery 54
'might is right' 156
Mikardo, Ian 7–8, 12, 16, 30, 72, 168, 242;
  political tactician 248; resignation of 12
Milburn, Alan 43
Miliband, Ralph 9, 31
Militant 264
militant trade unionism 28
Mills, John 256
miners' strike 176
Mitterand, François 138, 152, 181
mixed economy 20, 55, 71, 74, 152,
  180–82; 'third way' between Soviet
  communism and American capitalism
  74
modern state changes 220–22
modernisation 76, 81, 86, 140–41, 152,
  214, 220
Modernisation Select Committee 214
'modernizing juggernaut' 137
Monarchy 211–15; definition 213–14
Monday Club 42
Monetary Committee of Bank of England
  220
Monks, John 194
Monopolies Commission 165
monopolisation 36
moral crusade 156
Morrison, Herbert 7, 9, 15, 20, 71–4,
  210–213, 258; as leader of London
  County Council 210
Movement for Colonial Freedom 249
Mulgan, Geoff 131
Mullin, Chris 254
multilateralism 231
Mussolini, Benito 163
myth and reality of labourism 187–205

NAFTA 88
National Curriculum 240

National Economic Development
  Committees 169
National Enterprise Board 37, 58, 60, 172,
  180, 253
National Executive Committee 7, 18, 30,
  167, 176–9, 215; human rights 215;
  power of the unions 190
National Health Service 8, 14, 62, 71, 88,
  93, 165, 211, 241, *see also* Bevan,
  Aneurin
national insurance 7–8, 93, 125
National Manpower Service 57
National Minimum Wage 91, 128
National Plan 27, 49, 56–7, 76, 166, 168
National Recovery Programme 62
National Training Programme 61
nationalisation 8, 17–18, 37, 52, 71–3;
  efficiency of 17; moves towards land 52
nationalism 207
NATO *see* North Atlantic Treaty
  Organisation
Nazism 10
NEC Green Paper on National Enterprise
  Board 167, 176–8
Nenni, Peitro 12
neo-Conservatism 131
neo-liberal convergence 145
neo-liberal freedom 97
neo-liberal orthodoxy 146
neo-liberal trickle down theory 90, 127,
  130
neo-liberalism 94, 270–71
neo-revisionism 147–54
neo-socialism 26
Netherlands *see* Holland
neutrality 231
'New Agenda for Democracy' 215, 220–21
New Britain 55–6, 76, 220
New Deal for Communities 94, 99, 118,
  132
New Fabian Essays 72–3
new global informational capitalism 139
New Hope for Britain 50, 60
New Labour 86–102, 127–31, 178–80,
  268–73; and equality 127–31
New Labour's globalisation rhetoric 138–9
New Left 20, 24–46, 178–80, 251–6;
  character of the New Left 29–31;
  conclusions 41–4; development of the
  New Left 27–8; economic policy 251–2;
  introduction 24–7, 251; objectives of
  the New Left 32–6; other conflicts
  252–4; policies of the New Left 36–40;

pressure for constitutional change within Party 254–5; relevance today 256
new socialist orthodoxy 29
New Statesman 70
New Times 138–40, 145–6; globalisation as 139–40
New Welfare State 56
New Zealand 214
Nexos 180
NHS *see* National Health Service
NHS Direct 88
1945 7, 241
non-discrimination 115
Nordic capitalism 51
North American New Democratic ideology 83, 138, 155
North Atlantic Treaty Organisation 12, 82, 231, 236, 242, 253
Northern Ireland 208–9
Northern Ireland Act 1974 209
Northern Ireland Act 1998 209, 220
Northern Ireland Assembly 218
Northern Ireland Development Agency 180–81
Northern Ireland Human Rights Commission 209
Now Britain's Strong: let's make it great to live in 57
nuclear disarmament 16, 19, 21, 39
nuclear power 18, 49
Number 10 Downing Street 90, 170–71, 220, 224
Number 11 Downing Street 90
NUPE 28

objectives of New Left 32–6; democracy, accountability, participation 33–4; efficiency 32–3; equality 32; internationalism 34–6
OECD 149
Old Left: 1945–1960 7–23, 178–80, 247–50
Old Right 68–85, 121–6, 261–7; disintegration of social democracy, 1963–80 76–80; and equality 121–6; introduction 68–9; revisionist antecedents, 1935–55 69–72; since 1980 80–83; triumph of revisionism, 1955–63 72–6
oligopoly 164–5
One Way Only 16
OPEC 88, 172, 263

openness 216
Operation Dynamo 72
opportunity 73, 142–3
optimism 77
Orwell, George 13
Out of Crisis Project 181–2
outright nationalism 168
Owen, David 80, 219
ownership 163–86; democratising markets 172–4; NEC Green Paper on National Enterprise Board 176–8; New Left, Old Left and Old Labour 178–80; outcome 180–83; Planning Agreements 169–72; selective state shareholdings 163–9; Tony Crosland and birth of the social contract 174–6

pacifism 229, 239
Palestine 248
Pandit Nehru 21
Papandreou, Andreas 181
parity of sterling 123
Parliament Act 1911 211
Parliament Act 1945 211
parliament and the Monarchy 211–15; House of Commons 214–15; House of Lords 211–13; the Monarchy 213–14
Parliament (No. 2) Bill 1968 212
Parliamentary Labour Party 9, 25, 48, 86, 89, 99; abolition of House of Lords 213; election of cabinet ministers 221
parliamentary sovereignty 219
participation 33–4
parties and elections 217–19
Party Conference 1934 211
Party Conference 1942 17
Party Conference 1944 7
Party Conference 1948 9
Party Conference 1952 14, 76
Party Conference 1963 76
Party Conference 1973 171
Party Conference 1974 38, 207
Party Conference 1977 212
Party Conference 1983 212
Party Conference 1987 212
Party Conference 1994 212
Party Conference 2002 143
patriotism 240, 242
Paxman, Jeremy 90
Pensioner Guarantee 91
permissive society 95
personal conviction 86
pessimism 8

PFI *see* Private Finance Initiative
Phillips curve 60
Pirelli 166
Pitt, Terry 30
Plaid Cymru 207
Planning Agreements 163, 166, 173, 179;
    case for 169–72
Planning for Freedom 17
planning and markets 163–86
Plant, Raymond 217, 264, 271
Pol Pot 230
policies of New Left 36–40
policy review 80–81, 87, 138, 140, 233; on
    abolition of House of Lords 212
political economy of the Centre 47
political identity 105–119; historical
    background 105–113; identity of ends
    114–19
Political Parties, Elections and
    Referendums Act 2000 218–19
Politics of Democratic Socialism 70
Popular Front 230, 233
positions 5–102; the Centre 47–67; New
    Labour 86–102; the New Left 24–46;
    the Old Left: 1945–1960 7–23; the Old
    Right 68–85
post-revisionist social democracy 82
poverty 90, 97, 276; introduction of anti-
    poverty measures 128
Powell, Enoch 183, 212
power in the Party 190–93
PPERA *see* Political Parties, Elections and
    Referendums Act 2000
Practical Socialism for Britain 69–70
prerogative powers 213–14, 221
Prescott, John 43, 87, 94, 181, 209;
    supporter of regionalism 209
President of the European Council 220
Prime Minister's Department 220
Prime Minister's powers 215
prioritarianism 93
prioritisation 61
private education 75
Private Finance Initiative 179
privatisation 211
Privy Council 221
pro-deterrence stance 34
Progress Agreement 174
progressive political coalition 155
protest movements 28
Proto-New Labour 188–90
Prussia 237
pseudo-Conservative 70

Public Enterprise Group 30
public ownership 7–8, 10, 38–9, 41, 52,
    60, 70; extension of 58
public services 93, 98

race to the bottom 146
radical chauvinism 242
Radice, Giles 78, 81
Rank and File Mobilising Committee 31
rank-and-file 9, 192
Rawls, John 92–3, 114, 126, 264, 275–6
re-armament of Germany 17
re-nationalisation 9, 249
Reaganism 264
'real rights for citizens' 215
rearmament-disarmament-third force axis
    236
Redi, John 214
redistribution by stealth 127–8, 270, 277
Redistribution of Seats Act 1949 217
redistribution of wealth 32, 252
'Reds under the bed' 16
Refendums (Scotland and Wales) Act 1997
    208
reflation 36
Regional Assemblies (Preparations) Bill
    2002 209
Regional Development Agencies 94,
    209–210
rehabilitation 95, 150
Representation of the People Act 1948 217
resurgence of Old Right since 1980 80–83
revenge of globalisation 157
revisionism 17, 20–21, 24–5, 73
revisionist antecedents, 1935–55 69–72
Rhineland capitalism 51
Ricardo, David 165
'Rights Brought Home' White Paper 1997
    215
rights for women legislation 73, 95
Rodgers, Bill 80, 163, 171
Rolls-Royce 167, 178
Rousseau, Jean-Jacques 175
Royal Commission on Reform of the
    House of Lords 1999 212
'royal court' 75
Russell, Bertrand 22
Russia 233

sale of council houses 259
Salisbury convention 211
Scanlon, Hugh 28
Scargill, Arthur 24

schism 200, 233, 237
scientific socialism 76, 79
Scotland 116
Scottish Development Agency 180–81
Scottish Information Commissioner 217
Scottish National Party 207
Scottish Parliament 210, 215, 218
sea-change in Labour loyalties 259
Second World War 20, 89, 94, 112, 210,
    222, 232–3
secular logic 140
Sedgemore, Brian 30, 255
selective amnesia 167
selective state shareholdings 163–9
semi-Marxist thought 78
SERPS *see* State Earnings Related Pensions
    Scheme
sexism 43
Shaw, Eric 82, 239
Shaw, George Bernard 126
Shelter 27
Shore, Peter 171, 236
Short, Clare 43, 143, 242
siege economy 242
Siemens 171–2, 179
Signposts for the Sixties 55
Silicon Valley 180
Sinclair, Clive 180, 183
Single European Act 181
single proportional alternative system 217
Single Transferable Vote 209, 218
Skinner, Dennis 261
sleaze 218
Smith, Adam 166
Smith, John 81–2, 208, 216–17, 220–22;
    death of 215, 221; electoral reform
    217; legacy 215
social cohesion 241
Social Compact 176
Social Contract 59, 174–6
social democracy 28, 50, 54–5, 57–60, 62,
    77, 231; in context of Bernstein 111;
    conversion to European-style 82–3,
    106, 233, 240, 242; death throes 62, 83;
    disintegration of 76–80; and equality
    120–21; golden age 69; New Labour's
    politics as form of 87–9; renewal of
    139; ultimate goal of 98, *see also*
    democratic socialism; Keynesianism
Social Democratic Party 60, 80, 163, 264;
    failure of 80
social exclusion 129–30
Social Exclusion Unit 129

social inclusion 129, 133
social investment state 141, 152–3
social justice 83, 98, 107, 130
'Social Justice and Economic Efficiency'
    138
social legislation 54
social revolution 73
social welfare 54
socialism 7–23, 53, 68–9; Crosland's
    definition of 68; and Fabianism 73
Socialism Now 78, 123
Socialist Challenge 29, 38
Socialist Commentary 74
Socialist Commonwealth 53
Socialist League 69
'Sod Off Day' 79
solidarity 115–19, 143–4, 193
Soviet Union 10–12, 19, 21, 69, 232–3,
    258; blockade of Berlin 12
Spain 183
Spanish Civil War 230–31
Speaker's Committee 218
Special Advisers 220–21; Code of
    Conduct 221
'specialness' 241
Spokesman publishing house 29–30
Sputnik 17
stakeholding 86
Stalin, Josef 12, 19, 69
stasis 72
State Earnings Related Pensions Scheme
    126
state education 75
State Hydrocarbons Agency (Italy) 163,
    177
steel industry 8–9
stop-go cycle 27, 55–7
stop-stop cycle 27
Stormont parliament 209
Strachey, John 14, 47, 69, 72–4, 249
Strang, Gavin 43
Strasbourg 215–16
Straw, Jack 43, 87, 220, 243
strikes 28
STV *see* Single Transferable Vote
'substantial harm' test 216
'substantial prejudice' test (Scotland) 217
Suez crisis 20
super-powers 12, 240
supply-side measures 82, 139, 150
Supreme Court 223–4
Surestart 91, 118
Sweden 17, 146, 152–3, 174, 180, 232,

276; austerity policies 152; least
successful party of the left in Europe
201; negotiated governance 153

Taverne, Dick 78
Tawney, R.H. 50, 96, 115, 117, 121, 275;
link between equality and liberty 121
Tawneyite ethical socialism 50
Taylor, Anne 214
technological revolution 76
TGV system 170
Thatcher Government 80, 94, 127–8, 211
Thatcher, Margaret 26, 68, 150
Thatcherite Conservatism 21, 83, 87, 120,
146, 152; intellectual capital of 97
themes 103–244; constitutional reform
206–228; ends, means and political
identity 105–119; equality 120–36;
globalisation 137–62; internationalism
229–44; labourism: myths and realities
187–205; ownership, planning and
markets 163–86
Third Way: Politics for the New Century 93
'third way' 74
Third Way 131–2, 137–62, 211, 220
third world debt 242
TIGMOO 193
total effective demand 70
Townsend, Sue 26
Toyota 173
trade liberalisation 60
trade union block vote 48
trade unionism 17, 28, 190–93; Labour
and the trade unions 221–2; militant
28; and power in the Party 190–93
Trades Union Congress 18, 222
transformation 35–6
transnational corporations 58
transparency 216
Transport and General Workers' Union
13, 28, 177
Treatise on Money 52
Treaty of Maastricht 182
triangulation 270
Tribune 12–15, 20–22, 37, 70, 74;
association with policy demands 40
Tribunism 25, 253
triumph of revisionism, 1955–63 72–6
Trotskyist groupings 20, 232, 264
Truman administrations 13
Truman, Harry S. 13
Twentieth Century Socialism 74

Uncle Sam 236
unilateralism 18–19, 233
United Nations 234
United States 12, 19, 21, 28, 231–4
utopianism 144–5, 258

Vaizey, John 123
Valium 165
values 1–2, 105–119
Varley, Eric 180
Vietnam war 28, 230
vision 20
von Hayek, Friedrich 96–7, 132, 183
voting systems 217

wages freeze 27
Wakeham Commission 212
Walker, Patrick Gordon 234
Warde, Alan 28
wartime coalition 7
Washington 12
Webb, Sidney 210, 275
welfare capitalism 89
welfare payments 91, 128
Welfare State 55–6, 63, 211; debate on
funding of 128
Welsh Assembly 210, 215, 218
Welsh Development Agency 180–81
Welsh Language Act 1976 207
West Midlands Enterprise Board 181
Westminster model 206, 236
white heat 166, 238
Williams, Shirley 17, 80, 165; pro-Europe
Labour right 219
Wilson Governments 27–8, 30–31, 40, 92,
212
Wilson, Harold 9, 14, 16–18, 20, 75–80,
165, 242; advent as Labour Party
leader 55, 74; disintegration of social
democracy under 76–80; electoral
defeat of 24; leftist vision 49; race to
replace as leader 68; resignation of 14;
and scientific socialism 76; veto of
NEC Green Paper 168, 171
Winter of Discontent 68, 79
Wise, Audrey 254
Women's Action Committee 255
Working Families Tax Credit 91
world financial markets 87
WTO 143

xenophobia 43

XYZ Club 70

'Your Region, Your Choice' White Paper
    2002 209

'Your Right to Know' White Paper 1997
    216

Zilliacus, Konni 13, 247